Latinos and Public Policy in California:
An Agenda for Opportunity

David López and Andrés Jiménez, Editors

© 2003 by the Regents of the University of California. All rights reserved.

Library of Congress Cataloging-in-Publication Data

Latinos and public policy in California : an agenda for opportunity / David López and Andrés Jiménez, co-editors.
    p. cm.
  Includes bibliographical references.
  Contents: Introduction / David López and Andrés Jiménez -- Latinos in California / Belinda Reyes -- Rising tides and sinking boats / Manuel Pastor -- K-12 public education / Eugene Garcia -- Putting the cart before the horse / Patricia Gándara and Lisa Chávez -- Tipping the balance / Ed Kissam -- Illness and wellness / David Hayes-Bautista -- Access to illness care and health insurance / R. Burciaga Valdez -- Latino mental health in California / Kurt Organista and Lonnie Snowden -- Crime and justice / José Canela-Cacho -- Housing / Dowell Myers -- Latino political incorporation in California, 1990-2000 / Luis Ricardo Fraga and Ricardo Ramirez -- Conclusion / David López.
    ISBN 0-87772-409-1
    1. Hispanic Americans--California--Social conditions--20th century. 2. Hispanic Americans--Government policy--California. 3. Hispanic Americans--California--Politics and government--20th century. 4. California--Politics and government--1951- 5. California--Social policy. 6. California--Ethnic relations. I. López, David. II. Jiménez, Andrés.

F870.S75L38 2003
323.1168'0794--dc22
    2003057823

Contents

Foreword	vii
Introduction	xi
David López and Andrés Jiménez	
Chapter 1: Latinos in California: Population Growth and Diversity	1
Belinda I. Reyes	
Chapter 2: Rising Tides and Sinking Boats: The Economic Challenge for California's Latinos	35
Manuel Pastor, Jr.	
Chapter 3: K-12 Public Education: Bedrock or Barrier?	65
Eugene E. Garcia	
Chapter 4: Putting the Cart before the Horse: Latinos and Higher Education	87
Patricia Gándara and Lisa Chávez	
Chapter 5: Tipping the Balance: A Flexible, Integrated System of Adult Education	121
Edward Kissam	
Chapter 6: Illness and Wellness: The Latino Paradox	155
David E. Hayes-Bautista	
Chapter 7: Access to Illness Care and Health Insurance	189
R. Burciaga Valdez	
Chapter 8: Latino Mental Health in California: Implications for Policy	217
Kurt Organista and Lonnie Snowden	
Chapter 9: Crime and Justice: Developments in the Last Twenty Years and Priorities For the Next Twenty	241
José A. Canela-Cacho	
Chapter 10: Housing: Crisis or Opportunity?	279
Dowell Myers	
Chapter 11: Latino Political Incorporation in California, 1990–2000	301
Luis Ricardo Fraga and Ricardo Ramirez	
Conclusion: Latinos and Public Policy in California: An Agenda for Opportunity	337
David López	
About the Authors	343

Foreword

This volume originated in response to a series of policy discussions between University of California faculty and state legislative staff convened in late 2000 by the California Policy Research Center. The chapters were originally commissioned at a time of economic expansion and relative optimism about the state's role in contributing to improved health, education, and employment outcomes for California's Latinos. The state budgets of 1999 and 2000, fueled by capital gains of the dot-com industry and the stock-market-driven increases in tax revenues, reflected that optimism in the form of selected increases in health and education spending.

By early 2002, however, budget surpluses had turned into projected deficits. As this volume was prepared for press in early 2003, the state government was struggling to close an unprecedented $38 billion budget deficit for the current and forthcoming fiscal years. At the same time, the state and the nation have experienced political shocks and economic uncertainty that no one could have foreseen three years ago. Today, in an era of choices, the policy challenges discussed in this volume are more intractable than ever, as they depend on a strong economy for resolution.

This economic downturn and state budget crisis present us with new challenges for identifying policy innovations to address persistent inequalities. California has passed through and shaken off economic difficulties before, most recently only a decade ago. There is general agreement that in the current crisis the path of wisdom is to maintain essential state services, financing them with a combination of borrowing, judicious revenue increases, and cuts to nonessential programs. There is less agreement about what is essential and what we can live without.

With respect to a core concern of this volume—the integration of low-income Latinos into the state mainstream—the implication is clear: programs that contribute the most to improving the health and education of the state's "working poor" are among the essential programs. This includes programs aimed at improving the health of all children, as well as those that target the children of the working poor. In education, it means employing state resources to improve the schooling of the state's low-income children. We are under no illusion that somehow the state's usual balance of political forces will be suspended. Our point is that to abandon efforts to provide opportunity to the poorest third of our state's young population today will spell disaster in the future.

It is also worth reflecting on what has *not* happened in the past three years. First of all, the economic slide has not yet resulted in the sort of anti-immigrant sentiment that developed during the last major economic downturn in the early 1990s. This is all the more remarkable given the heightened concern for "secure borders" and the draconian steps taken by the U.S. Justice Department to strengthen enforcement of immigration regulations in light of the post-September 11 war on terrorism. To be sure, individual anti-immigrant and anti-Latino sentiments are still expressed, but these expressions have not found an echo among state officials and political campaigns. Both major political parties understand that Latino immigrants are not solely consumers of state services; they are taxpayers, public officials, and, increasingly, voters as well.

Second, state and local public officials remain committed to improvements in the state's education system and student achievement levels. It would be a terrible waste to abandon efforts that genuinely improve the capacity of schools to provide quality education for the state's low-income children just when recent reforms are beginning to show results.

The experience of the past three years leads us to more moderate and cautious prognostications of the future of Latinos in California. Demographic pressures have moderated somewhat, judging from the 2000 Census, which confirms previous evidence that Latino immigrants are now settling outside of traditional receiving areas. Larger proportions of immigrant workers are now settling in southern, eastern, and midwestern states, reducing somewhat the proportion of new arrivals to California. However, Latinos will continue to be a growing proportion of the state's population, due in large part to growth in the numbers of U.S.-born children of immigrants, who will represent a key component of the state's population growth over the next several decades. California's future is inextricably intertwined with the fate of its burgeoning Latino population. For the most part that fate will be determined by the hard work and determination of Latino families themselves, but the state's role in facilitating Latino success is even more important in times of crisis.

Foreword

The editors would like to acknowledge the cooperation and contributions of those who made this publication possible. We particularly thank Dr. María Chacón for her efforts in editing documents and coordinating communications among the authors, CPRC editorial staff, and the publications unit at the Berkeley Institute of Governmental Studies. The editing skills of Eileen Cohen, Russell Hoyle, and Joan Lichterman greatly improved the narrative, as did the work of IGS editors.

Introduction

David López and Andrés Jiménez

Both California and its Latino population are undergoing profound transformations at the beginning of the 21st century. California has become a "no majority" state. Latinos are already one-third of the population and the largest ethnic group among the state's school children. If current demographic trends continue, they will overtake non-Latino whites within the next 30 years and will become the absolute majority of the state's population sometime in the middle of this century.

Despite the state's Mexican origins, the Mexican/Latino presence in California was no more than three percent at the beginning of the 20th century. From 1910 to 1930 that number doubled with the first great migration north, but as late as 1940 Latinos were still very much a minority: six percent at most. Their presence grew slowly but steadily during the state's postwar population boom, but it was only in the last three decades of the 20th century that Latinos emerged as the most dynamic sector of the state's population. In the 1990s Latinos accounted for 85 percent of *all* population growth in the state. (Asians and Pacific Islanders accounted for most of the rest.)

In contrast, the state's non-Latino white population is actually declining not only in proportion, but in absolute numbers as well. (Changes in how the Census Bureau counts "race" make exact comparisons between 2000 and previous years difficult.) Although immigration continues to be a driving force of this population growth, by far the largest segment of Latino population growth is natural increase: the children of immigrant and native Latino families who require state-supported education and other services to grow up to be productive citizens.

Despite their growing presence, Latinos as a whole still constitute less than 20 percent of the electorate, possess a smaller share of wealth relative to other groups, and significantly lag behind other groups in educational attainment. Much of the apparent education gap is due to the presence of immigrants who grew up poor in Mexico and Central America, where only six to eight years of schooling is the norm. However, the children of immigrants, as well as Latino youth from families that have been here for generations, also lag behind in California's schools. These disparities are likely to persist into the foreseeable future and to frame a series of statewide policy debates on opportunity and access.

The UC Latino Policy Institute has commissioned this volume to address the effects of the growing Latino population on the state's policy agenda. In a series of 11 topical chapters, contributors from a variety of disciplines examine demographic trends, economic participation, education, job training, health care, mental health, criminal justice, housing, and political participation. The authors review the status of California Latinos in each of these areas and recommend policy approaches to enhance opportunities, improve service delivery, and make best or more efficient use of public resources.

The volume begins with a demographic overview of the state's Latino population. Drawing from the 2000 census and other sources, in Chapter 1 Belinda Reyes, research associate at the Public Policy Institute of California, presents key demographic trends and reviews a range of characteristics such as age distribution, employment, income, and geographic concentration. Reyes also examines the heterogeneity of the Latino population and identifies a set of shared socio-economic and other characteristics. In addition, she explores evidence of progress in educational attainment and earnings across generations, and examines trends in poverty, occupational segregation, and education gaps for segments of the Latino population.

Turning to issues of employment and economic opportunity in Chapter 2, Manuel Pastor, Jr., professor of Latin American and Latino studies at UC Santa Cruz, analyzes the role of Latinos in California's economy. Although the expanding Latino population has been an engine of growth, Latinos have not shared equally in the state's abundance, and some key indicators suggest they are falling increasingly behind other major ethnic groups. Pastor argues forcefully for educational and labor reforms that will increase access to the higher-income segments of the job market for Latinos growing up in California, and provide a just and safe workplace for immigrant workers. He puts special emphasis on the potential for Latino small-business entrepreneurs to make a significant contribution to the state's economic growth.

In Chapter 3 Eugene E. García, professor and dean of the School of Education at Arizona State University, examines the status of Latinos in the state's K–12 public school systems and stresses the need for specific reforms to increase educational equity. As the emerging majority of public school children, Latinos are poorly served by both state programs for "minority education" and the implementation of recent education reforms that threaten to put them at an even greater disadvantage in comparison with non-Latino white and Asian students. García argues that, properly implemented, bilingual/bicultural curricula are still the best path to academic success for Latino youth.

In Chapter 4 Patricia Gándara, professor of education at UC Davis, and Lisa Chávez, research associate at WestEd, a nonprofit education research agency, assess the status of Latinos in the state's public higher education system. Latino students, who are poorly served in K–12 education, are at a disadvantage at every step and in every segment of higher education. Attending a community college rarely leads to enrollment in a four-year college, CSU is easy to enter but hard to graduate from, and UC continues to be an impossible dream for the vast majority. Gándara and Chávez highlight programs that help Latinos make the transition to and remain in higher education, and point out that these programs are currently in jeopardy.

In Chapter 5 Edward Kissam, research associate at Aguirre International, reviews the operation of California's adult education system, which has pockets of excellence and effectiveness amid large areas of irrelevance and resource starvation. He surveys this vast and disjointed array of programs and makes concrete suggestions for improving coordination of services, particularly for immigrant workers, who represent a major component of enrollment in adult education. Kissam closes by assessing current proposals to reform state-supported adult education.

In Chapter 6 David E. Hayes-Bautista, professor of medicine and director of the Center for the Study of Latino Health and Culture at UCLA, explores the Latino health "paradox." Despite having higher risk factors for poor health, Latinos generally are healthy and have far lower death rates than non-Latinos from the three leading causes of death in the United States—heart disease, cancer, and stroke. Moreover, the closer they are to the experience of immigration, the healthier they are. The conditions and illnesses from which Latinos do suffer are distinctively different from the norm, and there is a short supply of culturally competent medical practitioners needed to treat their specific conditions. Hayes-Bautista makes a number of concrete suggestions for ameliorating this supply problem.

In Chapter 7 R. Burciaga Valdez, senior health scientist at RAND, continues the examination of health policy by focusing on the Latino health insurance crisis. Latinos are the most underinsured and underserved group in California, largely because they are concentrated in low-paying jobs in small companies in marginal industries. Valdez identifies a number of strategies for expanding health-insurance coverage that draw on existing public programs, employer tax subsidies, and assistance to low-income workers. He points out the limitations of a number of proposed reforms, noting, for example, that those aimed at more-affluent workers in larger companies bypass a large proportion of the Latino workforce.

In Chapter 8 Kurt Organista and Lonnie Snowden, both professors of social welfare at UC Berkeley, explore the oft-neglected topic of mental health among Latinos. Because even the affluent and insured find it difficult to obtain mental-health care, Latinos have an even greater struggle obtaining it. Added linguistic and cultural barriers make treatment especially serious for them, and the insecurity of life for so many immigrant families creates a mental health profile that may be distinct from the norm. The authors suggest ways to improve services, but also recognize the political difficulties of extending services to immigrants, especially those who are undocumented and may need them the most.

In Chapter 9 José Canela-Cacho, research associate at UC Berkeley's Earl Warren Legal Institute, explores the overrepresentation of Latinos at all levels of California's criminal justice system, as both offenders and victims. The situation is most extreme for juveniles. Canela-Cacho examines punishment and victimization statistics to reveal the challenge of improving both sanctioning and safety levels, and recommends a comprehensive strategy to reduce Latino victimization and incarceration rates simultaneously in order to avoid further polarization of criminal-justice policy along a racial and ethnic divide.

In Chapter 10 Dowell Myers, professor of policy, planning, and development at the University of Southern California, assesses the increasingly challenging issue of housing. The single greatest housing problem Latinos face stems from their low incomes and the high cost of real estate in urban California. In many ways, the housing problems of Latinos are those of the state as a whole, including sprawl and over-regulation that often creates artificial barriers to housing solutions. Even if Latino families do cooperate to rent and purchase housing, as some of the literature suggests, the gap between their demand and the supply of affordable housing has reached impossible levels. Myers singles out several specific policy changes that can help, but argues that low family incomes remain the key barrier to homeownership for Latinos.

In Chapter 11 Luis Ricardo Fraga, professor of political science at Stanford University, and Ricardo Ramírez, assistant professor of political science at the University of Southern California, examine political representation and participation. During the past decade Latino political participation has increased dramatically in terms of voting and office-holding, but the distribution of power in the state has not changed substantially. Latinos' low incomes and their low rate of citizenship will continue to work against full participation, but the direction of change is clear: Latino political participation will increase in the future. The authors point out that political participation can take a number of different forms, including unionization among noncitizen workers as well as more traditional forms like voting and office-holding. They suggest that the expansion of local office-holding in municipal and school jurisdictions may be one of the most important changes in Latino political participation that we will continue to witness in the decades to come.

In the conclusion, co-editors Andrés Jiménez and David López link the various strands of policy discussion woven throughout the volume and highlight common themes. Given the crucial role that Latinos play in the economy and polity, a policy agenda that expands their opportunities can benefit the state as a whole. They examine the importance of immigrant integration and the educational achievement of Latino children as leading state policy objectives, and underscore the importance of flexible approaches to policy issues, particularly given the heterogeneity of a Latino population that is characterized by differences in national origin, generation, nativity, language, and household income. Finally, they discuss how the contributors' proposed policy reforms in education, job training, housing, and other areas are beneficial across ethnic and population groups, thus creating opportunities for policy consensus.

Chapter 1

Latinos in California:
Population Growth and Diversity

Belinda I. Reyes

Latinos represent a growing proportion of California's population. In the last 10 years, the Latino population increased by 43 percent, reaching 11 million in 2000.[1] In the same decade, the non-Hispanic white population decreased relatively by seven percent, while reaching nearly 16 million in 2000. If these patterns of growth continue, Latinos will outnumber non-Hispanic whites as the largest racial and ethnic group in the state within 20 years.

In addition to constituting a numerous and growing segment of the state's population, Latinos have distinct characteristics that set them apart from other racial or national-origin groups. Latinos are a young population with a large proportion in the working-age years of 25 to 54. While many Latinos have low educational attainment and low incomes, they have high levels of employment and lower use of social services than would be expected given their higher levels of poverty. Most Latinos do not enjoy access to health benefits, but they have some of the best health outcomes of all racial and ethnic groups. While their rates of naturalization have been below those of other groups, these rates have been increasing in recent years, as has Latino representation in public office (see

---

[1] Throughout this chapter the words "Latino" and "Hispanic" are used interchangeably.

chapter 11). The future of California depends on how well the state is able to take advantage of the resources and opportunities the Latino population represents, and how effectively it responds to the needs of this key population group.

This chapter presents key demographic trends for California's Latino population. Given the importance of both similarities and differences among national-origin groups, when possible this chapter presents data for the major Latino subgroups—Mexicans, Caribbeans, and South or Central Americans.[2] In cases in which data sources do not allow for disaggregation, group characteristics are presented simply as Latino. The first section describes the growth and diversity of the Latino population. This is followed by a discussion of the population's characteristics and a quick review of the social and economic well-being of Latinos as compared to other racial and ethnic groups in California. The last section looks at the political participation of Latinos. Many of these topics are developed further in subsequent chapters.

Latino Population Growth

The Latino population increased fourfold between 1970 (2.4 million) and 2000 (11 million). This increase was greater than that of any other racial and ethnic group in the state, except for Asians, whose number increased by 460 percent in the same time period. Non-Hispanic whites experienced the lowest population growth, rising from 15.5 million in 1970 to 15.8 million in 2000 (see Figure 1.1).[3] The African-American and Native-American populations experienced modest growth in the same time period: The Native-American population doubled in size to 179,000 by 2000, and the African-American population grew by 58 percent, to 2.2 million in 2000.

Not only has the number of Latinos increased in the last 30 years, but the proportion of Latinos in the California population has also been increasing (see Figure 1.2). In 1970, 77 percent of the California population was composed of non-Hispanic whites, compared with 48 percent in 2000, while Latinos rose from only 12 percent of California's population in 1970 to 34 percent by 2000. Current patterns of population growth are expected to continue into the future. By 2021, Latinos are projected to be the largest racial and ethnic group in the state (Johnson, 2001).

---

[2]Ideally, data would be presented by national origin, but sample-size limitations prohibit further disaggregation.

[3]This figure selects people who were of only one race, not a combination of races. In 2000, only four percent of California residents identified as having more than one race.

Figure 1.1. California Population by Race and Ethnicity, 1970–2000

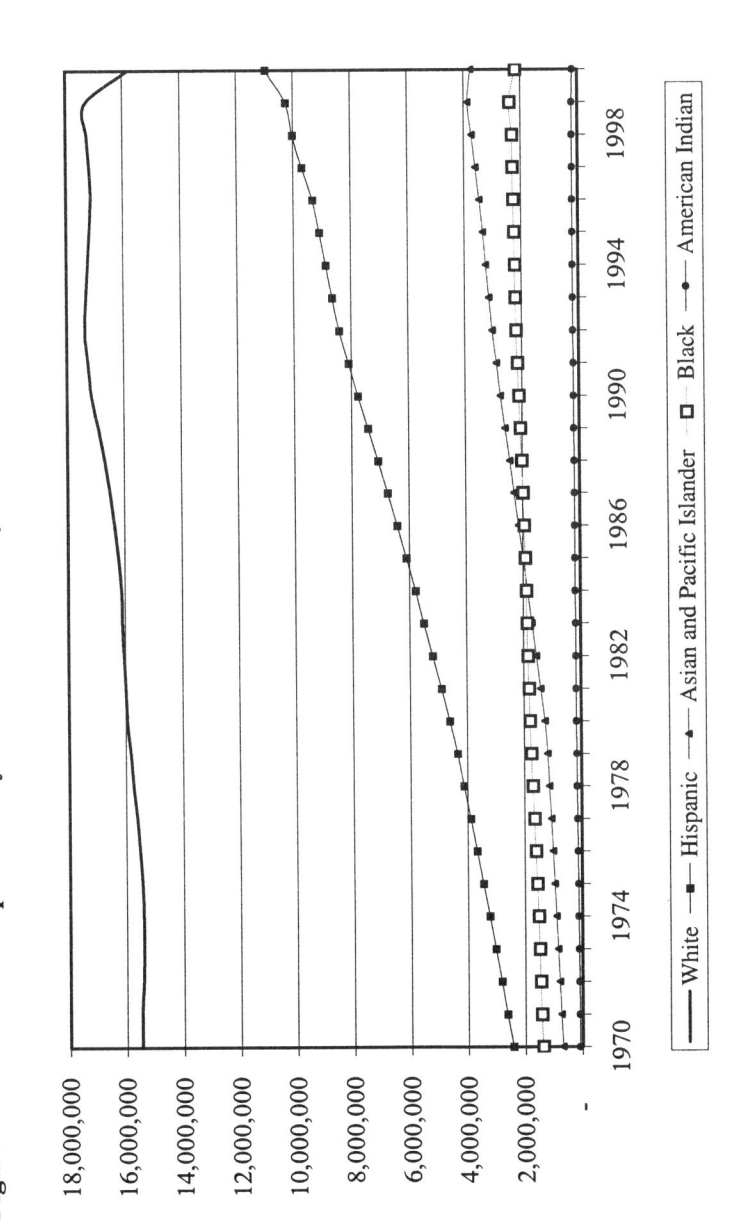

Source: Author's calculations from the California Department of Finance and 2000 U.S. Census.

Figure 1.2. Racial and Ethnic Distribution of the California Population, 1970-1998

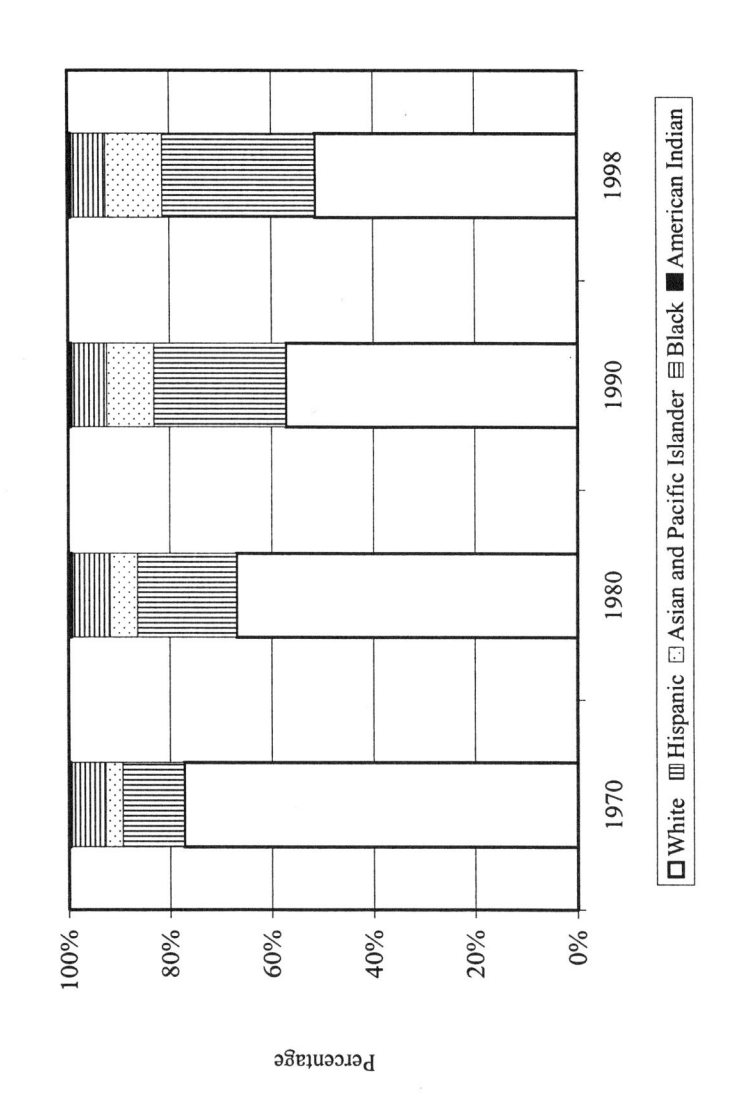

☐ White ☷ Hispanic ⊡ Asian and Pacific Islander ☰ Black ■ American Indian

Source: Johnson (2001) and author calculations from the 2000 U.S. Census.

Immigration

International migration has played an important part in the remarkable growth of the Latino population in California. The number of immigrants among the Latino population increased substantially in the last 30 years, from close to 600,000 people in 1970 to 4.6 million in the 1999–2001 period.[4] Foreign-born Latinos are a growing proportion of the state's overall Latino population (see Figure 1.3). In 1970, 27 percent of Latinos were born abroad, a proportion that increased to 44 percent by the 1999–2001 period. Nearly 80 percent of the Central and South Americans living in California in 1980 and 1990 were born abroad. This proportion declined to 70 percent by 1999–2001. There has been a radical decline in the proportion of immigrants among people of Caribbean descent (Cubans, Puerto Ricans, and Dominicans). In 1970, 62 percent of Californians of Caribbean descent were born abroad, but by 1999–2001 this had declined to 27 percent.

Birth Rates

Irrespective of immigration, Latino birth rates are very high, accounting for a significant proportion of the population growth (see Figure 1.4). In 1990, Latinos overtook non-Hispanic whites as the population with the highest number of births. Of the 519,000 births in California in 1999, 48 percent were to Latinos. The fertility rate for Hispanic women was substantially above that of other women in California.[5] In 1998, Latino women had, on average, 3.5 children, compared to 2 children for African-American women, 1.5 for white non-Hispanic women, and 1.9 for Asian women (Hill and Johnson, 2002).

Population Concentration within California

Although Latinos are concentrated in Southern California, especially in Los Angeles, growth in the Latino population can be seen in every county of the

---

[4]At the time this chapter was written the Census Bureau had not yet released data that would allow us to look at many outcomes by race/ethnicity and by ethnic subgroups. For this reason I combined the three years of the CPS—1999, 2000, and 2001—to generate a large enough sample to derive reliable statistics.

[5]The total fertility rate is the average number of children a woman will have in her lifetime (based on current age-specific fertility rates). Replacement-level fertility is 2.1 children per woman.

Figure 1.3. Proportion of California Latinos Who Are Foreign-Born, 1970, 1980, 1990, and 1999–2001

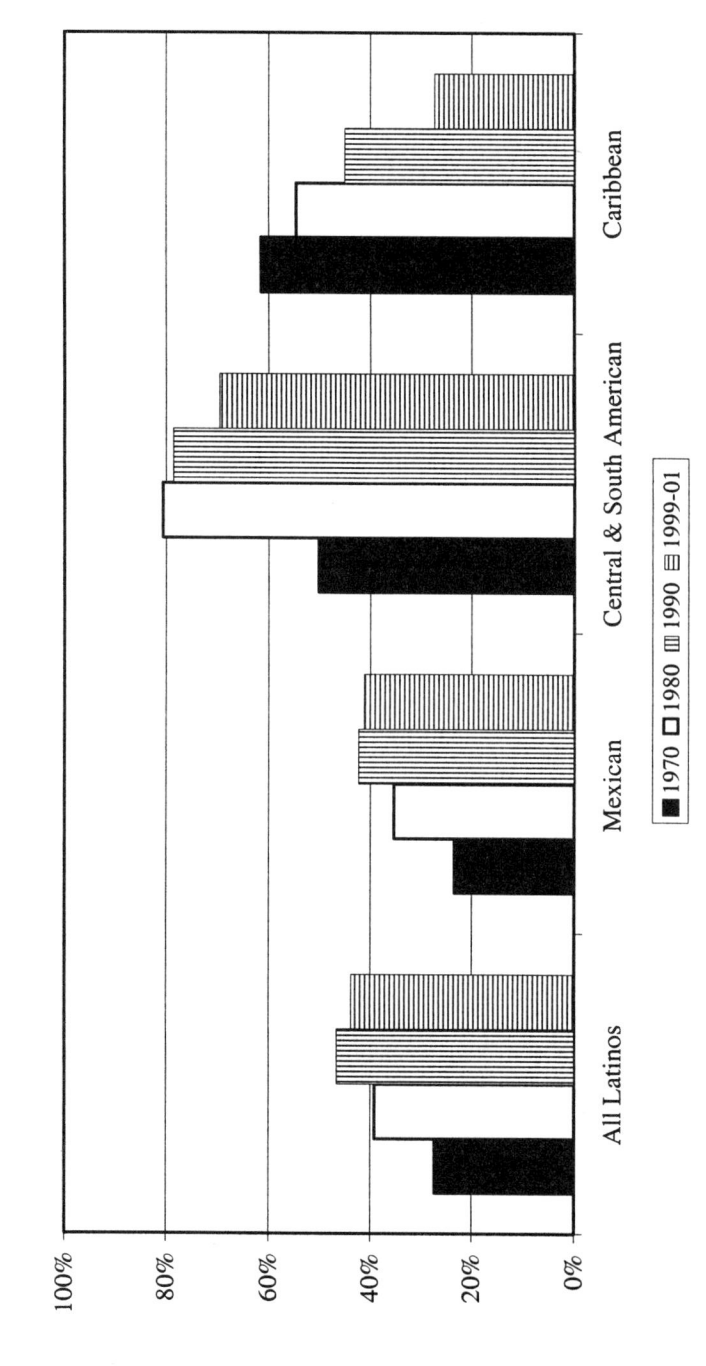

Source: Author's calculations from California Department of Finance and the Current Population Survey for 1999–2001

Figure 1.4. Births per Year for the Major Racial and Ethnic Groups in California, 1971–1999

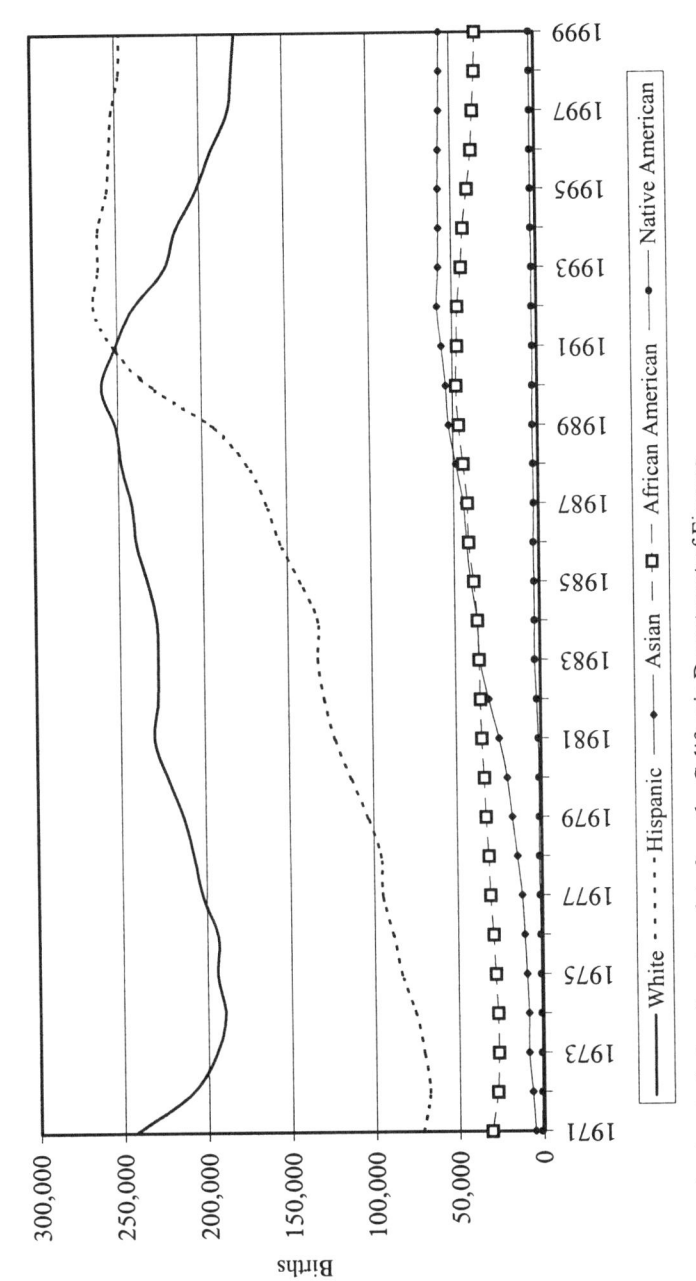

Source: Author's calculations based on data from the California Department of Finance.

state (see Figure 1.5). In 1970, Latinos were less than five percent of the population in over half of California counties. By 2000, only one county, Trinity, had a population that was less than five percent Hispanic. In 1970, Hispanics constituted more than 30 percent of the population in only two counties (Imperial and San Benito). By 2000, more than a third of California counties were over 30 percent Hispanic, and Imperial County's population was 73 percent Hispanic. In contrast, no county had a population that was over 20 percent African American, while Asians constituted more than 20 percent of the population in four counties and 32 percent of the population in San Francisco. The largest increases in the Latino population occurred in the less populous counties (i.e., Alpine, Mono, and Mariposa). Among the more populous counties, Riverside, Orange, San Bernardino, and San Diego counties experienced the greatest increase (absolute number) in the Latino population.

Characteristics of the Latino Population in California

Latinos are a heterogeneous population. They are of different races, and although they share a common language and cultural heritage, there is a great deal of variation in the experience of different Latino national-origin groups. For example, Cubans, Nicaraguans, and South Americans possess high levels of formal education, while Mexicans and other Central Americans have low levels of educational attainment. Differences in migration and settlement patterns, and the type of reception given these groups in the United States, have also affected the process of incorporation (Bean and Tienda, 1987; Portes and Bach, 1985; Portes, 1998). For example, Cubans and some Nicaraguans were provided with refugee status and received much support from the federal government. This, in addition to their advantageous economic status before migration, facilitated their incorporation into U.S. society. On the other hand, the continuous immigration of Mexicans, their concentration in low-skill occupations (including agriculture), and the presence of a sizeable number of undocumented immigrants have helped create a working-poor population. For Central Americans, the uncertainty of their immigration status, the experience of home-country civil conflict, and their recent arrival have constrained their economic progress in the United States.

Many scholars wonder if it makes sense to use the single term "Latino" to describe populations with such diverse experiences. Bean and Tienda (1987) argue that the term "Latino" is increasingly used pan-ethnically to identify people who may not consider themselves members of the same group, but who are labeled so by the dominant majority. In addition, the group's social status *vis-à-vis* the dominant majority produces an ethnic identification for people from previously distinct national-origin groups who share similar experiences in the United States, creating a common sense of national identity. Although par-

Figure 1.5. Proportion of Latinos in California's County Populations, 1970 and 2000

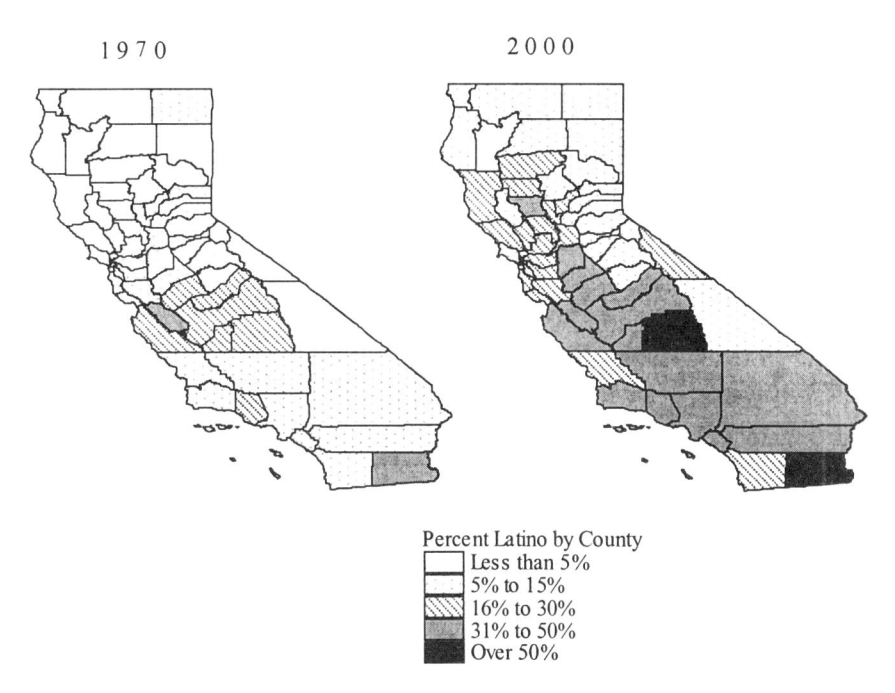

1970 2000

Percent Latino by County
- Less than 5%
- 5% to 15%
- 16% to 30%
- 31% to 50%
- Over 50%

Source: Author's calculations based on data from the California Department of Finance and the 2000 U.S. Census.

ticular issues may face each national-origin group, they are united by a common identity and a common set of concerns: immigration, voting rights and political participation, family preservation, education, business success, employment, language, and culture.

National Origin

Most of California's Latinos are of Mexican origin (see Figure 1.6). However, the proportion of Mexicans has been declining as the proportion of Central and South Americans has been increasing. In 1970, Mexicans were 87 percent of the state's Latino population, and by 2000 they made up 77 percent of the Latino population. Since the 1980s, a large influx of people from Central-American countries has increased their representation in California. In 1970, Central and South Americans were eight percent of the Latino population; by 2000 they made up 20 percent of the Latino population in California. In 2000 there were 8.4 million people of Mexican heritage, 2.3 million Central and South Americans, and 212,000 of Caribbean descent in California.

Among those of Central- and South-American origin, the largest groups are from El Salvador, Nicaragua, and Guatemala, as Figure 1.7 shows. With 440,000 California immigrants in 1999–2001, El Salvador ranked third among immigrant-sending countries to the state, and second among Latino immigrant groups in California. In the South- and Central-American subgroup there are also a substantial number of persons from Honduras, Peru, Argentina, and Colombia. Most of the Caribbean population is of Cuban and Puerto Rican descent.

Age Distribution

Figure 1.8 shows the age and gender distribution of the California Latino population as compared to that of the non-Hispanic white population. The baby-boom cohorts, those aged 35–55 in 2000, are especially evident in the age distribution of whites. One-third of non-Hispanic whites were between those ages in 2000. In contrast, Latinos have the youngest population of all racial and ethnic groups, with a median age of 25 in 2000. Hispanics outnumber non-Hispanic whites under age 25, and there are only 18,000 fewer Latinos than whites in the age 25–34 group. Whites outnumber Hispanics in the older cohort groups. For every four non-Hispanic white people older than 55 there is one Latino.

There is some variation in the age structure of Latino subgroups (see Figure 1.9). While 58 percent of all California Latinos were between 18 and 64 in 1999–2001, 84 percent of Latino immigrants were in this age group, and this

Figure 1.6. Populations of Selected Latino Groups in California, 1970, 1980, 1990, 2000

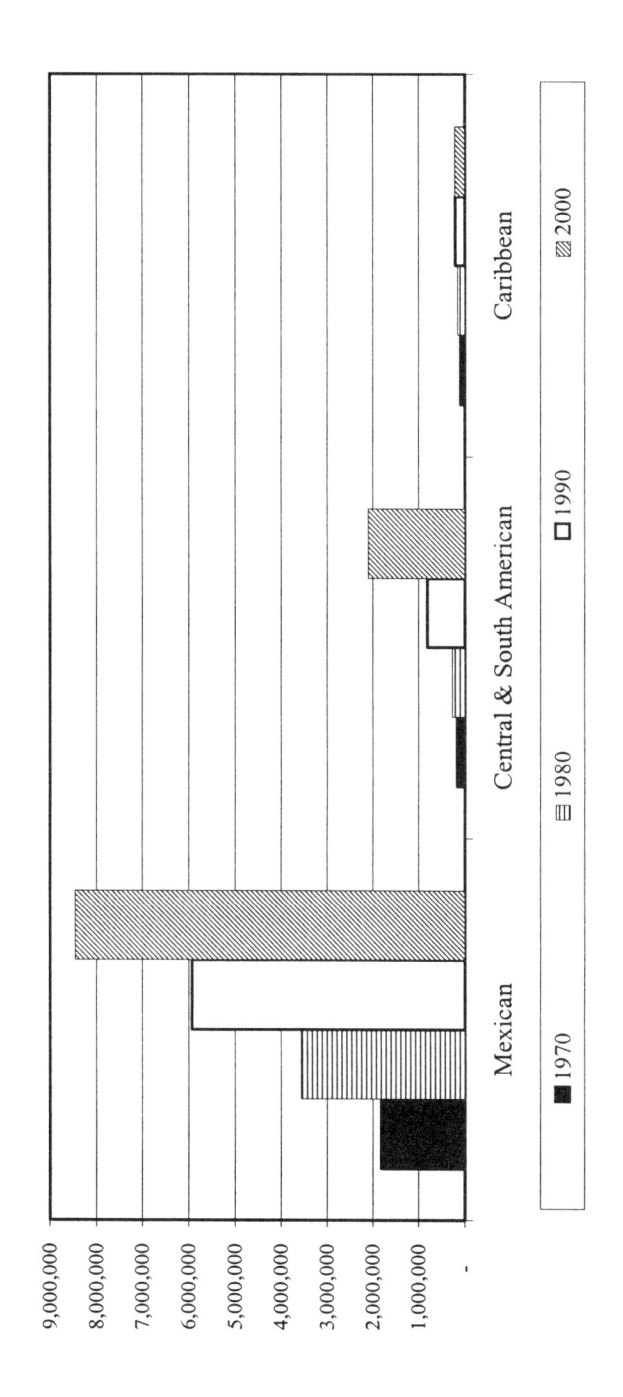

	Mexican	Central & South American	Caribbean

■ 1970   ☰ 1980   ☐ 1990   ▨ 2000

Source: Johnson (2001) and author calculations from the 2000 U.S. Census.
Note: People identified as "other Hispanic" were included in the Central- and South-American category, since it is possible that most of them did not select a country of origin because of changes in the way the Spanish-origin question was asked in the 2000 U.S. Census.

Figure 1.7. Home Countries of South- and Central-American Immigrants in California, Various Years 1970–2001

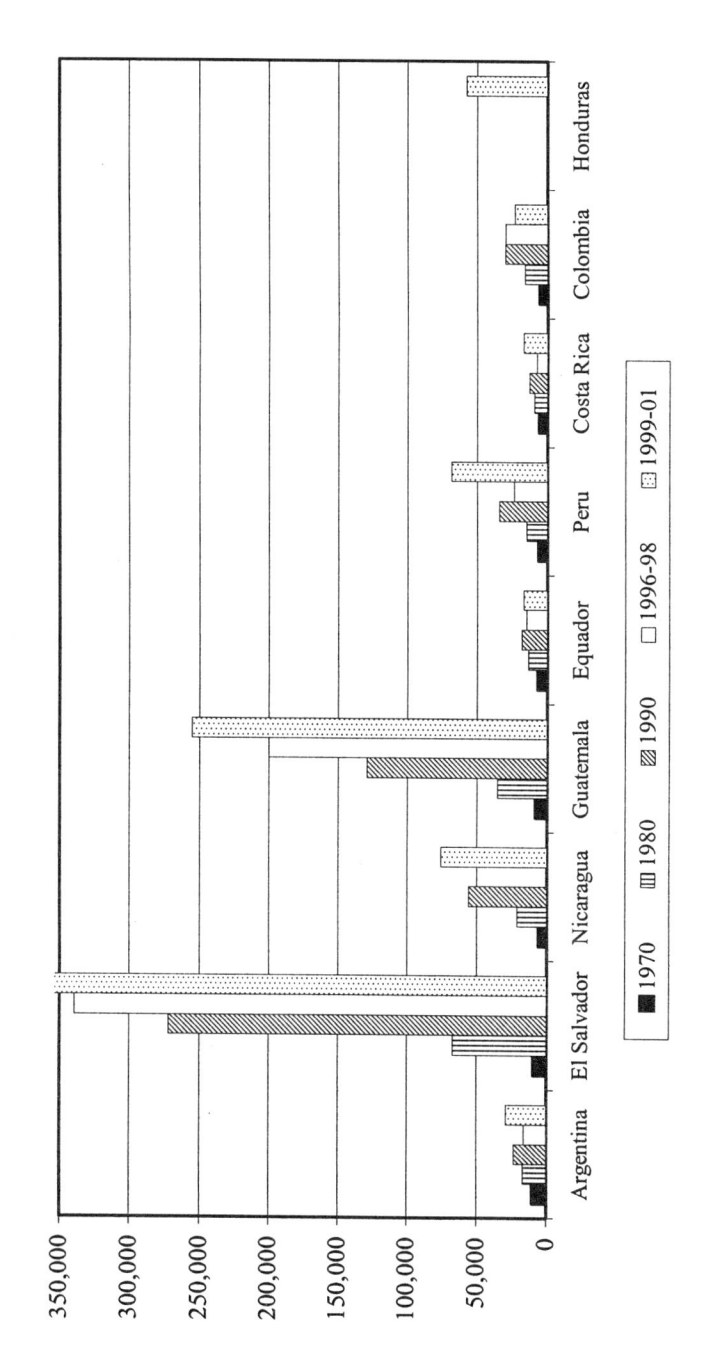

Source: Johnson (2001) and author calculations from the 1996–2001 CPS.

Population Growth and Diversity 13

Figure 1.8. Age and Gender Distribution for Latinos and Non-Hispanic Whites in California, 2000

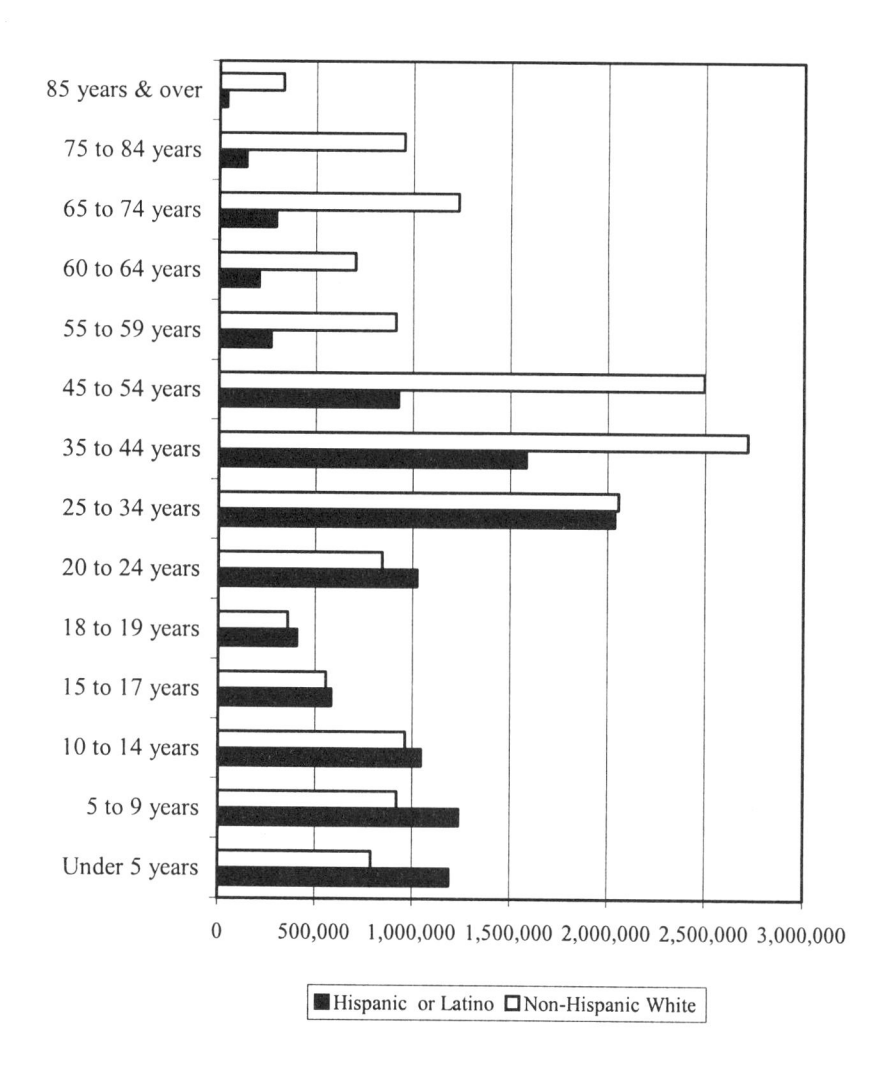

■ Hispanic or Latino   □ Non-Hispanic White

Source: Author's calculations based on data from the 2000 U.S. Census.
Hispanic: Males 5,615,031, Females 5,351,525
Non-Hispanic White: Males 7,008,532 Females: 8,808,258

Figure 1.9. Age Structures of Latino Subgroups in California, 1970, 1990, and 1999–2001

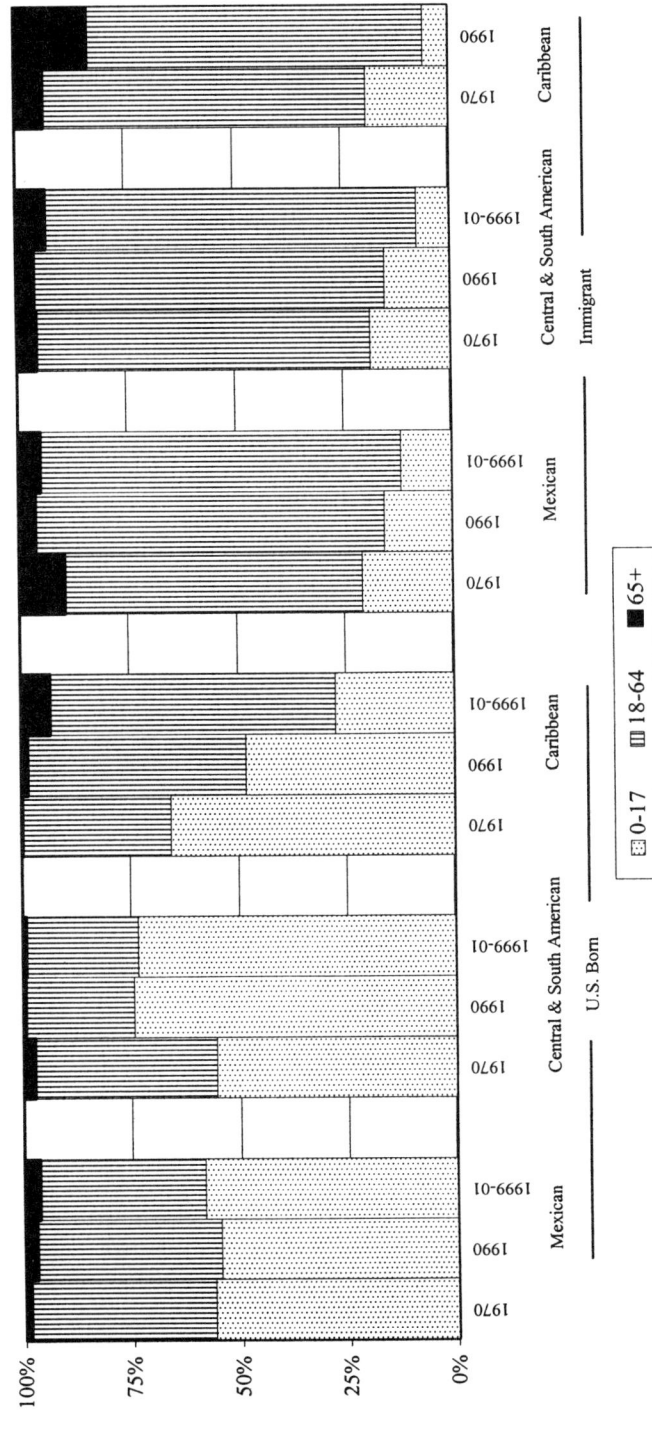

Source: Reed (2001) and author's calculations from the 1999, 2000, and 2001 CPS.

proportion has been increasing over time for immigrant subgroups. On the other hand, U.S.-born Latinos are a very young group, with 58 percent of them younger than 18. Seventy-three percent of U.S.-born Central and South Americans are younger than 18, reflecting the recency of their parents' arrival, as discussed below. Only a small proportion of Latinos are older than 65. Only among Caribbean immigrants do we see an elderly population profile similar to that of non-Hispanic whites.

Part of the explanation for the Latino age distribution in 2000 is the large proportion of recent arrivals among California Latinos (see Figure 1.10). In 1999–2001, 38 percent of Latino immigrants had been in the United States for less than 10 years. This is a decline from prior periods. In 1970, about half of the Latinos born abroad had been in the United States for less than 10 years. As for other outcomes, there is a great deal of variation across Latino subgroups. In 1970, about 80 percent of Caribbean immigrants and 70 percent of South- and Central-American immigrants had been in the United States for less than 10 years, but by 1999–2001 this proportion declined to 11 percent and 36 percent, respectively. By the 1999–2001 period, Mexicans had the largest proportion of recent arrivals among all Latino-immigrant groups, overtaking South and Central Americans, who had had the highest proportion of recent arrivals in the prior three decades.

English-Language Proficiency

The large proportion of recent immigrants may also account for the relatively low levels of English proficiency among Latinos. Twenty-seven percent of Latinos reported having limited English ability in 1990, with 10 percent completely unable to speak English (see Figure 1.11). However, this is not an issue for U.S.-born Latinos; overall only about six percent of U.S.-born Latinos had limited English-speaking ability in 1990. For U.S.-born Latinos of Central- and South-American descent, the proportion with limited English ability was slightly higher at nine percent, but this may be a result of their young age (see Figure 1.9). Among Latino immigrants, limited English-speaking ability is much more of a concern (see Chapter 5). Almost half of Mexican immigrants had limited English-speaking ability, with 20 percent completely unable to speak English. About 40 percent of Central and South Americans and 34 percent of Caribbeans had limited ability, with roughly 14 percent unable to speak any English in 1990.

Figure 1.10. Proportion of Latino Immigrants Who Are Recent (Less than 10 years) Arrivals in California, 1970, 1980, 1990, and 1999–2001

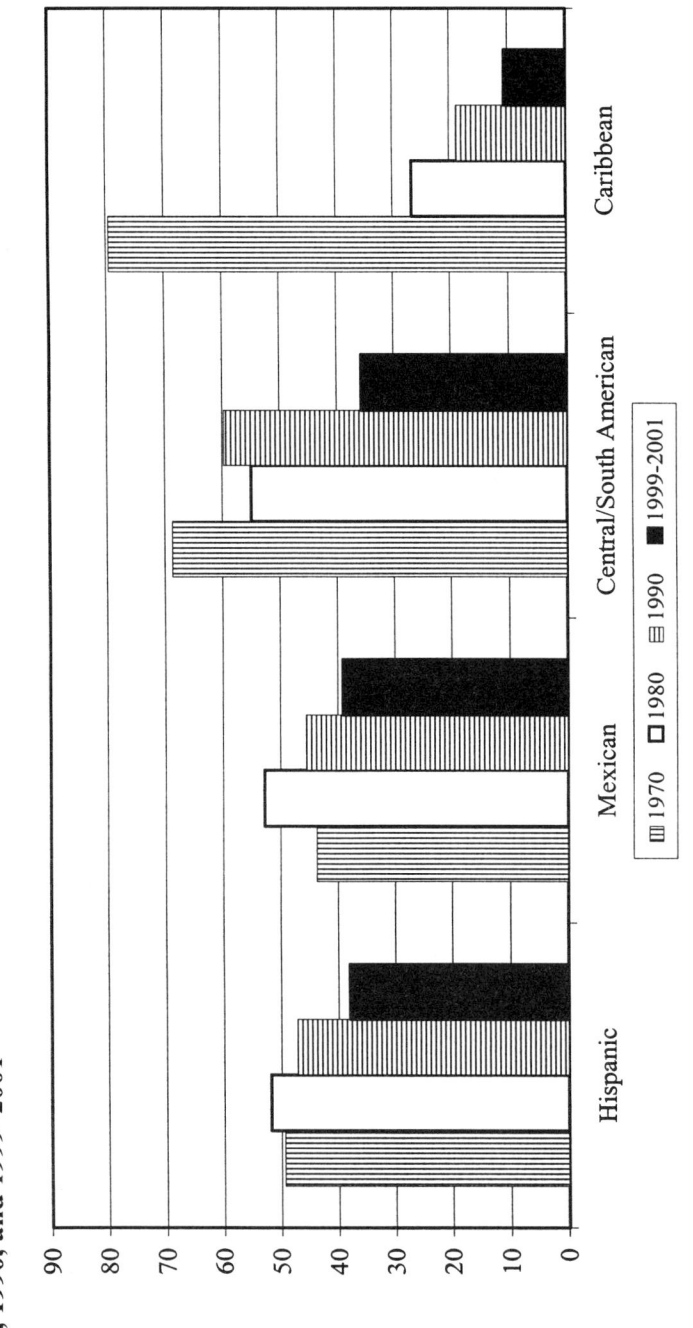

Source: Johnson (2001) and author's calculations from the 1999–2001 CPS.

Figure 1.11. English-Language Ability for Latinos in California, 1990

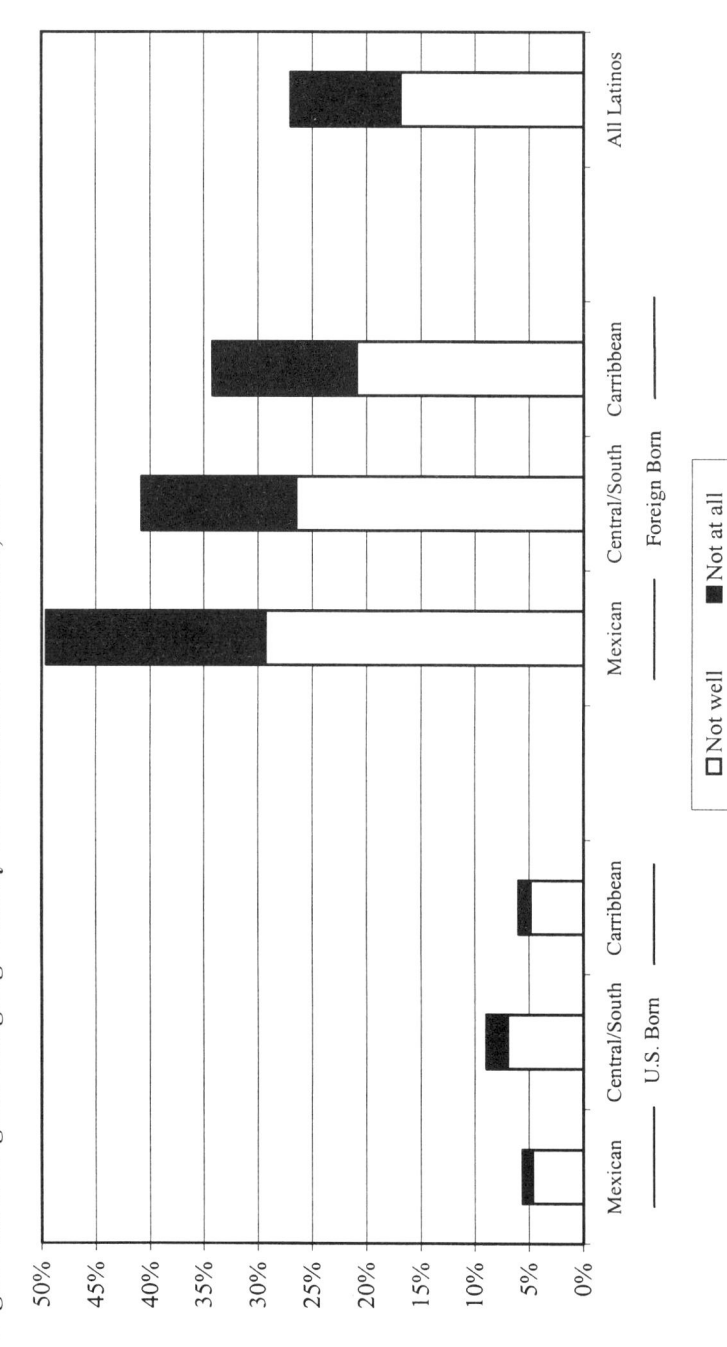

□ Not well ■ Not at all

Source: Reed (2001).

Educational Attainment

Educational attainment is associated with employment, earnings, family income, and health status. Lifetime opportunities are strongly linked to parental education and one's own education. Latinos had the lowest levels of education of all racial and ethnic groups as of 2001. I examined the educational attainment of adults 25–54 in order to capture the educational attainment of people in the labor force (see Figure 1.12). Currently, 46 percent of Latino adults have less than a high-school degree, an improvement from prior years: In both 1980 and 1990, 55 percent of Latino adults had no high-school diploma. Furthermore, there has been a substantial degree of intergenerational improvement in educational attainment, as seen by the differences in attainment between U.S.-born and foreign-born Latinos. While 61 percent of Latino immigrants had less than a high-school education, only 17 percent of U.S.-born Latinos had not completed high school in the 1999–2001 period. Even so, the educational attainment of U.S.-born Latinos still lags behind that of other racial and ethnic groups in the state. Only five percent of non-Latino whites and six percent of African Americans had less than a high-school education in 1999–2001.

A breakdown of Hispanic subgroups reveals a wide range of education levels across the different groups (see Figure 1.13). In the 1999–2001 period, 18 percent of U.S.-born Mexicans had less than a high-school education.[6] Among immigrant groups, the share with no high-school diploma was 44 percent for Central and South Americans, and 65 percent for Mexicans. However, all Latino groups experienced improvements in their educational achievement, especially U.S.-born Mexicans. The proportion that had completed high school more than doubled between 1980 and 1999–2001. The increase in the proportion of Central- and South-American immigrants with less than a high-school education in 1990 reflects the large influx of immigrants with low levels of education from that region in the 1980s.

Socio-Economic Status: A Brief Overview

As a group, Latinos exhibit some of the poorest economic outcomes in the state. They have the lowest median family income and highest child-poverty rates of all racial and ethnic groups in California. However, they have the highest rate of labor-force participation and the smallest proportion of low-income families

---

[6]Sample sizes for the 1999–2001 combined CPS are too small to generate reliable estimates of high-school completion rates for U.S.-born Central and South Americans and U.S.-born and foreign-born Caribbeans.

Figure 1.12. Proportion of California Adults 25–54 with Less than a High-School Education, 1980, 1990, and 1999-2001

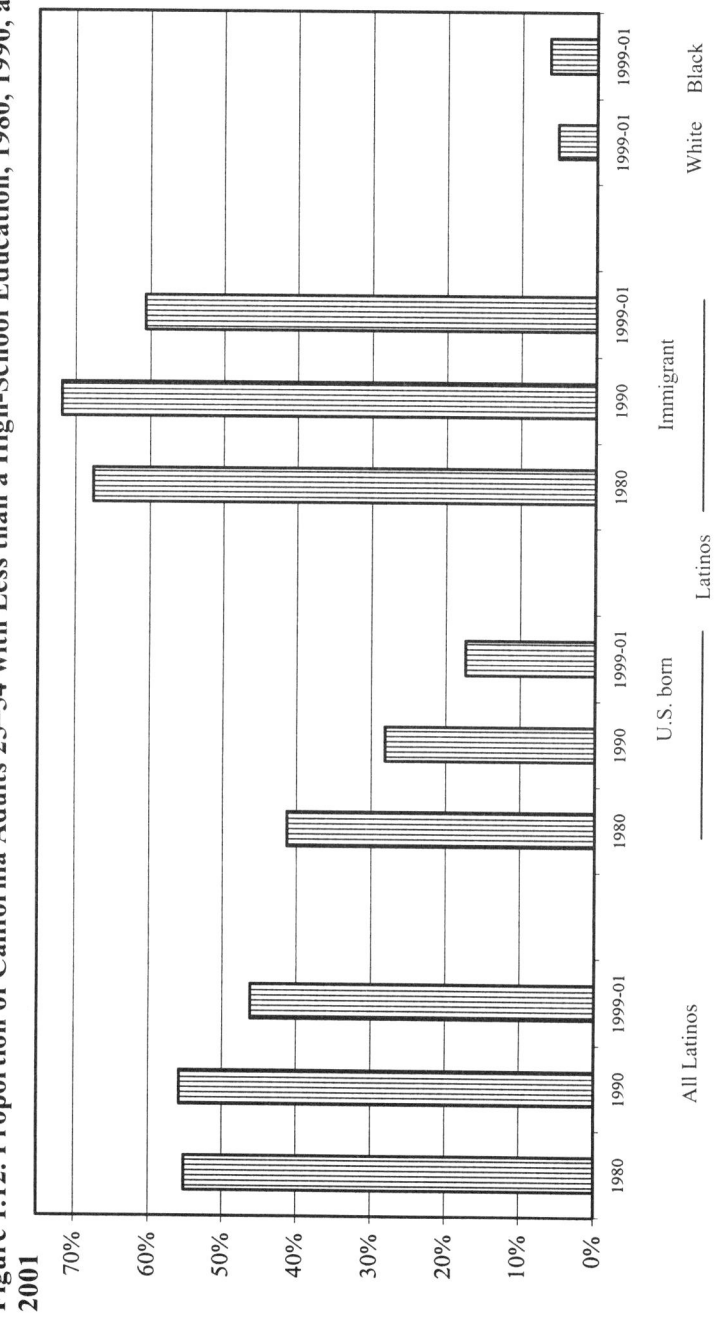

Source: Reed (2001) and author's calculations from the 1999–2001 CPS.

Figure 1.13. Proportion of California Adults 25–54 with Less than a High-School Education by Immigration Status, 1980, 1990, and 1999–2001

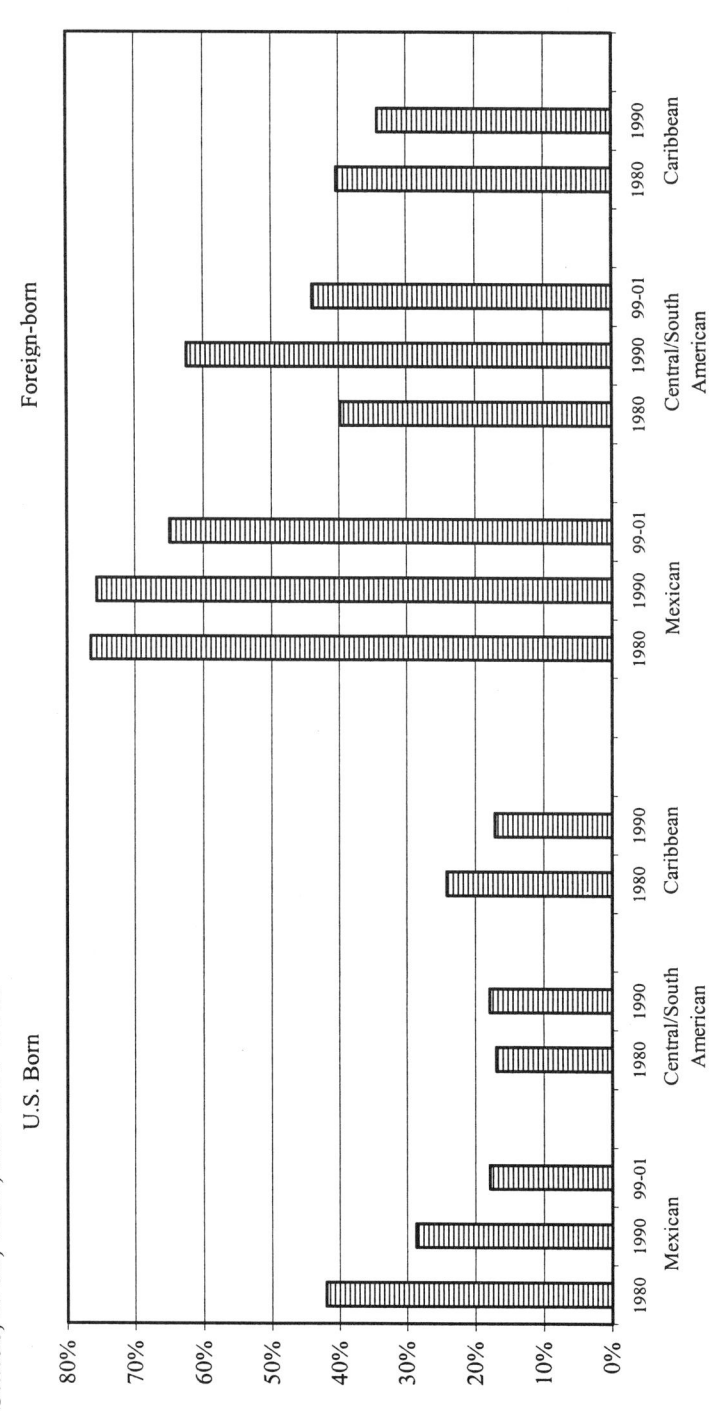

Source: Reed (2001) and author's calculations from the 1999–2001 CPS.

receiving welfare. There are also signs of socio-economic progress; with help from the state, greater improvements could be expected in the future. These trends will be reviewed briefly here and are discussed thoroughly in Chapter 2.

Latinos have the lowest family incomes of all racial and ethnic groups in California (see Figure 1.14). Since the late 1980s, median family income for Latinos has been below that of African Americans. In addition, the income of Latinos did not recover as quickly as that of other groups after the recession of the early 1990s; it took until 2000 for their median family income to reach the same level it had attained in the last peak in 1989. In contrast, by 2000 the median family income of white non-Hispanics had increased by nine percent above the 1989 levels. Among African Americans, median family income was five percent higher in 2000 than in the 1989 peak.

Part of the explanation for a decline in family income for Latinos is the increase in the proportion of Latinos who are foreign-born, as seen in Figure 1.3. On average, foreign-born residents earn less than U.S. natives. Hence, an increase in the proportion of immigrants among the Latino population would lead to a decline in median family income. But also at play is a decline in Latino earnings. As shown in Figure 1.15, between 1980 and 2001, median earnings declined for Latinos. This was true even for U.S. born Latinos (Reed and Cheng, forthcoming). Lower educational attainment, occupational segregation, and other factors in the U.S. labor market, such as discrimination, help explain the lower earnings of Latinos as compared to other groups (Reed and Cheng, forthcoming).

Although their earnings are low, Latinos participate in the labor force in large numbers (see Figure 1.16). Latino males participate at rates similar to those of non-Hispanic whites, and in the economic downturn of the early 1990s their rate of participation did not decline as rapidly as that of other groups. Latino women, however, participate at rates below those of other racial and ethnic groups.

Low earnings among those in the labor force limit the resources available to Latino households and increases poverty rates among Hispanics. In 2000, a third of Latino children lived in households with an income below the poverty line (see Figure 1.17). Furthermore, poverty rates among Latinos, as for African Americans, are very responsive to economic fluctuations, making children highly vulnerable to economic fluctuations in the future.

In spite of higher levels of Latino poverty than those of white and Asian households, the proportion of low-income Latino households in public assistance is similar to that of whites and Asians (see Figure 1.18). While a third of Latino children lived in poor households in 2000, only 12 percent of poor Latino households received public assistance.

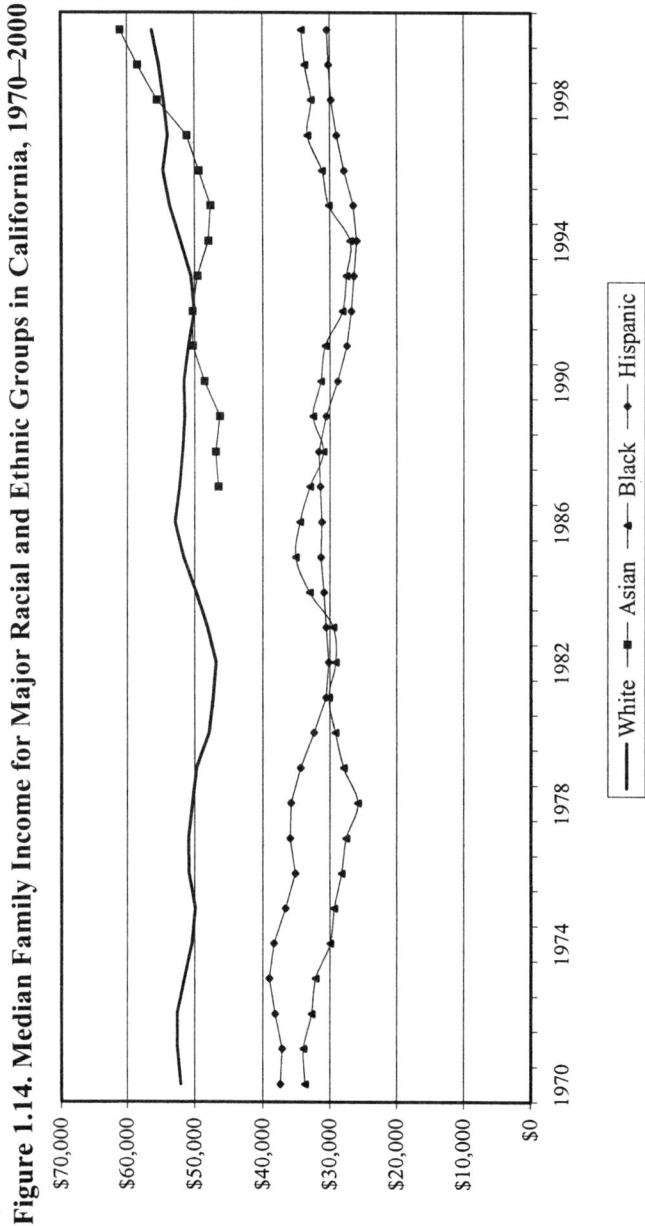

Figure 1.14. Median Family Income for Major Racial and Ethnic Groups in California, 1970–2000

Source: Author's estimate from the 1970–2001 CPS.
Note: Three-year moving average. Family income is the sum of the income of all family members, but it is measured at the individual level, and measures the mid-income available to Latinos in their families, not correcting for family size. Data for Asians are not available before 1988 in the CPS.

Figure 1.15. California Median Weekly Earnings of Hispanic Male Full-Time Workers Age 25 to 54 by Place of Birth, 1980–2001

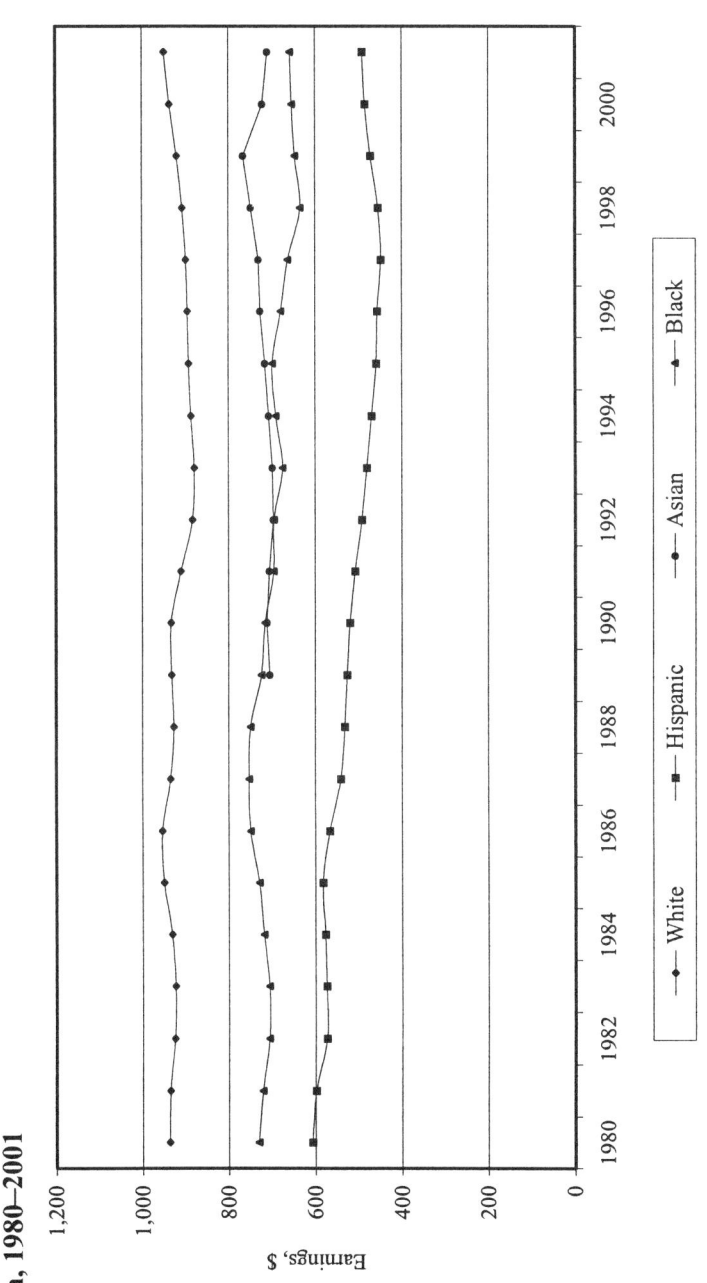

Source: Reed and Cheng (2001).

Figure 1.16. California Labor-Force Participation of Major Racial and Ethnic Groups, 1979–2000

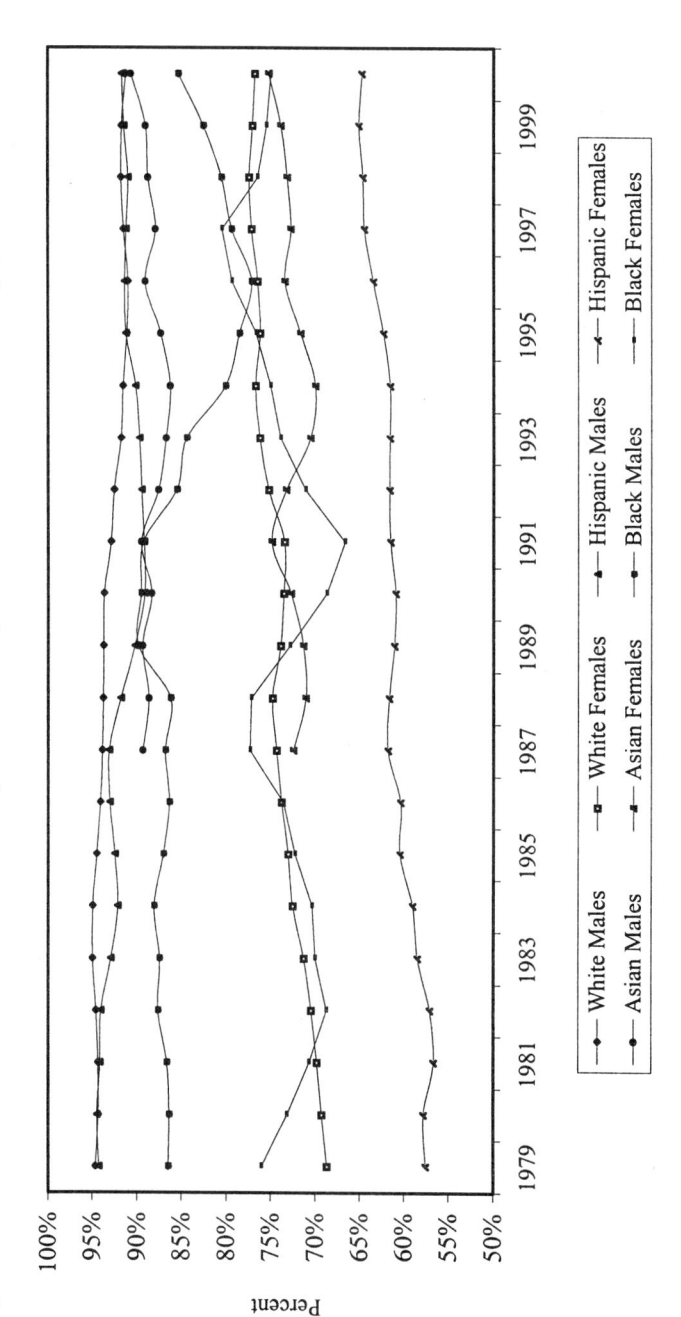

Source: Author's calculations from the 1979–2001 CPS.
Note: This is the percentage of the population employed or actively looking for work in the month prior to the survey. It is a three-year moving average. Data for Asians are not available prior to 1988 and are less reliable than for other racial and ethnic groups, because of sample limitations.

Figure 1.17. Poverty Rates of California Children 16 and Under by Race and Ethnicity, 1970–2000

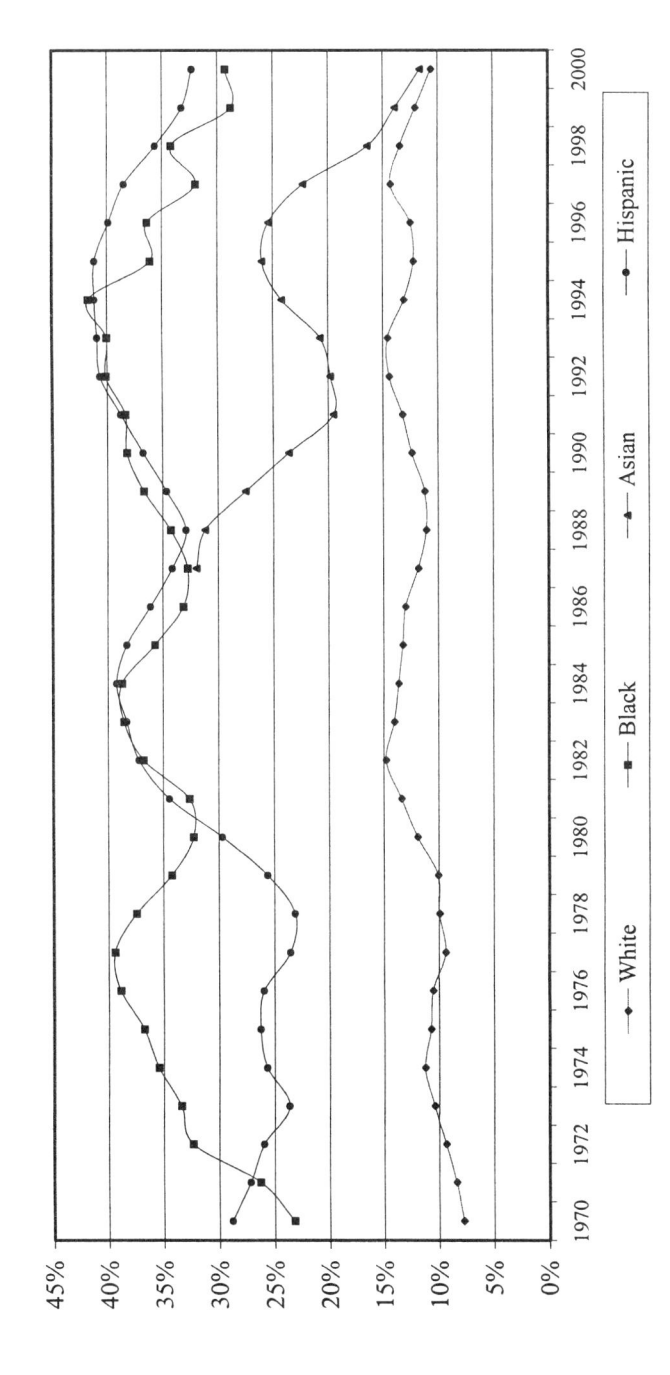

Source: Author's calculations from the 1970–2001 CPS.
Note: Numbers presented in three-year moving averages. Data for Asians are not available prior to 1988 and are less reliable than for other racial and ethnic groups because of sample limitations.

Figure 1.18. Proportion of California Low-Income Households That Received Some Income from Social Services, 1987–2000

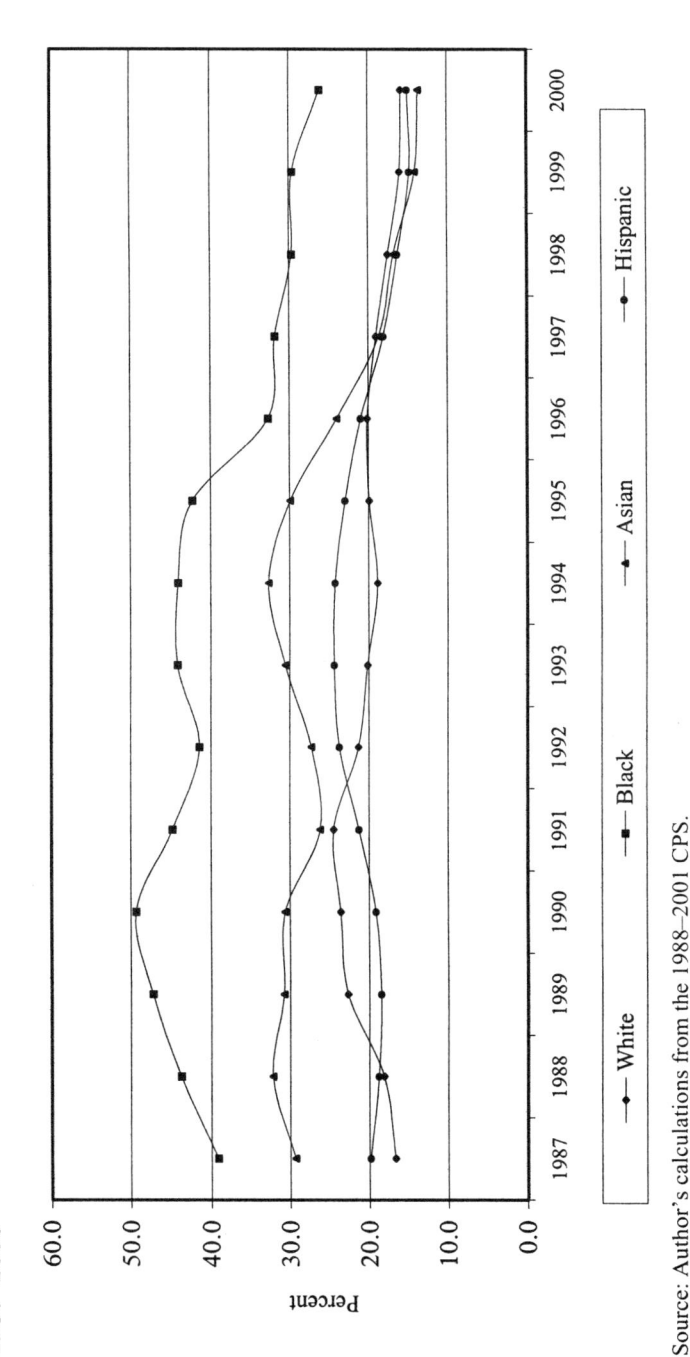

Source: Author's calculations from the 1988–2001 CPS.
Notes: Households are defined by the ethnicity of the head of household. Some of these households may be of mixed ethnicity. Low income is defined as 200% above the federal poverty line of $18,000 for a family of four (as of 2000).

Since the passage of the Personal Responsibility and Work Opportunity Reconciliation Act (PRWORA) of 1996, welfare use has declined for all racial and ethnic groups, especially African Americans and Asians. However, Latino usage appears to be less responsive to the change in policy and more responsive to economic fluctuations in the U.S. economy than that of other racial and ethnic groups.

It is important to point out that although PRWORA has significantly decreased the rate of public-assistance use among poor populations, it has had little effect on poverty rates. As shown in Figure 1.17, poverty rates remained high in 2000, and future economic fluctuations could have a devastating effect on the well-being of families without a safety net.

Political Participation

A high proportion of recent immigrants, the presence of many unauthorized immigrants, and a young population (many under 18) result in a high proportion of Latinos who are ineligible to vote.[7] Even the characteristics of those eligible—poor English proficiency and low educational attainment—are correlated with low participation in the political process. (See Chapter 11 for a full discussion of Latino political participation). Latinos have lower rates of registration and voting than other racial and ethnic groups, except for Asians. As Figure 1.19 shows, in 2000 Latinos were 31 percent of the California adult population but only 15 percent of those who voted.

However, recent years have shown tremendous growth in the Latino rates of naturalization, registration, and voting. After the passage of Proposition 187 in California in 1996, naturalization rates began to increase for Latinos (see Figure 1.20).[8] But as opposed to a short-term response to policy concerns of the time,

---

[7]To be eligible to vote a person must be a U.S. citizen who is 18 or older.

[8]I restricted the sample to people older than 18 who had been in the United States for more than five years. I also estimated the unauthorized population in order to estimate the number of eligible Latinos. I used Warren (1997) estimates of the unauthorized population and the growth in the unauthorized population. I assumed that 80 percent of unauthorized immigrants are Latinos and that a third of unauthorized immigrants stay longer than five years in the United States. Although a better estimate of the naturalization rate of eligible Latinos, this may still be an underestimate of the naturalization rate for Latinos, especially because many unauthorized Latinos entered the country in the late 1990s. See, for example, Belinda Reyes, Hans Johnson, and Richard Van Swearingen, "The Effect of the Recent Border Build-up on Unauthorized Immigration" (San Francisco, Calif.: PPIC Report, 2002); and Hans Johnson, Belinda Reyes, Laura Mameesh, and Elisa

Figure 1.19. California Population Proportions and Voting Population

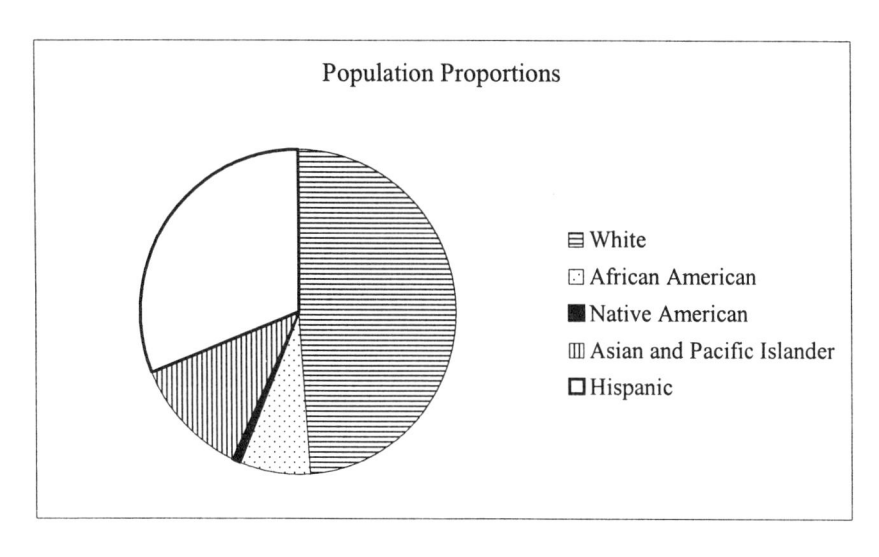

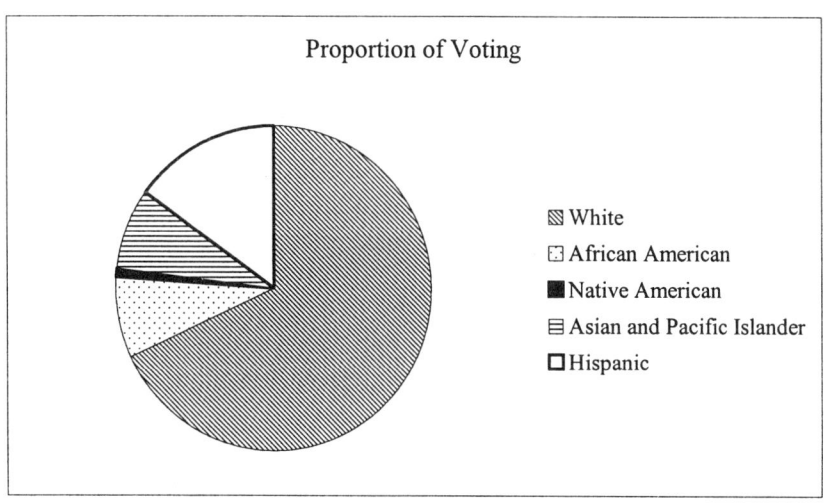

Population Proportions

- White
- African American
- Native American
- Asian and Pacific Islander
- Hispanic

Proportion of Voting

- White
- African American
- Native American
- Asian and Pacific Islander
- Hispanic

Source: Author's calculations from the 2000 November Supplement to the CPS.

Barbour, "Taking the Oath: An Analysis of Naturalization in California and the United States" (San Francisco, Calif.: PPIC Report, 1999).

Figure 1.20. Estimates of the Rate of Naturalization in California, 1996–2001

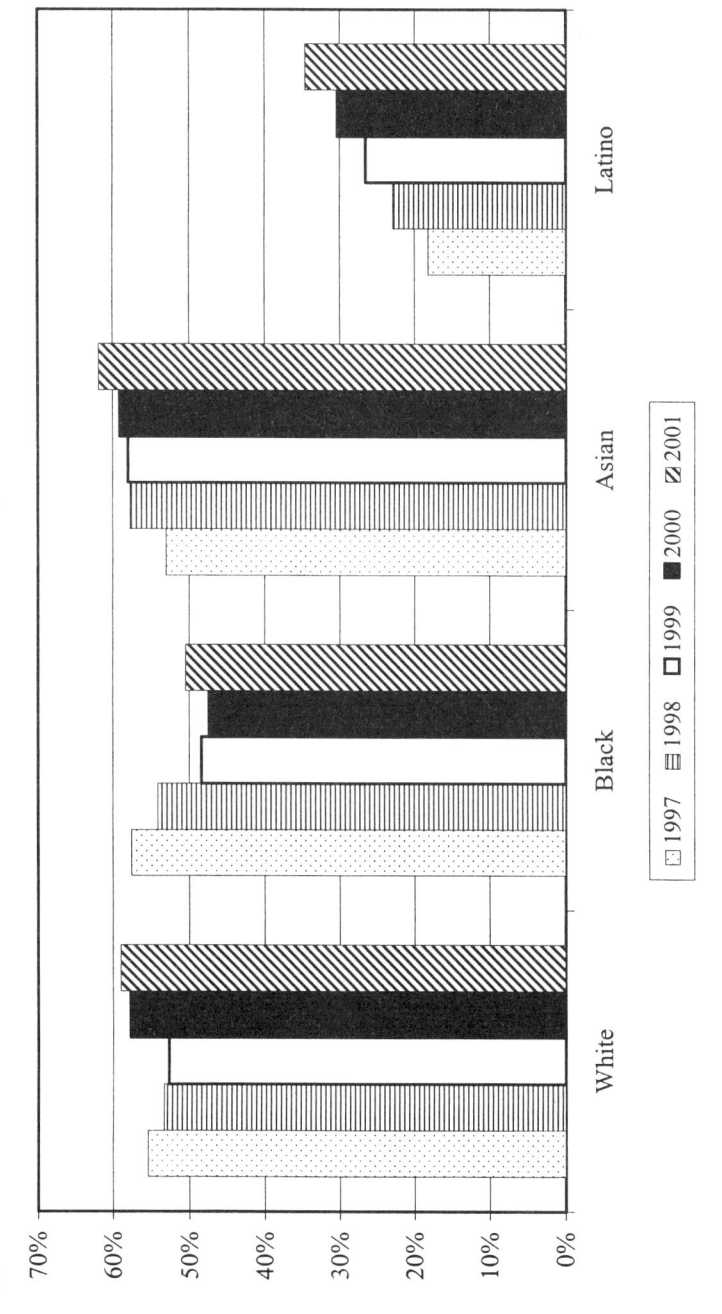

□ 1997 ▤ 1998 ☐ 1999 ■ 2000 ▨ 2001

Source: Author's calculations from the CPS for 1996–2001.

Figure 1.21. California Registration Rates and Voting Rates of Eligible Voters, 1972–2000

Registration Rates

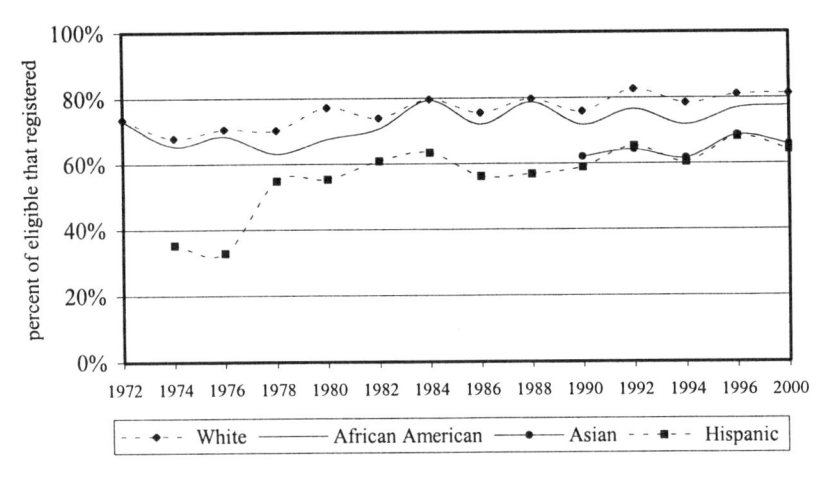

Voting Rates

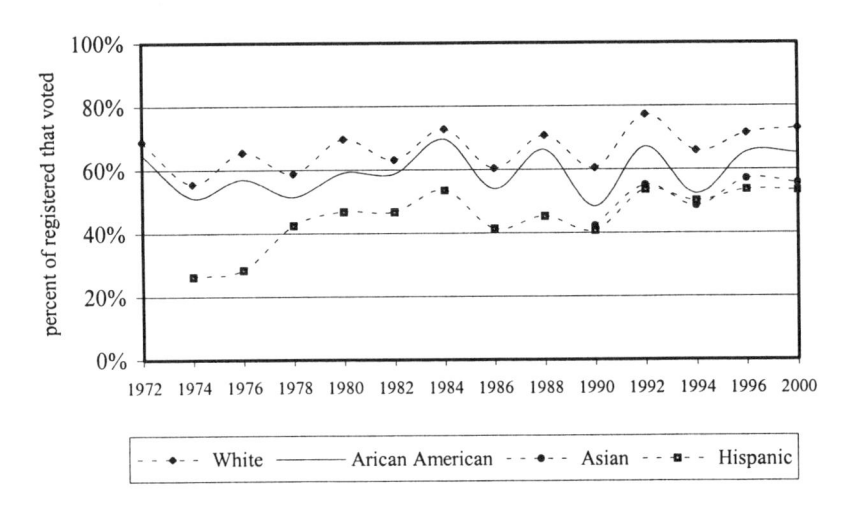

Source: Marco, Signoret, and Reyes (2001) and author's calculations from the November CPS for 1998 and 2000.

this trend has continued into the present. Yet even after the increase in the 1990s, naturalization rates among Latinos remain far below those of other immigrant groups.

Latino registration and voting rates have also been increasing faster than those of other racial and ethnic groups in the last 20 years (see Figure 1.21). In 1974, 35 percent of eligible Hispanics registered to vote. By 2000, this rate had increased to 64 percent. Voting rates among Latinos have historically been low. Only 26 percent of Latinos eligible to vote did so in 1974, but by 2000, 53 percent of eligible Latino voters participated in the election.

In addition to naturalizing, registering, and voting in greater numbers, Latinos have increased their political clout in the state. Since the 1980s, Latino elected officials have significantly outnumbered their African-American and Asian counterparts and have further increased their ranks. Rising from 460 in 1984, the number of Hispanics holding public office peaked in 1994 with 796 and decreased only slightly to 789 in 1998. While the number of Latino officials has increased over the last two decades, Latinos, along with Asians and African Americans, remain underrepresented in public office (see Figure 1.22). In 1998, Hispanics held 10 percent of all public-office positions, Asians 6.5 percent, and African Americans three percent. At best, these rates reflect only half of these groups' presence in the adult population (see Figure 1.19). These results, however, correspond closely with current Asian and Hispanic voting shares, while the representation of African Americans is less than half that of their voting population.

Summary

The Latino population will soon become the largest racial and ethnic group in the state of California. Most of the births in California are to Latino parents and Latinos already outnumber white non-Hispanics under age 25. In some parts of the state, such as Los Angeles County, they already constitute the largest racial and ethnic group.

In addition to being numerous, Latinos are a diverse population with a wide range of income and education characteristics. Some Latinos possess low levels of formal education. And although most have a strong desire to improve their lives and those of their children, they may lack the educational, social, and economic resources to advance in U.S. society. Others are highly educated professionals developing the infrastructure to build strong businesses here and abroad, expanding California's global influence.

Even though there has been a great deal of progress across generations, Latino levels of educational attainment, English proficiency, and earnings are still

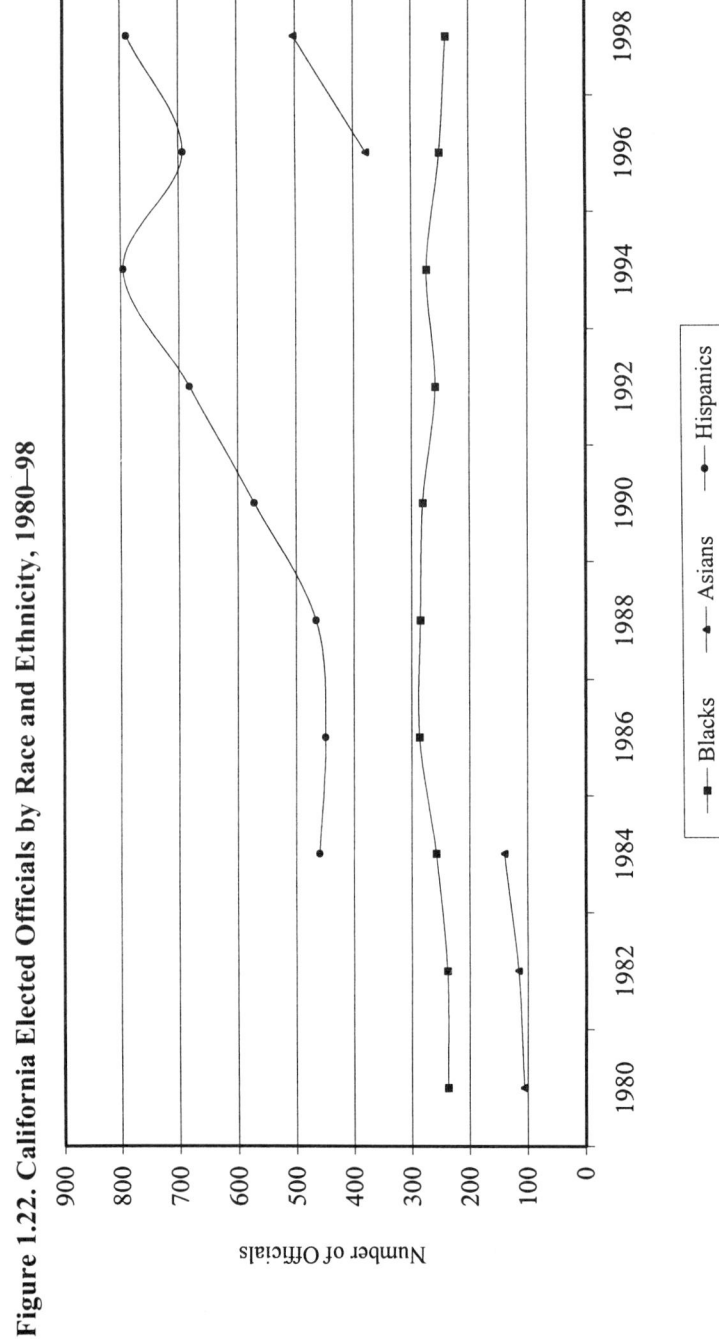

Figure 1.22. California Elected Officials by Race and Ethnicity, 1980–98

Source: Marco, Signoret, and Reyes (2001).

below those of other racial and ethnic groups, exemplified by the highest poverty rates in the state. For example, one of every three Latino children lived in a low-income household in 2000. Further, the fact that Latino families tend not to utilize social services as much as other low-income populations limits the resources available to them.

Despite traditional barriers such as ineligibility to vote due to immigration status and historically low rates of naturalization and political participation, Latinos in recent years have substantially increased their share of both the electorate and representation in public office.

The future progress of Latino communities, and the well-being of California, will depend on how well the state is able to make strategic investments that build on the resources and opportunities represented by these communities, and how effectively it responds to the needs of this key population group.

References

Bean, Frank, and Marta Tienda. 1987. *The Hispanic Population of the United States.* New York: Russell Sage Foundation.

Hill, Laura, and Hans Johnson. 2002. *Understanding the Future of California's Fertility: The Role of Immigrants.* San Francisco, Calif.: Public Policy Institute of California.

Johnson, Hans. 2001. "Demographics." In *A Portrait of Race and Ethnicity in California: Social and Economic Well-Being of Racial and Ethnic Groups,* ed. Belinda Reyes. San Francisco, Calif.: Public Policy Institute of California.

Johnson, Hans, Belinda Reyes, Laura Mameesh, and Elisa Barbour. 1999. *Taking the Oath: An Analysis of Naturalization in California and the United States.* San Francisco, Calif.: Public Policy Institute of California.

Macro, Elizabeth, Jose Signoret, and Belinda Reyes. 2001. "Political Participation." In *A Portrait of Race and Ethnicity in California: Social and Economic Well-Being of Racial and Ethnic Groups,* ed. Belinda Reyes. San Francisco, Calif.: Public Policy Institute of California.

Portes, Alejandro. 1998. "From South of the Border: Hispanic Minorities in the United States." In *The Immigration Reader: American in a Multidisciplinary Perspective,* ed. David Jacobson. Oxford, Mass.: Blackwell Publishers.

Portes, Alejandro, and Richard Bach. 1985. *Latin Journey: Cuban and Mexican Immigrants in the United States.* Berkeley, Calif.: University of California Press.

Reed, Deborah. 2001 "Educational Outcomes." In *A Portrait of Race and Ethnicity in California: Social and Economic Well-Being of Racial and Ethnic Groups,* ed. Belinda Reyes. San Francisco, Calif.: Public Policy Institute of California.

Reed, Deborah, and Jennifer Cheng. Forthcoming. *Racial and Ethnic Wage Gaps in the California Labor Market.* San Francisco, Calif.: Public Policy Institute of California.

Reyes, Belinda. 2001. "Economic Outcomes." In *A Portrait of Race and Ethnicity in California: Social and Economic Well-Being of Racial and Ethnic Groups,* ed. Belinda Reyes. San Francisco, Calif.: Public Policy Institute of California.

Reyes, Belinda, Hans Johnson, and Richard Van Swearingen. 2002. *The Effect of the Recent Border Build-up on Unauthorized Immigration.* San Francisco, Calif.: Public Policy Institute of California.

Warren, Robert. 1997. *Estimates of the Undocumented Immigrant Population Residing in the United States: October 1996.* Washington, D.C.: U.S. Immigration and Naturalization Services.

Chapter 2

Rising Tides and Sinking Boats:
The Economic Challenge for California's Latinos

Manuel Pastor, Jr.[1]

Introduction

After a sharp recession in the early 1990s, the California economy rebounded in the second half of the decade. Unemployment rates, after rising dramatically above the rest of the nation, tapered back down toward the national level. Employment growth was impressive, with 2.5 million jobs added over the 1993–2000 period. Although the "dot-bomb" collapse that began in 2000 and the energy crisis that erupted in 2001 put brakes on the expansion, most analysts concur that California's fundamental economic strengths are many: With Silicon Valley and multimedia in the north, and motion pictures and biotechnology in the south, California has been heralded as the home of high tech and the "new economy."

Yet any optimism about the recent boom and long-term economic future has been tempered by a rising awareness of the continuing trends toward inequality

---

[1] Thanks to the California Policy Research Center for supporting the research on which this paper is based. Thanks also to John Hipp, Karina Winata, Rachel Rosner, and Javier Huizar for research assistance.

in the state.[2] According to most researchers, the divergence between the top and the bottom of the income scale seems to be increasing even more rapidly in California than in the rest of the nation. While this is a worrisome pattern in general, it is especially challenging for California's Latinos, most of whom are disproportionately concentrated in the lower end of the distribution of income, power, and opportunities.

California's Latinos bring obvious assets to the economic table—especially a demonstrated work ethic and a strong desire to form both families and businesses—but in an economy that increasingly values skills and connections, Latinos remain handicapped by low education levels and limited social networks. The analysis below indicates that the current disparities may even worsen in the near future: While the non-Latino white population is disproportionately present in industries that enjoy high wages and high rates of projected employment growth, Latinos tend to be situated in industries that are likely to grow but in which lower wages are the norm. If unchecked, these trends could constitute a recipe for resentment and, eventually, social conflict.

This chapter offers a profile of the contemporary Latino experience in the California economy. I begin with a brief review of employment and distributional trends, stressing the widening gaps by class, race, and geography. I then profile key economic characteristics of California's Latinos, especially the striking contradiction between high rates of labor-force participation and high rates of poverty, as well as the relatively low level of job quality and educational attainment. I offer a brief regression analysis of the determinants of Latino economic performance, stressing that while gaps in human capital or education go a long way toward explaining Latinos' fortunes, these factors do not fully account for interethnic wage differences. I close this section by pointing to the power of social networks and the growing but still limited presence and small scale of Latino-owned firms.

I conclude the chapter by considering future trends and policy opportunities. Using a unique combination of three data sets to classify California's industries by both wages and projected employment increases, I note that Latino workers are well-positioned for growth, but in the low-wage sector of the economy. The challenge for Latinos and for California policymakers is to design an approach that will help Latino residents be better positioned for fuller participation and higher rewards in the state's new economy. This will surely involve a stress on helping Latinos advance up the economic ladder through improved access to education and training, specific assistance to Latino businesses, and enforcement of antidiscrimination legislation. Equally important will be the recognition that

---

[2]See, for example, Deborah Reed, *California's Rising Income Inequality: Causes and Concerns* (San Francisco: Public Policy Institute of California, 1999); and Chris Benner, Bob Brownstein, and Amy Dean, *Walking the Lifelong Tightrope: Negotiating Work in the New Economy* (San Jose: Working Partnerships, USA, 1999).

the new economy has brought an inevitable and intertwined mix of high- and low-end jobs, and that we must therefore raise basic labor standards for Latinos and others through increases in the state minimum wage, improved access to health care, a shift toward immigrant incorporation, and enhancements in the atmosphere for unionization. Taken together, these new policy directions can ensure that the state's economy will bring a brighter future for all our residents.

The California Economy: Diverging Fortunes in the Golden State

In March 1998, *The New Yorker* magazine published a special issue on California. The lead article, "The Comeback," teased readers with the subtitle "A few years ago, California's economy was a study in decline. Now it's the model of the future."[3] When even New Yorkers admit the center of economic gravity has shifted, something important is definitely afoot.

As Figure 2.1 shows, there were plenty of reasons for the earlier pessimism. The 1991–1993 dip in employment was initially driven by a national recession, but California was especially hard-hit by sharp cuts in defense and aerospace. As Figure 2.1's sectoral breakdown indicates, manufacturing fell sharply over the early 1990s; indeed, even after some recovery in the latter part of the decade, the 2000 employment level in manufacturing was still below that achieved in 1991.

While the early 1990s may have brought gloom and doom, the second half of the decade saw a dramatic recovery in the California economy. The state's high-tech firms launched the new Internet economy; labor shortages became the rule in many parts of the state; and housing prices surged to new highs, particularly in the rip-roaring Silicon Valley. The aftermath of the dot-com bubble has cast a pall over the short-run prospects for the California economy. However, even if the state's economic cooling should turn into a long and severe frost, the sectoral and distributional trends discussed here should continue.

Much of the recent growth in the economy has come in the area of services. Overall, services accounted for 80 percent of the job growth over the 1993–2000 recovery and over 90 percent of the longer-term job growth since 1983. Wholesale and retail trade has essentially followed employment, rising in tandem with Californians' ability to earn (see Figure 2.1). The sharpest increases have come in business services, a sector that includes software development; employment in this area grew over 80 percent over the 1993–2000 period—well above the

---

[3] John Cassidy, "The Comeback," *The New Yorker,* February 23 and March 2, 1998.

Figure 2.1 Employment in California, 1983–2000

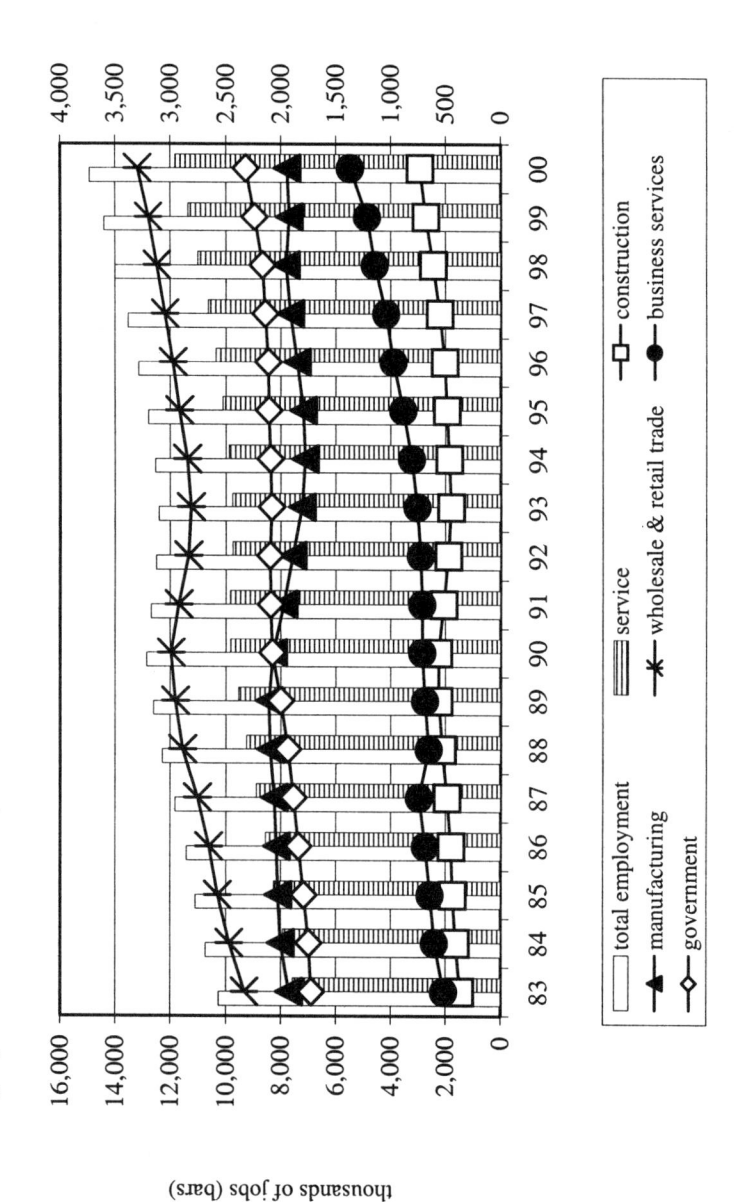

total employment increase of around 20 percent—and has risen 165 percent since 1983.[4]

Information industries have been a key driving force in California's new economy. While California's economy represents only 12 percent of the nation's total, the state accounts for 27 percent of the country's workforce in the computer industry, 21 percent in high-tech manufacturing, 20 percent in the nation's software industry, and over a quarter of workers in the country's biotechnology sector. Partly as a result of these new industries, California accounted for a whopping 37 percent of all venture capital invested in the U.S. in 1997.

The information industries are not necessarily the main generators of employment. Even in the heart of the new economy—Santa Clara County and the Silicon Valley—only 30 percent of the jobs are in high tech, even if one uses a broad definition of that sector to include all subsidiary manufacturing as well as direct information services, chip manufacture, and the like. Low-wage jobs in the local-serving sector have often been the flip side of high-tech growth: Software engineers working 16-hour days wind up needing restaurant, laundry, and childcare services. Moreover, the volatile markets of the new economy have led firms to rely more and more on temporary workers; nearly 12 percent of the total employment increase between 1993 and 1998 occurred within temporary help agencies, and contingent or independent-contract employment has been skyrocketing outside these agencies as well. Estimates suggest that temp work remained on the rise until the recent recession: Growth in what the state employment department terms the personnel supply industry rose 37 percent between 1997 and 2000, far outpacing the 10 percent rise in employment as a whole.

The rapidly changing economy has brought diverging fortunes to different classes, races, and regions. Figure 2.2 charts the median income for those in the top 20 percent and bottom 40 percent of all California households over the periods 1991–1994 and 1995–1998.[5] It shows huge gains at the top and a very modest improvement for those at the bottom, a pattern of disequalization that squares

---

[4]Data taken from the state's Employment Development Department; see www.calmis.cahwnet.gov.

[5]We cover only up until 1998 because this was the most recent year available at the time the original research for this chapter was completed. Subsequently available data for 1998–2000 show improvements in distributional measures due to the effects of low unemployment on labor markets; for an analysis of those years, see Manuel Pastor, Jr., and Carol Zabin, "Recession and Reaction: The Impact of the Economic Downturn on California Labor," in *The State of California Labor,* ed. Ruth Milkman (Berkeley, Calif.: University of California Press, 2002). We should also note that we use the median income for the income brackets pictured rather than the household average or share of total household income because the early years of the data used for this exercise include a "top

Figure 2.2 Median Household Income for Income Classes, California in the 1990s

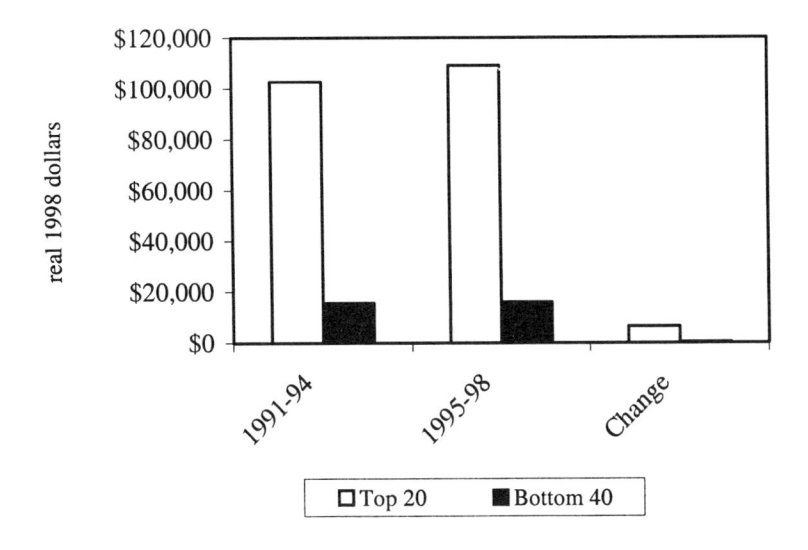

[Bar chart showing Top 20 and Bottom 40 income groups for 1991-94, 1995-98, and Change, in real 1998 dollars]

□ Top 20   ■ Bottom 40

with the results of several other studies.[6] If we break up the distribution by race rather than class, we see that Latino households posted the lowest dollar or percentage gain in household income over the 1990s (see Figure 2.3). While the usual supposition may be that immigration explains this pattern, Figure 2.4 reveals that even households headed by U.S.-born Latinos earn only about three-quarters of the income of their non-Latino white counterparts.[7]

There has also been a divergence in economic fortunes by region. Figure 2.5 reveals that much of the improvement over the 1990s was in the Bay Area and its red-hot Internet economy.[8] While modest improvement occurred in the

---

code" that reduces accuracy at the top ends of the income spectrum. See Appendix for details.

[6] Dan Galpern, "The Distribution of Income in California and Los Angeles," report by the Assembly Select Committee on the California Middle Class, June 16, 1998.

[7] The figure covers only the years 1993–1998 because the earlier years in the sample do not include the detail necessary to break ethnic groups by immigration experience.

[8] We can examine only four broad regions in the figure because the sample sizes for other regions (such as California's Central Coast) are too small to draw any reliable conclusions. In these calculations, San Diego is included in the Southern California (non–Los Angeles) rubric.

Figure 2.3. Shifts in Household Median Income by Race, California in the 1990s

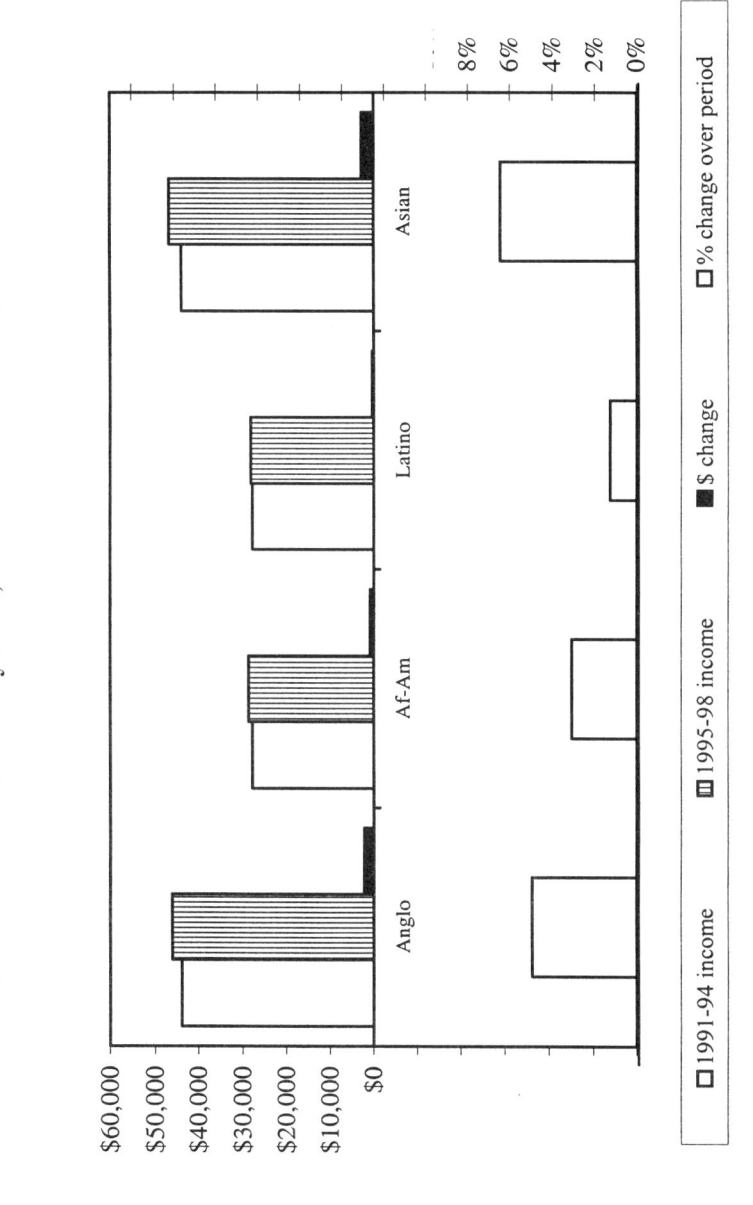

Figure 2.4 Relative Income of Anglos, U.S.-born Latinos, and Immigrant Latinos

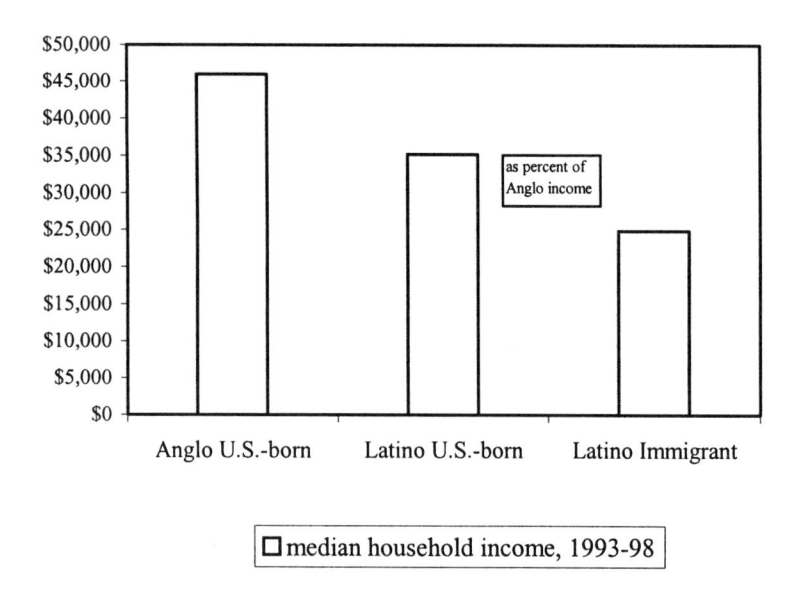

[Bar chart showing median household income, 1993-98:
- Anglo U.S.-born: ~$45,500
- Latino U.S.-born: ~$35,000 (as percent of Anglo income)
- Latino Immigrant: ~$25,000]

Central Valley,[9] household income for both Los Angeles and the rest of Southern California was essentially unchanged between these two periods of the 1990s (although Los Angeles has experienced a substantial job recovery in the last few years). The increasingly heterogeneous regional performance includes inequalities *within* the various areas. As Figure 2.6 indicates, the gap between the top 20 percent and the bottom 40 percent of households grew in nearly every region but the Bay Area; Los Angeles shows a particularly sharp increase, and the income of the bottom 40 percent of Los Angeles households actually fell in real terms over the period.

The ratio of non-Latino white household income to Latino household income generally held steady or even fallen across the various regions; the exception is Los Angeles, where the gap between these populations posted a sharp rise

---

[9]For a more detailed analysis of conditions for Latinos in the Central Valley, see Elaine M. Allensworth, and Refugio Rochín, "White Exodus, Latino Repopulation, and Community Well-Being: Trends in California's Rural Communities," Research Report No. 13, Julian Samora Research Institute, Michigan State University, 1996.

Figure 2.5 Income by Regents in California

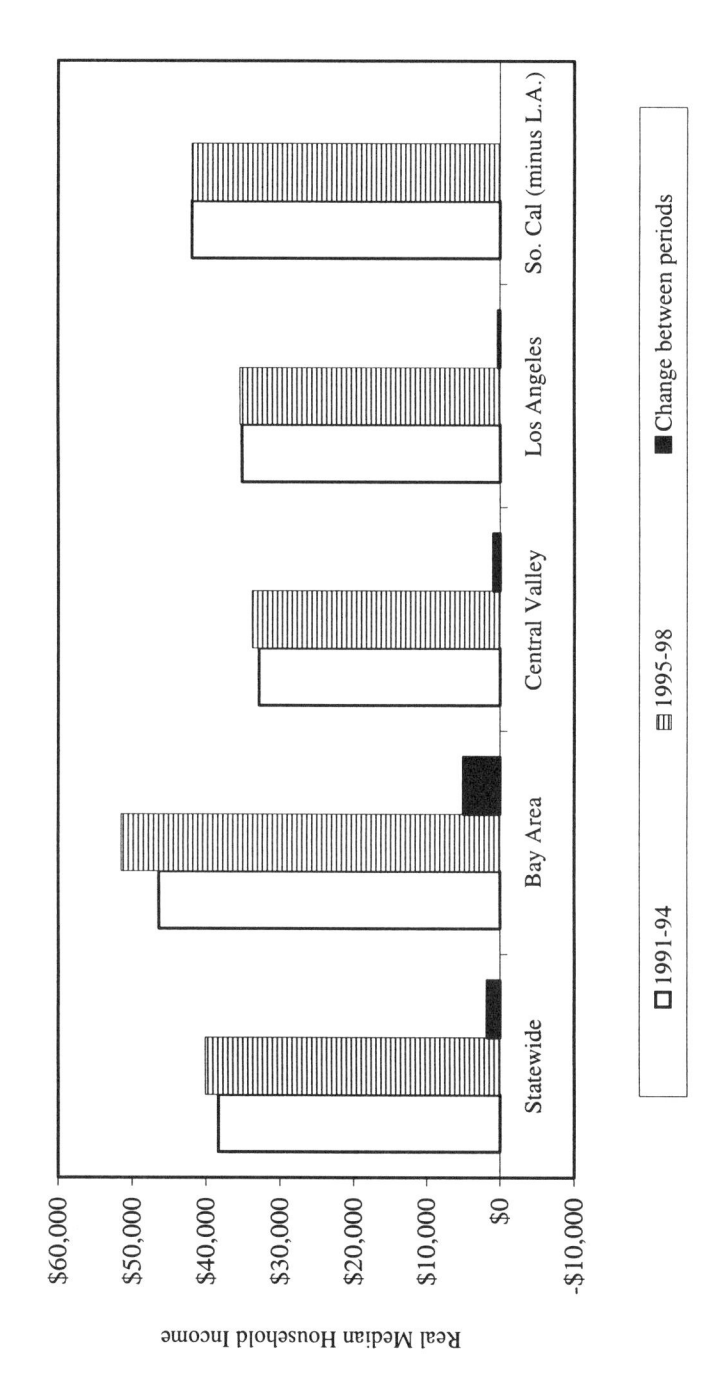

Figure 2.6. Ratio of Median Household Income: Top 20 Percent to Bottom 40 Percent by California Regions in the 1990s

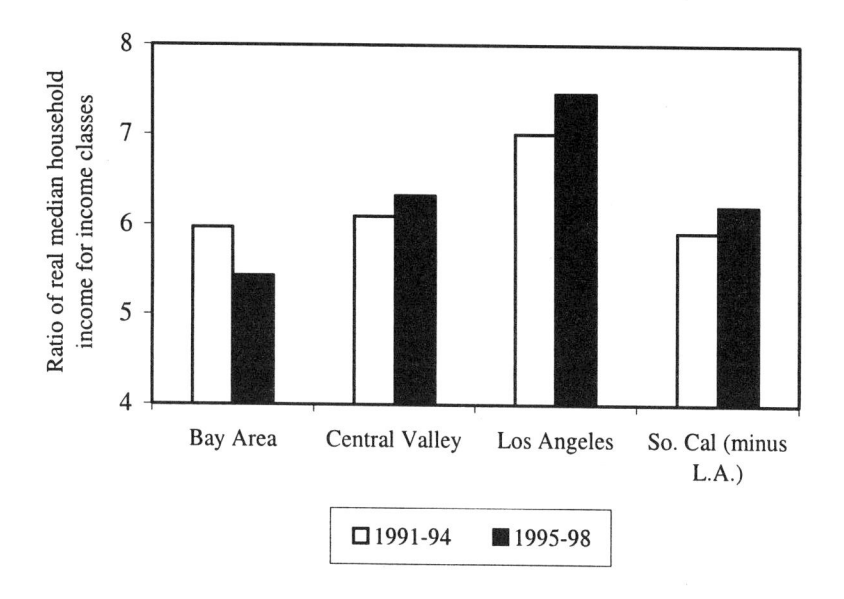

Figure 2.7. Ratio of Anglo to Latino Household Income by California Region over the 1990s

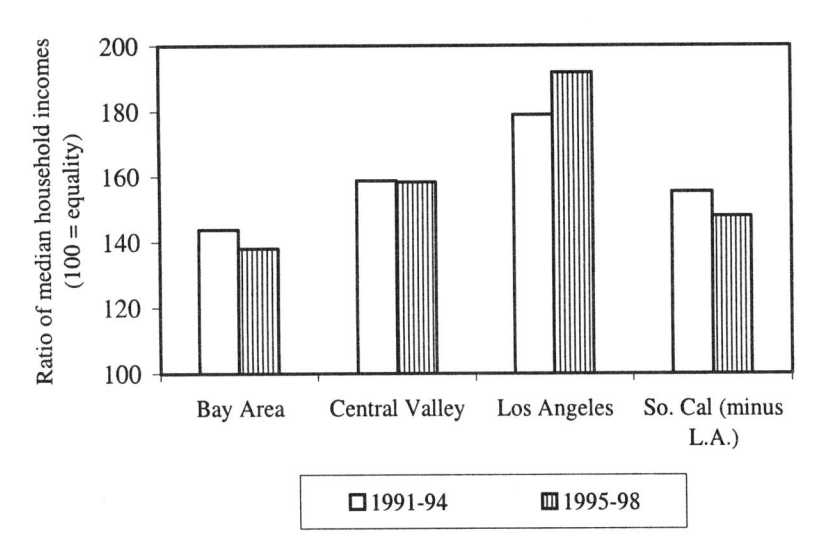

(see Figure 2.7). This suggests that part of the state's widening divide between Latino and non-Latino white households is driven by the pattern in Los Angeles, a county that contains over 40 percent of the state's Latino population.[10] Another part of the divide is driven by the dismal performance of the Central Valley, another key location for the state's Latinos. Thus, addressing both economic development in the Central Valley and the restructured and immigrant-dependent economy of Los Angeles would be a key part of any agenda to improve Latino economic fortunes in the state.

Latinos and the California Economy

While these geographic specifics help to explain Latino fortunes in the Golden State, other factors are at play in the persistent gap in income and poverty between non-Latino whites and Latinos (see Figure 2.8). As many authors have stressed, the poverty problem for Latinos is usually not due to joblessness. Latino males, especially immigrants, have the highest rates of labor-force participation of any males in the state, and the female labor-force participation rate is virtually the same as that of other ethnic groups despite the fact that Latinas are more likely to have children. Rather, the issue is generally low job quality and hence low wages.[11]

How do we measure job quality? One indicator is whether health insurance is available at work; while this is covered in more detail in Chapter 7, recent

---

[10]Rodriguez is far more optimistic about Southern California, stressing the emergence of a Latino middle class. His definition uses median household income as a cut point; this then includes many large households with multiple low wages earners. As Rodriguez notes, a majority of foreign-born Latino households have three or more workers, twice the number for Asian immigrants and more than three times that for Anglos. Thus, it is possible, depending on the number of earners and dependents, to be both be-*low the poverty level (which controls for the number in household) and squarely in the middle class (which does not). See Gregory Rodriguez, *The Emerging Latino Middle Class* (Institute for Public Policy, Pepperdine University, 1996). See also www. pepperdine.edu PublicPolicy/institute/middleclass/index.html.

[11]See, for example, David E. Hayes-Bautista, "Mexicans in Southern California: Societal Enrichment or Wasted Opportunity?" in *The California-Mexico Connection,* ed. Abraham F. Lowenthal and Katrina Burgess (Stanford: Stanford University Press, 1993), 131–46; Edwin Melendez, "Understanding Latino Poverty," *Sage Relations Abstracts,* vol. 18, no. 2 (1993); Rebecca Morales, and Paul Ong, "The Illusion of Progress—Latinos in Los Angeles," in *Restructuring and the New Inequality,* Rebecca Morales and Frank Bonilla (Beverly Hills: Sage Press, 1993); and Manuel Pastor, Jr., "Economic Inequality, Latino Poverty, and the Civil Unrest in Los Angeles," *Economic Development Quarterly,* vol. 9, no. 3 (August 1995).

Figure 2.8. Individual Poverty Rates for Latinos and Anglos in California, 1991–98

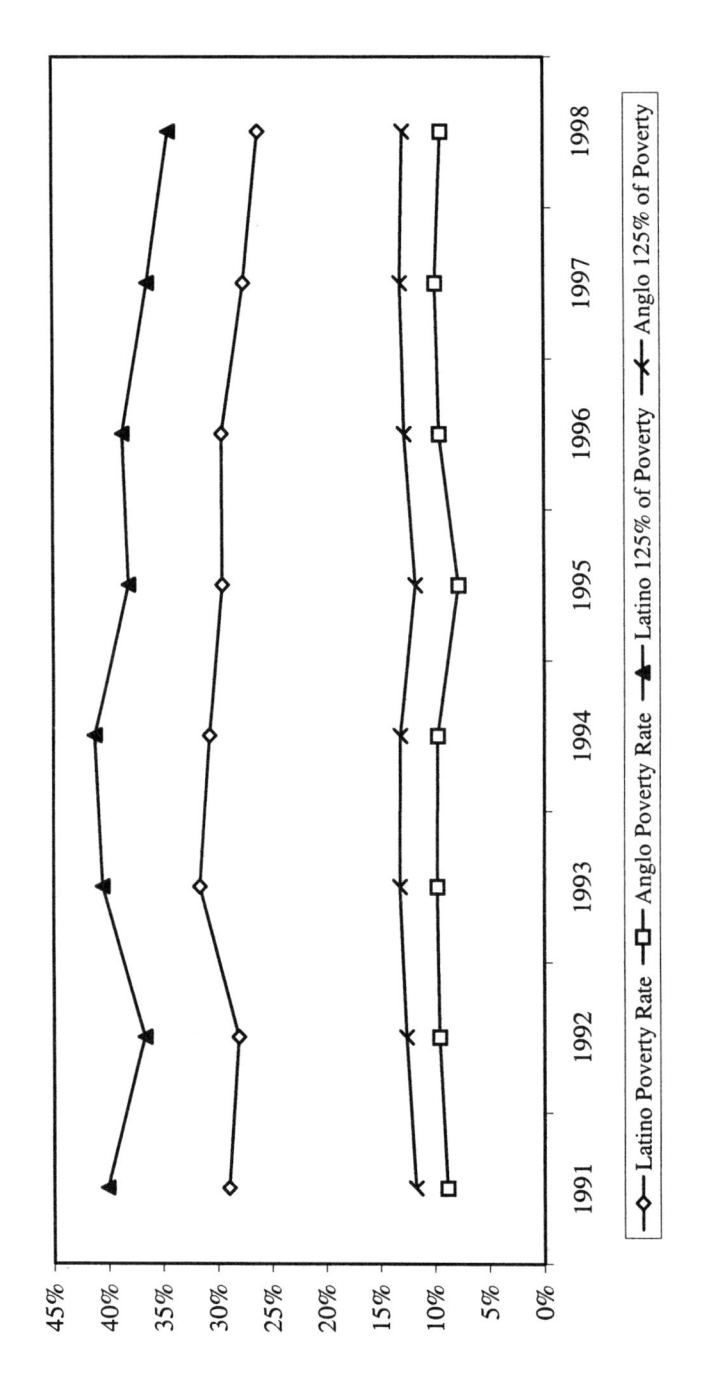

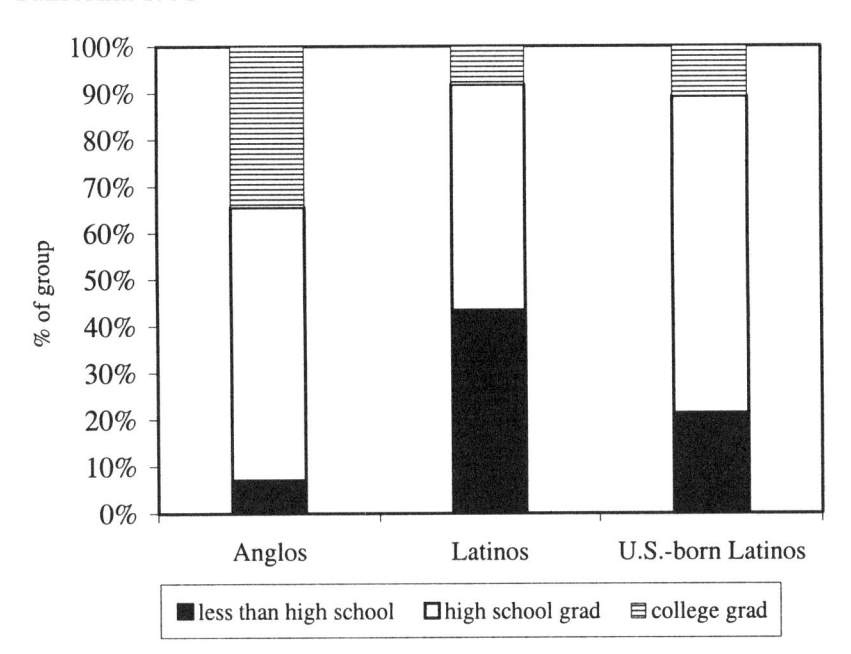

Figure 2.9. Educational Attainment for Those in the Labor Force, California 1998

statistics from the Current Population Survey (see Appendix) suggest that insurance rates fell over much of the 1990s in both non-Latino white and Latino households, reflecting the temporary and contingent nature of much of the work in the new economy, and that Latino households have at least twice the likelihood of facing the world without the security of health coverage.

Another indicator of job quality is unionization, principally because union jobs tend to pay a premium. Data from the Current Population Survey indicate that Latino unionization rates have, in recent years, sometimes crept above those of non-Latino whites. This may reflect the new emphasis of union organizers on Latino immigrant workers—and the apparent receptivity of such workers to union entreaties. Actual economic gains are modest because these union gains have been coming in the bottom end of the labor market, including industries like hotels, restaurants, and in-house health care.

Why do Latinos land in these jobs? One factor is skills or "human capital." Figure 2.9 looks at education levels for those in the labor force in 1998, breaking the pattern out by non-Latino whites, all Latinos, and U.S.-born Latinos only. As

Table 2.1. Determinants of Wages in California, 1997–98

Sample Variables	All % effect Sig.	All males % effect Sig.	All females % effect Sig.	Anglo males % effect Sig.	Latino males % effect Sig.	Anglo females % effect Sig.	Latina females % effect Sig.
High School Education	0.222[1]	0.202[1]	0.255[1]	0.135[2]	0.178[1]	0.255[1]	0.175[1]
Some College	0.381[1]	0.331[1]	0.437[1]	0.277[1]	0.310[1]	0.447[1]	0.386[1]
BA or More	0.772[1]	0.745[1]	0.801[1]	0.684[1]	0.697[1]	0.795[1]	0.719[1]
Work Experience	0.033[1]	0.036[1]	0.030[1]	0.038[1]	0.036[1]	0.037[1]	0.018[1]
Square of Work Exp.	−0.001[1]	−0.001[1]	−0.001[1]	−0.001[1]	−0.001[1]	−0.001[1]	0.000[1]
Full-Time Work	0.230[1]	0.227[1]	0.227[1]	0.277[1]	0.151[1]	0.279[1]	0.156[1]
Union	0.158[1]	0.156[1]	0.159[1]	0.170[1]	0.171[1]	0.149[1]	0.223[1]
Manufacturing	0.059[1]	0.082[1]	0.012	0.129[1]	−0.025	0.052	−0.053[4]
Married	0.104[1]	0.123[1]	0.074[1]	0.173[1]	0.106[1]	0.097[1]	0.071[2]
Immigrant '70s	−0.101[1]	−0.126[1]	−0.071[2]	−0.152[4]	−0.170[1]	0.164[4]	−0.150[1]
Immigrant '80s & '90s	−0.206[1]	−0.249[1]	−0.147[1]	−0.120[2]	−0.336[1]	−0.071	−0.218[1]
African American	−0.195[1]	−0.255[1]	−0.135[1]				
Latino	−0.152[1]	−0.165[1]	−0.131[1]				
Asian	−0.059[1]	−0.022	−0.095[1]				
Female	−0.142[1]						
Adjusted R-squared	0.43	0.44	0.40	0.38	0.39	0.34	0.39
Number in Sample	6282	3429	2852	1713	1117	1554	726
F-value	296.7[1]	183.7[1]	126.1[1]	88.7[1]	60.9[1]	66.6[1]	39.1[1]

[1] significant at the .01 level
[2] significant at the .05 level
[3] significant at the .10 level
[4] significant at the .20 level

Figure 2.9 indicates, the education gap is startling—and while a focus on only U.S.-born Latinos lowers the strikingly high percentage of those who have not finished high school, the percentage of college graduates is only slightly better than that for all Latinos and well below that for non-Latino whites. Indeed, education is so important that Trejo suggests that it accounts for virtually all the difference in wages between non-Latino whites and U.S.-born Latinos.[12]

How important is education compared to other variables in the determination of wages? To get at the answer to this question, I took a subsample of the Current Population Survey's Outgoing Rotation Group (ORG) files for California in 1997 and 1998 (for details, see Appendix) and regressed hourly wage outcomes on various characteristics standard in the labor-market literature.[13] Table 2.1 shows a panel of results; I examine all those in the civilian labor force, males only, females only, non-Latino white and then Latino males, and finally non-Latino white and Latina females. The explanatory power of the regressions, as evidenced by the adjusted R^2, is within the usual range for the literature, so I will focus attention on the coefficients, virtually all of which are significant at the one percent level.

Note that education, particularly higher education, clearly improves wage outcomes. However, while the coefficients for our education variables are similar for non-Latino white and Latino males, the positive effect of education for Latinas, particularly below a college education, is much less than that experienced by non-Latino white females. Work experience is positive, but the returns to seniority are significantly lower for Latinas; likewise, the returns to full-time employment are about half for both Latinos and Latinas, likely reflecting the tendency of both to be in high-turnover, low-reward secondary labor markets. Unionization yields a fairly uniform improvement for all classes of workers, but the effect is unusually strong for Latinas. A job in the manufacturing sector is a boost for non-Latino whites but a bust for Latinos: a probable reflection of non-Latino white participation in older high-wage industries and Latino participation in the newer lower-wage manufacturing sectors. Being a recent immigrant (entering the country in the 1980s or 1990s) has a negative impact across the board, but the effect is especially strong for Latino males.

---

[12] Stephen J. Trejo, "Why Do Mexican Americans Earn Low Wages?" *Journal of Political Economy,* vol. 105, no. 6 (1997): 1235–68.

[13] Per usual practice in labor economics, the actual dependent variable is the log of wages, allowing us to interpret the coefficients as the percent impact on wages. All regressions also included a constant and a variable for the year of the observation; neither control variable is reported in the table to avoid unnecessary clutter.

50   Manuel Pastor, Jr.

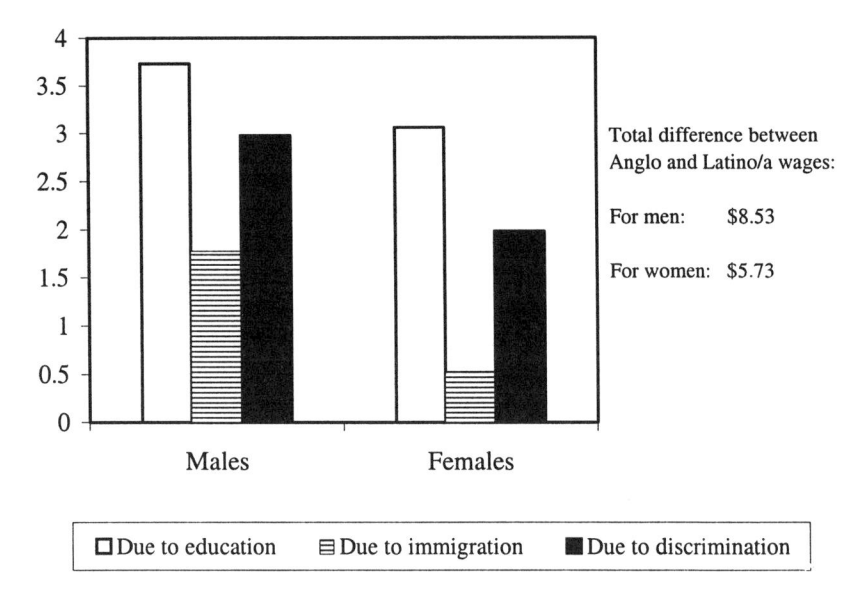

Figure 2.10. Accounting for Anglo and Latino/a Wage Differences

Total difference between Anglo and Latino/a wages:

For men: $8.53

For women: $5.73

□ Due to education   ☱ Due to immigration   ■ Due to discrimination

Following the procedures suggested in Reimers,[14] we decomposed the differences in non-Latino white and Latino wages using the coefficients from the regressions in Table 2.1. Basically, the strategy is to see what part of the wage differential can be accounted for by differences in each group's level of education, for example, and what part is attributable to the difference in returns (or coefficient values) for a certain level of education; since, in a perfect world, non-Latino whites and Latinos should obtain the same yield for education or training, analysts usually attribute this latter difference to discrimination. As Figure 2.10 indicates, the bulk of the actual wage differences between non-Latino whites and Latinos is due to education and recency of immigration, but there is a large "unexplained" difference, which analysts usually attribute to discrimination; the union, manufacturing location, and other variables explain part of the difference, but their impact is very small compared to the main three factors noted in Figure 2.10.

Both the discrimination and immigration impacts may be related to a variable we cannot measure using the available data—social networks. Most individuals obtain employment through various forms of personal contact, and Lati-

---

[14]Cordelia W. Reimers, "A Comparative Analysis of the Wages of Hispanics, Blacks, and Non-Hispanic Whites," in *Hispanics in the U.S. Economy,* ed. George J. Borjas and Marta Tienda (Orlando, Fla.: Academic Press, 1985).

nos are no exception. While researchers have made much of the strength of immigrant networks in securing jobs and generating community solidarity, statistical studies in Boston and Los Angeles—using different databases but similar techniques—found that Latinos who use such social networks may have more success securing employment, but they earn lower wages than those who find their employment through traditional job agencies and market techniques.[15] The reason is that "bonding" ties to those in a similar community or economic position may simply guarantee access to low-wage employment; what is needed are "bridging" ties to a world of higher-quality work.

How can public policy take account of these regression results? While politicians tend to focus on educational improvements, investing in human capital is not enough; moreover, it is a very long-term strategy, and the problems of poverty are immediate. In the shorter term, there are important and relatively uniform (across Latinos and non-Latino whites) returns from work experiences and union membership, suggesting that shorter-term policy efforts might be devoted to connecting people to consistent employment and insuring a supportive environment for unions to organize and represent the burgeoning Latino labor force. Of particular importance might be the development of "bridging" networks that cross geographic, class, and often ethnic boundaries. When communities are boxed in by residential segregation, racial discrimination, and weak educational structures, such network bridges to better opportunities are few, and public policy needs to be directed toward finding useful substitutes, such as community-based employment and training agencies.

Latino Business in California

While the previous discussion focused on wages and workers, ethnic-owned businesses are also crucial for economic and community advancement. Such firms offer one vehicle for accumulating assets and often meet consumer needs unsatisfied by mainstream firms (for example, in the ethnic food industry). Ethnic firms are more likely to hire ethnic workers, providing key entry points to the world of employment. Finally, ethnic entrepreneurs can often provide the kind of middle-class anchor necessary to secure community revitalization and political empowerment. For all these reasons, the future of the Latino community is dependent in part on the health of Latino-owned businesses.

---

[15] See, for example, Luis Falcón, "Social Networks and Employment for Latinos, Blacks, and Whites," *New England Journal of Public Policy,* vol. 11, no. 1 (1995): 17–28; and Manuel Pastor, Jr., and Enrico Marcelli, "Men N the Hood: Skill, Spatial, and Social Mismatch for Male Workers in Los Angeles County," *Urban Geography*, vol. 21, no. 6 (2000).

From 1987 to 1992, the U.S. Census reports that the number of U.S. Latino-owned businesses grew 83 percent, significantly higher than the 26 percent growth rate for all businesses, with gross receipts rising by 195 percent, compared to 67 percent for all firms.[16] Growth continued through 1997, with an estimated 30 percent increase in the number of Hispanic-owned firms since 1992, compared to an increase of 6.8 percent for all firms.[17]

Part of the reason for the spectacular growth in the earlier period is that the base was small: Even after the rapid growth between 1987 and 1997, Latino firms made up just 5.8 percent of all firms in the U.S. (while Latinos were around 11 percent of the population in that year) and only one percent of all receipts.[16] In California, the numbers are higher, reflecting the increased presence of Latinos in the state: Latino-owned firms are 13.1 percent of the total although they earn only about 2.4 percent of total business receipts.

These low values as a percentage of total revenues reflect the smaller size of Latino firms. Across the U.S., 40 percent of Latino-owned firms had receipts of less than $10,000 in 1997, and average receipts for Latino-owned businesses were slightly over $155,000—well below the nearly $900,000 average reported for all firms.[16] In the service industry, Latino-owned firms garnered average receipts of $78,000, about 27 percent of the average for all firms; the receipt disparity was greatest in manufacturing, where the average Latino firm earned less than 10 percent of the average for all firms, likely reflecting the difficulty of entering the manufacturing industry at sufficient scale to compete with mainstream firms. Construction is a field in which Latino firms are closest to equity, achieving 36 percent of the industry average in sales.

California had the largest number of Latino-owned firms (336,405) and receipts ($51.7 billion) in the country, accounting for 28 percent of all Latino-owned firms and an equivalent share of their receipts. The Los Angeles-Long Beach area was the largest metropolitan area in the U.S. in terms of number of firms (136,678) and contained 41 percent of California's Latino-owned firms and 31 percent of Latino business gross receipts. Still, Miami was bigger in terms of gross receipts: With only 120,605 firms, Miami's Latino business owners garnered $26.7 billion, compared to $16.3 billion in Los Angeles. A similar-scale dynamic can be seen when we consider the top 500 Latino firms in the country: While 25 percent are located in California, only one of the top 10, and

---

[16] U.S. Department of Commerce, Economics, and Statistics Administration, Bureau of the Census, *1992 Economic Census, Survey of Minority Owned Business Enterprises—Hispanic* (MB92-2), 1996.

[17] U.S. Department of Commerce, Economics, and Statistics Administration, Bureau of the Census, *1997 Economic Census, Survey of Minority Owned Business Enterprises—Hispanic*, 2001. The figure excludes Schedule C corporations.

17 of the top 100, have a California base.[18] Clearly, California-based firms, enjoying one of the largest and most dynamic markets in the world as well as a huge Latino consumer base, have significant room to grow.

How are these firms positioned in the market? Table 2.2 compares all U.S. firms, all U.S. Latino firms, all California firms, and all California Latino firms. Compared to the U.S. average, Latino firms are disproportionately concentrated in agriculture and transportation; they are underconcentrated in manufacturing and wholesale trade, and severely underrepresented in finance. These latter industries have exhibited the fastest growth in the number of Latino firms over recent years, suggesting a process of catch-up is occurring. Still, the overall pattern suggests a relative shortage of Latino firms in some significant higher-value-added sectors.

The distribution of Latino firms against the distribution of Latino receipts for California suggests that the service sector (which has, for example, over 47 percent of California's Latino firms but only 18 percent of the revenues) is populated with small and relatively unproductive Latino firms—a phenomenon that probably reflects the ease of entry into that sector (see Figure 2.11). Manufacturing firms are only three percent of California's Latino firms but a whopping 37 percent of the total revenue; while these firms have only about half the receipts of the average manufacturing firm in the state, they are quite sizeable compared to, for example, the Latino-owned businesses in the service sector, where the average Latino firm earns only 19 percent of the industry mean.

In the future, retail niches, particularly given the state's growing Latino population, represent a real opportunity for business expansion.[19] However, it is important to ensure that Latino firms secure a foothold in the growing and high-value-added sectors of the economy, an issue of concern given the overwhelming concentration of Latino businesses in low-end service.

Latinos and the Future of the California Economy: Directions for Policy

What will the future bring for Latino workers and firms? The evidence suggests that, despite some degree of economic recovery, the distribution of income has

---

[18]See the Hispanic Business 500 Directory 2000 from *Hispanic Business;* www.hispanicbusiness.com/research/companies/hb2000-500.asp. The figures do show improvement from 1998, when only 18 percent of the top 500 and 13 percent of the top 100 Hispanic firms were located in California.
[19]For more on the nature of the Latino market and expenditure patterns, see Geoffrey D. Paulin, "A Growing Market: Expenditures by Hispanic Consumer," *Monthly Labor Review* (March 1998): 3–21.

Table 2.2. Sectoral Distribution of All U.S., U.S. Latino, and California Latino Businesses, 1997

Industry	All firms US % of revenue	Latino firms US % of revenue	All firms CA % of revenue	Latino firms CA % of revenue
Agriculture	1.3%	1.5%	1.0%	2.4%
Construction	5.1%	11.8%	4.7%	12.2%
Manufacturing	21.7%	15.4%	18.3%	37.0%
Transportation, communication, utilities	6.4%	4.5%	5.4%	3.9%
Wholesale trade	23.0%	21.7%	26.3%	9.7%
Retail Trade	14.3%	17.3%	13.4%	13.2%
Finance, insurance, real estate	13.8%	3.6%	12.7%	3.0%
Services	14.1%	21.0%	17.9%	17.7%
Industries not classified	0.3%	3.3%	0.3%	1.1%

	All firms US % of firms	Latino firms US % of firms	All firms CA % of firms	Latino firms CA % of firms
Agriculture	3.0%	3.5%	2.5%	5.5%
Construction	11.2%	12.7%	8.1%	9.4%
Manufacturing	3.3%	2.1%	3.7%	2.7%
Transportation, communication, utilities	4.4%	7.0%	3.5%	6.1%
Wholesale trade	3.8%	2.6%	4.3%	2.2%
Retail Trade	13.8%	12.9%	12.5%	13.6%
Finance, insurance, real estate	10.7%	4.7%	10.3%	4.9%
Services	42.6%	41.7%	49.2%	47.2%
Industries not classified	7.1%	12.7%	6.1%	8.4%

Figure 2.11. Latino Business Receipts by Industry Relative to Average, California 1997

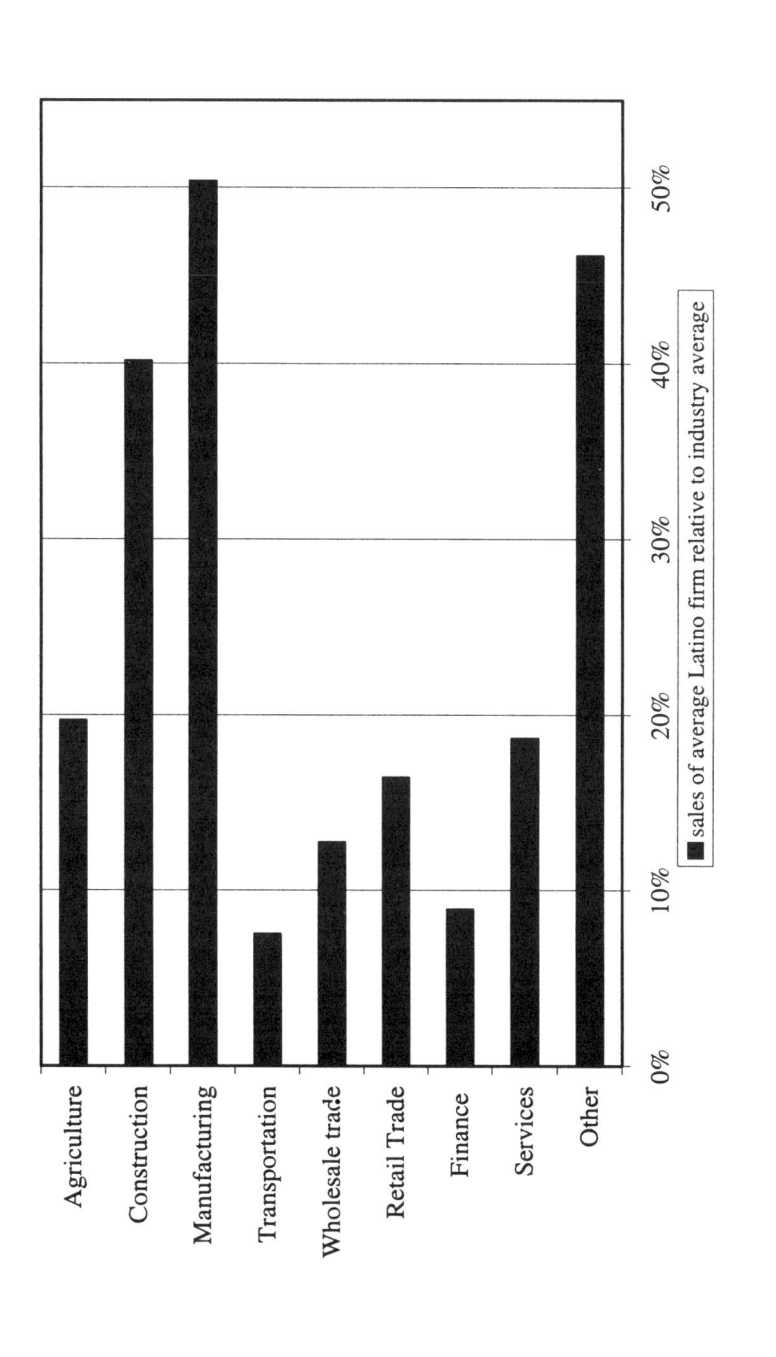

■ sales of average Latino firm relative to industry average

deteriorated over the long haul and there are persistent gaps by race and ethnicity. Latinos are faring especially poorly, the key explanatory factors being a lack of education, recent immigrant status, social networks, and location in the labor market, as well as continuing discrimination. Latino businesses offer a ray of hope, but excessive attention on the spectacular growth in the number of Latino firms masks their small size relative to the market and other firms.

Moreover, simply being in a high-growth sector does not necessarily guarantee positive economic prospects. As Benner, Brownstein, and Dean (1999) point out, some of the fastest-growing industries over the 1990s were temporary help and restaurant work, neither of which generally offers high pay and reasonable benefits. Growth, in short, needs to be charted against projected returns.

To do exactly that, I began with the state's estimates for job growth by industry between 1996 and 2006, as provided by the Labor Market Information Division (LMID) of the state's Employment Development Department.[20] See the Appendix. I then matched those industries to the two-digit industry categories used in the Current Population Survey, a task that required devising a common coding system or crosswalk to link the two series. I applied these new industry categories to the Current Population Survey's ORG for California for 1996 and 1997 to obtain average hourly wages, deflating these measures by the California consumer price index to obtain real levels. I then matched the projected industry growth rates and real wages to the demographic data in the March supplement of the Current Population Survey for 1997 and 1998, the first two years of the projected growth period.

For the 43 industries for which I had all measures in this matched database, I used the median growth rate and median hourly wage rate to break the industries into four categories: (1) high-wage, fast-growth, (2) low-wage, fast-growth, (3) high-wage, slow-growth, and (4) low-wage, slow-growth.[21] For example, category one includes health services, entertainment, industrial machinery, and professional services; category two includes eating and drinking establishments, auto repair, and low-end business services; category three includes older, established industries such as aircraft, paper, and transportation equipment; and category four includes furniture, metal finishing, apparel, and miscellaneous manufacturing.

Figure 2.12 shows wage and growth profiles for Latinos and non-Latino whites, the two most populous groups in the state. Non-Latino whites are disproportionately in the high-wage, slow-growth sector; this reflects their presence

---

[20] Again, more recent projections are available but these were the most recent at the time the original research was conducted for this piece.

[21] The medians are actually taken from a weighted sample, with the weights being the sum of sectoral employment in 1996 and projected sectoral employment in 2006.

The Economic Challenge for California's Latinos

Figure 2.12. Location of Anglo and Latino Labor Force in Industry by Wage and Growth Levels in California's Future Economy

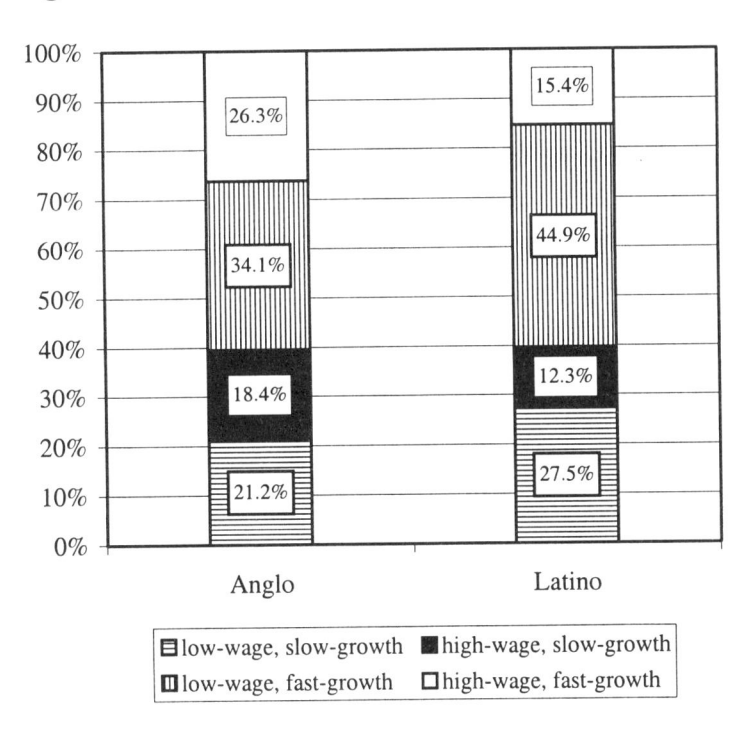

Anglo:
- high-wage, fast-growth: 26.3%
- low-wage, fast-growth: 34.1%
- high-wage, slow-growth: 18.4%
- low-wage, slow-growth: 21.2%

Latino:
- high-wage, fast-growth: 15.4%
- low-wage, fast-growth: 44.9%
- high-wage, slow-growth: 12.3%
- low-wage, slow-growth: 27.5%

Legend: ☐ low-wage, slow-growth ■ high-wage, slow-growth / low-wage, fast-growth ☐ high-wage, fast-growth

in older manufacturing firms that are no longer on the rise but still provide for a decent standard of living for incumbent workers. As for the high-growth sectors, non-Latino whites and Latinos have about the same percentage of each group's labor force in fast-growth industries—but non-Latino whites are much more likely to be in high-income, fast-growth sectors, while Latinos are much more likely to be in low-income, fast-growth sectors.

This analysis suggests that the current non-Latino/white-Latino income divides may, in the absence of public policy, become wider in the future, simply as a result of the evolution of economic sectors. To improve the situation, it is important to realize that there are three basic approaches to labor market enhancement: rapid economic growth, new methods of placement and training, and new labor standards.

Growth is clearly necessary: While economic expansion does not guarantee benefits to lower-income individuals, recession is a sure recipe for poverty and despair. However, being in the right growth sectors is critical. To obtain more Latino employment in the higher-end industries, educational attainment must be improved, particularly in the public schools that train the lion's share of Latino youth. While education is discussed elsewhere in this volume, it is useful to stress here the very high payoff from a college education: Outreach programs for the University of California and the California State University systems are therefore especially important for Latino economic advancement.

While formal education is a long-term strategy, training and job connections can have more immediate payoffs. Improvements in training programs, including an expansion of community college opportunities and incentives for direct employer on-the-job training, would help both those seeking employment and those who are currently employed but want to move up. Workers also need better placement mechanisms; relying on social networks when there is a pattern of racial segregation by industry will simply project the past into the future. Community-based placement agencies are one vehicle for creating new bridges between low-income communities and better employment opportunities; the state could work with the federal government and local agencies to ensure that such groups are actively and authentically involved in the new Workforce Investment Boards that have emerged from recent federal legislation.

Latino businesses could also use a boost, perhaps through enhancing small-business programs and improving community development and neighborhood retail strategies. Also important is access to the financial system. Many Latino firms are undercapitalized, and recent reports suggest that Latino firms face higher interest rates on loans and are often reluctant to apply for credit. While Proposition 209 places a limit on the use of affirmative action, outreach efforts to ensure that ethnic businesses join the pool for state business contracts are still allowed and should be encouraged.

Setting new labor standards is critical to Latino economic fortunes. As successful as training and placement may be, such strategies do not alter the bottom end of the labor market where many workers languish while hoping and training for a shot at advancement. Conditions could be improved by raising the state minimum wage, implementing a state "living wage" law (by which firms receiving subsidies from the state would be required to pay decent wages and/or provide health insurance), and expanding health-care access for low-wage workers (perhaps through a combination of stiffer requirements for employers, more incentives to small businesses, and an increase in publicly supported health insurance). Further unionization could also help, particularly given the demonstrated high returns for Latinas (see Table 2.1); while changes in federal law are needed to make labor organizing less difficult, state and local governments could help by at least asking that firms receiving development and other subsidies be required to demonstrate that they have allowed workers full access to potential union representation.

Immigrants need more help to incorporate their talents and energies successfully into the labor and business sides of the economy. Such incorporation is in everyone's interests; California will continue to depend on immigrant labor, and new evidence even suggests that immigrant workers help the wages of many U.S.-born workers by keeping jobs and labor demand within the state.[22] Devoting resources to helping new residents find employment, connect with naturalization and other services, and start micro-enterprises may be a worthy investment. In addition, the evidence offered above—that there is apparently still some degree of discrimination against immigrant and native Latinos—suggests that enforcement of civil-rights law should remain a key priority for the state.

These are not especially radical policy changes, and a determined governor and state legislature could accomplish all of them. Forging the political will to do so would require two sorts of alliances, one with the middle class, the other with labor. To gain middle-class support, it is important to stress two facts: The negative effects of labor-market changes on Latinos are a harbinger of what may affect more privileged workers down the road, and the low-income profile of the growing Latino workforce has a very negative effect on tax revenues available to the state and federal governments for retirement and infrastructure spending. As for labor, Latino communities and labor leaders have increasingly come together on issues of mutual concern, especially the alleviation of working poverty. As a result, Latino labor leaders have become major players in state and local politics; Latino voters have been crucial to recent labor advances (such as the 1998 defeat of a state initiative designed to limit unions' ability to use member funds for political causes); and labor's most recent organizing successes in California, such as those with janitors and home care workers in Los Angeles, have been with Latino workers.

This new political resolve requires more than just tactics and alliances; change will require a renewed commitment to inclusion and basic shifts in social attitudes. The significant challenges facing Latino communities in California have sometimes led analysts to treat Latinos as a sort of problem to be solved. Yet the high rates of labor-force participation and apparent eagerness to form businesses suggest that the Latino population may be a key asset as the state's economy continues to expand and transform. With the right sort of policies, California's new economy could build on these obvious strengths, reversing the rising inequality of recent years and serving as the vehicle for all the residents of California to realize their dreams of better lives for themselves and their children.

---

[22]See, for example, Enrico Marcelli, "Undocumented Latino Immigrant Workers: The L.A. Experience," in *Illegal Immigration in America*, ed. David W. Haines and Karen E. Rosenblum (Westport, Conn.: Greenwood Press, 1999); Enrico A. Marcelli and David M. Heer, "Unauthorized Mexican Workers in the 1990 Los Angeles County Labour Force," *International Migration*, vol. 35, no. 1 (1997): 59–83; and Enrico A. Marcelli, Manuel Pastor, Jr., and Pascale M. Joassart, "On the Labor Market Effects of Informal Economic Activity in Los Angeles County," *Journal of Economic Issues*, vol. 38, no. 3 (1999).

Appendix: Data Sources

The primary data source for most of this paper is the March Supplement of the Current Population Survey (CPS) as downloaded from *www.bls.census.gov* for each of the years examined. Since the time the original research was completed for this paper, several additional years of the CPS have become available; while the long-run trends are essentially the same, there was an important narrowing of some wage gaps, as is typical of the last phases of a recovery. We stick with the original sample here for a variety of reasons: to preserve symmetry with the two four-year periods of the 1990s, because of the complex way earlier years in the March CPS series are connected with the Outgoing Rotation Group (ORG) files for the wage regressions as explained below, and because the process of editing the overall book manuscript was longer than anticipated.

We use median income rather than average income in many of the graphs and comparisons. Average-income figures in the CPS files are problematic because prior to the March 1996 releases (covering the year 1995), the top-code values were a set cap rather than the current average of the underlying top-coded values. This procedural shift ensures that the aggregate income, obtained by totaling the reported income figures, matches the real values after 1994; prior to this, annual aggregate income, calculated by adding up the household-income figures in the CPS data, is lower than the actual value. This implies that income-share calculations between 1991 and 1994 are somewhat problematic, which explains why we have opted for explicating the median income in each income category. For calculating median income for each period, I simply pooled all the observations and took the medians for various categories, as in Lopez and Feliciano;[23] a procedure that instead uses the average of the medians for the periods and produces similar results.

For some calculations, particularly the labor-force attachment rate, I rely on data derived from the Public Use Microdata Sample (PUMS) as reported in Stiles et al.[24] This is far more reliable than the CPS, but is also increasingly out of date. The numbers in this analysis should be redone when the PUMS for 2000 becomes available.

The regressions are done using the CPS ORG file as provided to me by Working Partnerships USA (San Jose) and the Economic Policy Institute (Washington, D.C.). This database is precleaned, including checks against top codes, recalculations of wage rates to eliminate obvious outliers and mistaken entries,

---

[23] David Lopez and Cynthia Feliciano, "Who Does What? California's Emerging Plural Labor Force," in *Organizing Immigrants,* ed. Ruth Milkman (Ithaca: Cornell University Press, 2000).

[24] Jon Stiles, Jonathan Cohen, Zachary Elkins, and Fredric Gey, *California Latino Demographic Databook* (Berkeley: California Policy Seminar, University of California, 1998).

and a filter to include only those in the labor force. Unfortunately, the filtered database does not include a designation for whether the individual is a migrant and, if so, when he or she entered the United States. Since this migration history is important in determining Latino destinies, I pulled the migration codes from the March Supplement files and linked them by household and individual identifiers (including race, gender, and age of the individual as well as the ID numbers to avoid mislinking) for the last two years of the ORG sample; Trejo[11] uses a similar procedure for matching CPS sources. Because not all those in the ORG were in the March supplement, this misses some of the observations, but it was the quickest approach to tagging the prefiltered sample with the extra data. I also ran a sweep to clean out duplicate entries, counting only individuals who were in the final month of being in the ORG sample. As noted, Trejo uses a similar procedure to match outgoing rotation data and monthly CPS information, and also a similar technique to drop duplicate observations.[11]

The job projections by industry were taken from downloadable tables available on the Web site of the state Employment Development Department's LMID. Job projections by occupation are also available, but the relationship between the state's occupational categories and the CPS categories is quite problematic and involves significant recalculation at the three-digit (and below) levels. For the purposes of this chapter, I have stuck with industry calculations that were available at a two-digit level for both the LMID data and the CPS; the two-digit data is also aggregated enough to enjoy sample sizes large enough to calculate reliable sectoral composition figures from non-Latino whites and Latinos without entirely losing specificity to the broad one-digit categorizations. More recent job-projection figures have become available since the original research was completed for this paper, but because of our linking of this data to the CPS files used in the wage regressions, we have stuck with the earlier projections. As I noted in the text, the median cutoffs used in calculating our four broad industry projects come from a sample weighted by actual employment by sector in 1996 and predicted employment by sector for 2006.

References

Allensworth, Elaine M., and Refugio Rochin. 1996. "White Exodus, Latino Repopulation, and Community Well-Being: Trends in California's Rural Communities." Research Report No. 13, Julian Samora Research Institute, Michigan State University.

Benner, Chris, Bob Brownstein, and Amy Dean. 1999. *Walking the Lifelong Tightrope: Negotiating Work in the New Economy.* San Jose, Calif.: Working Partnerships, USA.

Falcón, Luis. 1995. "Social Networks and Employment for Latinos, Blacks, and Whites." *New England Journal of Public Policy*, vol. 11, no. 1 (Spring/Summer): 17–28.

Galpern, Dan. 1998. Senior Consultant, "The Distribution of Income in California and Los Angeles." Report by the Assembly Select Committee on the California Middle Class, Assembly Member Wally Knox, Chair, June 16.

Hayes-Bautista, David E. 1993. "Mexicans in Southern California: Societal Enrichment or Wasted Opportunity?" In *The California-Mexico Connection*, ed. Abraham F. Lowenthal and Katrina Burgess. Stanford, Calif.: Stanford University Press.

Lopez, David, and Cynthia Feliciano. 2000. "Who Does What? California's Emerging Plural Labor Force." In *Organizing Immigrants*, ed. Ruth Milkman. Ithaca: Cornell University Press.

Marcelli, Enrico. 1999. "Undocumented Latino Immigrant Workers: The L.A. Experience." In *Illegal Immigration in America*, ed. David W. Haines and Karen E. Rosenblum. Westport, Conn.: Greenwood Press.

Marcelli, Enrico A., and David M. Heer. 1997. "Unauthorized Mexican Workers in the 1990 Los Angeles County Labour Force." *International Migration*, vol. 35, no.1: 59–83.

Marcelli, Enrico A., Manuel Pastor, Jr., and Pascale M. Joassart. 1999. "On the Labor Market Effects of Informal Economic Activity in Los Angeles County," *Journal of Economic Issues*, vol. XXXIII, no .3 (September).

Melendez, Edwin. 1993. "Understanding Latino Poverty." *Sage Relations Abstracts*, vol. 18, no. 2.

Morales, Rebecca, and Paul Ong. 1993. "The Illusion of Progress—Latinos in Los Angeles." In *Restructuring and the New Inequality*, ed. Rebecca Morales and Frank Bonilla. Beverly Hills, Calif.: Sage Press.

Pastor, Manuel, Jr. 1995. "Economic Inequality, Latino Poverty, and the Civil Unrest in Los Angeles." *Economic Development Quarterly*, vol. 9, no. 3 (August).

Pastor, Manuel, Jr., and Enrico Marcelli. 2000. "Men N the Hood: Skill, Spatial, and Social Mismatch for Male Workers in Los Angeles County." *Urban Geography*, vol. 21, no. 6 (August): 474–96.

Pastor, Manuel, Jr., and Carol Zabin. 2002. "Recession and Reaction: The Impact of the Economic Downturn on California Labor." In *The State of California Labor,* ed. Ruth Milkman. Berkeley, Calif.: University of California Press.

Paulin, Geoffrey D. 1998. "A Growing Market: Expenditures by Hispanic Consumer." *Monthly Labor Review* (March): 3–21.

Reed, Deborah. 1999. *California's Rising Income Inequality: Causes and Concerns.* San Francisco, Calif.: Public Policy Institute of California.

Reimers, Cordelia W. 1985. "A Comparative Analysis of the Wages of Hispanics, Blacks, and Non-Hispanic Whites." In *Hispanics in the U.S. Economy,* ed. George J. Borjas and Marta Tienda. Orlando, Florida: Academic Press, Inc.

Rodriguez, Gregory. 1996. *The Emerging Latino Middle Class.* Institute for Public Policy, Pepperdine University. http://www.pepperdine.edu/PublicPolicy/institute/middleclass/index.html.

Stiles, Jon, Jonathan Cohen, Zachary Elkins, and Fredric Gey. 1998. *California Latino Demographic Databook.* Berkeley, Calif.: California Policy Seminar, University of California.

Trejo, Stephen J. 1997. "Why Do Mexican Americans Earn Low Wages?" *Journal of Political Economy,* vol. 105, no. 6: 1235–68.

U.S. Department of Commerce, Economics and Statistics Administration, Bureau of the Census. 2001. *1997 Economic Census, Survey of Minority Owned Business Enterprises—Hispanic.*

———. 1996. *1992 Economic Census, Survey of Minority Owned Business Enterprises—Hispanic* (MB92–2).

U.S. Small Business Administration (SBA), Office of Advocacy. 1999. *Minorities in Business,* Washington, D.C.: U.S. SBA.

K–12 Public Education:
Bedrock or Barrier?

Eugene E. García

Introduction

During the past two decades, the linguistic and cultural diversity of California's schools and the specific growth of Latino students have increased dramatically, and they are expected to increase even more in the next several decades. California's population growth has included a significant increase in immigrant populations, with more immigrants from south of our border, including countries beyond Mexico. Today, two out of three California children are from an ethnic or racial minority group, one in two speaks a language other than English at home, and one in three was born outside the United States (see Tables 3.1 and 3.2).

California's adult population has deep concerns about the quality of K–12 public education. For example, Policy Analysis for California Education (PACE) polls in 1992, 1994, and 1998 consistently report that over 70 percent of adults polled indicate the schools are not "doing a good job."[1] Confronted with

---

[1] Policy Analysis for California Education, *Californians Speak on Education and Reform Options: Uneven Faith in Teachers, School Boards, and the State as Designers of Change* (Berkeley: University of California, Berkeley, and Stanford University, 1998).

this public perspective and continued evidence of underachievement and low rates of college participation by certain sectors of the state's Latino student population, policymakers, administrators, teachers, parents, the business community, and other private-sector partners urge one another to do something different to promote student achievement—change teaching methods, adopt new curricula, enhance standards and accountability, build bridges between school and work, and allocate more strategic funding.

Although such actions may be needed, they will not be meaningful unless we begin to think differently about the educational needs of our students and the systems that we have organized to serve them. This is particularly the case for the growing number of Latino students in California. Thinking differently involves viewing these students and these systems in new ways that may contradict conventional notions. This change in thinking, already reflected to some degree in the systemic-reform era we are in today, will allow us to come to a new set of realizations about the value and importance of schooling experiences.

Reform initiatives aimed at Latino students in California have become more rigorous in the last 10 years. This chapter will deal with two substantive challenges regarding the schools' response to Latino students. At one level, "change" has been to take on different roles and responsibilities regarding global economic realities and new values of equity and excellence. Another "change" has been in ways that would lead to a new and different culture and society for California. In addition, educational institutions have been asked to change their own behavior or culture in light of new theories of teaching and learning and the diversity of students served now and in the future. The responses to these two challenges have not generated a coherent, cohesive, and integrated change or reform agenda. This incoherent set of changes has produced significant conflicts that need resolution if the latest wave of reform is to have significant influence on the general society and on Latino children. The following discussion will address issues of policy and theory insofar as they concern educational practice.

Policy

Within my own professional sphere, whether at the local, state, or national level, I have confronted a cohort of policies that govern the education of Latinos. The policies are not always guided by theories of teaching and learning. Yet they are important determinants of student expectations, instructional practices, and resource distribution that significantly affect the type of education provided to students. This has been particularly true for the Spanish/English bilingual and immigrant students of California. Although this chapter will emphasize the workings of education theories and practice, I begin with the assertion that a set of policies—not theories or education research—has driven the education practice received by Latinos. In the conclusion of this chapter I will present a set of policies that are firmly grounded in theory and research that I believe will generate a better future for Latino students in the state.

Theory and Practice

Theoretical and conceptual notions of how children learn guide the fundamental aspects of how we organize teaching in our schools. Teachers also have theories of how children develop and learn, as well as theories about their own role in such processes.[2] Whether we articulate them or not, we all have theories that guide us in making sense of the world we live in; theories are important to all of us, not just to scientists. In an effort to understand how theory and policy come together in classrooms, researchers have tried to document instructional practices that have important effects on Latinos as they experience the schooling process in the new era of educational reform.[3] Such practices are sometimes linked directly or indirectly to theories of learning and development and to conceptual frameworks related to language acquisition. In this chapter I will attempt to expand on my own perceived linkages of theory and practice as they relate to the educational treatment of Latino students.

To reiterate, the foundations of schooling initiatives targeted at Latino students in California are the focus of this chapter. My perspective is that of a professional educator interested in the intersection of theory, practice, and policy in the classroom. More specifically, the chapter will address educationally related conceptual/theoretical pursuits that attempt to explain, and lay the foundation for, educational action. An attempt will be made to highlight state policy priorities that can lead to a brighter educational future for Latino students in California. It seems most appropriate to begin addressing the educational and related demographic circumstances of our Latino students.

---

[2]E. Garcia, *Student Cultural Diversity: Understanding and Meeting the Challenge* (Boston, Mass.: Houghton Mifflin, 1999); T. Stritikus and E. Garcia, "Education of Limited English Proficiency in California Schools and Assessment of the Influence of Proposition 227 on Selected Teachers and Classrooms," *NABE Journal* 14, 1 (2000): 165–81.

[3]In addition to Garcia's *Student Cultural Diversity: Understanding and Meeting the Challenge,* see: E. Garcia, "Attributes of Effective Language Minority Teachers: An Empirical Study," *Journal of Education* 173 (1991): 130–41; E. Garcia, "Promoting the Contributions of Bilingual Students," in *Educational Policies and Practices for Students Learning English as a New Language,* ed. S. H. Fradd and O. Lee (Tallahassee, Fla.: University of Florida and the Florida State Department of Education, 1997), Vii 1–Vii 13; and H. Romo, *Reaching Out: Best Practices for Educating Mexican-Origin Children and Youth* (Charleston, W.Va.: Clearinghouse on Rural Education and Small Schools, 1999).

The Demographic Picture

The U.S. Census Bureau, in its attempts to document the racial and ethnic heterogeneity of our country's population, has arrived at a set of highly confusing terms that place individuals in separate, exclusionary categories: white, white non-Hispanic, black, and Hispanic (with five subcategories of Hispanics). Unfortunately, most of these terms are highly ambiguous and do not represent the true heterogeneity that the Census Bureau seeks to document. These categories are useful only as the most superficial reflection of our nation's true diversity. Some census-identified "whites," "blacks," and "Hispanics" might not believe they match these designations, but they are constrained by the forced-choice responses allowed in census questionnaires. Racially and culturally we are not "pure" stock, and any separation by the U.S. Census Bureau, the Center for Educational Statistics, or other social institutions that attempt to address the complexity of our diverse population is likely to result in a highly ambiguous sketch.

Despite this significant limitation in efforts to document this country's population diversity, an examination of the available data in this arena does provide an incomplete but useful portrait of our society and the specific circumstances of various groups within our nation's boundaries. That sketch is one of consummate vulnerability for nonwhite and Hispanic/Latino (usually referred to as "minority") families, children, and students. Nonwhite and Hispanic families, at-risk children, and students are likely to fall into the lowest quartile on indicators of "well-being": family stability, family violence, family income, child health and development, and educational achievement. Yet, this population has grown significantly in the last two decades and will grow substantially in the decades to come.

Chapter 1 in this book provides an overview of ethnic change and the growing centrality of Latinos in California. Here I focus on the state's school-age population, which is substantially more Latino than even the state's adult population. In 2000, 32 percent of the state's total population was Latino; 43 percent of the children aged 5 to 17, and at least 47 percent of those entering kindergarten, were Latino. The trend is clear: In the decades to come, half the state's schoolchildren and then young adults will be Latinos who have grown up in California.

Table 3.1 provides the latest available breakdown of the ethnicity and language background of children enrolled in California's public schools. (Private schooling, which is beyond this chapter's purview, enrolls approximately 10 percent of the state's children.) Latinos are already the single largest group of public-school students. They are not spread equally across all grade levels. Instead, each new cohort entering kindergarten is about two percent "more Latino" than the previous component. Thus, while half of the newcomers today are

Table 3.1. Ethnicity and Language at Home of California's Children Enrolled in Public School, 1998–1999

	K–12 Enrollees Number	K–12 Enrollees Percent	Speaks Language Other than English at Home (Percent)
Latino	2,481,000	42	78
White	2,181,000	37	10
Asian	656,000	11	64
Black	497,000	8	n.a.
Other	50,000	2	n.a.
Total	5,865,000	100	44

Note: n.a. = not available.
Source: School enrollment figures from California Department of Finance Web site; language at home rates are from the Census Supplemental Survey Web site, for children aged 5 to 17, excluding those in private school.

Latino, whites still outnumber Latinos at the highest grades, especially because Latinos are much less likely than whites to finish high school.

The last column of Table 3.1 is especially significant: 78 percent of Latino children are reported to speak Spanish at home. The vast majority of these and other children who do not speak English at home are growing up in immigrant households (see Chapter 1). This does not mean that 78 percent of Latino children cannot speak English well; after the first few years the vast majority become effective English speakers. But it does mean that all the qualities—the challenges as well as the opportunities—of bilingualism, in which the language of schooling is not the usual home language, are a fact of life for the majority of Latino (and Asian) public-school children in California. This is not a "minority" issue: 44 percent of all the state's schoolchildren speak a language other than English at home, and the rate rises each year.

Table 3.2 provides the ethnic breakdown and more-detailed language data for California's kindergarteners in 1998. The increase in Latino enrollment and drop in white enrollment is even more striking at this point of entry. The language statistics are especially important. Each spring schools assess the English ability of children who are not English monolinguals, categorizing them as either English language students (ELS) or fluent English proficient (FEP) bilinguals. In the spring of 1998, 65 percent of all Latinos were categorized as ELS, 10 percent as FEP, and 25 percent as English monolinguals. There has been

Table 3.2. Ethnicity and Language Designation of California Public School Kindergarteners, Spring 1998

	Enrollees		ELS*		FEP*		Monolingual	
	Number	Percent	Number	Percent	Number	Percent	Number	Percent
Latino	220,000	47	141,000	65	22,000	10	55,000	25
					All Others Combined			
			26,000	11	11,000	4	209,000	85
White	156,000	34						
Asian	44,000	10						
Black	38,000	8						
Other	4,000	1						
Total	464,000	100	167,000	36	33,000	7	264,000	57

*ELS = English Language Student (formerly LEP); FEP = Fluent English Proficient.
Source: School enrollment figures and language designation rates from California Department of Education Web site.

much debate about the accuracy of such categorizations, but they do provide a rough guide to the linguistic situation of students. Perhaps the most important point is that the vast majority of Spanish-at-home kids are not fluent bilinguals at this stage of their development, but rather must still rely on Spanish for effective communication. The rates for other language groups (not reported in Table 3.2) varied enormously: Mandarin-speaking kindergarteners were equally divided between ELS and FEP, while most other Asian-language groups, like Spanish speakers, were predominantly ELS.

Taken together, Tables 3.1 and 3.2 show the importance of immigration and language in understanding the educational issues related to Latino children in California. Language has always been an important issue for Latino education, but with the great increase in immigrant households in the last four decades it has taken center stage: The vast majority of the largest ethnic group among California's schoolchildren (as well as important segments of smaller groups) do not speak English at home and enter first grade with limited English skills.

Of course language is only part of the story. As Chapter 1 details, Latino households have lower incomes, and Latino parents have much less education, than most other groups. To a large extent this simply reflects their status as poor immigrants, though there is evidence of significant income and educational disparities even among native-born Latino adults (see Figure 1.15 in Chapter 1). There are certainly important exceptions: There are thousands of well-educated and affluent Latino immigrant families in California who are able to nurture their young children carefully to be effective bilinguals at the outset of their school careers. (Remember that 10 percent of the Latino kindergarteners are FEP, effective bilinguals). But the vast majority are not effective bilinguals when they start school, and the majority of these children come from poor immigrant households.

The demographic transformation that has become more evident in the last decade was easily foreseen long ago. With regard to schooling, high school or equivalent completion rates are alarmingly low for these emerging-majority student populations. With regard to academic achievement, in 1994, 30 percent of 13-year-old students were one grade level below the norm on standardized achievement measures. This differed significantly for emerging-majority and white students: 27 percent of white students, 40 percent of Hispanic students, and 46 percent of black students were one grade level below the norm.

Combined with the contemporary educational zeitgeist, which embraces excellence and equity for all students as best reflected in *A Nation at Risk*,[4] and the

---

[4]National Commission on Excellence in Education, *A Nation at Risk: The Imperative for Education Reform* (Washington, D.C.: U.S. Department of Education, 1983).

more recent national goals statement,[5] attention to Latino children, families, and students has been significant. The major thrust of any such effort aimed at these populations has been on identifying why such populations are not thriving and how institutions serving them can be reformed or restructured to meet this educational challenge. Recent analyses and recommendations include:

- The California State Department of Education's efforts to train infant and toddler caregivers in state-supported programs[6]
- The U.S. Department of Education's reforms for federally funded education programs[7]
- The National Academy of Education's discussion of standards-based reform[8]
- Efforts of the Roundtable on Head Start Research of the National Research Council to provide an issue analysis of research needed to produce a thriving future for Head Start for a highly diverse population of children and families[9]
- The National Council of Teachers of English and the International Reading Association's treatment of language-arts standards[10]
- The National Association for the Education of Young Children's position statement regarding linguistic and cultural diversity[11]

More directly related to this discourse are the contributions of the White House Initiative on Educational Excellence for Hispanic Americans. All these articulations have attended to the "vulnerabilities" of Latinos and have addressed issues of language and culture, given this country's past treatment of

---

[5]Goals 2000: Educate America Act. Pub. No. L. (103–227), 108 Stats. 125 (1994).

[6]California Department of Education, *Fostering Development in a First and Second Language in Early Childhood: Resource Guide* (Sacramento, California Department of Education, 1998).

[7]E. Garcia and R. Gonzalez, "Issues in Systemic Reform for Culturally and Linguistically Diverse Students," *College Record* 96 (1995): 418–31; and U.S. Department of Education, *No More Excuses: Final Report of U.S. Hispanic Dropout Project* (Washington, D.C.: U.S. Department of Education, 1998).

[8]M. W. McLaughlin and L. A. Shepard, "Improving Education through Standards-Based Reform," A Report by the National Academy of Education Panel on Standards-Based Education Reform. (Stanford, Calif.: National Academy of Education, 1995).

[9]D. A. Phillips and N. J. Cabrera, eds., *Beyond the Blueprint: Directions for Research on Head Start's Families* (Washington, D.C.: National Academy of Sciences, 1996).

[10]National Council of Teachers of English and International Reading Association, *Standards for the English Language Arts* (Urbana, Ill. and Newark, Del.: NCTE/IRA, 1996).

[11]National Association for the Education of Young Children, NAEYC Position Statement: Responding to Linguistic and Cultural Diversity—Recommendations for Effective Early Childhood Education (Washington, D.C.: NAEYC, 1996).

this population and the present conceptual and empirical understanding of how institutions must be more responsive. Much of this thinking related to policy and practice is based on the issues and research findings in the following discussion.

New Theory and Practice for Schooling: Educational Reform

The Present Status of Educational Reform for Latinos in California

The profound need for school reform at the local level and in the classroom is best communicated by an e-mail message I received from a practicing teacher:

> Hi . . .
> *Here's the report from the Western Front. Please pass it around.*
> In short, this school and school district are nightmares.
> Reading and writing levels are grotesque. I have only four students who are operating above grade level who could function in an honors program. That's out of 150 on the rolls.
> Teacher support is nil. I still don't have a stapler or even file folders for portfolio writing assessment. The trash is emptied maybe once a week. The floors are filthier than some bars I've been in, and the bathrooms and stairwells stink. Half the lights are out in most classrooms and every third and fourth light works in the dark hallways. There is one computer lab for Math, four or five computers in the library and that's about it. The textbooks left for me to use were 1980 copyright 10th grade lit books, and there were only enough for a classroom set. And, of course, all except one of the short stories was about teenage white (male) characters, and these kids Just Don't Relate to that. Plus, despite this being a major ESL school, no supplementary resources "enrichment" materials exist that I can find that contain black or brown or multinational short stories or poems.
> There are few AP classes but few students pass the tests. Kids who miss school for field trips and football games are not listed on an excuse sheet nor is there any other official notification. They just tell you they were on a field trip and you mark the grade book accordingly.
> These kids are sweet. It's too bad this system here just processes them through, like the Pink Floyd mechanized conveyor belt "We don't need no education" song, but on a bad drug trip.

A recent federal report relevant to these issues provides a more formal assessment. Concluding that the educational failure of Hispanic students in the U.S. was reaching crisis proportions, the U.S. Department of Education assembled a group of experts to assess the educational circumstances of Hispanic students, the reasons for these circumstances, and the educational practices that were effective and/or promising. I was fortunate to serve on the Hispanic Dropout Project that guided the work of this endeavor and participated in developing its final report.[12] I can take no credit for the report's eloquent conclusion:

> We submit this report with a sense of urgency and impatience because of the slow pace of improvement.... There are dozens of proven programs, replicable programs capable of increasing Hispanic students' achievement, increasing high school completion, and increasing their college going rate.... Why, then, the persistent gap in Hispanic student achievement? Many explanations have been offered: student characteristics such as social class, language, and entering achievement levels, especially among recent immigrants; school-based forces such as student retention, ability grouping, and tracking; and, non-school forces such as family and/or neighborhood violence and criminal activity, lack of community-based opportunity, and the historical and social and political oppression of different ethnic and racial groups. Many of these "reasons" have assumed mythic proportions. They are used to explain a phenomenon that is portrayed as too large and too complex for schools to address. In short, these reasons have become little more than excuses for our schools and society's failure to act. We as a people, need to say: *No more excuses, the time to act is now* (pp. 61–62).

Coupled with a sense of urgency, this report recommended specific practices that were in need of attention. In an effort to be comprehensive in its practice-reform agenda, the report included separate recommendations for teachers and for the schools that serve Latinos.

Like other research and synthesis on Latino school failure and success, this report identified teachers as crucial to the intellectual and academic development of Hispanic students. They were urged to:
1. Teach content so that it interests and challenges students.
2. Communicate high expectations, respect, and interest in each of their students.
3. Understand the roles of language, race, culture, and gender in schooling.
4. Engage parents and community in the education of their children.
5. Become knowledgeable about and develop strategies to educate students and to communicate with their parents.
6. Seek and obtain the professional development needed to engender these attitudes, knowledge bases, and specific instructional skills.

Schools serving these students were similarly urged to adopt the programmatic features and attributes of effective programs that had been replicated in various school settings:
1. Schools should emphasize the prevention of academic problems. They need to become more aggressive in responding to early warning signs that a stu-

---

[12] No More Excuses: The Final Report of the Hispanic Dropout Project.

dent may be doing poorly, losing interest, or in some other way becoming disengaged from school.
2. Schools, especially high schools, need to personalize programs and services that work with language-minority students.
3. Schools should be restructured to ensure that all students have access to high-quality curricula. They should recognize time, space, and staffing patterns that provide students with the support necessary to achieve.
4. Schools should replicate programs that have proven effective. In addition, by using new and present funding, schools should re-deploy resources to run these programs.
5. Schools should carefully monitor the effectiveness of what they do for Hispanic students requiring the disaggregation of student-progress data and acting on that data to improve or replace failing strategies. (Adapted from pp. 35–38.)

Such a listing of specific actions has been reinforced by more direct research.[13] It is also echoed in other syntheses of research that have considered the linguistic and cultural character of the language-minority student and particular education practices.[14] Over and over again a similar call to action resonates in

---

[13] In particular, see, in addition to Romo's *Reaching Out: Best Practices for Educating Mexican-Origin Children and Youth,* R. J. Rossi, "Education Reform and Students at Risk," Volume III: Synthesis and Evaluation of Previous Efforts to Improve Educational Practice and Development of Strategies for Achieving Positive Outcomes, Studies of Education Reform (Washington, D.C.: American Institutes for Research, 1995); L. Olsen, *Made in America: Immigrant Students in Our Public Schools* (New York: The New Press, 1997); H. Romo and T. Falbo, *Latino High School Graduation: Defying the Odds* (Austin: University of Texas Press, 1996); K. Larson and R. Rumberger, PACT Manual: Parent and Community Teams for School Success. ABC Dropout Prevention and Intervention Series (University of California at Santa Barbara, Graduate School of Education, 1995); A. C. Zentella, *Growing up Bilingual: Puerto Rican Children in New York* (Malden, Mass.: Blackwell Publishers, 1997); M. Rose, *Possible Lives: The Promise of Public Education in America* (New York: Penguin Books, 1995); L. D. Soto, *Language, Culture, and Power: Bilingual Families and the Struggle for Quality Education* (New York: State University of New York Press, 1997); and H. Trueba, *Latinos Unidos* (Lanham, Md.: Rowman and Littlefield, 1998).

[14] The report of the National Research Council regarding the education of language minority students in 1997 (D. August and K. Hakuta, *Improving Schooling for Language-Minority Children: Research Agenda* (Washington, D.C.: National Council Research, 1997); the report of the National Academy of Sciences regarding the teaching of reading, particularly to non-English-speaking students (National Research Council, *The New Americans: Economic, Demographic, and Fiscal Effects of Immigration,* [Washington, D.C.: National Academy Press, 1997]); the report of the University of California Task Force on Latino Student Eligibility (University of California, *Latino Student Eligibility and Participation in the University of California.* YA BASTA! Report No. 5 of the Latino Eligibility Task Force. [Berkeley: University of California, Chicano/Latino Policy

these reports and directs educational institutions to take on specific practices that can enhance Latino student achievement.

Preparing Latino Students for the Future: State Policy Priorities

As California enters the 21st century, it is even more important to understand the seismic changes in technology, globalization, and democratization that are reflected in similarly seismic demographic changes—particularly the significant growth of Latino students in all our schools. Unfortunately, our general population is far more attuned to and comfortable with engaging in aspects of the technological, global, and political challenges than those that confront us because of this demographic reality. They can almost be characterized as having a "blind spot" when it comes to this new reality.

However, changes are all inextricably intertwined. Some 60 percent of new jobs in the near future will be in information technology and communications. To those students who master and control this new technology—locally, regionally, nationally, and internationally—go the spoils. They will be like those who controlled capital and labor in the 20th century. This link creates an obvious imperative to educate those who will either help this country to prosper or serve as its growing weak link. Those students who master and control the new technology will serve as our foundation for national preeminence in the fields of high technology in a global workplace that promotes democratic principles and practices.

These circumstances pose a particular challenge to educators and those among us who look to educational agencies for help in realizing the moral imperatives of equity and social justice. These agencies are being called on to develop and implement models of culturally competent practices in treating and delivering services to growing numbers of Latino students and families.

If these agencies are successful, then one could predict that as more Latino students enter the "right" kinds of schools, barriers to their academic, social, and economic success and mobility will fall. Likewise, as non-Latinos become more attuned to the cultural diversity around them and the resources inherent in that diversity, cultural distinctions will blend with other features of our society to create a more egalitarian, multicultural society. This is of course a highly optimistic scenario of the future for Latino students and California in general. Yet it is most certainly a preferable prediction to one that argues that California could

---

Project, 1997]); and the Report of the National Task Force on Minority High Achievement (College Board, *Report of the Task Force on Minority High Achievement* [New York: College Board, 1999]).

become another Bosnian nightmare, where racial and ethnic conflicts could escalate into major social unrest.

This optimistic scenario cannot exist without immediate integration of our new theoretical and educational understanding regarding the education of Latino students and the policies that now guide California in its education of Latino children and families. Very specifically, state policies that address English-only philosophies create accountability systems that disadvantage Latinos. Such policies do not maximize educational investments that enhance the teaching and learning opportunities of Latino and other low-income and underachieving student populations.

English-Only State Policies

Proposition 227's "one-size-of-English-only-instruction" for Latino students who come to school proficient in Spanish but lacking English-language proficiency has no foundation in modern linguistic or cognitive theory, in state or national research, or in what we might call "best educational practices." This form of English-only policy also is out of line with federal policies articulated in the Improving American Schools Act of 1994 and specifically in the Bilingual Education Act within this same legislation. Federal policy is quite clear that programs serving language-minority students should be: (1) aimed at ensuring high academic achievement; (2) formulated to be "additive" (adding English proficiency without the loss of native-language proficiency), not subtractive (adding English without regard for maintaining proficiency in the native language); and (3) flexible in allowing local school districts and schools to implement instruction programs to meet the first two goals.[15] U.S. Department of Education Secretary Richard Riley, in the announcement of a new U.S. Department of Educational initiative, called for the funding of 1,000 new, national bilingual-education programs that are "additive" in nature.

In practice, recent analyses of California's implementation of Proposition 227 indicate that school districts, schools, and teachers are artfully creating ways (such as the use of parent waivers, shifting to charter-school status, and defining ambiguous aspects of the new Proposition 227–generated regulations to maximize native-language instruction) to develop flexibility in order to align instruction with sound theory, research, and "best practices."[16] These same analyses

---

[15] A. Wiese and E. Garcia, "The Bilingual Education Act: Language Minority Students and Equal Educational Opportunity," *Bilingual Research Journal* 22 (1998): 1–18.

[16] R. Rumberger and P. Gandara, *Crucial Issues in California Education 2000: Are the Reform Pieces Fitting Together* (Berkeley: University of California and Policy Analysis for California Education, 2000); and P. Gandara et al., *The Initial Impact of*

indicate that as Latino students begin to receive more instruction in English, teachers are reporting more negative attitudes from their English-only colleagues toward any instruction in Spanish. This negative climate is reported to have negative effects on both teachers and Latino students.

Although it seems an impossible task to call for the political mobilization necessary to overturn Proposition 227, it is imperative that state policies be constructed to allow school-level flexibility. Such policies would allow teachers to use their best professional judgment regarding educational programs and instructional strategies while being held to educational standards that ensure student progress. This would require a sound accountability system that recognizes local flexibility while at the same time providing reliable and valid information on the educational progress of Latino language-minority students.

Accountability

California, under the leadership of Governor Davis, is rightly devoting much of the state's new education spending to building the capacity of schools and students to meet the state's educational challenges. But those investments need time to pay off. Latino students and parents have a right to expect that schools deliver on their charge of preparing the next generation of workers and citizens; taxpayers have a right to expect progress in return for their investment.

The state is right in focusing on accountability. We should be testing to ensure that schools raise student performance and that students have the necessary knowledge and skills. But the development and implementation of such a system in California has been, and continues to be, too simplistic and particularly disadvantageous to Latino students. Too many policymakers equate accountability with testing, thinking that the signals sent by tests about performance are enough to spark instructional improvement and better student learning. Schools vary tremendously in their ability to respond to these signals. On this point research could not be clearer. It is shortsighted to assess performance without investing in support for teaching and learning. The discussion should address important questions about the testing itself, about who is included, and about how performance is measured.

A full-fledged and appropriate accountability system must focus on:
- **A fair and technically sound assessment system.** To account for student differences and subject-matter variation, systems should include multiple measures of performance. They should incorporate accommodations for non-English-proficient students, students with special needs, and very young students. Tests should measure what states and districts want to see

---

Proposition 227 on the Instruction of English Learners (Santa Barbara: Language Minority Research Institute, 2000).

incorporated in the curriculum, not generic skills included in some off-the-shelf assessments like the SAT 9. As an example of some of these points, states such as Washington and Vermont are requiring individually administered oral-reading assessments in the primary grades. These assessments accommodate the skills of young readers and add to the information provided by traditional paper-and-pencil tests. In Texas, the accountability system includes testing in Spanish for students who may require it.
- **Adequate preparation for the assessments.** For tests to be meaningful, students must have prior instruction in the subject area. For students' learning to reach desired achievement levels, instruction must improve. That requires investment in teacher development and curriculum. It means that instruction must be focused on the standards for learning that guide the assessments, and that schools must have time to develop instruction aimed at the standards before they are judged as successful or failing. Students who need extra support must be given it, through early-intervention and extra-help programs. Such a consideration is not now part of California's plan for an accountability system.
- **Appropriate uses of assessments.** Assessments need to inform a number of decisions, including teacher plans for individual students, school curriculum designs, teacher professional-development needs, and what to do when school performance lags. Different tests are needed for different purposes; there's no such thing as an all-purpose measure. Educators and policymakers both need assistance in interpreting and using assessment information. California's present use of only one standardized test in its accountability system of "high-stakes" decisions and consequences is sorely deficient.
- **Responsibility for all.** Good accountability systems include incentives and consequences for everyone in the system. In California, schools are rewarded if they "succeed," or they can be taken over or closed if they "fail." Teachers are "rewarded" if students' test scores improve, and, in a new proposal by the governor, students would receive postsecondary scholarships on the basis of their test scores, or potentially be held back or denied graduation on the basis of these same test scores. But others should be held accountable as well—school districts for policies and practices that enhance or prohibit student progress, and colleges and universities that prepare new teachers and provide continued support to the profession. Finally, policymakers must assume responsibility for attending to the necessary investments, and not just to the punishments.

The state also needs to invest resources and time in the testing system itself. It needs to recognize that there are differences in how students demonstrate competence and that ignoring the student's primary language in the testing process ignores a well-documented variable in making testing valid, reliable, and fair. Therefore, the state needs to give students multiple ways to show what they know. Such a system also needs to make provisions for language minorities and for students with special needs.

Educational Investments for Failing Schools

From the previous review of educational data, it is clear that too many California public schools serving Latino students are failing. There is a moral as well as an educational imperative to take immediate action. California policy options to deal directly with this set of circumstances typically include three broad remedies to fix failing schools. Some have called for vouchers that would enable parents of children in poorly performing schools to attend private or religious schools, paid for with public funds. Others advocate using the state's accountability system to reward "successful" schools and shut down (or reconstitute) "failing" schools, reopening them with a new principal, new teachers, additional resources, and a new school-improvement plan. California policy also supports variants of public-school choice, especially charter schools—publicly funded but privately operated schools that are subject to varying degrees of public oversight.

Unfortunately, these policy options are rooted more in ideology than in fact. For example, vouchers are decried by some as undermining public education, and hailed by others as the solution to public-school failure. Research has shown that each of these remedies has its own strengths and weaknesses. As Romo discusses in *Reaching Out: Best Practices for Educating Mexican-Origin Children and Youth,* none is a magic bullet for a policy to deal with failing schools and underachieving Latino students in those schools.

With regard to vouchers, there is evidence of small gains in math achievement for minority children, including Latino students, and strong evidence of high parental satisfaction with these programs. On the other hand, overall achievement gains have been uniformly small and, in areas such as reading, results have been mixed. In addition, there are consistent findings that vouchers do not attract the most disadvantaged applicants, and instead appeal to the most-involved parents. The second policy option, reconstituting schools, has been tried most notably in Chicago's high schools. Research has found that reconstitution encourages greater effort among teachers who put in more hours on the job and participate in more professional development. On the negative side, teachers in reconstituted schools did not change their classroom practices, and achievement levels remained low. In addition, there was an inadequate supply of qualified teachers to restaff the schools. Charter schools have proven to be a popular and bipartisan policy option. Unfortunately, the jury is still out on whether charter schools improve student achievement. We do know that provisions for accountability in California's enabling legislation have a profound effect on the number and character of charter schools. Consequently these schools differ dramatically in terms of quality. Recent California evidence shows substantial variation in the levels of achievement, degrees of segregation, and the extent to which charter schools skim off the most able students from public schools.[17]

Beyond the lack of evidence that supports the belief that these remedies will solve the problem of failing schools, the trouble with all of them is that they focus on changing governance and structure, rather than on improving teaching and learning in schools. For 30 years, research has shown what makes an effective school where teaching and learning takes place: high expectations and standards for all students, curricula that mirror the standards, appropriate methods of standards-based assessment, strong principals, a safe and orderly environment, a high degree of parental involvement, teachers who are well-prepared in content and pedagogy, ongoing professional development for all teachers, and accountability throughout the school. As Garcia discusses in *Student Cultural Diversity: Understanding and Meeting the Challenge,* these characteristics can be found in the best schools, be they public, private, religious, charter, or reconstituted.

A recent RAND state-by-state analysis of standardized test results suggests that policy initiatives to boost student achievement have been effective, with math scores climbing steadily across the country at an average rate of about one percentile point each year from 1990 to 1996. Texas and a handful of other states that were among the leaders in adopting new standards, enhancing state investments in education, and adopting comprehensive accountability systems have demonstrated particular gains, including significantly higher scores by poor students and Latino students. According to a national study released in September 2000, smaller class size in early grades and access to preschool appear to increase student achievement, particularly in impoverished communities, more than the salaries, education, or experience of teachers.[18]

The study linked scores on a national standardized test to census data and variables such as per-pupil spending and social class. Specifically, the study looked at seven math and reading tests administered in 44 states through the National Assessment of Educational Progress, a federal program that tests samples of fourth-, eighth-, and twelfth-graders. The results indicate that there continues to be a wide disparity in performance across the states for students from socio-economically similar families, with students from poorer families scoring at lower levels. With regard to Latino, big-population states, Texas topped the list, with students scoring an average of 11 percentile points higher than their counterparts in last-ranked California. The states succeeding in this measure

---

[17]G. Wells, "Language and Education: Reconceptualizing Education as Dialogue," *Annual Review of Applied Linguistics* 19 (1999): 135–55.

[18]D. Grissmer, Ann E. Flanagan, Jennifer H. Kawata, and Stephanie Williamson, *Improving Student Achievement: What State NAEP Test Scores Tell Us* (Los Alamitos, Calif.: RAND Corporation, 2000).

tended to spend more money per student, have lower student-teacher ratios and less teacher turnover, provide more public prekindergarten classes, and have teachers report satisfaction with their classroom resources. Such sophisticated policy studies confirm what research findings have been reporting: poor children, particularly Latino children, achieve at lower rates because they are given an inferior education.

A recently filed lawsuit based on this presupposition (*Williams et al. v. State of California et al.*) will move this policy discussion directly into the California courts. It puts forward the very specific evidence that poor students, particularly Latino and African-American students in urban schools, are receiving educational opportunities that are substantially inferior to those available to more-privileged children attending the majority of California's public schools. The plaintiffs contend that state officials responsible for ensuring equal and adequate educational opportunities for every child in California have failed to develop and implement appropriate procedures to identify and correct the substandard conditions—physical, fiscal, professional, and instructional—at the schools these children attend.

Creating schools that work for Latino students will not be accomplished by focusing on structural reforms alone, and it won't be accomplished at all if we continue to have a divisive, ideological debate in which remedies are dismissed out of hand or accepted with little or no evidence. There is only one way to improve failing schools, and that is to ensure that any reform maintains a focus on the classroom, the characteristics of effective schools, and the resources necessary to address the present educational inequities.

Conclusion

The treatment of Latino students in California's educational institutions can be compared to a seismic indicator of an impending earthquake, an indicator that is now sending signals of coming dangers. We can ignore those signals, but they will not go away. We can respond to them minimally, study them some more, and prepare for the worst. Or we can marshal our resources in ways that will make the inevitable an opportunity for action from which we can benefit. Simply put, our challenge for the students of this state is to help them help California arrive at a truly multiracial, multi-ethnic democracy. We must learn about and create new ways to (1) honor diversity and the social complexity in which we live—acknowledge the integrity of the individual and of the social circumstances where he or she develops as a human being; and (2) unify, but not insist upon it without recognizing that the underpinnings of unification are individual and collective dignity, coupled with educational, social, and economic success.

References

August, D., and K. Hakuta. 1997. *Improving Schooling for Language-Minority Children: Research Agenda.* Washington, D.C.: National Council Research.

California Department of Education. 1998. *Fostering Development in a First and Second Language in Early Childhood: Resource Guide.* Sacramento, Calif.

College Board. 1999. *Report of the Task Force on Minority High Achievement.* New York, N.Y.: College Board.

Gandara, P., J. Maxwell-Jolly, E. Garcia, T. Stritikus, J. Curry, K. Gutierrez, and J. Asato. 2000. *The Initial Impact of Proposition 227 on the Instruction of English Learners.* Santa Barbara, Calif.: Language Minority Research Institute.

Garcia E. 1999. *Student Cultural Diversity: Understanding and Meeting the Challenge.* Boston, New York: Houghton Mifflin Company.

———. 1991. "Attributes of Effective Language Minority Teachers: An Empirical Study." *Journal of Education,* vol. 173: 130–41.

Garcia, E., and R. Gonzalez. 1995. "Issues in Systemic Reform for Culturally and Linguistically Diverse Students." *College Record,* vol. 96, no. 3: 418–31.

Goals 2000: Educate America Act. Pub. No. L. (103–227), 108 Stats. 125 (1994).

Grissmer, D., Ann E. Flanagan, Jennifer H. Kawata, Stephanie Williamson. 2000. *Improving Student Achievement: What State NAEP Test Scores Tell Us.* Los Alamitos, Calif.: RAND Corporation.

Larson, K., and R. Rumberger. 1995. *PACT Manual: Parent and Community Teams for School Success.* ABC Dropout Prevention and Intervention Series. California University, Santa Barbara. Graduate School of Education.

McLaughlin, M. W., and L. A. Shepard. 1995. "Improving Education through Standards-Based Reform." A Report by the National Academy of Education Panel on Standards-Based Education Reform. Stanford, Calif.: National Academy of Education.

National Association for the Education of Young Children. 1996. NAEYC Position Statement: Responding to Linguistic and Cultural Diversity—Recommendations for Effective Early Childhood Education. Washington, D.C.

National Commission on Excellence in Education. 1983. *A Nation at Risk: The Imperative for Education Reform.* Washington, D.C.: United States Department of Education.

National Council of Teachers of English & International Reading Association. 1996. *Standards for the English Language Arts.* Urbana, Ill. and Newark, Del.

National Research Council. 1997. *The New Americans: Economic, Demographic, and Fiscal Effects of Immigration.* Washington, D.C.: National Academy Press.

Olsen, L. 1997. *Made in America: Immigrant Students in our Public Schools.* New York: The New Press.

Policy Analysis for California Education. 1998. *Californians Speak on Education and Reform Options: Uneven Faith in Teachers, School Boards, and the State as Designers of Change.* Berkeley, Calif.: University of California, Berkeley, and Stanford University.

Phillips, D. A., and N. J. Cabrera, eds. 1996. *Beyond the Blueprint: Directions for Research on Head Start's Families.* Washington, D.C.: National Academy of Sciences.

Romo, H. 1999. *Reaching Out: Best Practices for Educating Mexican-Origin Children and Youth.* Charleston, W. Va.: Clearinghouse on Rural Education and Small Schools.

Romo, H., and T. Falbo. 1996. *Latino High School Graduation: Defying the Odds.* Austin, Tex.: University of Texas Press.

Rose, M. 1995. *Possible Lives: The Promise of Public Education in America.* New York: Penguin Books.

Rossi, R. J. 1995. "Education Reform and Students at Risk. Volume III: Synthesis and Evaluation of Previous Efforts to Improve Educational Practice and Development of Strategies for Achieving Positive Outcomes." *Studies of Education Reform.* Washington, D.C.: American Institutes for Research.

Rumberger, R., and P. Gandara. 2000. *Crucial Issues in California Education 2000: Are the Reform Pieces Fitting Together?* Berkeley, Calif.: University of California, Berkeley and Policy Analysis for California Education.

Soto, L. D. 1997. *Language, Culture, and Power: Bilingual Families and the Struggle for Quality Education.* N.Y: State University of New York Press.

Stritikus, T., and E. Garcia. In press. "Education of Limited English Proficiency in California Schools and Assessment of the Influence of Proposition 227 on Selected Teachers and Classrooms." *NABE Journal.*

Trueba, H. 1998. "*Latinos Unidos.*" Lanham, Md.: Rowman and Littlefield.

United States Department of Education. 1998. *No More Excuses: Final Report of U.S. Hispanic Dropout Project.* Washington, D.C.: Author.

University of California. 1997. *Latino Student Eligibility and Participation in the University of California. YA BASTA!* Report No. 5 of the Latino Eligibility Task Force. Berkeley, Calif.: University of California, Chicano/Latino Policy Project, July.

Wells, G. 1999. "Language and Education: Reconceptualizing Education as Dialogue." *Annual Review of Applied Linguistics,* vol. 19: 135–55.

Wiese, A., and E. Garcia. 1998. "The Bilingual Education Act: Language Minority Students and Equal Educational Opportunity." *Bilingual Research Journal* 22(1): 1–18.

Zentella, A. C. 1997. *Growing up Bilingual: Puerto Rican Children in New York.* Blackwell Publishers: Great Britain

Chapter 4

Putting the Cart before the Horse:
Latinos and Higher Education

Patricia Gándara and Lisa Chávez

Introduction

Making good public policy requires an appropriate sense of timing. Removing a public "safety net" before individuals have a fair opportunity to compete in society, the workplace, or school is like putting the proverbial cart before the horse. It reverses the appropriate order of events. We argue in this chapter that Proposition 209, the state referendum that prohibited affirmative action in public higher education as well as in state hiring and contracting, is an example of exactly that—putting the cart before the horse—and as such, is bad public policy. Although the campaign for Proposition 209 claimed that it "equalized" opportunity for every citizen, prohibiting special consideration for any person on the basis of his or her racial or ethnic background,[1] in fact it increased disparities in access to higher education. At a time when the combination of a stressed K–12 public education system and the arrival of large numbers of poor immigrant children should have called for measures to improve access to higher education, Califor-

---

[1] Lydia Chávez, *The Color Bind: California's Battle to End Affirmative Action* (Berkeley: University of California Press, 1998).

nia took a giant step in the opposite direction. A difficult and troubling situation—the highly disproportionate access of different ethnic groups to higher education—was made worse; in ending affirmative action, the state lost a valuable tool for equalizing educational opportunity. This chapter reviews the data on the effect of unequal educational opportunity for Latinos and others, the current situation with respect to higher education in California, the principal barriers that stand in the way of equal access, and the policy implications of the foregoing.

A History of Slow Progress in Higher Education

High-school dropout rates are declining—at least officially—for Latino students in California, from 7.8 percent annually in 1991 to 3.8 percent in 1999,[2] and more Latino students are going on to college.[3] Nonetheless, the results are mixed regarding Latinos access to higher education in recent times, as Table 4.1 illustrates. Some highlights are:

- In 1980, nine percent of the undergraduates in the three public institutions of higher education in California were Latinos; by 1999 that figure had grown to 24 percent. However, Latinos constituted just 16 percent of the public high-school graduates in California in 1980, and by 2002 their representation had doubled to more than 32 percent.
- Latino representation in each of the state's segments of the public higher-education system has increased at a higher rate than Latino representation among the state's public high-school graduates.
- However, the growth in higher education has occurred primarily in the lower two segments of the public higher-education system. The California State University (CSU) system saw the greatest percentage increase in Latino representation over the period—191 percent—while the community-college system saw an increase of 163 percent. The University of California system posted only a 124 percent increase in the representation of Latino students among its undergraduates.
- This growth in higher-education participation for Latinos still falls short of reaching parity with the high representation of Latinos among the state's high-school graduates. Most troubling is Latino representation at the Uni-

---

[2]California Department of Education, *Graduation Rates in California Public Schools by Ethnic Group, 1984–85 through 1998–99* (2000). www.cde.ca.gov/demographics/reports/statewide/ethgrate.htm.

[3]Much controversy surrounds the methodology for counting dropouts in California. Thus, while the annual dropout rates appear to be down dramatically over previous figures, the actual graduation rate for Latinos remains low. The four-year graduation rate—the percentage of students who graduated 12th grade as a proportion of those who entered in the ninth grade—was only 55.3 percent. This was the lowest for all ethnic groups.

Table 4.1. Historical Representation of Latinos Among High-School Graduates and Undergraduate Enrollment at California Community Colleges, California State University, and the University of California, 1980–2000

Latino Representation	1980 Number	1980 Percent	1990 Number	1990 Percent	2000 Number	2000 Percent	Percent Increase In Representation
Public high-school graduates	38,698[a]	16.0	55,152	23.3	100,637	32.5	103.0
Community colleges[b]	111,173	9.7	192,679	15.0	333,953	25.5	163.4
California State University	17,640	7.1	35,658	12.1	60,156	20.6	190.7
University of California	5,335	5.5	14,191	11.4	17,324	12.3	123.7
All three public institutions	134,148	9.0	242,528	14.2	411,433	25.7	185.1

Sources: California Department of Education, 2000, "Number of Graduates from California Public Schools by Ethnic Designation, 1980–81 though 1997–98." www.cde.ca.gov/demographics/reports/statewide/gradste.htm; and California Postsecondary Education Commission, *Eligibility of California's 1996 High School Graduates for Admission to the State's Public Universities* (Sacramento: California Postsecondary Education Commission, 1998).

[a]Data are for June 1981 graduates, the earliest year available.
[b]Data are for undergraduates only. Concurrent high school students and "unknown student level" enrollees not included.

versity of California (UC), which in the year 2000 was only 38 percent of the Latino proportion of high-school graduates. The Latino presence at UC barely changed from 1990 (11.4 percent) to 2000 (12.3 percent).

Access to higher education for Latinos and other underrepresented minorities was dealt a major blow when the Regents of the University of California passed SP-1, the resolution that barred the consideration of race or ethnicity in admissions, and the voters followed this with the passage of Proposition 209, which extended the ban statewide. Neither the community colleges nor the CSU system was greatly affected by Proposition 209, but the impact on Latino enrollment at the University of California system was severe. In 1998, the year that the ban went into effect, 53 percent fewer Latinos were admitted to UC Berkeley and 33 percent fewer were admitted to UCLA than the year before. Thus, while the two flagship campuses of the UC system had also been the standard-bearers of diversity in the system, their share of Latino undergraduates dropped from a high of about 15 percent in 1997 to 8.6 percent in 1998. Latinos were already underrepresented in the UC system before 1998; SP-1 and Proposition 209 only increased their underrepresentation.

What Is at Stake?

Access to quality higher education is critical for the welfare of the Chicano/Latino[4] community and for the welfare of California. With a 41.5 percent share of the state's public-school population, Latinos are the largest ethnic group in the schools and are growing at the rate of almost one percent per year. Latinos are expected to constitute more than half of the K–12 public-school students in California within a decade.[5] Thus, California's future well-being is intimately tied to the well-being of the Latino population. A recent report issued by the California Research Bureau details in stark terms the consequences of Latino undereducation for the California economy. While Latinos constituted 28 percent of the labor force in 1998, they represented only 19 percent of the wage income. The primary reason for this discrepancy is the relatively low level of education of Latino workers. In California, as in the nation as a whole, a striking correlation exists between educational attainment and income: In 1998, the median income for households headed by someone without a high-school diploma was less than $20,000, while the median income of households headed by someone with a bachelor's degree was three times that figure. The median income of households headed by someone with a professional degree was nearly five times

---

[4]The term Chicano/Latino includes all Hispanic groups, and "Hispanic" is synonymous with "Latino." The term Chicano refers to individuals of Mexican origin, as does the term Mexican American.

[5]California Department of Finance, *California Public K–12 Enrollment Projections by Ethnicity, 2001 Series* (Sacramento, Calif., 2001).

higher. Among white wage earners, 33 percent have at least a bachelor's degree. Among Latinos, only eight percent are similarly well educated. Because Latinos make up an ever larger share of the labor force, overall wage income can be expected to decline proportionately if this education gap does not close. The current strength of the California economy cannot be sustained under such circumstances.[6]

Moreover, a RAND Corporation study on the economic returns of increasing the educational level of Latinos concluded that "Hispanics with a bachelor's degree will pay more than twice as much in taxes as those with only a high-school diploma, and Hispanics with a professional degree will pay an estimated three times as much as those with a bachelor's degree."[7] With increased education of Latinos, the state of California can anticipate significant savings in expenditures for public services such as welfare, Medi-Cal, and jails and prisons.[8] In a study of the costs and benefits of closing the education gap for minorities in California and the nation, Vernez found that the *public benefit* gained, versus the cost of increased education, in all cases favors providing more education.[9] For example, if Latinos were educated at the same level as whites, every additional dollar spent on education would save the state about $1.90. About one-third of this savings would come from public expenditures and two-thirds from increased taxes on earnings. When *societal benefits*—public benefits plus the increased disposable income that accrues to individuals—are computed, benefits more than double to over four dollars for every dollar spent on education.

As important as the economy is for all Californians, there are other compelling reasons to increase Latino access to higher education. Beyond the pecuniary benefits of a college education are numerous social benefits to increasing the education levels of underrepresented groups. People with higher levels of education enjoy better health and longer lives,[10] are more likely to attend arts activities, to vote, and to provide leadership in their communities.[11] Latinos' fellow

---

[6]Elías López, E. Ramírez, and R. Rochin, *Latinos and Economic Development in California* (Sacramento: California Research Bureau, 1999).

[7]Stephen Sorensen, Dominic J. Brewer, Stephen J. Carroll, and Eugene Bryton, *Increasing Hispanic Participation in Higher Education: A Desirable Public Investment* (Santa Monica, Calif.: RAND Corporation, Institute for Education and Training, 1995).

[8]Lynn A. Karoly, Peter W. Greenwood, Susan S. Everingham, Jill Houbé, M. Rebecca Kilburn, C. Peter Rydell, Matthew Sanders, and James Chiesa, *Investing in Our Children: What We Know and Don't Know about the Costs and Benefits of Early Childhood Interventions,* MR-898 (Santa Monica, Calif.: RAND Corporation, 1998).

[9]George Vernez, *Closing the Education Gap* (Santa Monica, Calif.: RAND Corporation, 1999).

[10]Laura Perna and Watson Scott Swail, "Early Intervention Programs: How Effective Are They at Increasing Access to College?" Paper presented at the annual meeting of the Association for the Study of Higher Education, Miami, Fla., November 7, 1998.

[11]Thomas Mortensen, Postsecondary Education Opportunity, 61, 1997.

students in higher education benefit directly: Diversity within educational settings has been shown to confer cognitive advantages on students schooled in such settings, especially when this occurs during students' late adolescence.[12] Political benefits are also important: Education makes for better citizens, as measured by increased voter participation, and genuine equality of educational opportunity can be expected to reduce social tensions.

Latino Students in the State's Higher-Education Institutions

Table 4.2 shows the distribution of California 1998 public high-school graduates enrolling in the three segments of the state's public higher education. Latinos enter community colleges and the CSU system at rates similar to white students, but there is a striking white/Latino gap in rates for entry into the University of California. But even the apparently similar rates for the lower and middle segments mask ethnic inequities. While the community colleges represent an important pathway to higher education for some students, they are a dead end for many others. Approximately one-third of all 1998 community-college students matriculated with the intention of transferring to a four-year university, yet only about three percent of these students transfer in any given year.[13] Latinos are underrepresented among the small proportion of students who do transfer. For example, Latinos constituted 24 percent of the 1996 community-college enrollment. However, two years later, they were only 12.6 percent of the transfer students to the University of California, and only 17.9 percent of the transfers to the CSU system.[14]

Although the ban on affirmative action has not yet had a profound effect on the CSU system, the immediate future may hold a very different scenario. Increasing enrollment pressures on some CSU campuses have resulted in moving the less competitively eligible students, who in most cases are African American and Latino, to the less sought-after campuses. This phenomenon has become known as "cascading." For example, the CSU San Diego and California Polytechnic campuses set higher admissions criteria and turn away significant numbers of CSU-eligible students because of the high demand to attend these schools. In turning away less "competitively eligible" applicants, CSU San Diego saw a 23 percent drop in Latino freshman enrollment from 1,010 in

---

[12]Patricia Gurin, *Expert Testimony in the Cases Gratz, et al., v. Bollinger, et al. and Grutter, et al., v. Bollinger, et al.*, University of Michigan, 1999.

[13]Terr Hardy, "Fewer Community College Students Make Leap to UC, CSU," *The Sacramento Bee*, March 27, 2000.

[14]California Postsecondary Education Commission, "College-Going Rates of California Public High-School Graduates, by Racial/Ethnic Group, Fall 1996 to Fall 1998," *Higher Education Performance Indicator Report* (Sacramento: California Postsecondary Education Commission, 1999).

Table 4.2. Percentage of Public High-School Graduates Enrolling in the Three Segments of California Public Higher Education, Fall 1998

Ethnicity	Community Colleges	California State University System	University of California	Combined
White	29.6	7.3	5.1	42.0
Asian	31.1	3.3	16.4	60.8
Latino	30.4	7.0	2.7	40.1
Black	29.4	8.4	2.8	40.6
All	31.2	9.7	7.5	48.4
Group eligible for admission	All graduates	Top 34% of graduating class	Top 12.5% of graduating class	–

Source: California Postsecondary Education Commission, *First-Time Freshmen in California Colleges and Universities, Fall 1998. Fact Sheet 2000–03.* (Sacramento: California Postsecondary Education Commission, 2000).
Notes: Only new freshmen in public institutions are included. CPEC estimates that about 15% of high-school graduates attend either private institutions of higher education in the state or an institution out of state.

1998 to 715 in 1999. Admissions criteria for transfer students are also stricter than for the CSU system as a whole, with CSU San Diego now requiring a 2.8 grade point average for students wishing to transfer from a community college, as opposed to the 2.0 required systemwide. As pressure intensifies for the CSU to accommodate more students, similar cascading can be expected at the more coveted campuses. For the system as a whole, the total representation of Latinos and blacks among CSU freshmen dropped slightly from 1997 to 1999, suggesting that cascading eventually may result in declining minority enrollment overall.[15]

In contrast to the muted effect of Proposition 209 on the CSU system, the loss of affirmative action as a tool in admissions has had a profound effect on the UC system. In 1997, while affirmative action was still in effect, 13.2 percent of the entering UC freshmen were Latino (of these, 11.9 percent were Mexican

---

[15] California Postsecondary Education Commission, *Total Enrollment by Segment by Student Level by Ethnicity,* 2002. www.cpec.ca.gov.

American).[16] This dropped to 11.8 percent (and 8.8 percent for Mexican Americans) in 1998, the first year in which the provisions of Proposition 209 were imposed. The numbers rebounded slightly in 1999 with intensive efforts to recruit students of color who met the university's eligibility requirements, and systemwide figures showed a Latino enrollment of 12.4 percent (9.3 percent of whom were Mexican-origin students). Some within the university applauded themselves for the rapid turnaround in the declining numbers of underrepresented students enrolling. However, this small increase obscured a more troublesome trend—the increasing segregation of the UC campuses. Most of the gains in the UC system in 1999 came from increased enrollment at the smaller campuses, while enrollment at the system's most prestigious campuses, UCLA and UC Berkeley, decreased. This is another example of cascading.

As Table 4.3 shows, the Latino share of incoming freshmen at both UCLA and UC Berkeley dropped dramatically in the wake of Proposition 209. In 1997, 15.8 percent of UCLA's and 14.6 percent of UC Berkeley's freshman class consisted of Latinos. In 1998, Latino representation at these institutions was, respectively, 11 percent and 8 percent—a 30 percent and 45 percent decrease. Latino representation at UCLA was close to pre-Proposition 209 levels as of 2001 (14.4 percent), yet still remained lower at UC Berkeley (10.7 percent).

Such segregation of students by campus serves to create a two-tiered system within the University of California, with important implications for student and faculty recruitment and ability to attract important research grants. Universities' reputations rely to a large extent on the qualifications of the students they attract as measured by test scores and incoming GPA, and colleges are ranked accordingly by several noted publications. These rankings can come to take on critical importance as ambitious students seek to be associated with the most renowned schools, and ambitious faculty seek to be affiliated with institutions that have the most "qualified" students. Research dollars follow top-ranked faculty as well as institutions with reputations for excellence. Thus, the ratcheting up of student "numerical" qualifications perpetuates a vicious cycle. As individual campuses are weakened, so is the university system as a whole. Moreover, the recent research on the cognitive benefits of education in diverse settings adds a further dimension to this problem. It is becoming increasingly clear that all students stand to lose from being educated in segregated educational settings.

While California's public universities lost students of color—and Latinos in particular—in the aftermath of SP-1 and Proposition 209, it appears that private colleges and universities in the state have made some gains. The states' accredited private institutions of higher education enrolled approximately 100,000

---

[16]We note in several cases the separate figures for Mexican-origin students, because while Mexican Americans constitute between 80 and 85 percent of the California Latino population, they generally represent only about two-thirds of the "Hispanic" or "Latino" enrollees in the state's four-year institutions.

Table 4.3. Latino Freshman Enrollment at UCLA and UC Berkeley, Fall 1997–2001

	1997		1998		2001		Percent change, 1997–1998
	Number	Percent	Number	Percent	Number	Percent	
UCLA	565	15.8	434	11.0	574	14.4	-30.3
UC Berkeley	469	14.6	266	8.0	379	10.7	-45.3

Source: University of California Office of the President, 2002a, *University of California Application, Admissions and Enrollment of California Resident Freshman for Fall 1995 through 2001*. http://www.ucop.edu/news/factsheets/flowfrc9501.pdf.

Note: Data for both Chicanos and Latinos are included in "Latino" above.

new students in 1998, and while many were not from California, it is probably safe to assume that the majority of Latino students were from the state.[17] Most Latinos stay in state for both financial and cultural reasons. Rather than experiencing the decline in Latino enrollment between 1997 and 1998 that UC did, private colleges and universities experienced a slight increase from 15.3 percent to 15.6 percent of their student body. A more significant point is the rapid growth in Latino undergraduate enrollment in California private higher education. From 1990 to 2000, the representation of Latino students rose in the private colleges and universities in the state from 9.2 to 16.5 percent (see Table 4.4). It is also significant that much of this increase came during the recession years of the mid-1990s, when the cost of a private education was especially difficult to finance for lower-income students. Such growth in minority populations had to be accompanied by a significant commitment of financial aid.

Graduate Education and Faculty

The attention given to freshman enrollments has masked to some extent the even greater declines in Latino enrollment in the state's graduate and professional schools. This is especially discouraging because Latinos received 13.6 percent of the bachelor's degrees from UC in 1997–98 and 18.8 percent of the degrees from CSU, creating a significant pool of future Latino graduate and professional students (see Table 4.5).[18]

Notwithstanding the growth in undergraduate degrees for Latinos, their enrollment in professional schools declined considerably since the mid-1990s. For example, in 1994, 14.6 percent of all UC medical school first-year enrollees were Latino. This figure declined steadily through the decade to eight percent in 2001.[19] Similar trends have been noted at the state's law schools. In 1994, the

---

[17]Data are not broken down by geographic origin of Latino students in the private postsecondary system.

[18]By contrast, in 1984–1985 Latinos received just five percent of the undergraduate degrees from UC, and only 9.6 percent from CSU in 1990–1991, the earliest year for which we were able to obtain data.

[19]University of California Office of the President, *University of California Medical School Applicants, Admits and First-Year Class Enrollment Percentages*, 2002. www.ucop.edu/acadadv/datamgmt/meddata. This number combines both Mexican-origin and all other Latinos.

Table 4.4. Domestic Undergraduate Enrollment in California Private Higher Education, by Percent Ethnicity, 1990–2000 (73 institutions)

Year	African	Latino	Asian	White	Total
1990	5.6	9.2	10.4	66.1	96,019
1991	5.2	8.7	10.7	64.1	85,081
1992	5.7	10.6	12.7	59.6	98,192
1993	5.8	11.7	12.7	58.2	85,227
1994	5.8	13.3	13.8	56.2	119,594
1995	6.3	13.9	14.3	54.2	120,943
1996	6.2	13.8	14.4	54.0	125,747
1997	6.9	15.3	13.8	51.7	130,785
1998	6.6	15.6	15.3	50.0	149,016
1999	6.7	15.7	15.6	49.8	152,205
2000	6.6	16.5	15.1	49.2	171,909

Source: California Postsecondary Education Commission, 2002, *Total Enrollment by Segment by Student Level by Ethnicity.* www.cpec.ca.gov.

three UC law schools registered a high of 14.5 percent Latinos, but by 2001 this figure had fallen to 6.9 percent.[20] More than five percentage points were lost in the year after Proposition 209.

Such a decline in the representation of Latinos in the professional-school pipeline has serious consequences for representation in the professions and in academe. A recent report from UCLA noted that fewer than five percent of physicians statewide are Latino[21]—a meager number to serve the burgeoning Latino population that often depends on Latino health professionals for their "cultural competence" and ability to communicate effectively in Spanish. Indeed, minority physicians have been shown to be more likely to practice in underserved

---

[20] University of California Office of the President, *University of California Law School Applicants, Admits and First-Year Class Enrollment Percentages,* 2002. www.ucop.edu/acadadv/datamgmt/lawdata/.

[21] David E. Hayes-Bautista, Paul Hsu, Robert Beltrán, and Juan Villagómez, *The Latino Physician Shortage in California, 1999* (Center for the Study of Latino Health, UCLA, 2000).

Table 4.5. Bachelor's Degrees Conferred: University of California and California State University, 1997–1998

Ethnicity	University of California Number	Percent	California State University Number	Percent
White	12,512	45.2	24,534	53.4
Asian American	10,124	36.6	9,480	20.6
African American	987	3.6	2,716	5.9
Latino	3,754	13.6	8,619	18.8
Native American	275	1.0	558	1.2
All	27,652	100.0*	45,907	100.0*

*Includes only students who reported race/ethnicity.
Sources: California State University Office of the Chancellor, *Degrees Granted by Ethnic Group and Sex, Systemwide, 1997–98*, Analytic Studies Statistical Reports, 2002. www.calstate.edu/AS/stat_reports/1997-1998/degree97-98.html; and California Postsecondary Education Commission, 2002, *Total Degrees Awarded by Segment by Degree Type by Ethnicity.* www.cpec.ca.gov.

communities than nonminority physicians.[22] Given the effects of Proposition 209 on the UC Berkeley and UCLA campuses, we can expect to see a continuing decline in minority medical-school enrollees because these two campuses were among the top five contributors of minority medical-school enrollees in the nation.[23] Likewise, the percentage of Latino faculty in the UC system fluctuated between a scant 4.1 percent and 4.5 percent for most of the 1990s, settling at 4.6 percent in 2001.[24] Although increasing numbers of Latino students have been graduating from high school, going on to college, and completing doctoral degrees (seven percent of UC doctorates went to Latinos in 1984–1985 and nine

---

[22]M. Komaromy, K. Grumbach, M. Drake, K. Vranizan, N. Lurie, D. Keane, and A. B. Bindman, "The Role of Black and Hispanic Physicians in Providing Health Care For Underserved Populations," *New England Journal of Medicine* 334(20) (1996): 1305–10; and J. C. Cantor, E. L. Miles, L. C. Baker, and D. C. Barker, "Physician Service to the Underserved: Implications for Affirmative Action in Medical Education," *Inquiry* 33(2) (1996): 167–80.

[23]The other three institutions are Xavier of Louisiana and Howard University (both historically African-American colleges) and the University of Texas at Austin.

[24]University of California Office of the President, *Graduate Academic Programs: Fall 1995 through Fall 2001, New Registrants*, 2002c. http://www.ucop.edu/acadadv/datamgmt/graddata/acadnreg.html.

percent in 1997–1998), relatively little progress has been made in diversifying the state's higher-education faculty.

The usual response to the question of why higher education has been so slow to diversify its faculty is that the pool of minority Ph.D.'s is so small. A recent study calls into question the extent to which this may be true.[25] In her study of 298 Ford, Mellon, and Spencer fellowship recipients, 93 percent of whom received their Ph.D.'s from elite, research universities, Smith found that although they were perceived to be "sought after," the great majority of these individuals (89 percent) had few if any offers for tenure-track appointments—54 percent of the science Ph.D.'s took postdoctoral positions or sought other positions outside of academe because no tenure-track offers were forthcoming. In her summary statements, Smith quotes the representative comments of one Chicana who holds a Ph.D. in American history:

> I would say that I find it a little surprising that I do not regularly get phone calls with regards to recruitment. We are so few, it's amazing that most universities will say, "We can't find anybody," yet persons like myself are not recruited. I think I should be getting phone calls, and I don't get phone calls (p. 134).

While Latino faculty are almost certainly important in helping to create a more hospitable campus climate for Latino students, university administrators often hold more power in decision making and have access to budgets, which enables them to have a direct impact on minority student recruitment, retention, and well-being. Hence, the hiring of high-level Latino administrators must be viewed as an important priority in raising the profile of Latino issues within academe. A study by Haro of university CEO hiring practices found that, although the popular perception was that Latino candidates were highly sought after, they fared more poorly in the hiring process than both white men and white women.[26] The reason most often given for not making offers to highly qualified Latino applicants was a difference in "style" that did not fit with the expectations of the recruitment committee. Among the components of style that were especially significant to respondents in this study were appearance and access to important networks, two attributes that were almost certainly affected by the candidates' ethnicity.

Finally, the consequences of higher-education policy in California are not confined to California. The University of California produces the largest proportion of minority doctorates in the nation. As UC cuts back on its minority en-

---

[25] Daryl Smith, *Achieving Faculty Diversity, Debunking the Myths* (Washington, D.C.: Association of American Colleges and Universities, 1996).

[26] Roberto Haro, "Epilogue Held to a Higher Standard: Latino Executive Selection in Higher Education," in *The Leaning Ivory Tower,* ed. Raymond Padilla and Rudolfo Chávez (Albany: State University of New York Press, 1995).

rollments, the nation's supply of minority scholars and professionals will surely be affected. For example, in 1997, UC produced 10.2 percent of all Latino Ph.D.'s in the nation, higher than its seven percent of Ph.D.'s overall. UC also produces about 10 percent of all Asian-American and African-American Ph.D.'s.[27] Since UC doctorates are more likely than average to be attractive candidates for faculty positions, these numbers underestimate the University of California's significance in building minority faculties nationwide. Clearly, UC has a major role in the production of minority scholars nationally, and anything that reduces this production has a national impact.

Structural Barriers to Accessing Four-Year Institutions

Given the low transfer rates of community-college students to four-year colleges, and the large percentage of Latinos who attend community colleges, overall Latino college-graduation rates are unlikely to improve without major innovations. The proposed "parallel" or dual admissions system is certainly a positive step forward, in that students who do well in their high-school work but are not qualified for direct admission to UC are given a promise of admission as transfer students if they complete the two-year community-college program successfully. But it remains to be seen how this will work in practice. Since it still requires students to be in the top 12.5 percent of their high-school graduating classes, it will still not solve the problems grounded in poor K–12 education and the high dropout rates in community colleges. For this reason, understanding the reasons behind the underrepresentation of Latinos at the state's public four-year institutions is crucial. We argue that college-bound Latino high-school graduates are not "choosing" to attend community colleges over four-year colleges. Instead, their choices are *limited* to community colleges primarily because they lack the traditional academic eligibility requirements needed for admission to the state's four-year institutions, and they lack the financial resources to move away from home. Lack of preparation is rooted in unequal opportunities in schooling and access to information regarding appropriate college preparation, both of which are grounded in the low levels of socio-economic status found among Latinos. Table 4.6 displays parental education and income for several ethnic groups. Of course, the students in this sample are those who intend to go to four-year colleges and thus are among the highest achievers in their respective ethnic groups.

Nearly all of the African American, Native American, and white students' parents have high-school diplomas among this college-going group. Likewise, a relatively high percentage of these parents have at least some college education. Notable, however, are the very low levels of parent education among the Mexi-

---

[27]National Science Foundation, *WebCASPAR Database System*, 2000. http://caspar.nsf.gov.

Table 4.6. California College-Bound Students' Parental Education and Income, by Ethnicity, 1998

	No High School Diploma	Some College (%)	Income <$20K (%)	Income >$100K (%)
African American (31,068)	3	48	30	5
Mexican American (33,288)	36	25	34	4
Native American (3,366)	4	56	18	10
Asian American (41,389)	13	60	27	10
White (177,015)	1	73	6	22

Source: Unpublished SAT administration data from the College Board, 1998.

can American sample: A stunning 36 percent of parents do not have high-school diplomas, and only 25 percent have some college—less than half the percentage for Asians and about one-third of that for whites. Because Latino students are disproportionately poor and often do not bring the social and economic advantages with them to school that are enjoyed by white and middle-class students, schools that serve these youths must be prepared to help close the gap. Fundamentally, these schools need to be prepared to do more, but they often do much less than schools serving middle-class students. Enormous inequalities exist in the schooling of low-income Latinos when compared to more economically advantaged white and Asian students.

Eligibility Criteria as Barriers

The California Postsecondary Education Commission (CPEC) conducts a transcript study of the state's graduating class every four years in an effort to document issues related to eligibility among the state's public high-school graduates. Low levels of eligibility for admission to four-year institutions are a primary reason why Latinos and African Americans are underrepresented at the state's two public four-year institutions. For example, while the California State University system is mandated to accept the top 33 percent of California's public high-school graduates, only 13 percent of all Latino graduates in 1996 were fully eligible for admission to CSU. Only four percent were fully eligible for admission to the University of California system.[28] The majority of Latinos are ineligible because they have not completed the "A–G" high-school curriculum (those classes required for eligibility to the University of California, and the CSU system). Beyond this, their grade point averages (GPA) tend to be significantly lower than those of white and Asian students (see Table 4.7).

In addition to the evident disparities in GPA by ethnicity, it should be noted that grades of all students have improved since the CPEC first collected these data in 1983. While GPAs of both African American and Latino students are significantly below those of white and Asian students, the gap between their grades is growing larger with time. Latinos showed the smallest increase in GPA over the period. This is due, at least in part, to differences in course-taking patterns. Latinos are less likely to be offered, and to take, advanced-placement and honors courses that confer extra points for the purpose of computing GPA.

Poor Latino children tend to go to qualitatively poor, underfunded schools that are attended largely by other poor children. These schools, often in the overcrowded urban centers, have been shown to enjoy fewer resources, have more disciplinary problems and higher turnover of both students and staff, and to have less-qualified teachers who generally have lower aspirations for their students.[29] Latino students in such situations are also more likely than their middle-class white and Asian peers to have low aspirations for themselves.[30]

---

[28]California Postsecondary Education Commission, *Eligibility of California's 1996 High School Graduates for Admission to the State's Public Universities* (Sacramento: California Postsecondary Education Commission, 1998). Eligibility for admission to the University of California system is determined by the following factors: (1) completion of a minimum number of college-preparatory courses' "A–G" curriculum in English, math, science, foreign languages, and other electives; (2) minimum GPA of 3.3 in these courses; (3) college-entrance exams such as SAT or ACT and three achievement tests. The California State University system has similar but less stringent requirements (such as lower minimum GPAs and exams are not necessary if the GPA is 3.0 and over. Moreover, CSU has traditionally been more flexible in allowing students to meet some requirements while enrolled).

[29]See, for example, P. Shields et al., *Teaching and California's Future by the Center for the Future of Teaching and Learning* (Santa Cruz, Calif.: Center for the Future of Teaching and Learning, 1999); and National Center for Education Statistics, *The Condition of Education* (Washington, D.C.: U.S. Department of Education, 1998). Twenty percent of teachers in high-poverty schools (where the vast majority of Latino students are found) have no teaching credential, and that English-language learners (about 80 percent of whom are Latino) are the most likely of all children to be taught by a teacher without a credential or other appropriate preparation to teach them.

[30]Grace Kao and Marta Tienda, "Educational Aspirations of Minority Youth," *American Journal of Education* 106 (1998): 349–84; Patricia Gándara, Susan O'Hara, and Dianna Gutiérrez, "The Changing Shape of Aspirations: Peer Influences on Achievement Behavior," in *Peers, Schools, and the Achievement of U.S. Mexican Youth,* ed. M. Gibson, P. Gándara, and I. Koyami (New York: Teachers College Press, in press).

Table 4.7. Grade Point Averages of California High-School Graduates by Ethnicity, 1983, 1986, 1990, and 1996

Ethnicity	1983	1986	1990	1996	Gain, 1983–1996
White	2.69	2.65	2.74	2.90	.21
Asian	2.96	2.96	3.11	3.19	.23
Black	2.26	2.29	2.33	2.41	.15
Latino	2.42	2.44	2.44	2.55	.13

Source: California Postsecondary Education Commission, *Eligibility of California's 1996 High School Graduates for Admission to the State's Public Universities* (Sacramento: California Postsecondary Education Commission, 1998).

Another area where Latinos face educational inequity is in coursework offerings, particularly in math and science. This affects their potential college eligibility. Adelman argues that the kind of education to which students are exposed in the K–12 years may be more effective at predicting their postsecondary options and outcomes than any other variable, including their families' socioeconomic status (SES).[31] For example, no single factor, including test scores and GPA, better predicts college completion for underrepresented students than the rigor of courses students have taken in high school. The best proxy of rigorous coursework is the highest math course completed. Students who take at least one math course beyond algebra II in high school are significantly more likely to complete college, across all ethnic groups. Given the importance of high-school curriculum for long-term postsecondary outcomes, we are compelled to ask how precollege curriculum differs between students from low-income and minority backgrounds and all other students.

Only half as many Latino students enroll in intermediate algebra as do all other students, thus significantly reducing their eligibility for selective four-year colleges and curtailing their preparation in mathematics.[32] Likewise, they are

---

[31] Clifford Adelman, *Answers in the Tool Box. Academic Intensity, Attendance Patterns, and Bachelor's Degree Attainment* (Washington, D.C.: U.S. Department of Education, Office of Educational Research and Improvement, 1999).

[32] These data mirror national-level statistics on Latinos and math course-taking patterns. According to a recent National Center for Education Statistics report, Latinos graduate from high school having completed fewer advanced math courses than their white and Asian counterparts. While they have nearly closed the gap with whites with respect to taking geometry (69 percent vs. 73 percent), only 51 percent of Latinos have

only about half as likely to enroll in chemistry or physics as non-Latino students. While some might argue that these course-taking patterns represent preferences exercised by students, evidence suggests that students must make "choices" within the limited opportunities offered within their schools. First, inner-city schools and schools with predominantly low-SES and minority students offer fewer advanced math and science courses.[33] Also, nationwide, students who are in college-preparatory programs but attend high schools with predominantly low-SES students take fewer academic courses compared with college-preparatory students who attend higher-SES schools.[34] Therefore, being "college prep" or "college bound" does not guarantee that students are taking the best set of courses. Latinos are lacking in completion of academic coursework that is crucial for eligibility for admission to CSU and UC. The evidence suggests that one reason for this is that they are not offered the opportunities to take advanced courses.

Unequal opportunities to take rigorous coursework also have implications for eligible students who compete for admission to the highly competitive flagship campuses. The availability of advanced-placement (AP) courses is a serious issue because UC awards an additional grade point for each AP or honors course taken and passed with at least a C grade. Thus, on a four-point scale, taking these courses can increase a student's GPA considerably. A recent study by the Public Policy Institute of California showed a considerable disparity both in A–F[35] courses and in AP courses across schools. Only 52 percent of the lowest-income schools' classes met A–F requirements, while 63 percent of courses in the highest-income schools met these requirements. Similar patterns held up

---

taken an algebra II course, compared with 62 percent of whites and 67 percent of Asians. Likewise, only 14 percent of Latinos have taken a trigonometry class, compared with 19 percent of whites and 25 percent of Asians. See U.S. Department of Education, *The 1994 High School Transcript Study Tabulation* (Washington, D.C.: NCES 98–532, 1998). This also has implications for persistence: Students who take at least one math course beyond algebra II in high school are significantly more likely to complete college, across all ethnic groups. See Adelman's *Answers in the Tool Box*.

[33] Jeanie Oakes, Tor H. Ormseth, Robert M. Bell, and Patti Camp, *Multiple Inequalities* (Santa Monica, Calif.: RAND Corporation, 1990).

[34] D. Rock, H. Braun, and P. R. Rosenbaum, *Excellence in High School Education: Cross-Sectional Study, 1980–1982, Final Report* (Princeton: Educational Testing Service, 1985).

[35] The entering class in 2002 was required to add an additional requirement to their preparation for entering UC. This included a course in fine arts, which changed the old A–F requirement pattern to A–G. As such, studies published prior to 2002 looked at data for the old A-F requirement.

when the analysis was done by percent of nonwhite students in the school.[36] Likewise, this study found that "the median high-SES school has over 50 percent more AP courses than the median low-SES school" (p. 72). The lack of AP courses not only lowers GPA; it is also reflected in lower test scores on standardized tests used for college admission. This in turn reduces Latino students' competitiveness for the most highly competitive state campuses.

In sum, Latino students are disadvantaged with respect to eligibility at every point: GPA, test scores, adequacy of precollege preparation, and rigor of coursework. Thus, any reworking of quantitative admission formulas can have only very limited effects with respect to increasing Latino access to higher education. Fundamental problems of inequality in schools create barriers that are not addressed in current admissions procedures. Two lawsuits were filed in 1999 that address these issues. The first, *Daniel v. the State of California,* argues that minority and low-income students are not given enough AP course options in their high schools and that this negatively affects chances for admission to the University of California. The second, *Rios v. the University of California Board of Regents,* argues that UC Berkeley's admissions practice of giving extra weight to AP test scores favors white and Asian students. As this is written these cases are unresolved, and in themselves they may achieve little, but they have increased public awareness of the very serious problem of curriculum inequities.

Lack of Information Regarding College Requirements

Much of the racial-ethnic variance in eligibility is explained by significant variation in socio-economic status, particularly in parental education. Family-background characteristics have long been associated with students' educational achievement, and many studies have concluded that family background explains the largest portion of the variance in student achievement.[37] An important way by which low parental education translates into low achievement is lack of information regarding college requirements and necessary preparation. A vast and

---

[36]Julian Betts, Kim Rueben, and Anne Danenberg, *Equal Resources, Equal Outcomes? The Distribution of School Resources and Student Achievement in California* (San Francisco: Public Policy Institute of California, 2000).

[37]See, for example, James Coleman, *Equality of Educational Opportunity* (Washington, D.C.: U.S. Government Printing Office, 1966); Christopher Jencks, and Susan Meyer, "The social consequences of growing up in a poor neighborhood," in *Inner-City Poverty in the United States,* ed. Laurence E. Lynn, Jr., and Michael G. H. McGeary (Washington, D.C.: National Academy Press, 1990); and Michael Puma, Nancy Karweit, Cristofer Price, Anne Ricciuti, William Thompson, and Michael Vaden-Kiernan, *Prospects: Final Report on Student Outcomes* (Washington, D.C.: U.S. Department of Education, Office of the Under Secretary, 1997).

expanding qualitative literature based largely on interviews with students, teachers, and parents has shown that college-educated parents are crucial sources of information as their children go through the educational system. For example, highly educated parents are keenly aware of the implications of taking algebra versus basic math in junior-high school and actively intervene when they disagree with their children's placement.[38] In contrast, parents with lower levels of education are largely unaware of the implications of being tracked into a low math course and tend to trust the school personnel's decisions.[39] McDonough's study of college-bound girls in Northern California showed that girls from working-class families applied to fewer schools and rarely considered prestigious colleges or universities (private as well as public) as feasible choices.[40] Instead, they tended to apply to CSU campuses. Furthermore, they received little guidance from school counselors, who were overworked and hardly knew them at the large schools they attended. Girls from upper-middle-class families with similar grades and SAT scores, on the other hand, applied to many different prestigious private schools, rarely considered the CSU system an option, and treated flagship UC schools as "backups" in case they did not get accepted to their first choices. Their parents understood the significance of selectivity of college on potential earnings and encouraged them to apply to a variety of schools. Their high-school counselors also communicated the idea that certain schools were more desirable than others.

In 1998, only 25 percent of Mexican American college-bound students in California came from families in which at least one parent had some college experience. This is almost half the percentage of parents with some college education for the next lowest group—African Americans (see Table 4.6). This indicates that Latinos have less access to important information and resource networks to represent their children's interests adequately. Most Latino students cannot rely on their parents for crucial information. Instead, they must rely on institutional agents such as teachers and counselors within the educational system to facilitate their postsecondary preparation. As a result, their choices, knowledge, and outcomes are largely reliant on forming these relationships.[41]

---

[38]Elizabeth L. Useem, "Middle Schools and Math Groups: Parents' Involvement in Children's Placement," *Sociology of Education* 65 (1992): 263–79.

[39]For similar research that contrasts middle- and low-SES parents' approaches to their children's schooling, see Annette Lareau, "Social Class Differences in Family-School Relationship: The Importance of Cultural Capital," *Sociology of Education* 60 (1987): 73–85.

[40]Patricia McDonough, *Choosing Colleges, How Social Class and Schools Structure Opportunity* (Albany: State University of New York Press, 1997).

[41]Ricardo Stanton-Salazar, "A Social Capital Framework for Understanding the Socialization of Racial Minority Children and Youths," *Harvard Educational Review* 67 (1997): 1–40.

One study of 70 Chicano professionals from working-class and lower-income backgrounds showed how the instrumental knowledge necessary to navigate the educational system came, in large part, from teachers or white middle-class classmates.[42] Thus, while Latino parents are often described as providing little support and encouragement for their children's education, Gándara's research showed that having high aspirations and high parental encouragement is not necessarily enough to ensure the success of Latinos from low-SES families.

California high schools provide only about one counselor to every 850 high-school students statewide, and in the crowded inner-city high schools that most Latinos attend, the ratio is often much higher. Thus, Latino students often receive little or no counseling about how to prepare themselves for college. Many low-income Latino students see their counselors not as allies or sources of support, but as gatekeepers who all too often refuse them admission to the courses that would prepare them for college. Considerable evidence has accumulated that counselors in low-income schools often underestimate the abilities of their students and track them into noncollege-preparatory courses on the assumption that they lack the ability to undertake more rigorous coursework.[43] Of course, this is a vicious circle: Once these students are tracked into the slower groups it is difficult, if not impossible, for them ever to compete with peers who have become proficient in material to which low-income Latino students have never even been exposed.

A relatively new feature on the educational landscape is the mushrooming business of private college-admissions consultants. Given the inadequate counseling resources on the high-school campuses, parents with sufficient means have increasingly been paying for counseling services outside the schools. These counselors can increase a student's chances of acceptance into competitive colleges by advising on effective application strategies. They can also increase the chances that even mediocre students will find colleges that meet their needs.[44]

---

[42]See, for example, Patricia Gándara, *Over the Ivy Walls: The Educational Mobility of Low-Income Chicanos* (Albany: State University of New York Press, 1995); and Gary Orfield and John Yun, *Resegregation in American Schools* (Cambridge, Mass.: Harvard Civil Rights Project, 1999). Latino students are increasingly likely to be educated in segregated schools that provide fewer opportunities for interracial contact and the development of personal and social networks that can increase cultural capital and promote social mobility. Latino students today are more likely to be attending segregated schools than in 1972 when desegregation efforts were at their height.

[43]See, for example, Jeanie Oakes, *Keeping Track. How Schools Structure Inequality* (New Haven, Conn.: Yale University Press, 1985); and Harriet Romo and Toni Falbo, *Latino High School Graduation. Defying the Odds* (Austin: University of Texas Press, 1996).

[44]Patricia Korn McDonough and E. Yamasaki, "Admissions Advantage for Sale: Private College Counselors and the Students Who Use Them," *Review of Higher Education* 20 (1997): 297–317.

Such advantages are not normally available to low-income Latinos and serve to maintain inequality of access to higher education.

Limited Financial Resources

In 2000, Senate Bill 1644 (Ortiz) was signed into law, guaranteeing a college scholarship to every graduating high-school senior and some college transfer students who meet both financial-need requirements and a minimum GPA. When signed by the governor, SB 1644 took effect in the 2001–2002 academic year. However, the response was much less than hoped for. There was no immediate surge of applicants for the Cal Grants, and the numbers of grants awarded fell more than 10,000 short of the number budgeted.[45] The California Student Aid Commission has tried to understand why the numbers of applicants did not materialize, and many observers lay the blame on counselors who failed to direct students to the applications. Given the extreme shortage of counselors in California schools, however, it is more likely that students never came into contact with a counselor who could have provided the information. Several significant glitches were found that also accounted for the shortfall in awards, including schools' failure to provide accurate GPA information on students.[46] The Cal Grants are a potentially important instrument for achieving greater equity in higher education, but to realize their potential will require a strengthening of the information systems at the secondary and community college levels, and more personalized counseling to help students fill out the necessary forms.

Confronting the Problem of Insidious Higher-Education Policies

The Racial Privacy Initiative

Recently, the same regent who effectively brought an end to affirmative action at the University of California has backed what is called the *racial privacy initiative,* which will appear on the California ballot in March of 2004. Under the guise of creating a color-blind state, the initiative would prohibit the collection of racial/ethnic data by the state. This would, of course, make it impossible to chart our progress toward equal opportunity and identify the areas in which we fall short. Those who favor the initiative argue that it is time to do away with

---

[45] R. Trounson, "The State Cal Grant Recipient Total to Fall Short of Goals," *The Los Angeles Times,* April 17, 2002.

[46] M. Health, "More Cal Grants Awarded after Error Resolved," *The Daily Californian,* April 30. 2002.

classifications of individuals that serve to label and divide the population. However, as much as most people share the vision of a color-blind society in which everyone has a truly equal opportunity, the data clearly indicate that we are not there yet. The only way to get there is by being able to identify the problem and address it where it exists. If we cannot identify the problem, we cannot fix it. Depriving researchers and policymakers of the information needed to measure inequality does not make it go away. It could be argued, that it will only make it worse. But, we would not have a way of knowing this. The racial privacy initiative could have particularly pernicious effects on opportunity in higher education.

Remediation

Recent trends toward strengthening the standards at all levels of education have resulted in policies to decrease or eliminate remedial classes for students who do not meet university standards in certain core academic areas. The CSU system has adopted a policy to reduce the demand for remedial courses to 10 percent by 2007. The goal is to compel high schools to send better-prepared students to college, but this policy is sure to reduce access to the state university system, at least in the short run. Given that nearly half of all students entering CSU in 1998 needed remedial instruction, a decrease in availability of such courses means that many students will not be able to enroll. A high proportion of these rejected students will be Latinos.

The Shell Game of Shifting Standardized Test Weights

The use of the SAT I test as a significant portion of the UC eligibility formula came under intense fire in late 1990s, culminating in a conference in the spring of 2001 at UC Santa Barbara that focused on the role of the SAT in college admissions. At this conference, UC President Atkinson indicated his intention of moving away from the SAT I toward achievement tests that would more accurately reflect the curriculum to which students had been exposed, considering this to be a fairer measure of students' abilities. In the interim, the University of California has shifted the weighting of its admissions formula to place 75 percent emphasis on the SAT II (achievement tests) and 25 percent on the SAT I (aptitude test). Analyses conducted by UC Office of the President suggest that this (interim) measure may increase access to the University of California for all students by about an additional two percent. A similar percentage increase would result for Latino students. However, critics of this interim policy have noted that a chief reason that many Latino students are found ineligible for UC is that they fail to take the full battery of SAT II tests. The extensive requirements for standardized testing, along with the expense of such tests, cause many Latino students to opt for CSU or other colleges where such tests are not required.

Whether or not this interim policy shift has actually resulted in any increase in absolute numbers of Latino students eligible for UC (their proportion of the eligibility pool would theoretically remain the same) is not yet known. The potentially more meaningful change in admissions testing—establishing a curriculum-based achievement test aligned with California standards that would replace the current SAT battery—is probably more fair, but students will still be dependent on the quality of their schools to compete favorably on this test. And, Latino students, as a group, attend the poorest-quality high schools in the state.[47] Without a strengthening of the education to which these students are exposed, it is doubtful that any shift in testing policy will yield significantly more eligible students.

Socio-Economic Status as a Substitute for Ethnicity in Admissions Formulae

With the prohibition of affirmative action, greater emphasis has been placed on selecting students from low socio-economic backgrounds instead of on race or ethnicity, with the assumption that this will increase the numbers of ethnic minorities as well. This policy is, however, fraught with problems. Using socio-economic status as a consideration does not capture significant numbers of Latinos for a variety of reasons. One important issue is the extent to which "middle-class" Latinos are really middle class. Often, Latino middle-class families are no more than one generation out of poverty, have low levels of accumulated capital, and have an educational background that includes inferior public schooling and less-competitive postsecondary institutions. Their children are not well prepared to compete with their solidly middle-class white and Asian peers. In fact, Latinos from the highest income bracket perform only slightly better than whites from the lowest income bracket on SAT tests, reflecting more limited educational experiences than are assumed to accompany the label of "middle class."[48] Moreover, using income as a measure of socio-economic well-being often obscures as much as it reveals. Income measures generally fail to account for factors such as the responsibilities that accrue to large (and extended) families, indebtedness that results from lack of capital, and the numbers of breadwinners

---

[47]Julian Betts, Kim Rueben, and Anne Danenberg, *Equal Resources, Equal Outcomes? The Distribution of School Resources and Student Achievement in California* (San Francisco: Public Policy Institute of California, 2000).

[48]Scott Miller, *An American Imperative: Accelerating Minority Educational Advancement* (New Haven, Conn.: Yale University Press, 1995).

required to maintain a middle-class income. The profile of the middle-class white family and the middle-class Latino family may be very different.

Management of Enrollment Pressures Brought on by Tidal Wave II

Because of the increasing numbers of baby boomers' children who are reaching college age, higher-education institutions in California are anticipating a surge in enrollment—Tidal Wave II. The CSU system will need to accommodate about 130,000 more students by 2010, and the UC system is expected to accommodate another 56,000 by that date.[49] There are not enough spaces in these institutions to assimilate that number of students. To date, enrollment pressures have resulted in the turning away of thousands of qualified Latino students from the most competitive campuses. For example, in 1998, UC Berkeley turned away 616 Latinos with GPAs of 4.0 or better and average SAT scores of 1170. These students were not considered "competitive" at UC Berkeley and were rerouted to campuses where the enrollment pressures were not as great. As the pressure increases on the five institutions—Irvine, Santa Cruz, Riverside, Santa Barbara, and Davis—that do not experience the same pressures as Berkeley, UCLA, and San Diego, the University of California will have to find new ways to accommodate students. The University of California is currently reviewing its options, which include year-round schedules, distance learning, and increased class sizes. One can assume, however, that the least-competitive students will be given the fewest, and least attractive, options. This can also have the effect of reducing the attractiveness of UC campuses for those students.

Policy Options

There have been two major responses to the demise of affirmative action in university admissions. On the heels of the Hopwood decision,[50] Texas implemented

---

[49] California Postsecondary Education Commission, *Riding the Tidal Wave. Analysis of Growth and Resources for California Higher Education in the First Decade of the Third Millennium* (Sacramento: California Postsecondary Education Commission, 2000).

[50] Jorge Chapa and Vincent Lazaro, "Hopwood in Texas: The Untimely End of Affirmative Action," in *Chilling Admissions: The Affirmative Action Crisis and the Search for Alternatives,* ed. G. Orfield and E. Miller (Cambridge, Mass.: The Civil Rights Project at Harvard University, 1998). The Hopwood case was filed by four white students who were denied admission to the University of Texas Law School. In 1996, the Fifth Circuit Court of Appeals agreed with them that they had suffered discrimination because the law school had considered race in the acceptance of some Black and Latino applicants who had lower admissions scores than the plaintiffs.

the 10 percent plan, making the top 10 percent of students from each high school in Texas eligible for the University of Texas. Early returns suggest that this approach may be at least modestly successful in that state. Admissions of Latino students have increased to levels commensurate with the pre-Hopwood period, and retention of Latino students is higher, primarily because of an extensive web of support programs put into place along with the 10 percent plan.[51] Unfortunately, the circumstances that exist in Texas and make the 10 percent plan a viable alternative for that state do not hold in California. With the capacity to accept the top 10 percent of each high school's graduates in the state, and an institution that is less selective than UC, the University of Texas is able to accommodate the yield from this strategy without turning away any qualified students. California does not have this additional capacity. A four percent plan known as "Eligibility in Local Context" (ELC), modeled on the Texas experiment, was implemented for the fall of 2001, but was expected to increase the yield of new Latino admittees by only about 750 students. A recent report from UC Office of the President suggests that as many as 1,080 Latino students were added to the pool of students accepted to UC in the fall of 2001 as a result of the ELC plan, although the precise number is not known because of difficulties in separating these students from those who would otherwise be eligible under normal circumstances.[52]

The second strategy, and the one implemented most widely by the University of California, is extensive student outreach. The outreach strategy, first implemented in its present form in 1998, incorporates a panoply of activities that can be categorized by two types: student-centered strategies that focus on providing individual students with academic support, guidance, and information about preparing for and applying to college, and school-centered activities geared toward curricular and teaching reform in the schools that these students attend. The University of California contends that it spent $250 million on its outreach activities in 1999–2000. In 2002, before an extensive evaluation could be conducted of these efforts, the state legislature radically reduced the budget for outreach, defunding most of the school-centered efforts. Ironically, while school-centered interventions are notoriously difficult to implement and slow to take hold, they may be the best chance for real increases in college-going for underrepresented students. A recent review of outreach programs nationwide raises concerns about the extent to which they can be expected to contribute to short-term increases in *competitive eligibility* for Latino and other underrepresented students, because the data fail to demonstrate significant gains in GPA or test scores for program participants. The authors concluded that significant gains

---

[51]B. Walker, "University of Texas Enrollment and Retention Data," presented at the Higher Education Access Seminar, University of California, Berkeley, March 31, 2000.

[52]University of California Office of the President, *University of California Eligibility in Local Context Program Evaluation Report* (Oakland: University of California Office of the President, 2002).

are probably dependent on the ability of schools to incorporate the best practices of outreach into their own routines and practices—a reform that will not happen overnight.[53]

What options, then, hold hope for significantly increasing access to higher education for Latino students? We suggest several.

First, we suggest that even an incremental shift in the definition of merit—from a *developed-abilities model,* which defines students' merit on the basis of what they have already been able to achieve, to a *value-added model,* based on what students can be expected to achieve and contribute to the campus and to the society—could begin to help us think more broadly about the goal of college admissions. Bowen and Bok explicate this model well, arguing that students' contribution to enriching the campus environment through diverse perspectives and experiences, and contributions to society through community leadership, are important reasons for admitting students.[54] Moreover, Astin has argued powerfully that the true worth of a higher-education institution can be measured not by its ability to select students who are already achieving maximally, but by selecting and educating those who have not reached their potential and providing a value-added experience so that they might do so.[55]

Second, to decrease the problem of cascading, and increase access to the most competitive campuses, the University of California could withhold a portion, perhaps 30 percent, of its admissions slots to be distributed equally across campuses by the Office of the President. In this way, students who are eligible for UC, whether competitively eligible or not, could have an equal chance at being assigned to a campus of their choice. An alternative strategy would be to provide a "stipend" to the campus for each student admitted who falls into the lower tier of eligibility. This would help to defray costs associated with providing academic support for these students and possibly create an incentive for more equally distributing the full range of eligible students.

Third, given the limited impact of long-term outreach strategies for increasing access to selective institutions for Latino students now in California high schools, a more immediate yield could be expected from a significant increase in the resources applied to those Latino students most likely to meet eligibility criteria. A recent evaluation study of the University of California's Puente program, which serves primarily Latino students, found that the most significant impact of the program may have been on high-achieving Latino students who were assumed to be "on track" for matriculating to a four-year institution but

---

[53]Patricia Gándara and Deborah Bial, *Paving the Way to Higher Education* (Washington, D.C.: National Center for Education Statistics, NCES 2001).

[54]William Bowen and Derek Bok, *The Shape of the River* (Princeton, N.J.: Princeton University Press, 1998).

[55]Alexander Astin, *Achieving Educational Excellence* (San Francisco: Jossey-Bass, 1985).

would not actually have done so in the absence of the program's intervention.[56] Because even high-achieving Latinos are at risk for not matriculating successfully to four-year colleges, nominally middle-class Latino students should be included in the pool to be targeted with special resources and attention.

Fourth, to increase the overall yield of Latino college students over the long term, outreach efforts will have to engage schools in significant reform activities, consistent with the lessons learned from effective outreach programs, but in an intensive and comprehensive approach. Strategies should include experimental coursework involving collaboration between university and high-school faculty to create better linkages between high-school offerings and university expectations. Fundamental reforms in K–12 schools will be necessary to reduce the need for remediation at the college level and increase the eligibility of more Latino students to selective four-year institutions. In a period of restricted funds and tight budgets, it is not clear that the public will be present to make this happen.

Fifth, efforts must be redoubled to capture more students in the community-college pipeline by providing early admission to the four-year institutions dependent on the completion of a prescribed course of study.[57] This must be accompanied by intensive monitoring of these students and financial aid to make the transition possible. The University of California is currently launching the Dual Admissions Program (DAP), an extension of the Eligibility in Local Context (four percent) Plan. The DAP provisionally accepts those students from each high school who fall between the top four percent and top 12.5 percent of all graduating seniors. These students must complete their first two years at a community college, but are automatically enrolled in the University of California upon completion of required courses with a minimum grade point average. This program holds large potential for increasing the diversity of the UC campuses, *if sufficient resources are applied to it.* The program must provide a qualitatively different experience for these students as compared to regular community college attendance. It must create a "campus on a campus" so that students are kept in a cohort where they can build relationships with each other and be monitored.

Last, following the Texas example, the UC campuses must put into place an extensive academic support system to ensure that Latino students who are admitted to the university can not only survive, but also succeed in this environment. A recent report conducted for the College Board points to some of the strategies that colleges across the country have used effectively to foster high

---

[56]Patricia Gándara, "A Study of High School Puente: What We Have Learned about Preparing Latino Youth for Postsecondary Education," *Educational Policy* 16 (2002): 474–95.

[57]Some community colleges use this strategy very effectively, but the implementation is very uneven across the state.

achievement among underrepresented students.[58] Such strategies include summer bridge programs, adjunct instruction to ensure success in gatekeeper courses, reorganization of undergraduate curricula, and organized peer study groups that support both social and academic adaptation of underrepresented students. A greater emphasis on high achievement among underrepresented students is necessary if we are to successfully diversify the university's faculty.

Conclusion

Thoughtful public policy aimed at equalizing access to higher education in California would incorporate strategies that are specific to different cultural groups. Mounting evidence suggests the importance of attending to culturally specific knowledge and circumstances in closing the achievement gap for students and in paving the way to successful postsecondary outcomes.[59] Intervention programs to increase college access and success have found repeatedly that they are most successful with those students with whom they are able to make effective cultural connections.[60] However, SP-1 and Proposition 209 put the cart before the horse in California, and we find ourselves trying, with very limited tools, to equalize opportunities for specific groups of students. Given existing admissions criteria, there are no proven strategies for making both quick and significant gains in access to highly competitive campuses for Latino students. In the absence of a redefinition of merit or a total reform of the schools that serve these students, progress will be slow at best. Wise investment of our resources, however, incorporating both short- and long-term strategies, can maximize the yield.

---

[58] Patricia Gándara and J. Maxwell-Jolly, *Priming the Pump: Strategies for Increasing the Achievement of Underrepresented Undergraduates* (New York: The College Board, 1999).

[59] Luis Moll and Norma González, "Lessons from Research with Language Minority Children," *Journal of Reading Behavior* 26 (1994): 439–56.

[60] See, for example, Patricia Gándara and Deborah Bial, *Paving the Way to Higher Education* (Washington, D.C.: National Center for Education Statistics, NCES 2001205, 2000); and Patricia Gándara and J. Maxwell-Jolly, *Priming the Pump: Strategies for Increasing the Achievement of Underrepresented Undergraduates* (New York: The College Board, 1999).

References

Adelman, Clifford. 1999. *Answers in the Tool Box. Academic Intensity, Attendance Patterns, and Bachelor's Degree Attainment.* Washington, D.C.: U.S. Department of Education, Office of Educational Research and Improvement.

Astin, Alexander. 1985. *Achieving Educational Excellence.* San Francisco: Jossey-Bass.

Betts, Julian, Kim Rueben, and Anne Danenberg. 2000. *Equal Resources, Equal Outcomes? The Distribution of School Resources and Student Achievement in California.* San Francisco: Public Policy Institute of California.

Bowen, William, and Derek Bok. 1998. *The Shape of the River.* Princeton, N.J.: Princeton University Press.

California Department of Education. 2000a. *Graduation Rates in California Public Schools by Ethnic Group, 1984–85 through 1998–99.* http://www.cde.ca.gov/demographics/reports/statewide/ethgrate.htm.

California Department of Education. 2000b. *Number of Graduates from California Public Schools by Ethnic Designation, 1980–81 through 1997–98.* http://www.cde.ca.gov/demographics/reports/statewide/gradste.htm.

California Department of Finance. 2001. California Public K–12 Enrollment Projections by Ethnicity, 2001 Series. Sacramento, California.

California Postsecondary Education Commission. 1999. *College-Going Rates of California Public High School Graduates, by Racial/Ethnic Group, Fall 1996 to Fall 1998.* Higher Education Performance Indicator Report. Sacramento: California Postsecondary Education Commission.

———. 1998. Eligibility of California's 1996 High School Graduates for Admission to the State's Public Universities. Sacramento: California Postsecondary Education Commission.

———. 2000a. *First-Time Freshmen in California Colleges and Universities, Fall 1998.* Fact Sheet 2000–03. Sacramento: California Postsecondary Education Commission.

———. 2000b. Riding the Tidal Wave. Analysis of Growth and Resources for California Higher Education in the First Decade of the Third Millennium. Sacramento: California Postsecondary Education Commission.

———. 2002a. "Total Enrollment by Segment by Student Level by Ethnicity." http://www.cpec.ca.gov.

———. 2002b. "Total Degrees Awarded by Segment by Degree Type by Ethnicity." http://www.cpec.ca.gov.

California State University Office of the Chancellor. 2002. "Degrees Granted by Ethnic Group and Sex, Systemwide, 1997–98." *Analytic Studies Statistical Reports.* http://www.calstate.edu/AS/stat_reports/1997-1998/degree97-98.html.

Cantor J. C., E. L. Miles, L. C. Baker, and D. C. Barker. 1996. "Physician Service to the Underserved: Implications for Affirmative Action in Medical Education." *Inquiry* 33(2): 167–80.

Chapa, Jorge, and Vincent Lazaro. 1998. "Hopwood in Texas: The Untimely End of Affirmative Action." In *Chilling Admissions: The Affirmative Action Crisis and the Search for Alternatives,* ed. G. Orfield and E. Miller. Cambridge, Mass.: The Civil Rights Project at Harvard University.

Chávez, Lydia. 1998. *The Color Bind: California's Battle to End Affirmative Action.* Berkeley: University of California Press.

Coleman, James. 1966. *Equality of Educational Opportunity.* Washington, D.C.: U.S. Government Printing Office.

Gándara, Patricia. 1995. *Over the Ivy Walls: The Educational Mobility of Low-Income Chicanos.* Albany: State University of New York Press.

Gándara, Patricia, and Deborah Bial. 2001. *Paving the Way to Higher Education.* Washington, D.C.: National Center for Education Statistics. NCES. Report No. 2001205.

Gándara, Patricia, and J. Maxwell-Jolly. 1999. *Priming the Pump: Strategies for Increasing the Achievement of Underrepresented Undergraduates.* New York: The College Board.

Gándara, Patricia, Susan O'Hara, and Dianna Gutiérrez. In press. "The Changing Shape of Aspirations: Peer Influence on Achievement Behavior" in *Peers, Schools, and the Achievement of U.S. Mexican Youth,* ed. P. Gándara and I. Koyami. New York: Teachers College Press.

Gándara, Patricia. 2002. "A Study of High School Puente: What We Have Learned about Preparing Latino Youth for Postsecondary Education." *Educational Policy* 16:474–95.

Gurin, Patricia. 1999. Expert Testimony in the Cases *Gratz, et al. v. Bollinger, et al.* and *Grutter, et al. v. Bollinger, et al.* University of Michigan.

Hardy, Terr. 2000. "Fewer Community College Students Make Leap to UC, CSU." *The Sacramento Bee,* March 27.

Haro, Roberto. 1995. "Epilogue Held to a Higher Standard: Latino Executive Selection in Higher Education." In *The Leaning Ivory Tower,* ed. Raymond Padilla and Rudolfo Chávez. Albany: State University of New York Press.

Hayes-Bautista, David E., Paul Hsu, Robert Beltrán, and Juan Villagómez. 2000. *The Latino Physician Shortage in California, 1999.* Los Angeles: Center for the Study of Latino Health, UCLA.

Health, M. 2002. "More Cal Grants Awarded after Error Resolved." *The Daily Californian,* April 30.

Jencks, Christopher, and Susan Meyer. 1990. "The Social Consequences of Growing up in a Poor Neighborhood." In *Inner-City Poverty in the United States,* ed. Laurence E. Lynn, Jr., and Michael G. H. McGeary. Washington, D.C.: National Academy Press.

Kao, Grace, and Marta Tienda. 1998. "Educational Aspirations of Minority Youth." *American Journal of Education* 106: 349–84.

Karoly, Lynn A., Peter W. Greenwood, Susan S. Everingham, Jill Houbé, M. Rebecca Kilburn, C. Peter Rydell, Matthew Sanders, and James Chiesa. 1998. *Investing in Our Children: What We Know and Don't Know about the Costs and Benefits of Early Childhood Interventions*, MR-898, Santa Monica, Calif.: The RAND Corporation.

Komaromy M., K. Grumbach, M. Drake, K. Vranizan, N. Lurie, D. Keane, and A. B. Bindman. 1996. "The Role of Black and Hispanic Physicians in Providing Health Care for Underserved Populations." *New England Journal of Medicine* 334(20): 1305–10.

Lareau, Annette. 1987. "Social Class Differences in Family-School Relationship: the Importance of Cultural Capital." *Sociology of Education* 60: 73–85.

López, Elías, E. Ramírez, and R. Rochín. 1999. *Latinos and Economic Development in California*. Sacramento: California Research Bureau.

McDonough, Patricia. 1997. *Choosing Colleges. How Social Class and Schools Structure Opportunity*. Albany: State University of New York Press.

McDonough, Patricia Korn, and E. Yamasaki. 1997. "Admissions Advantage for Sale: Private College Counselors and the Students Who Use Them." *Review of Higher Education* 20: 297–317.

Miller, Scott. 1995. An American Imperative: Accelerating Minority Educational Advancement. New Haven: Yale University Press.

Moll, Luis, and Norma González. 1994. "Lessons from Research with Language Minority Children." *Journal of Reading Behavior* 26: 439–56.

Mortensen, Thomas. 1997. Postsecondary Education Opportunity. 61.

National Center for Education Statistics. 1998. *The Condition of Education*. Washington, D.C.: U.S. Department of Education.

National Science Foundation. 2000. *WebCASPAR Database System*. http://caspar.nsf.gov/.

Oakes, Jeanie. 1985. *Keeping Track. How Schools Structure Inequality*. New Haven: Yale University Press.

Oakes, Jeanie, Tor H. Ormseth, Robert M. Bell, and Patti Camp. 1990. *Multiple Inequalities*. Santa Monica: RAND Corp.

Orfield, Gary, and John Yun. 1999. *Resegregation in American Schools*. Cambridge: Harvard Civil Rights Project.

Perna, Laura, and Watson Scott Swail. 1998. "Early Intervention Programs: How Effective Are They at Increasing Access to College?" Paper presented at the annual meeting of the Association for the Study of Higher Education, Miami, Fla., November 7.

Puma, Michael, Nancy Karweit, Cristofer Price, Anne Ricciuti, William Thompson, and Michael Vaden-Kiernan. 1997. *Prospects: Final Report on Student*

Outcomes. Washington, D.C.: U.S. Department of Education. Office of the Under Secretary.

Rock, D., H. Braun, and P. R. Rosenbaum. 1985. *Excellence in High School Education: Cross-Sectional Study, 1980–1982. Final Report.* Princeton: Educational Testing Service.

Romo, Harriet, and Toni Falbo. 1996. *Latino High School Graduation. Defying the Odds.* Austin: University of Texas Press.

Shields, P., et al. 1999. *Teaching and California's Future by the Center for the Future of Teaching and Learning.* Santa Cruz, Calif.: Center for the Future of Teaching and Learning.

Smith, Daryl. 1996. *Achieving Faculty Diversity, Debunking the Myths.* Washington, D.C.: Association of American Colleges and Universities.

Sorensen, Stephen, Dominic J. Brewer, Stephen J. Carroll, and Eugene Bryton. 1995. *Increasing Hispanic Participation in Higher Education: A Desirable Public Investment.* Santa Monica, Calif.: RAND Corporation. Institute for Education and Training.

Stanton-Salazar, Ricardo. 1997. "A Social Capital Framework for Understanding the Socialization of Racial Minority Children and Youths." *Harvard Educational Review* 67: 1–40.

Trounson, R. 2002. "The State Cal Grant Recipient Total to Fall Short of Goals." *The Los Angeles Times,* April 17.

University of California Office of the President. 1999. *Composition of Graduate Students and Faculty at the University of California by Race and Sex.* Oakland: University of California Office of the President.

———. 2002c. Graduate Academic Programs: Fall 1995 through Fall 2001, New Registrants. http://www.ucop.edu/acadadv/datamgmt/graddata/acadnreg.html.

———. 2000b. University of California Law School Applicants, Admits and First-Year Class Enrollment Percentages. http://www.ucop.edu/acadadv/datamgmt/lawdata/.

———. 2000a. University of California Medical School Applicants, Admits and First-Year Class Enrollment Percentages. http://www.ucop.edu/acadadv/datamgmt/meddata.

———. 2002a. University of California Application, Admissions and Enrollment of California Resident Freshman for Fall 1995 through 2001. http://www.ucop.edu/news/factsheets/flowfrc9501.pdf.

———. 2002b. *University of California Eligibility in Local Context Program Evaluation Report.* Oakland: Office of the President of the University of California.

———. 2002. University of California Law School Applicants, Admits and First-Year Class Enrollment Percentages. www.ucop.edu/acadadv/datamgmt/lawdata/.

———. 2002. University of California Medical School Applicants, Admits and First-Year Class Enrollment Percentages. www.ucop.edu/acadadv/datamgmt/meddata.

United States Department of Education. 1998. *The 1994 High School Transcript Study Tabulation.* Washington, D.C.: (NCES 98–532).

Useem, Elizabeth L. 1992. "Middle Schools and Math Groups: Parents' Involvement in Children's Placement." *Sociology of Education* 65: 263–79.

Vernez, George. 1999. *Closing the Education Gap.* Santa Monica, Calif.: RAND Corp.

Walker, B. 2000. "University of Texas Enrollment and Retention Data." Presented at the Higher Education Access Seminar, University of California, Berkeley, March 31.

Chapter 5

Tipping the Balance:
A Flexible, Integrated System of Adult Education

Edward Kissam

Introduction

Adult basic education is a critical service-delivery system for California Latinos. The structure of the current system is so fragmented that there are many areas of disagreement about where the boundary between adult education and employment training is best drawn; however, the consensus is that the core-area mission of adult basic education is to support adult learners in developing a set of functional competencies in communication, acquisition, and management of both textual and quantitative information, in analytic thinking and in developing a sense of the wide range of contemporary systems that are the backbone of the information society.[1] This core skills set is the necessary foundation for contin-

---

[1] There are two widely accepted national frameworks for visualizing the functional competencies targeted by core adult-education programs. The first is the three-volume SCANS framework developed in the early 1990s by the Secretary's Commission on Achieving the Necessary Skills ("Teaching the SCANS Competencies," "What Work Requires of Schools: A SCANS Report for America 2000," and "Learning a Living: A SCANS Report for America 2000"); the second is the more recent EFF (Equipped for the Future) framework developed by the National Institute for Literacy.

ued lifelong learning. This complex of adult-learner needs and these educational opportunities are the primary focus of this chapter—although other adult-learning opportunities, such as technical training in corporate or community-college settings, are certainly relevant.

Building high-performance information-handling and communication skills is critical as an avenue for Latinos to achieve economic and political parity with other Californians. The basic skills-development needs of Latinos who have immigrated to California differ significantly from those of native-born Latinos, but both are key groups of adult-education customers. Not surprisingly, the majority of California's four million foreign-born Latinos need to develop English-language communication skills, and about 150,000 California-born Latinos also have some limitations in English. Forty-one percent of Latino workers in California have only a high school diploma, and at least another 45 percent (most of them Mexican and Central-American immigrants) have even lower levels of educational attainment.[2]

While the current need for adult-learning opportunities is tremendous, Latinos' need for adult-learning services will increase in the coming decade because in 2000 about 1.2 million limited-English, Spanish-speaking students were in the K–12 school system.[3] There is also a consensus that second-generation Latino immigrants face serious problems in the public-school system and that English-language acquisition may well be further hampered in the wake of Proposition 227.[4] Thus, demand for adult-education services from Latino youth and young adults—both those born and raised in California and those who are immigrants—is likely to escalate rapidly in the near future.[5]

---

[2] Elias Lopez, Enrique Ramirez, and Refugio Rochín, "Latinos and Economic Development in California," California Research Bureau, June 1999.

[3] Sonya Tafoya, "The Linguistic Landscape of California Schools," The Public Policy Institute of California, vol. 3, no. 4 (February 2002).

[4] The provisions of Proposition 227 were designed to eliminate bilingual education in California, although there were provisions for parents to specifically request waivers so their children could receive bilingual instruction beyond the one-year period of "transitional" bilingual education that the proposition allowed. Uncertainties regarding the actual instructional methodologies being used in the wake of Proposition 227 make it unclear what its impact will be.

[5] In addition to service demand from California-born youth and young adults, a significant number of Mexican and Central-American immigrants are youth who have dropped out of school to migrate to work in California. On the basis of interviews with teenagers working in farmwork, I estimate that about 30,000 teenage Latino farmworkers come to work in California agriculture each year. See Edward Kissam, et al., "No Longer Children: Case Studies of the Living and Working Conditions of the Youth who Harvest America's Crops," Aguirre International Report to Office of Policy, U.S. Department of Labor, May 2001.

Latinos make up one-third (about 10.9 million persons[6]) of the California population and more than one-half of the total population of adults in the state who need basic skills improvement.[7] Although Latinos appear to be slightly overrepresented in California adult-education enrollment (making up about 65 percent of the total adult-education population[8]) the question remains whether this represents equitable access to services in view of the fact that Latinos have such serious English-language and basic skill-development needs.[9] Even more worrisome is the fact that it is not clear if the courses they enroll in are adequate to provide Latino adult learners the skills they need to communicate effectively with their non-Spanish speaking neighbors, to participate fully in California civic life, or to move out of the population of working poor in which both immigrant and native-born Latinos are disproportionately concentrated.[10]

During late 2001 and early 2002, the state initiated a major effort to carefully analyze the performance of the adult-education system and propose a range of strategic initiatives. One of these initiatives, an administrative reorganization sketched out as part of the governor's 2002–2003 budget, would create a new state department of labor and shift responsibility for adult education from the California Department of Education to the California Community Colleges system. Another, a report developed by the Adult and Noncredit Education Subgroup as part of a comprehensive planning process under the aegis of the Joint Committee to Develop a Master Plan for Education, puts forward a more substantive set of recommendations. In 2003, the state legislature established a select committee on adult education. The long-overdue attention now being given to the overall adult-education system has the promise of greatly improving prospects for Latino adult learners. Nonetheless, I will argue that still bolder and more decisive action will be needed to help Latinos achieve full equity in the civic and economic landscape of California society.

---

[6]Census 2000. Census estimates of limited-English, educationally disadvantaged Latinos are very low because low educational attainment, recent arrival in California as an immigrant, linguistic enclosure, and crowded housing are all predictors of differential undercount (Fein 1993).

[7]Estimate by the author based on findings of the National Adult Literacy Survey, 1993.

[8]California Department of Education, "Student Progress and Goal Attainment Report: Federally Funded WIA/AEFLA Programs in California 1999–2000." Enrollment is reported by ethnicity only for programs receiving federal adult basic education funding and thus may slightly exaggerate overall Hispanic enrollment.

[9]As I discuss below, I estimate that eight out of 10 Latinos in California could benefit from improvements in their basic literacy skills.

[10]Janet Wells, "Racial Divide in Boom Time, Study Reports," *San Francisco Chronicle*, September 5, 2000, an article based on findings from a Field Institute telephone poll conducted May–July 2000.

Policy responses to problems of quality and appropriateness of educational service should not be formulated simply in terms of new regulatory guidelines for provider accountability, new training initiatives, or new funding-allocation formulas. Instead it will be necessary to move forward boldly to re-engineer the current system in California and provide greater value to Latino adult-education customers, California communities, and employers—all major stakeholders in adult learning. California needs a new policy framework, new planning priorities, and aggressive follow-up to ensure effective implementation. With courage, innovation, and commitment such an initiative can be a win-win situation. Continuation of the status quo will be a recipe for failure, ensuring that California Latinos, a population now at risk of becoming information "have-nots," will fall behind other groups and be condemned to the bottom tier of an information-intensive economy and society.

The Response to Latino Adult-Learning Needs Matters to All Californians

Latinos are at risk in this contemporary information-based society for two underlying reasons. The first is that Latino immigrants, most of them from Mexico, El Salvador, and Guatemala, have very low levels of educational attainment.[11] The second is that second-generation Latinos are very likely to drop out of school or attend schools where they cannot receive a high-quality education.[12]

Broad concerns about haves and have-nots in an information society and adult education's role in fostering social and economic equality are not new, but

---

[11]For example, 59 percent of Mexican immigrants and 39 percent of Central-American immigrants legalized under the Immigration Reform and Control Act of 1986 (IRCA) had only an elementary-school education. U.S. Department of Justice, Immigration and Naturalization Service, "Report on the Legalized Alien Population," March 1992. This tabulation is consistent with slightly different tabulations that break out educational attainment for special agricultural workers or SAWs (immigrants whose statuses were regularized based on qualifying work in agriculture) and other legal permanent residents (LPRs) in California. See CASAS, *A Survey of Newly Legalized Persons in California,* California Health and Welfare Agency, 1989.

[12]See, for example Patricia L. de Cos et al., "K–12 Performance" in *A Coordinated Approach to Raising the Socio-Economic Status of Latinos in California,* ed. Lopez, Puddefoot, and Gándara, California Research Bureau, March 2000; Alejandro Portes, "Immigration's Aftermath," *American Prospect* (April 2002); and Liz Guillen, "California Latino Students: Continuing Challenges That Cannot Be Ignored," Testimony to Senate Education Committee Informational Hearing on the Status of Latino Public School Students, January 31, 2001.

the specifics have changed.[13] The information-handling competencies referred to as literacy have constantly evolved in response to social and technological change. What is different about California in the 21st century is the *rate* of technological and social change and the very real challenges inherent in forging a new multicultural society of almost unprecedented scale. For example, seven of the 10 most diverse metro areas in the U.S. are in California, and Latinos are the second-largest ethnic group (after non-Hispanic whites) in each.[14]

The emergence of a multi-ethnic, multilingual, pluralistic "new California" is part of California's strength, but it places a premium on higher-order communication and problem-solving skills among coworkers and neighbors.[15] As California moves toward becoming a majority-minority state, all segments of California society will need to rely on Latinos for leadership—in community life, science, the arts, and business. By 2025, Latinos will make up almost half of California's population, becoming the largest ethnic group in a pluralistic society.[16] Latino civic engagement is critical for two related but separate reasons. First, the persistent exclusion of such a large population group would deform the overall processes of governance; second, Latino immigrants bring a wealth of social capital, which, if successfully mobilized in addressing California community problems, can make the difference between vibrant and decaying communi-

---

[13]National Center on Education and the Economy, "America's Choice: High Skills or Low Wages!" Commission on the Skills of the American Workforce, June 1990; Secretary's Commission on Achieving Necessary Skills, "Learning a Living: A SCANS Report for America 2000," U.S. Department of Labor, 1992; BW Associates, "Mobilizing for Competitiveness: Linking Education and Training to Jobs," California Business Roundtable, January 1994; Sondra Stein, *Equipped for the Future: A Reform Agenda for Adult Literacy and Lifelong Learning,* National Institute for Literacy, February 1997; and Anthony P. Carnevale and Donna M. Desrochers, "Getting Down to Business: Matching Welfare Recipients' Skills to Jobs that Train," Educational Testing Service, 1999.

[14]William H. Frey, "The Diversity Myth," in *Diversity in America—A Supplement to American Demographics,* 2000.

[15]California's Little Hoover Commission recommends establishment of a Golden State Residency Program that would invest in building immigrants' skills and other efforts to facilitate the process of integrating immigrants into California life—not simply on the basis of benefiting individual immigrants but, rather, because these investments can be expected to enhance entire communities' ability to address the problems they face. Adult education investments highlighted in the commission's report include: English as a Second Language (ESL) and citizenship instruction.

[16]Hans Johnson, "How Many Californians? A Review of Population Projections for the State," Public Policy Institute of California, October 1999.

ties.[17] Improved adult education for California Latinos will benefit all Californians.

Another concern is that California's labor market is highly segmented, with Latinos disproportionately represented in the lower rungs of career ladders in most occupational clusters. To achieve economic equality Latino immigrants will need opportunities to develop career awareness, communication, and analytic skills to move out of the tertiary labor market and into emerging occupations.[18] Upward career mobility and economic equity are not only of crucial economic importance for Latinos themselves but for their employers and for California society as a whole.

Even industrial sectors such as agriculture, where about 800,000 mostly immigrant Latinos are employed as farmworkers, need skilled labor—for supervising large and complex labor-intensive operations, for installing, operating, and maintaining high-technology equipment used in contemporary agricultural production, and for management and administrative tasks. Although agriculture is generally regarded as a low-skill industry, California's competitiveness in the hemispheric and world economy stems, in part, from a technological and organizational infrastructure that makes the state's production competitive with low-wage production regions such as Mexico and China.

California's ability to compete in the global market in both low-tech industrial sectors such as agriculture and high-tech sectors such as electronics requires larger pools of Latino workers with solid basic skills in information handling and analytic thinking. Upward career mobility for Latinos who did not have an opportunity to participate in higher education is important not simply for Latinos themselves but for all Californians—in part because employment instability compromises families' ability to fund their children's educations and leads to increased public-support costs as the now-young Latino population ages.

The third factor is California's nature as a region where there has been extensive "peripheralization of the core," i.e., creation of third-world enclaves in close proximity to affluent areas. This has resulted in residentially segregated communities and tremendous economic and institutional disparities in access to

---

[17]Edward Kissam, et al., "Evaluation of the Central Valley Partnership," Final Report to the Civic Culture Program, James F. Irvine Foundation, The Aguirre Group, December 1999.

[18]Some labor-market analysts use the term "tertiary labor market" to refer to segments of the labor market where employment is characteristically on a day-to-day basis or at the employer's will, where provisions of labor laws, for example, those relating to minimum wage, safe working conditions, or overtime are at best enforced unevenly, and where benefits such as health insurance, vacation pay, sick leave, and retirement benefits are not available. Employment training practitioners and labor market analysts consider "emerging occupations" to be those where there is both increasing demand, relatively good pay, and upward career ladders. Most, but not all, of these "emerging occupations" are the result of changes in technology.

education between subregions such as Silicon Valley and the Central Valley.[19] As a state, California faces tremendous challenges in social integration and in bringing together such socio-economic, cultural, and linguistic extremes.

Visualizing Latinos' Adult-Learning Needs

An adequate understanding of California Latinos' skills-development needs is a crucial foundation for developing effective strategies to respond to these needs, in terms of legislative policy response, program-implementation guidelines, and capacity-building efforts. Because demand for services is so high, even in the best of economic circumstances California will need to focus on developing a highly cost-effective system of support for adult continuing education.

In many respects, Latinos' adult-learning needs are no different from those of other groups of economically and educationally disadvantaged adults. For all adult-education customers, the key factors in determining social, civic, and economic equality in 21st-century California are their ability to access information and their agility in analyzing, managing, and using it to create and communicate new information. Because Latinos are the largest cohort of adult learners in the state, from a rational policy perspective, the ideal system would be one configured to provide a broad range of educational services designed explicitly to meet Latino learners' needs. But the adult-education system faces a special challenge in overcoming stereotypes from the past, *vis-à-vis* Latino adult learners' needs. In past decades, adult education most commonly visualized Latinos' adult-learning needs as centering around "survival English."

It would be dangerous to assume that California Latinos would be well served by a "one size fits all" adult-education policy. It is becoming increasingly clear that Latinos' adult-education needs require access to diverse opportunities to acquire the generative communication skills and proactive analytic competencies needed for them to advocate and chart their own course, not simply to survive. In order for workers and citizens to lead, and not simply respond to what others want of them, they need the information-handling competencies to prevail, not simply to survive. In this quest, one of the unique challenges faced by Latino adult learners is access to opportunities for accelerated intensive adult education and for self-directed learning. Because most Latino adult learners are

---

[19]Elaine M. Allensworth and Refugio I. Rochin, "The Mexicanization of Rural California: A Socio-Demographic Analysis 1980–1997," Julian Samora Research Institute, Michigan State University, January 1999; and Edward Kissam and Stephen Reder, "Responding to Diversity: Strategies and Initiatives to Support Lifelong Learning for Limited English Adults in California," Final Report to Adult Education and Planning Unit, California Department of Education, Aguirre International, April 1997.

among the "working poor," they face very high opportunity costs in taking time out from low-paid work to participate in adult-learning programs.

The diversity of Latino immigrants in California must also be taken into account in analyzing adult-learning needs. Particularly striking are the differences in the educational experiences of immigrants from urban and rural Mexico. California farmworkers have mean educational levels of about six years of schooling—but even within this population there are great variations, related to community of origin.[20] As migration of indigenous ethnic minorities increases from remote, rural areas of the Mexican states of Oaxaca, Guerrero, Veracruz, and Chiapas, and from Maya areas of Guatemala, immigrants' educational disadvantages are likely to increase.[21] Although educational attainment is much higher among U.S.-born Latinos than among immigrants, second-generation Latinos are also educationally disadvantaged. About two-fifths (41 percent) have less than a high-school education, and probably an even greater number have skills deficits despite having attended or graduated from high school. The educational disadvantages of California-born Latinos stem both from problems of educational quality in the inner-city and rural K–12 school districts in which they live, and from tensions arising in the course of acculturation.[22] However, in assessing the complex dynamics of the problems encountered by Latino youth who have attended school in California, it is useful to remember that many U.S.-born Latino schoolchildren are from immigrant families[23] and that school enrollment is growing very rapidly in the districts where Latino students go to school.

Indices of Latinos' Adult-Learning Needs

The National Adult Literacy Survey (NALS) provides valuable insights into the need for literacy-skills development in relation to the functional competencies required to achieve economic stability and effectively engage in civic life. This is due to the NALS framework, which is based on real-world competencies,

---

[20] Unpublished analyses of the 1999 California data from the National Agricultural Worker Survey (NAWS), the Aguirre Group, 2002.

[21] Edward Kissam, et al., "No Longer Children: Case Studies of the Living and Working Conditions of the Youth who Harvest America's Crops," Aguirre International Report to Office of Policy, U.S. Department of Labor, May 2001.

[22] Ruben Rumbaut and Wayne A. Cornelius, eds., *California's Immigrant Children,* Center for U.S.-Mexican Studies (San Diego: University of California, San Diego, 1995); and Carola and Marcelo Suárez-Orozco, *Transformations: Migration, Family Life, and Achievement Motivation among Latino Adolescents* (Stanford: Stanford University Press, 1995); Alejandro Portes and Rubén Rumbaut, *Legacies,* Berkeley: University of California Press, 2001.

[23] Michael Fix and Wendy Zimmerman, "All Under One Roof: Mixed-Status Families in an Era of Reform," The Urban Institute, June 1999.

Table 5.1. Adult Latinos' Need for Literacy-Skills Improvement as Assessed in NALS

Literacy Level	California Latinos %	Overall Population %	Ratio of Latinos to Overall Population
NALS Level 1	59	24	2.5
NALS Level 2	22	22	1.0
Needing basic skills improvement	81	46	2.1

Source: Based on data from the National Adult Literacy Survey/California.

not arbitrarily developed educational indicators.[24] The findings convey a stark picture of educational inequality for Latinos.[25] Table 5.1 shows the proportion of California Latinos lacking baseline information-handling skills as compared to the state as a whole. The last column of Table 5.1 estimates Latinos' relative need for adult-education services in comparison to the overall state population. The table illustrates the particularly heavy concentration of Latinos—mostly the more-recent immigrants—with very low English-language literacy (NALS Level 1), and the need for services for adult learners with somewhat higher functional literacy (NALS Level 2)—native-born Latinos and long-time immigrants.

The key distinction that makes the divide between NALS Level 2 and higher levels the watershed for social and economic equity is that only at these higher levels of literacy can individuals begin to manage information proactively. Only then can they integrate information from different sources, draw inferences from analyses of disparities among information sources, and find the relevant mathematical information to solve the quantitative problems that are the most critical in making hard individual or community decisions.

The labor-market implications of these findings are ominous for Latinos. Persons functioning at NALS Level 1 or 2 may find temporary safe havens in a

---

[24] Arbitrarily developed educational indicators are scales or items in scales that seek to test competencies in isolation, as distinguished from competencies in carrying out real-world tasks. At the worst, these indicators report reading competencies, for example, in grade-level equivalents.

[25] Lynn B. Jenkins and Irwin S. Kirsch, *Adult Literacy in California: Results of the State Adult Literacy Survey,* Educational Testing Service, 1994.

labor market demanding increasingly complex skills, but they remain at risk of being displaced by industrywide changes or technological development.[26] For example, NALS interviewers asked unemployment-insurance claimants to assess whether their literacy skills were adequate for their most recent job. The mean scores of those who felt their skills were adequate fell consistently into the NALS Level 3 range where, for example, reading tasks involve interpreting text without organizational headings and integrating information from different text sources, and mathematical tasks require readers to locate relevant quantitative information within a textual passage. Those who felt their skills were inadequate scored in Level 1 for reading and in Level 2 for writing and mathematics—the skills range typical for California Latinos.

English-Language Demands in Immigrant Enclaves versus Full-Fledged Social Mobility

In 1990, about 1.8 million California Latino adults had limited English comprehension and speaking skills.[27] Still more—about 2.2 million—had some problems in reading. Not surprisingly, even more—about 2.9 million—had difficulties in writing English. Adjusting these gross numbers to capture only those over 16 not enrolled in high school or college, it is likely that the population of Latinos in need of adult-learning opportunities to improve their English is now more than 2.2 million.

A 1996 survey of limited-English, Spanish-speaking households provides a more detailed analysis of the educational needs of this large subpopulation of adult Latinos.[28] Survey respondents were queried about their ability to manage the day-to-day challenges they faced in four critical domains of adult functioning—the workplace, family life, community life, and lifelong learning. In reflecting on the implications of these findings it is critical to recognize that these are means, and that many subgroups among Latinos (e.g., recent immigrants from rural areas and middle-aged married women with minimal schooling) have more serious skills barriers to social and economic equity than other groups

---

[26]Irwin S. Kirsch, Ann Jungeblut, and Anne Campbell, *Beyond the School Doors: The Literacy Needs of Job Seekers Served by the U.S. Department of Labor,* Educational Testing Service, September 1992.

[27]Lynn B. Jenkins and Irwin S. Kirsch, *Adult Literacy in California: Results of the State Adult Literacy Survey,* Office of Educational Research and Improvement, U.S. Department of Education, 1996.

[28]Edward Kissam and Stephen Reder, "Responding to Diversity: Strategies and Initiatives to Support Lifelong Learning for Limited English Adults in California," Final Report to Adult Education and Planning Unit, California Department of Education, Aguirre International, April 1997.

(e.g., young Mexican and Central-American immigrants from urban areas who came to California with at least eight years of home-country schooling).

Skills Needed for Employment Stability, Career Advancement, and Economic Equity

Table 5.2 shows the survey respondents' assessment of their abilities (and consequently skills-development needs) in the domain of employment stability, career advancement, and economic equity. It highlights the degree to which these limited-English Latinos are at-risk workers, constantly threatened by the possibility that the establishments where they work will go broke, leave town, or force workers to leave work as a result of on-the-job conflicts, poor working conditions, or job demands that can be met only by younger workers in excellent health. In this regard, an important policy dimension to be considered is that aging Latinos who remain in the tertiary labor market throughout their work life may find themselves ineligible for Social Security benefits in their old age and, even before then, be increasingly disadvantaged by lack of access to health insurance. The reason is that reliance on networks of extended family and *compadres*[29] is increasingly difficult in the contemporary California environment, where families can no longer cluster in *colonia*-style[30] settlements or find time to participate in traditional systems of mutual reciprocity such as those described by Lomnitz.[31]

Skills Needed for Civic Engagement, Community Problem-Solving, and Political Equity

The often-rhetorical issue of civic involvement is a practical concern for Californians living in communities that are deeply divided by race, ethnicity, language, and economic class. Researchers such as Robert Bach have argued that interethnic collaboration is a critical challenge for social policy.[32] But motivation is not enough; effective involvement in community life requires a wide range of skills: the acquisition and evaluation of information, problem-solving, negotiation, and teamwork. Table 5.3 shows that the domain of community life

---

[29]Mexican systems of *compadrazgo* are social networks based on ties between *compadres*, described formally by anthropologists as "fictive kinship systems."

[30]*Colonias* are settlements of Mexican immigrants that grew up in the absence of zoning regulations or enforcement of such regulations, making it possible for extended-family members or multiple generations to build houses in clusters on land owned by the family that originally settled it.

[31]Larissa Lomnitz, *Networks and Marginality: Life in a Mexican Shantytown* (New York: New York: Academic Press, 1977).

[32]Robert Bach, "Report of the Changing Relations Project," Ford Foundation, 1990.

Table 5.2. Self-Assessment of Workplace Competencies (Percent of Total Respondents)

How confident are you that you can do what it takes to meet your own and others' expectations?

Workplace Domain	In Current Environment			In English-Only Environment		
	Very or Extremely	Somewhat	Not Very or Not at All	Very or Extremely	Somewhat	Not Very or Not at All
In the work you're doing now*	66	22	12	8	15	77
For communicating with your supervisor, boss, or the company owner	47	21	32	7	11	82
For getting a job in some new kind of work (occupation)	43	17	40	7	11	82
For getting a better position in the kind of work you're doing now	40	15	45	5	9	86

*This question was coded "not applicable" for persons not currently in the labor force, i.e., neither employed nor looking for work. Sixty-nine percent of the survey respondents (174) were in the labor force.

Table 5.3. Self-Assessment of Ability to Participate in Community Life (Percent of Total Respondents)

To what extent do you feel you're able to deal with or contribute to community responses to the following issues you face:

Community Life Domain	Current Environment			English-Only Environment		
	Great Extent	Some Extent	Not Very Well or Not at All	Great Extent	Some Extent	Not Very Well or Not at All
Dealing with ongoing community problems—e.g., help from police to decrease crime, better housing	42	28	30	2	10	88
Joining with friends and neighbors to have a say about how organizations respond to your needs	34	20	46	2	7	91
For understanding the community issues you hear about, see in the newspapers, or that people vote on	25	27	48	3	4	93
For communicating your opinion or viewpoint to local leaders, your state or congressional representatives	26	18	55	3	5	92

is a particularly problematic one for limited-English Latinos because they do not feel well qualified in either Spanish or English to deal with the community-life demands they face.

Table 5.3 reflects the reality that critical processes in California community life and governance tend to take place in English whether or not the majority of community residents know English. Survey respondents feel they are less able to function in dealing with California civic life than in any other domain. Building the foundation skills for Latino civic engagement is central to efforts to ensure Latino equity. Without such a basis for ongoing civic involvement, it becomes markedly more difficult to leverage sporadic political involvement to advance a policy agenda of desirable responses to issues of special importance to Latinos. Adult education will need to develop active and innovative strategies to fulfill its crucial role in making the idea of participatory democracy more than a hollow dream for limited-English Latinos.

Navigating Change—Building the Skills Needed for Lifelong Learning

In the area of lifelong learning, adult-education programs have a unique contribution to make to the well being of California Latinos. An important part of the adult-education mission is to establish a *foundation* for Latinos to manage their lifelong learning, which may include selective enrollment in different specialized courses (typically vocational training) in combination with self-directed study. Here survey respondents felt somewhat prepared to function in their current environments but only minimally prepared to function in English-language environments.[33] Table 5.4 presents survey findings about skills in this domain.

The most striking pattern in Table 5.4 is limited-English Latinos' recognition that building skills in the area of computer-based and library-based access to information (a subset of reference skills in general) is an important area for development. As a commitment to the principle of ongoing learning, programs must build limited-English Latino learners' ability to acquire and analyze the information they need to navigate an information-based economy and society deserve high priority.

---

[33]Bilingual vocational-training designs work well, and program designs such as those used for more than three decades by programs such as the Center for Employment Training, in which program participants move from "feeder" vocational English as a Second Language (VESL) courses into English-language technical instruction are an option; however, in the current policy environment they are not likely to be well funded.

Table 5.4. Self-Assessed Ability to Develop New Skills and Learn New Information (Percent of Total Respondents)

How confident are you that you can do what it takes to develop new skills or get the information you need to get ahead in life?

Lifelong Learning Domain	Current Environment			English-Only Environment		
	Very or Extremely	Somewhat	Not Very or Not at All	Very or Extremely	Somewhat	Not Very or Not at All
For participating and succeeding in a program to learn a new trade or occupation?	51	18	31	7	9	84
For using magazines, manuals, or books to find out information you want or need (at work or in your daily life)	45	18	37	5	11	84
Using other resources to get the information you need, e.g., computers or libraries	24	13	63	4	7	89
Deciding if you want to improve your educational skills and how you might best go about doing that	44	20	36	5	9	86

Implications of Multidimensional Assessment of Functional Competencies

The preceding needs profile in three critical domains of social functioning supports the idea that adult education must address the needs of Latino limited–English-proficient adults through skills development oriented specifically toward building a foundation for the personal, social, and economic mobility needed to do what one wants, live where one wants, and have and express the opinions one wants to have in contemporary America. The insights of researchers who emphasize the extent to which Latinos are a healthy population, due in large measure to the ability to draw on resources of social capital, are important.[34] However, the current analysis questions Latinos' ability to draw effectively on these reserves of social capital in an unfamiliar and often hostile English-dominant social and legal context. Without the ability to transfer the social technology that makes up Latinos' store of social capital into an unfamiliar sociopolitical context, Latinos are compromised in their ability to deploy these skills. This suggests a need for interventions in the form of adult-education services that coach learners to adapt their cultural know-how to successfully navigate the fast-paced and often turbulent mix of work, family, and community life in 21st-century California.

California's Current Adult-Education Service-Delivery System

As in most states, California's adult-education service-delivery system is made up of diverse service providers: adult-school programs run by K–12 districts; community-college programs; community-based literacy, English-as-a-second-language (ESL), and civics programs run by libraries, community groups, and employment-training providers; special programs run by agencies such as the California Conservation Corps; and programs for incarcerated persons run by the California Department of Corrections, the California Youth Authority, and county jail systems. In several counties, most notably San Francisco, an interagency agreement designates the local community college as the primary service

---

[34]Latino immigrants' social capital that can be deployed to enhance health status includes funds of knowledge related, essentially, to preventive healthcare; information imparted by *curanderas,* by *compadres,* and through a variety of informal networks; and services available at low cost or through barter when no money is available to access the mainstream system. See Bonnie Bade, "Is There a Doctor in the Field? Underlying Conditions Affecting Access to Health Care for California Farmworkers and their Families," paper presented to CPAC Conference, California Policy Research Center, September 1999.

provider, but 84 percent of adult-education enrollees statewide are served by K–12 adult schools.

Adult education received about $566 million in apportionment funding in 2001–2002.[35] About three-quarters of the funding goes to K–12 adult schools and the balance goes to community colleges.[36] Another $90 million per year in funding for adult basic-skills development is provided under the Workforce Investment Act (which now incorporates federal funding for adult education), the Carl D. Perkins Act, and related work-oriented funding to support a variety of employment-training and employability-enhancement programs. The specific amount available for adult education (i.e., basic-skills development), as distinguished from employment training (i.e., skills-specific training) is difficult to determine because most programs include some amount of remedial education.

A program under the Workforce Investment Act (WIA) that is of particular importance for California's immigrant Latinos is the English Literacy/Civics (EL/Civics) program that was funded at a level of $20 million in 2000–2001 to provide instruction in citizenship preparation and/or civics in conjunction with English. Additional programs such as the federal Even Start program provide some additional adult-learning opportunities, and WIA funding targeted to migrant and seasonal farmworkers contributes to the services available to California Latinos—but they are funded at relatively low levels and are not generally considered to be part of the adult-education system.

The funding structure for California adult education has several anomalies that give rise to chronic problems in service delivery. The first of these problems is that funding is provided on the basis of hours of classroom attendance by a student; the current "adult revenue limit"[37] is $2,099 for 525 hours of instruction (just under $4.00/contact hour)—a level far below the authorized level per hour of instruction in either regular K–12 classrooms or in community college for-credit courses.[38] This tends to undercut instructional quality since the primary management challenge for administrators is to provide some kind of instruction without the financial leeway to make adequate investments in systems that would assure instructional quality. Problems include: burgeoning class size for

---

[35]Sum of 2001–2002 entitlement column for 11 state regions. California Department of Education, Adult Education Data, 2002. www.cde.ca.gov/adulteducation/datacollect/capadaindex.html.

[36]Based on tabulation of funding for 1996–1997 in Joint Board Task Force on Non-credit and Adult Education, "Challenges Opportunities Changes," Final Report, December 1998. http://www.otan.us/webfarm/jbtf/index.html.

[37]The term "adult revenue limit" refers to the amount of funding generated by one student contact hour. This limits reimbursement to adult education service providers for the costs of providing service. While the actual cost of an hour of instruction in various adult education courses can vary greatly, the adult revenue limit controls the average expenditure per student hour.

[38]This is being addressed in current (2002) policy proposals (see discussion below).

high-demand courses such as ESL—since these will generate surplus revenue, which is then used to subsidize smaller, less-popular classes; reliance on part-time teachers who have little time for preparation; and pro-forma systems of teacher supervision and observation that provide no way to deliver targeted in-service training to teachers.

The second service-delivery problem is that Proposition 13 tied adult-education funding in subsequent years to the levels of service that were provided when the proposition passed in 1978. Thus, funding is not linked to the extent of need for services (although highly reliable methods have been developed, using census data, to generate estimates of the extent and severity of need for adult-education services).[39] This is a particularly serious problem for Latino adult learners seeking to enroll in ESL or ESL/citizenship courses in rural counties where ongoing immigration rates are high. Despite legislative efforts to address the problem of "zero-capped" adult-education programs (i.e., those that did not offer any level of adult-education services when Proposition 13 passed), difficulties continue in delivering programs in jurisdictions with very low levels of funding because there is no way to build service-delivery capacity. Unfortunately, many of the communities and counties with the most rapid increases in Latino population are the same communities and counties that had not developed adult-education programs at the time of Proposition 13.[40]

The third problem is that adult education, like K–12 education, is funded on the basis of attendance (actual contact hours). Because the funding structure is linked to inputs rather than outcomes, a built-in mechanism discourages giving priority to effectiveness—because longer courses generate more revenue than shorter courses that might achieve the same outcomes. A mismatch occurs between the needs of Latino adult learners and those of program providers: Program providers are biased toward providing a greater quantity of less-effective instruction in teacher-centered classrooms, while Latino learners are inclined to drop out of adult-education programs that take too much of their time (because the opportunity costs in lost wages, transportation, and child care are very high).

Another closely related problem is that it is difficult for adult-education providers to build programs around alternative-learning modalities such as Internet-based, self-directed learning, because regulatory barriers discourage implementation of such designs. For example, current provisions in the education code allow school districts to allocate up to five percent of their available adult-education funding for alternative-learning delivery systems. This provides some flexibility but few incentives to develop effective program designs. Although the five percent provisions allow distance learning, they require that al-

---

[39]Stephen Reder, "Synthetic Estimates of NALS Literacy Proficiencies from 1990 Census Microdata," Northwest Regional Educational Laboratory (for Office of Vocational and Adult Education/U.S. Department of Education), August 1994.

[40]This serious problem is also being addressed in current (2002) policy proposals.

ternative learning strategies be linked to some sort of use of educational technology for distance learning, making it difficult for providers to afford both the technology and investments in alternative staffing patterns required for field trips, coaching, and team-teaching. Although some adult-education programs provide counseling and guidance to help adult learners, the fact that this sort of support service generates no revenue is a strong disincentive to provide it. This is particularly problematic for Latino immigrants enrolled in adult education because the majority dropped out of school in the elementary grades and have little experience in effective learning, in navigating the complexities of course catalogues, and in planning and pursuing a course of self-directed learning on their own.

During 1999–2000, the California K–12 adult-education system served about 1.1 million students enrolled in core basic-skills and vocational-education courses.[41] The community-college system served more than 800,000 adult-education students. Thus, it is likely that about one million California Latinos— perhaps one in six of California's educationally disadvantaged Latinos—are enrolled in core-area adult- and continuing-education courses in any year. However, despite a high level of service-delivery inputs to Latino adult learning (measured in hours of instruction), outcomes are much less impressive.[42] Among Latinos enrolled in ESL, for example, only one-third are on record as having moved to a higher level. Of the remaining two-thirds, about one in five has achieved his or her personal learning objectives, although it is not clear that this means these persons have acquired the skills they need to function adequately. They have not moved to a higher level because their immediate needs were met. The remaining enrollees (slightly more than half of the total) appear to have had an unsuccessful experience.

Learner-Centered Instruction: A Framework for New Policy Directions

The foundation for improving the adult-learning opportunities available to California Latinos must be leadership in the political and policy arena that insists on

---

[41] California Department of Education, "Enrollment Report," 1999–2000. By core basic-skills classes I mean students enrolled in nonfee courses in the following of the 10 authorized areas: elementary, high school, ESL, citizenship, and vocational training. This is about 74 percent of the total adult-education enrollment.

[42] ESL classes are usually larger than any other adult-education courses, making them moneymakers for school districts because they generate more revenue than costs. Thus, while the inputs into service for Latino (and other) ESL learners may seem high, their value is exaggerated because instructional quality may often be inferior because of class size.

a reconceptualization of what adult education is, what it is to accomplish, and how it is to accomplish its objectives. This leadership must recognize that tinkering with time-worn service-delivery systems and administrative concepts or incrementally fine-tuning current funding strategies is inadequate. Such reconceptualization is needed to develop the administrative mechanisms for re-engineering and reorienting programs to deliver cost-effective outcome-oriented interventions.

Systemwide commitments are required but, at the same time, it would be wise to review a broad range of effective program designs to gain insights into best practices that may contribute to overall adult-education reform efforts. These include designs that are used only with special populations or in programs with low levels of funding. The environmental scan used in the California policymakers' and educational administrators' strategic planning in connection with intermittent efforts to achieve systemwide reform is generally too narrow. In reconsidering options for California Latinos, attention might be given not only to promising designs that are explicitly educational but not used systemwide (e.g., workplace literacy programs such as those piloted under the National Workplace Literacy Program, Even Start, EL/Civics), but to interventions from other fields, e.g., health-promotion campaigns, corporate training, and community-organizing programs for low-income families designed to build effective communication skills as well as an awareness of how "the system" works.[43] Such efforts will benefit adult learners from all ethnic groups.

Below I highlight critical system-improvement missions that must be undertaken to result in reform that would significantly improve adult-learning opportunities for California Latinos. I describe the policy initiatives already underway and new policy initiatives needed to make these system-improvement missions feasible. These system-development initiatives should be considered unilaterally by state government (whether the lead agency for adult education continues to be the California Department of Education or is a newly created department of labor). They should also be used to structure an agenda for public debate about the new directions that are necessary for adult-education reform in California. Such reform will benefit all adult-education customers. Such an ambitious and challenging adult-education reform agenda provides, at the very least, a way to frame dialogue between policymakers (the legislature, the administration) and

---

[43]By recommending instruction oriented toward understanding how "the system" works I mean the full range of organizational systems that govern contemporary social and economic life, e.g., government bureaucracies, private-sector employers' systems for hiring and promoting workers, the electoral system, functioning of the legal system, etc. The Secretary's Commission on Achieving the Necessary Skills framework officially identifies "Understanding Systems" as one of five broad areas of "high-performance" competencies.

the stakeholders in adult education—employers, civic leaders, social-program planners and administrators, and adult learners.

Systemic Initiative 1:
Better Manage Individual Clients' Learning Programs

A problem facing Latino immigrants, as well as inner-city and rural U.S.-born Latinos from economically disadvantaged families, is that their personal experiences have given them only minimal preparation for understanding how to navigate the institutional and informational systems that provide the scaffolding for achieving personal goals in contemporary society. Across all domains of endeavor, pursuing career mobility, managing lifelong learning, working to solve community problems, or working to make one's perspective prevail in the political process, sound understanding of the shape and the dynamics of these systems is needed as the basis for sound personal decisions and for transforming analytic or creative thinking into effective action. At the same time, the skills gap between the average Latino adult-education student's English-language communication, literacy, and information-management skills and the competencies he or she needs for agility and resiliency in contemporary society is so tremendous that lifelong learning should be seen not as a luxury but as a necessity. The adult-education system needs to find ways to provide ongoing support for lifelong learning (or, at the very least, protracted learning over a period of several years of intense personal skills development).

One priority in developing such a system must be to create systematic approaches for service providers to better understand students' skills-building needs and learning styles, and to help students to gain these insights themselves. This suggests a shift toward a system of interactive diagnostic assessment designed to provide the framework for developing a personal learning plan for each student, as opposed to testing or formal assessment. Such a system will need to provide not simply an initial assessment of where to place a student, but ongoing consultation and exit assessment and one-time consultation when a student leaves the formal-learning system. This information could be used for lifelong case management and for helping learners develop a strategy and navigate the challenges of learning in different kinds of environments (e.g., formal classroom, self-study, and distance learning).

Assessment is necessary in order to provide the foundation for counseling and coaching services that support self-directed learning. Counseling support to learners needs to include opportunities for reflection on what students have learned, discussion of options (including tradeoffs and ways to manage time for learning), and personal coaching support to help individual students understand how their aspirations and learning activities fit into their lives.

Systemic Initiative 2:
Enhance English-Language Instructional Strategies

Adult education's role in building Latino immigrants' English-language communication skills must be reconceptualized as a series of strategic investments to support *sustained* English-language learning to move from pidgin to proficiency—as distinct from so-called "survival English." To achieve such a transformation, the adult-education system needs to make systematic and focused investments in a mixture of improved teacher training, more time for such training, more time for developing appropriate curricula, and a commitment to genuinely individualizing and contextualizing language learning. Much more instructional attention must be given to the ability to communicate proactively, to express one's own perspectives and style, and to pursue one's own goals, for example, in negotiating with others, inspiring team members, providing reflective feedback, and working collaboratively to understand or rephrase texts so others can understand them.

It will be critical to develop program models designed to extend learning beyond the classroom; "seat time" is not magic. Ultimately, the service-delivery system for ESL must be transformed into one in which English learning begins with an individualized, intensive, formal orientation to principles for effective English learning, coupled with a commitment to providing access to a continuous stream of followup services after a learner has begun to familiarize himself or herself with English and initiated an informal, but serious, course of personal skills development. These services include guidance, coaching, and support for self-directed ongoing learning. Adoption of such a two-phase service-delivery strategy will make ESL instruction more effective and more cost-effective—for both learners and taxpayers.

Systemic Initiative 3:
Focus the System on Building Learning-to-Learn Competencies

Latino immigrants who left school at a very early age are disproportionately harmed by adult-education-programs' inattention to developing "learning-to-learn" skills. Because most Latino adult-education students are elementary-school dropouts, they have little experience with effective strategies for developing skills on their own.[44] California-educated Latino youth whose skills development faltered or who dropped out of high school are also very likely to benefit from adult basic education (ABE) instruction with a focus on learning-to-

---

[44]Traditional "stand and deliver" instruction in rural areas of Mexico places less of an emphasis on skills-building and learning-to-learn than on covering a set curriculum of obligatory bits of knowledge.

learn—because for them school attendance was often more a matter of going into a chaotic arena of conflicting social pressures and subtexts than of entering an environment that fostered learning. In particular, attention to enhancement of learning-to-learn skills can provide these youths, many of whom are English-proficient, easier access to vocational-training programs and a greater likelihood of success in completing them.

There are several promising service-delivery strategies for overcoming the problems of inexperienced or resistant learners, but a shift in adult-education policy will be necessary if they are to be adopted throughout the system. For example, it would be useful to rely more on tutoring and mentoring to take an adult learner through the process of solving a set of problems, or struggling to build new competencies—in part because the tutor or mentor can help the learner formulate learning strategies that are fashioned to their particular needs. This sort of intense, personal interaction is also a key to helping inexperienced and tentative learners engage in a sustained effort without getting stalled at "bumps in the road" that, from the learner's perspective, look like washed-out bridges. To develop programs that effectively use this design, emphasis will need to shift from reliance on professional certification as the basis for effective instruction to forming instructional teams with complementary skills sets. Such teams might include, for example, former adult-education students or Latino college students who "know what it's like" but who have had personal success in their learning endeavors. Designs built on cooperative learning, where the learning team is made up of student peers also have promise. California has extensively experimented with workplace literacy programs, a program design that, in addition to an emphasis on contextual learning, relies on coworkers participating as members of a learning team. Yet another instructional design, Family English Literacy (the basis of the federal Migrant Even Start program) has been used very effectively in some California communities.

Systemic Initiative 4:
Encourage Program Designs that Provide Intensive, Accelerated-Learning Opportunities

The Latino population, because of a large number of young working-poor adults, incurs substantial opportunity costs in attending adult-education classes. This makes the lack of intensive instruction problematic. We need systematic and serious attention to developing program designs that support accelerated learning. Promising strategies include greater use of team teaching (despite higher hourly instructional costs) to increase learning efficacy, smaller class size, and investments in support for out-of-class self-directed learning to supplement classroom experience. Locating adult-education programs in public-housing venues or even in privately owned housing where Latino adult-education students are concentrated would permit more-intensive class attendance, particularly in urban areas where increasing numbers of adult-education students feel it is dangerous to go out to attend night school.

Increased use of cooperative-learning strategies to extend learning beyond the classroom has promise because it builds flexibility in communicating, provides opportunities for reflecting on and trying out learning techniques, and reaffirms the relevance of traditional Latino values about the importance of mutualism and cooperative action. Adult-education commitment to mutualism, in addition to its utility as a technique for teaching a group of learners at widely varying levels of communication competency, has the benefit of underscoring the utility of social capital, of providing personal collaboration and support, and as being a resource to rely on in order to succeed in the unfamiliar domains of mainstream institutions such as adult schools and community colleges.

Systemic Initiative 5:
Adopt New Strategies to Ensure Instructional Quality

Two primary approaches have traditionally been used for adult-education quality assurance—reliance on certification to monitor program performance, and reliance on educational credentials and in-service training to ensure instructional quality. These are sensible strategies but they are not adequate.

Current program-monitoring procedures for quality assurance are increasingly divorced from serious analysis of real-world learning outcomes. Of special importance in improving instructional quality for Latino adult learners with low levels of literacy and little experience in a formal educational setting are customer-satisfaction surveys and analyses of actual skills-development gains in relation to learner characteristics to determine which subgroups of students are being served effectively and which are not. Such analyses (e.g., customer surveys or focus groups at the end of a course), in which students are encouraged to reflect on how the adult education has concretely and practically affected their skills levels (and where it has failed to have an impact), could generate information that is immediately and practically relevant for instructional improvement. This information could also help students assess what they may need to do to reach their desired learning goals. These types of program-evaluation tools have been used effectively in a wide range of settings but are not used at all in the California adult-education system because skills gains, as measured by the Comprehensive Adult Student Assessment System (CASAS) tests, have become the centerpiece of performance-based accountability. One difficulty is that standardized measurement systems such as CASAS, which generates a numerical scale score, are bureaucratically attractive because they provide an easy tool for comparing and statistically analyzing the performance of multiple programs, but the tool is not very credible in assessing what that "performance" actually entails, i.e., what learners will actually be able to do in a real-world context after an X-point gain on the scale.[45] The other difficulty is that these sorts of measurements provide no insights to instructors about how to teach better or to students about how to learn better. A high priority must be to require multidimensional approaches to assessing adult-education program performance instead of relying on a single-flawed measure with uncertain relevance to desired real-world skills outcomes.

Current adult-education staff recruitment and skills-development training efforts are hampered by their reliance on credentials as the basis for staff recruitment and on episodic short-term training (i.e., workshops on selected educational topics) for in-service training. They are also compromised in that they give little weight to assessing cultural competence as an element in adult-education instructors' skills repertoire, even though a critical concern is instructors' ability to help Latino students bridge the cultural, linguistic, and cognitive distance between very different social and cognitive universes. Staff-development strategies, as currently implemented, are particularly problematic in the rural and inner-city areas where Latinos are concentrated because they place the full burden of program quality improvement on instructors, many of whom are part-time employees juggling two or more jobs.

In-service training should move away from intermittent individual training toward practical team-based collaborative skills development whereby instructors work together to develop new curricula, new resource materials, and new ways to provide one another with peer support. For example, adult-education instructors, as part of their in-service training, could work with colleagues in a local adult school to develop resources for inquiry-oriented learning that would facilitate Latino adult-education student efforts to move from traditional passive learning to active exploratory learning. Or in areas with growing numbers of indigenous Latino immigrants whose first language is Mixtec or Maya, the practical focus of instructor skills development could be to develop materials to respond to the special ESL learning needs of these hard-to-serve populations.

---

[45]CASAS attempts to overcome this problem by publishing "crosswalks," i.e., a table that relates CASAS numerical scores to other adult-education competencies, such as the framework developed by the Secretary's Commission on Achieving the Necessary Skills. The difficulty here is that there is little empirical basis for such inferences, in particular because there has not been an adequate effort to determine how cultural and linguistic backgrounds might modulate the purported equivalence between CASAS scores and a poorly defined cluster of skills in interacting with systems that have a distinctively mainstream U.S. character.

Systemic Initiative 6:
Provide Incentives for Public-Private Collaboration in Providing Adult-Learning Opportunities

Because so many Latino adult learners are working poor with little free time for attendance in formal classroom instruction, workplace-learning program designs have particular promise in responding to their needs. During the 1990s, much was learned about the appropriate strategies for customizing instruction to target specific, practical functional-competency development—including English-language communication. Analytic and communication skills built in the context of workplace learning, if curricula are developed thoughtfully, can be transferred to managing family life and participating effectively in civic life. Using the SCANS framework to inventory high-performance, multipurpose skills needed for success has tremendous promise for programs that can leverage immediate skills gains, dramatically increasing worker productivity and upward career mobility and, at the same time, providing the basis for all-around personal-skills development.[46]

Policy Initiatives to Make Adult-Education System Redesign a Reality

In early 2002, the Adult-Education Sub-Group put forward several recommendations, made as part of ongoing revisions to California's Master Plan for Education. These recommendations, made under the auspices of the Joint Committee to Develop a Master Plan for Education—Kindergarten Through University, represent a promising first step in adult-education reform. Major recommendations include the following:

- Revise the state framework of authorized areas of instruction to respond better to contemporary needs and to emphasize civic participation, workforce-based learning, and improved integration of oral communication, literacy, and practical life skills in ESL;
- Use multiple indicators to assess students' skills gains and longitudinal assessment of students' skills gains as they progress through a series of courses and learning experiences (not simply within the context of a single course);
- Develop a more seamless service-delivery system, building closer interagency collaboration among adult schools, community colleges, and com-

---

[46]Lauren Resnick, "Literacy in School and Out," in *Daedalus* (special issue: Literacy in America), (Spring 1990).

munity-based adult education providers, as well as investments in distance-learning infrastructure;[47]
- Make available additional resources for support services and programs available to all adult learners to provide guidance in ongoing education to match students' personal and educational goals (i.e., lifelong learning);
- Allocate funding for adult-education on the basis of local indicators of need for service (e.g., population, levels of educational attainment, limited English proficiency, income levels, and economic conditions); and
- Increase adult-education funding to match the revenue limit for the K–12 system.

These recommendations point in the right direction but, as is commonly the case in consensus documents, the details for policy reform are not always clearly articulated. We will ultimately need a full set of specifications for systemic change as the framework for a coherent set of policy initiatives. Interestingly, the Master Plan recommendations regarding funding are the most explicitly articulated ones. They are well justified and would be likely to make a major difference in systemwide priorities by allowing service providers in affected areas (particularly those with high rates of Latino immigration) to focus less on making do with available resources and more on designing population-appropriate adult-learning programs. To enhance this initial policy agenda we need to develop administrative and funding guidelines that reshape the adult-education system. Instructional effectiveness should be a key element in efforts to respond affordably to very high levels of need for skills development (i.e., with a focus on outcomes, not simply on inputs or level of services made available).

Below I suggest additional policy initiatives for improving adult-education services for California Latinos and all adult-education enrollees. These policy options range from working within the framework of the State Master Plan (and current policy-reform efforts) to enacting fundamental changes in system funding or administrative guidelines.

- Further modify the system of funding based on average daily attendance (ADA) to encourage investments in counseling. From a systems-analysis perspective, increased unit costs for counseling are likely to be economically justified by: decreased course dropout rates and improved slot utilization, more-rapid skills development, and, during the postprogram phase, low-cost benefits—assuming that with some support students can more successfully persist with self-directed learning. Policy options include authorizing funding for cost-reimbursement of optimal levels of counseling in rela-

---

[47]This recommendation is superior to the governor's 2002–2003 proposal, which is flawed in that it envisions creation of a super-agency, an administrative reorganization initiative that does little to address the challenges in achieving the consensus objective of developing a more "seamless" system for providing adult-learning options.

tion to direct instruction, and more indirect strategies, such as adjustment to funding level based on customer satisfaction and real-world outcomes.
- Pursue partnerships and cofunding opportunities. Because adult education can make tangible contributions to civic life in California, it is appropriate for local governments to invest in developing the civic competencies of those who live in their jurisdictions. Policy initiatives should be undertaken to explore programs that combine state adult-education funding with federal funding from grants to local municipalities such as Community Services Block Grant and Community Development Block Grant funds. Efforts should be initiated to make adult basic-skills development an integral part of Proposition 10–funded services for families with young children. Increased attention should be given to special-purpose adult education in key areas such as health promotion where, for example, funding from private foundations such as The California Endowment could be used in conjunction with state and/or federal adult-education funding to improve Latino adults' ability to communicate effectively with English-speaking healthcare personnel.
- Increase investments in quality instruction and capacity building. Although the systems currently invest a substantial amount (almost $5 million annually) on in-service training, a minority of adult-education instructors attend this training. There are unanswered questions as to whether the instructors who have the most need for skills development are able to participate in this training because many adult schools still rely heavily on part-time instructors moonlighting from other jobs. For these employees, it is difficult to find the time to attend training workshops, and it may well be that there are not adequate incentives to make such workshops worthwhile. Investments in teacher training should increase, and adult-education providers should be required to plan more carefully to integrate in-service training into service-improvement efforts. As my discussion of systemic initiatives outlined, investments in project-based staff development that link skills enhancement to collaborative work in planning and developing resources—if they respond to specific local learners' needs—can be a win-win situation for service providers who pay for staff training, for instructional staff, and for their students who make use of newly developed instructional resources.
- Remove funding and regulatory barriers to deployment of instructional teams that combine certified and noncertified personnel. In addition to addressing the problem of limited financial resources for adult education, removing the requirement that contact hours must entail face-to-face contact between students and a certified teacher would tend to support instructional strategies with more finely textured attention to individuals' learning needs, provide more opportunities for modeling effective teamwork and collaborative-literacy practices, and permit greater use of project-based learning strategies with learners. In this context, volunteers should be considered as

significant resources for supporting Latino adults' lifelong learning. California-born teenagers and young adults who are bilingual have been recruited as volunteer instructors in ESL/citizenship classes. This experience has been quite promising. Removal of this barrier would also be likely to have the positive impact of increasing the range of potential adult-education service providers, thereby facilitating Latino students' access to adult-learning opportunities, increasing levels of cultural competence among service providers, and encouraging innovative designs such as those currently being piloted in EL/civics programs (where funding rests on a formula combining cost reimbursement and outcome-based payment for service without requiring student contact with certified staff).

- Authorize establishment of adult charter schools. The charter-school mechanism offers an alternative means to provide new governance and fresh perspectives on adult-learning services. Ideally, municipal or county government might be charged with authorizing such entities, or the decision might be made by referendum to overcome the obvious self-interest that would lead local educational agencies to oppose such changes in administrative structure. In Latino-majority communities, an adult charter school movement might lead to a rebirth of the popular movement in the 1960s and 1970s to create *calmecacs*[48] as culturally appropriate institutions for responding to Latinos' learning objectives and revaluing of traditional cultural resources. While the public debate on charter schools points to socialization of children in a public institutional context as one of the great benefits of even mediocre public schools, this argument is less compelling with respect to adult learners and provision of adult-learning opportunities.

Conclusion

In the long run, the general strategy for adult education in California will need to move from the current piecemeal system toward an affirmative and comprehensive effort to convey a vision of the adult-education system needed for California's well-being in the 21st century.[49] Latinos will be major beneficiaries of sys-

---

[48] *"Calmecac"* is a Nahuatl term referring to "houses of learning" in pre-Columbian Mexico. In the 1960s and 1970s Chicano activists experimented with these alternative-learning institutions, which relied on Freirian theory and popular education strategies of inquiry-based learning while emphasizing exploration of traditional Mesoamerican concepts as a source of inspiration for cultural revitalization.

[49] Although this refers primarily to efforts to fine-tune the current system of ADA-based reimbursement, isolated solutions, such as recommendations for increased resources for distance-learning, cannot be expected to yield real improvements in Latinos' adult-learning opportunities unless comprehensive efforts are made to link adult educa-

temic reform, and it is not unreasonable to expect Latino legislative representatives to take a leadership role in defining the direction and mechanisms to be used in adult-education reform. The key to successful adult-education reform will be to propose an integrated package of logically related funding and regulatory initiatives that address all of the major components that need to be fixed: provisions for allocating financial resources to adult-education providers, framework for defining allowable activities to contribute to lifelong learning, processes for staff recruitment, deployment, and in-service training, and methods for assessing individual student progress and evaluating programmatic success. Although it will be tempting to address these disparate aspects of service-delivery system dynamics on a piecemeal basis, it is not clear that this strategy will be sufficient to bring about the changes that are so urgently needed.

Because learning is an intensely personal experience and because the information-handling demands of California society are escalating so rapidly, the needs of Latino adult learners can be addressed effectively only with a new, culturally responsive vision of what adult-education services are and how they should be customized to address the specific skills development of different subpopulations of adult learners. Whatever specific policy options are explored, it will be crucial to focus on excellence in order to ensure that Latino adult learners are not relegated to second-class socio-economic status because the only learning opportunities they can access are second-rate ones.

Equitable funding for adult education is a critical social-policy goal. It must be coupled with systematic efforts to ensure that enhanced funding for adult-learning programs is used effectively to configure a system that is responsive to the particular needs of diverse learners, offers more modalities for adult learning, and focuses squarely on the challenge of initiating and providing ongoing support for lifelong learning. California Latinos' social, economic, and political equality is compromised by their educational disadvantage. For millions, the adult-education system represents a lifeline in a turbulent sea of rapid change. It will be crucial for all stakeholders—Latino adults in search of quality adult-learning opportunities, California employers, and the general public—to insist on a 21st-century system of quality adult learning for educationally disadvantaged Californians, including Latinos.

---

tion to other community efforts and resources. In the case of distance learning, for example, this would necessarily include attention to the promise of community technology centers, multi-agency efforts to overcome the digital divide, and availability of software appropriate for low-literate Spanish-speaking adult learners.

References

Allensworth, Elaine M., and Refugio I. Rochín. 1999. "The Mexicanization of Rural California: A Socio-Demographic Analysis 1980–1997." Julian Samora Research Institute, Michigan State University, January.

Bach, Robert. 1990. "Report of the Changing Relations Project." Ford Foundation.

BW Associates. 1994. "Mobilizing for Competitiveness: Linking Education and Training to Jobs." California Business Roundtable, January.

California Department of Education. 1999. "Federal Report 1998–1999." Report to Division of Adult Education and Literacy, U.S. Department of Education, December. http//www.cde.ca.gov.

———. "California State Plan 1999–2004." Plan submitted to Division of Adult Education and Literacy, U.S. Department of Education, April 9, 1999, under provisions of Workforce Investment Act, Title II. http//www.cde.ca.gov.

———. "Student Progress and Goal Attainment Report: Federally Funded WIA/AEFLA Programs in California 1999–2000." http//www.cde.ca.gov.

California's Little Hoover Commission. 2002. "We the People: Helping Newcomers Become Californians." www.lhc.ca.gov.

Carnevale, Anthony P., and Donna M. Desrochers. 1999. "Getting Down to Business: Matching Welfare Recipients' Skills to Jobs that Train." Educational Testing Service.

CASAS. 1989. *A Survey of Newly Legalized Persons in California.* California Health and Welfare Agency.

de Cos, Patricia L., et al. 2000. "K–12 Performance." In *A Coordinated Approach to Raising the Socio-Economic Status of Latinos in California,* ed. Lopez, Puddefoot, and Gándara. California Research Bureau, March.

Fein, David. 1989. "The Social Sources of Census Omission: Racial and Ethnic Differences in Omission Rates in Recent U.S. Censuses." Ph.D. dissertation, submitted to Department of Sociology, Princeton University, June.

Fein, David, and Kirsten West. 1988. "The Sources of Census Undercount: Findings from the 1986 Los Angeles Test Census," *Survey Methodology Journal* 14(2): 223–40.

Fix, Michael, and Wendy Zimmerman. 1999. "All Under One Roof: Mixed-Status Families in an Era of Reform." The Urban Institute, June.

Frey, William H. 2000. "The Diversity Myth." In *Diversity in America—A Supplement to American Demographics.*

Guillen, Liz. 2001. "California Latino Students: Continuing Challenges That Cannot Be Ignored." Testimony to Senate Education Committee Informational Hearing on the Status of Latino Public School Students, January 31.

Jenkins, Lynn B., and Irwin S. Kirsch. 1994. *Adult Literacy in California: Results of the State Adult Literacy Survey.* Educational Testing Service.

———. 1996. *Adult Literacy in California: Results of the State Adult Literacy Survey.* Office of Educational Research and Improvement, U.S. Department of Education.

Johnson, Hans. 1999. "How Many Californians? A Review of Population Projections for the State." Public Policy Institute of California, October.

Joint Board Task Force on Noncredit and Adult Education. 1998. "Challenges Opportunities Changes." Final Report, December. http://www.otan.us/webfarm/jbtf/index.html.

Kirsch, Irwin S., Ann Jungeblut, and Anne Campbell. 1992. "Beyond the School Doors: The Literacy Needs of Job Seekers Served by the U.S. Department of Labor." Educational Testing Service, September.

Kissam, Edward. 1995. "Reconsidering Literacy in a Transnational Context." Paper presented in National Center for Adult Literacy Panel, 3d Binational Conference on Adult Education, May.

Kissam, Edward, and Stephen Reder. 1997. "Responding to Diversity: Strategies and Initiatives to Support Lifelong Learning for Limited English Adults in California." Final Report to Adult Education and Planning Unit, Aguirre International, April.

Kissam, Edward, et al. 1999. "Evaluation of the Central Valley Partnership." Final Report to the Civic Culture Program, James F. Irvine Foundation, The Aguirre Group, December.

———. 2000. "No Longer Children: Case Studies of the Living and Working Conditions of the Youth Who Harvest America's Crops." Aguirre International Report to Office of Policy, U.S. Department of Labor, May 2001.

Lomnitz, Larissa. 1977. *Networks and Marginality: Life in a Mexican Shantytown.* Academic Press, N.Y.

Lopez, E. S. 1995. "Education and Integration Prospects in Rural California." *Immigration and the Changing Face of Rural California.* Asilomar.

Lopez, Elias, Enrique Ramirez, and Refugio Rochín. 1999. "Latinos and Economic Development in California." California Research Bureau, June.

National Center on Education and the Economy. 1990. "America's Choice: High Skills or Low Wages!" The Commission on the Skills of the American Workforce, June.

Portes, Alejandro. 2002. "Immigration's Aftermath," *American Prospect,* April.

Stephen Reder. 1994. "Synthetic Estimates of NALS Literacy Proficiencies from 1990 Census Microdata." Northwest Regional Educational Laboratory (for Office of Vocational and Adult Education/U.S. Department of Education), August.

Resnick, Lauren. 1990. "Literacy in School and Out." *Daedalus* (Special issue: Literacy in America), Spring.

Rumbaut, Ruben, and Wayne A. Cornelius, eds. 1995. *California's Immigrant Children.* Center for U.S.-Mexican Studies, University of California, San Diego.

Secretary's Commission on Achieving Necessary Skills. 1993. "Teaching the SCANS Competencies." U.S. Department of Labor.

———. 1991. "What Work Requires of Schools: A SCANS Report for America 2000." U.S. Department of Labor.

———. 1992. "Learning a Living: A SCANS Report for America 2000." U.S. Department of Labor.

Stein, Sondra. 1995. "Equipped for the Future: A Customer-Driven Vision for Adult Literacy and Lifelong Learning." National Institute for Literacy, July.

———. 1997. "Equipped for the Future: A Reform Agenda for Adult Literacy and Lifelong Learning." National Institute for Literacy, February.

Suárez-Orozco, Carola and Marcelo. 1995. *Transformations: Migration, Family Life, and Achievement motivation Among Latino Adolescents.* Stanford University Press.

Tafoya, Sonya. 2002. "The Linguistic Landscape of California Schools." The Public Policy Institute of California, vol. 3, no. 4 (February).

U.S. Department of Justice, Immigration and Naturalization Service. 1992. "Report on the Legalized Alien Population." March.

Wells, Janet. 2000. "Racial Divide in Boom Time, Study Reports." *San Francisco Chronicle*, September 5.

Chapter 6

Illness and Wellness:
The Latino Paradox

David E. Hayes-Bautista

Introduction

The health of California Latinos presents perhaps the clearest example of an asset at risk. Lingering stereotypes to the contrary, their health is generally quite good, with far lower death rates from the three leading causes of death in the United States—heart disease, cancer, and stroke—than those of non-Latinos. This laudable health outcome is achieved with very low health expenditures and low use of physicians and hospitals. If all Californians shared the same level of health as Latinos, the state would lose nearly 50,000 fewer lives per year to the three leading causes of death, and at far lower cost than at present.

Latino populations, however, face grave health risks for the following reasons:
- Cultural assimilation appears to erode healthy behaviors and is accompanied by a general decrease in health status.
- Latino physicians, who are generally better able to communicate with Latino patients, are in short supply.

- A large percentage of Latinos are not covered by health insurance. (See Chapter 7)

"Minority Health-Disparity" Policy

On February 21, 1998, President Clinton announced, via national radio address, a new initiative to achieve a self-described ambitious goal: to eliminate long-standing health disparities experienced by racial and ethnic minority populations in the United States. He condemned the fact that minorities had not fully shared in the general improvement in the nation's health status, citing a number of indicators he vowed to change:

> Minorities suffer from certain diseases at up to five times the rate of white Americans. For example, infant mortality rates are 2½ times higher for African-Americans and 1½ times higher for Native Americans. African-American males under 65 suffer from prostate cancer at nearly twice the rate of whites; Vietnamese women suffer from cervical cancer at nearly five times the rate of whites; and Latinos have two to three times the rate of stomach cancer.[1]

On Clinton's initiative, the federal government was to mobilize its resources, seek the cooperation of the private sector and local communities, and eliminate—once and for all—health disparities that had for too long been treated as intractable.

This initiative was based on the policy model of minority health, often referred to as the "race and ethnic health disparities" model, that drives most health policy at the federal level today. As is so often mentioned by the Office of Minority Health, a number of national health problems appear to be related to the sole fact of race and ethnicity:

> Compelling evidence that race and ethnicity correlate with persistent, and often increasing, health disparities among U.S. populations demands national attention.[2]

Race, ethnicity, and poverty tug at each other in the inner city, with some health problems more the result of race and ethnicity, and others more the result

---

[1] Health and Human Services Press Office, White House Fact Sheet, February 21, 1998.

[2] U.S. Department of Health and Human Services Web site, Office of Minority Health, "Eliminating Racial and Ethnic Disparities in Health," 1998. Available at: http://raceandhealth.hhs.gov/sidebars/sbinitover.htm. Accessed August 17, 2000.

of poverty and low levels of education. However, all problems implicate a resonance between the two:

> Urban health problems arise from the complex interaction of socioeconomic factors, behavior, environment, and disease that is related to race and ethnicity.[3]

Irrespective of their origin in either race and ethnicity or poverty and low level of education, the health problems created by the urban health burden are increased illness, early death, higher mortality, higher infant mortality, and shorter life expectancy. Although this is the model that many policymakers have in mind when they begin to address the health-care issues of Latinos, it is not supported by health data.

The Latino Epidemiological Paradox

Although it has become customary to speak of "minority health" in this country in terms of "health disparities," with minority health status being depicted as worse than nonminority, Latino health has not fit this pattern. Rather, Latino health in California (as in Arizona and Texas) presents a picture that has become labeled the "Latino epidemiological paradox": In spite of higher risk factors (e.g., lower income, lower educational status, less access to health care), the Latino health profile is generally stronger than that of non-Latinos, with a few notable exceptions.

This paradox is measured in many ways. One common method is to use death rates, since every death is recorded, by means of a death certificate. The death rate for heart disease is not quite the same as the prevalence of heart disease. However, since we do not know how many people have nonfatal heart disease, absent a major survey that includes extensive laboratory work, we will never know the prevalence of heart disease, so instead we use deaths as one means of determining the difference between Latino and non-Latino health status. This type of analysis rests on the assumption that there is some relationship between the prevalence of a disease (e.g., heart disease) and deaths that are due to that disease. California's mortality profile for 1995 provides an illustration of this Latino epidemiological paradox.[4]

---

[3] American College of Physicians, "Inner City Health Care," *Annals of Internal Medicine* 15(126), (March 1997): 485–90.

[4] D. E. Hayes-Bautista and P. Hsu, *Health of Latino California: Chartbook 1997*. UCLA: Center for the Study of Latino Health, 1998.

All Causes of Death

The usual comparative metric for causes of death is the age-adjusted number of deaths for every 100,000 persons. The following data from the California Department of Health Services, Summary Death file, show how many persons died in 1995 out of 100,000 Latinos and 100,000 non-Latinos. The non-Latino population is predominantly white, but includes African-American, Asian and Pacific-Islander, and Native-American populations. Age adjustment controls for the fact that the Latino population is much younger than the non-Latino population—eliminating the disparity between younger and older populations. Any younger population, irrespective of ethnicity, will have fewer deaths than an older population.

California's non-Latino death rate in 1995 was 458.9 of every 100,000. By contrast, among Latinos it was only 334.6 of every 100,000 (see Figure 6.1). The important observation is that even though the Latino population generally has far lower income, education, and access to care (as detailed in other chapters in this book), its overall death rate is lower. This contravenes the conventional model, which holds that lower income, lower education, and lower access to care result in higher mortality. The Division of Disadvantaged Assistance, in its 1990 *Health Status of the Disadvantaged Chartbook,* asserted: "The age-adjusted death rates for other races were higher than those for Whites."[5] Although this may hold for some populations, it is not the pattern observed for Latinos.

Specific Causes of Death

The leading causes of death in California, as in the U.S., are heart disease, cancer and stroke. These are the leading causes of death for Latinos, but at rates far lower than the non-Latino population. (see Table 6.1).

Relative Risk

While the Latino rates are lower than the non-Latino rates for most causes of death, there are a few causes for which the Latino rates are higher. These mortality patterns can be summarized quickly using a *relative risk* ratio, which shows whether one population is at higher or lower risk than another for a specific cause of death. If the Latino and non-Latino populations had the same age-adjusted mortality rate, the relative risk for Latinos would be 1.00; that is, the

---

[5]Division of Disadvantaged Assistance, *Health Status of the Disadvantaged Chartbook,* HHS: DHHS publication No. (HRSA) HRS-P-DV 90–01, 1990.

Figure 6.1. Non-Latino and Latino Age-Adjusted Mortality Rates per 100,000 Californians, 1995

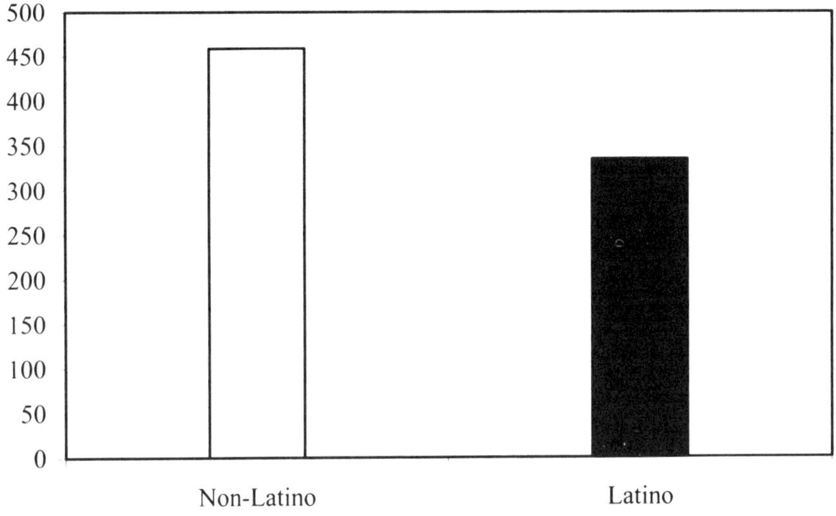

Source: California, Department of Health Services, Summary Death File, 1996.

chances of a Latino dying of that disease would be the same as a non-Latino's. A relative risk of 0.50 means that a Latino is half as likely to die of that cause as a non-Latino. If the relative risk were 2.00, a Latino would be twice as likely to die as a non-Latino.

Figure 6.2 shows the relative risk, comparing Latinos to non-Latinos, for 11 causes of death. Some patterns are immediately noticeable.

Lower relative risk.

In Figure 6.2, the clear bars indicate causes from which Latinos are less likely to die than non-Latinos. Latinos have the lowest relative risk (r.r.) for chronic obstructive pulmonary disease (COPD): At 0.32, this means that Latinos are about one-third as likely to die from this cause as non-Latinos. In ascending order, the other causes of death are: suicide (r.r. = 0.44), cancer (r.r. = 0.58), heart disease (r.r. = 0.67), pneumonia (r.r. = 0.71), AIDS (r.r. = 0.74), and cerebrovascular disease (r.r. = .75).

Table 6.1. Age-Adjusted Death Rates, Non-Latino and Latino, California, 1995

Cause of Death	Non-Latino	Latino
1. Cancer	120.9	70.1
2. Heart disease	120.5	80.2
3. Cerebrovascular disease	26.4	19.9
4. Unintentional injuries	26.1	25.7
5. Chronic obstructive pulmonary disease (COPD)	22.0	7.0
6. AIDS	19.5	14.4
7. Pneumonia	15.4	10.9
8. Suicide	12.6	5.6
9. Diabetes	9.9	16.8
10. Homicide	9.3	16.8
11. Cirrhosis		13.9
	8.7	

Source: Deaths as categorized by the California Department of Health Services, Summary Death File, 1995.

Same Relative Risk

Unintentional injuries (e.g., motor-vehicle accidents, industrial accidents, etc.) are the one cause of death for which the Latino risk is virtually identical to the non-Latino risk (death rate 25.7 compared to 26.1). The relative risk of 0.98 means that Latinos are as likely as non-Latinos to die of this cause. Given that Latino death rates are usually 30 percent lower than non-Latino rates, a cause of death for which the Latino rate is nearly identical to the non-Latino rate should be an area of concern.

Motor-Vehicle Accidents

In a disturbing subtrend, the Latino male death rate for motor-vehicle accidents, (a subset of unintentional injuries), is higher than the non-Latino male death rate (20.4 compared to 16.7). The Latina female rate of 8.1 is higher than the non-Latino female rate of 7.9.

Higher Relative Risk

The Latino risk is substantially higher than the non-Latino risk for some causes. Latinos are nearly half-again as likely as non-Latinos to die (r.r. = 1.59) from cirrhosis, which may be caused by either drinking or hepatitis. Diabetes has often been considered a Latino disease, and the risk of dying of this cause is nearly 70 percent higher (r.r. = 1.70) than the non-Latino risk. In Table 6.1, the

Figure 6.2. Latino to Non-Latino Rate of Relative Risk for Major Causes of Death in California, 1995

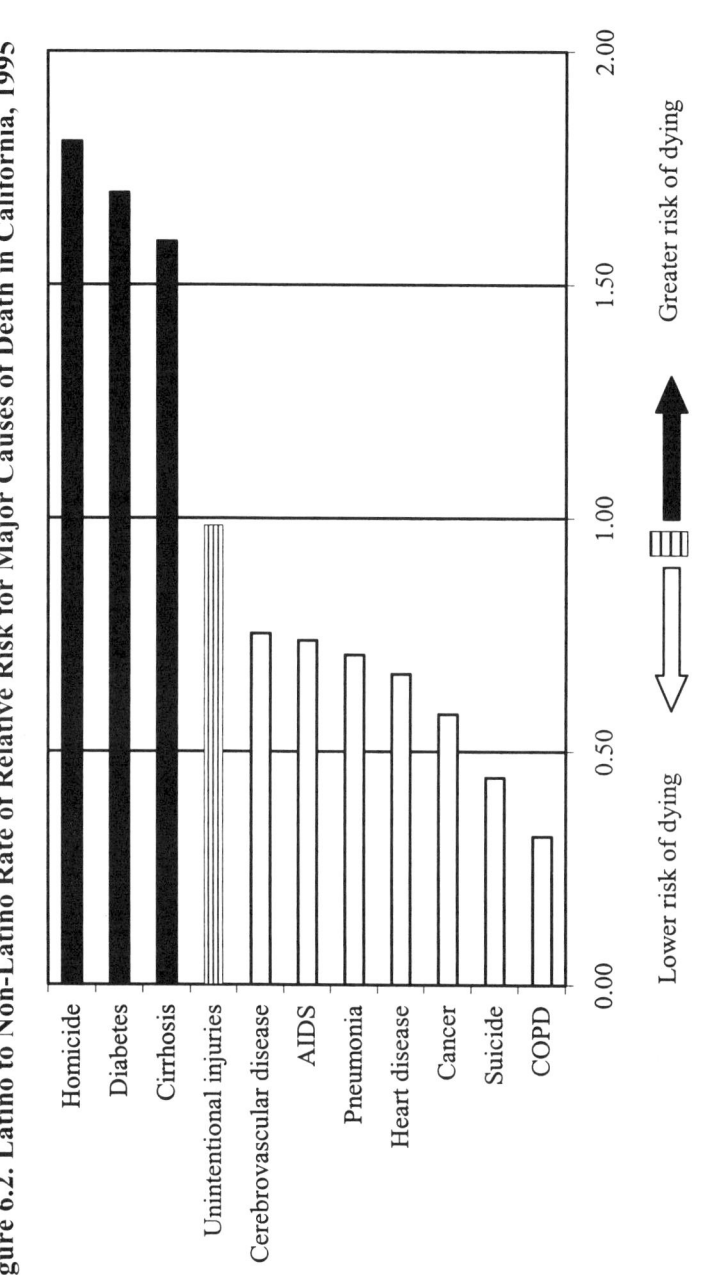

Source: California, Department of Health Services, Summary Death File, 1996.

Latino homicide death rate is nearly identical to the Latino diabetes death rate. However, Latinos are somewhat more likely than non-Latinos to die of homicide (r.r. = 1.81) than of diabetes. Clearly, cirrhosis, diabetes, and homicide should be considered priority areas for Latino health-prevention efforts.

Greater Latino risk factors—lower income, lower education, and less access to care—have led many federal programs to announce that Latinos suffer the same health disparities as other minority populations. Data consistently show just the opposite. Thanks to the Latino epidemiological paradox, the overall Latino health profile is quite strong.

Latino health priorities need to be normed on variances from the Latino norm. Some gender-related patterns, age-group patterns, and occupational patterns—specifically for farmworkers—vary from this norm and require special attention from policymakers.

Gender Variations

U.S. males have a higher mortality rate than U.S. females. This general mortality pattern holds true for California for both Latinos and non-Latinos. Among Latinos, males have an overall relative risk of 1.47 compared to Latinas—meaning Latino males are 47 percent more likely to die than Latinas. Among non-Latinos, the male relative risk is 1.33; that is, non-Latino males are 33 percent more likely to die than non-Latino females. In comparing the genders across ethnicity, the Latino male mortality rate is 39.3 percent lower than the non-Latino male rate (see Figure 6.3). The Latina mortality rate is 44.7 percent lower than the non-Latino female rate.

Specific Causes Of Death
While Latino males are generally 47 percent more likely to die than Latinas, Latino males are strikingly more at risk for some causes of death than Latinas. Figure 6.4 shows Latino male-to-female relative risk for five causes of death. The differences are sobering:
- Latino males are more than 10 times as likely to die from AIDS than Latinas (r.r. = 10.54).
- Latino males are more than six times as likely to die from homicide than Latinas (r.r. = 6.42).
- Latino males are more than three times as likely to die from cirrhosis than Latinas (r.r. = 3.41).
- Latino males are more than twice as likely to die from motor-vehicle accidents than Latinas (r.r. = 2.52).

Figure 6.3. Age-Adjusted Mortality Rates per 100,000 People by Gender in California, 1995

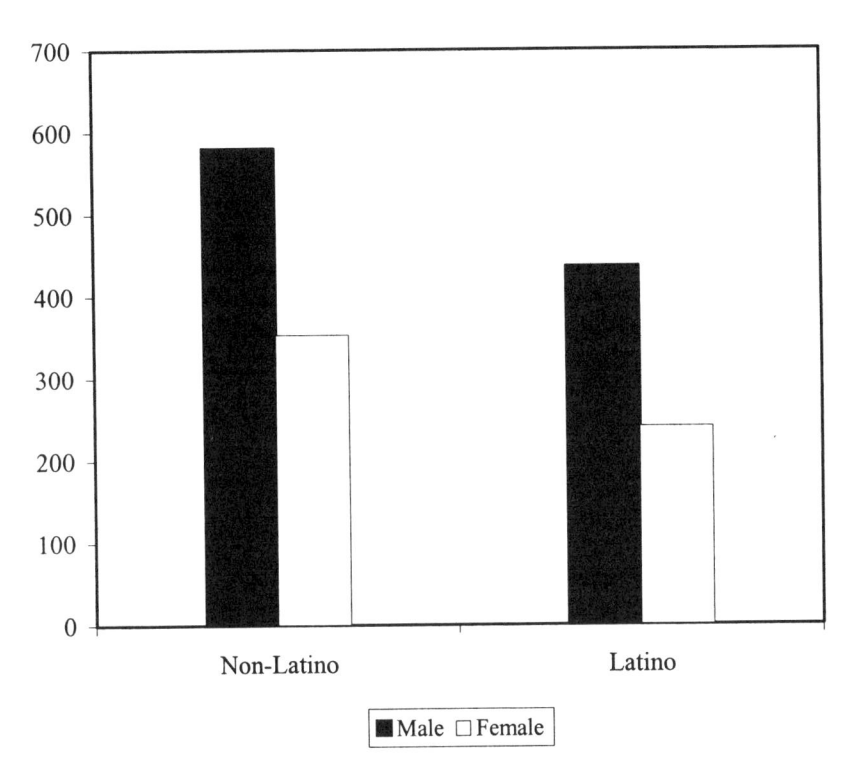

Source: California, Department of Health Services, Summary Death File, 1996.

Gender and Diabetes

Diabetes is an issue of special concern for everyone. While for nearly all other causes of death the Latina rate is 47 percent lower than that of the Latino male rate, for diabetes the Latina death rate of 16.3 is nearly identical to the Latino male rate of 17.3—almost twice as high as the non-Latino female rate of 9.0.

Age-Specific Death Rates

The lower Latino mortality rate occurs all across the age spectrum, in all age groups, with one exception: late adolescents age 15–24. Figure 6.5 provides

Figure 6.4. Latino Male-to-Female Rate of Relative Risk for Causes of Death in California, 1995

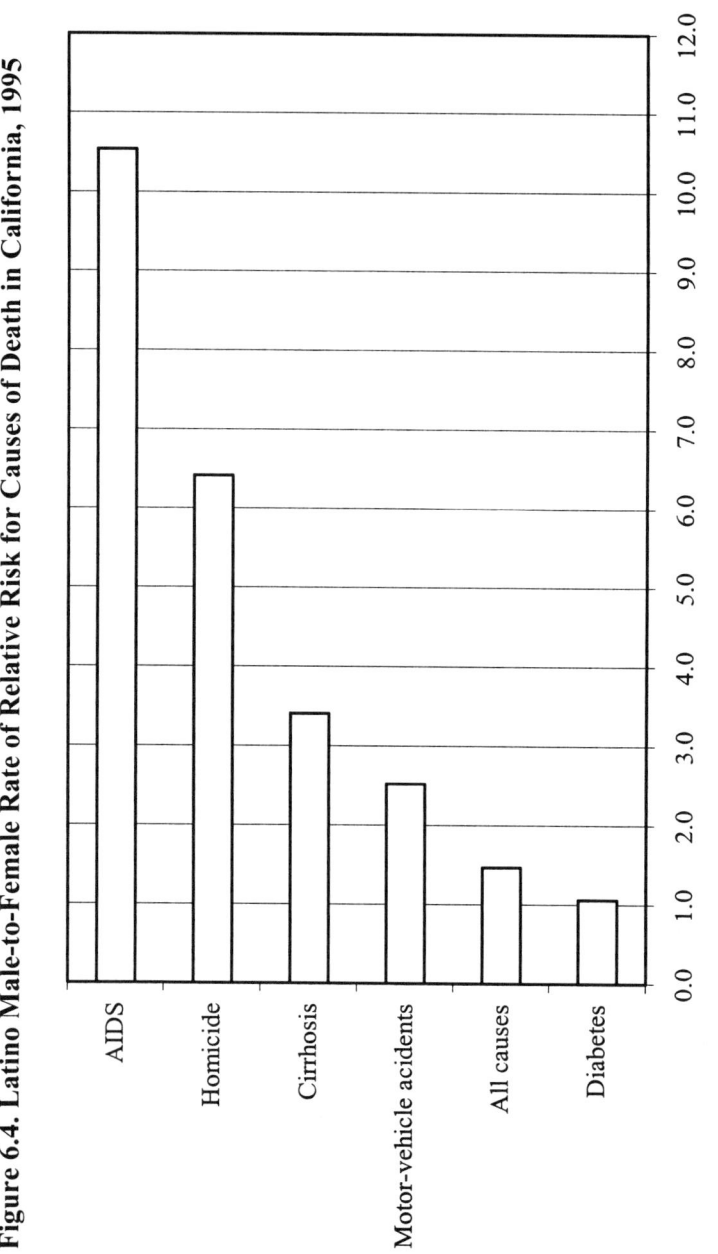

Cause	Ratio
AIDS	~10.7
Homicide	~6.3
Cirrhosis	~3.4
Motor-vehicle accidents	~2.6
All causes	~1.5
Diabetes	~1.1

Source: California, Department of Health Services, Summary Death File, 1996.

Illness and Wellness: The Latino Paradox 165

Figure 6.5. Comparative Death Rates per 100,000 People by Age Group in California, 1995

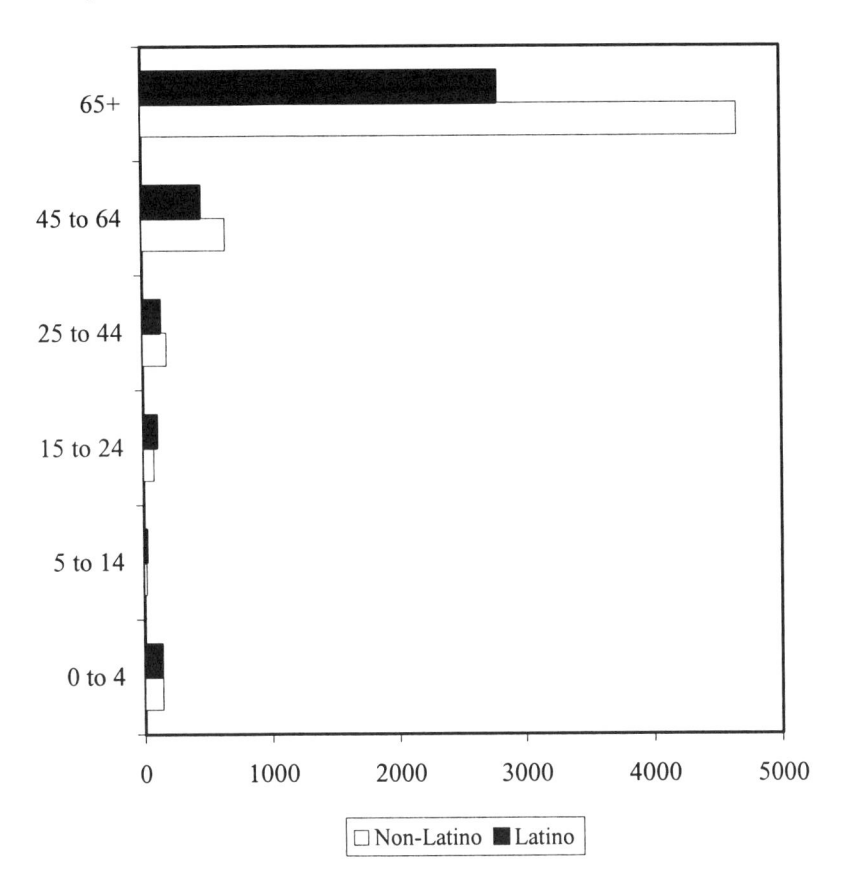

Source: California, Department of Health Services, Summary Death File, 1996.

a cross-section of mortality throughout the life spectrum. Overall, those over 65 have the highest mortality, reflecting the end of life that all humans must face; although most Latinos live long enough to die in their old age.

In the youngest age groups, 0–4 and 5–14, the young-adult (25–44), middle-adult (age 45–64), and older-adult (65 and older) groups, the Latino mortality rate is lower than the non-Latino rate. Only in the adolescent age group (15–24) is the Latino death rate higher. This requires significant social policy attention.

Farmworker Death Rates

The health profile of California Latino farmworkers presents a special case of risk. An analysis, of the mortality of Latinos in 38 designated "farmworker ZIP codes" compared to all other Latinos (largely urban) in the rest of the state, showed that farmworkers have a higher overall mortality than urban Latinos, with special risk for the following (see Figure 6.6):

- Farmworkers were more than twice as likely to die from motor-vehicle accidents (r.r. = 2.03).
- Farmworkers were almost twice as likely to die from diabetes (r.r. = 1.88).
- Farmworkers were almost 50 percent more likely to die from unintentional injuries (r.r. = 1.47).
- Farmworkers were over one-third more likely to die from pneumonia (r.r. = 1.35).
- Farmworkers were 20 percent more likely to die from Chronic Obstructive Pulmonary Disease (COPD; r.r. = 1.21).
- Farmworkers were 15 percent more likely to die from cerebrovascular disease (r.r. = 1.17).[6]

A more thorough analysis with non-Latino rural populations is beyond the scope of this paper, but certainly should be a priority research topic. In general, an examination of the death rates shows that the Latino epidemiological paradox is applicable to most Latino mortality. However, some Latino subgroups have cause-of-death profiles that do not hew to the Latino epidemiological paradox. The major causes of death, in California, for Latino males age 15–24 are homicide, motor-vehicle accidents, and other unintentional injuries. For Latinas diabetes is a particular problem, along with cervical cancer. For farmworkers, motor-vehicle accidents, unintentional injuries, and heart disease are especially troublesome.

Culture, Assimilation, and Health: Birth Outcomes

Understanding Latino social dynamics—health, family, employment, business development, and education—is the key to understanding the future of California. The pie chart on the right-hand side of Figure 6.7 provides an important theme for understanding Latino social dynamics: the role of immigrants and their cultural patterns of behavior. We shall see that while Latina immigrants have less education and access to care (and, as Chapter 2 discusses, less income), their birth outcomes are better than those of their more-assimilated counterparts, U.S.-born Latinas. The roles of culture and assimilation are suggested

---

[6]Environmental Defense Center, "The Central Coastal Environmental Health Project Baseline Assessment" (Ventura: EDC, 2000).

Figure 6.6. Rate of Relative Risk for Causes of Death in California Among Latino Farmworkers and Other Workers, 1989–91

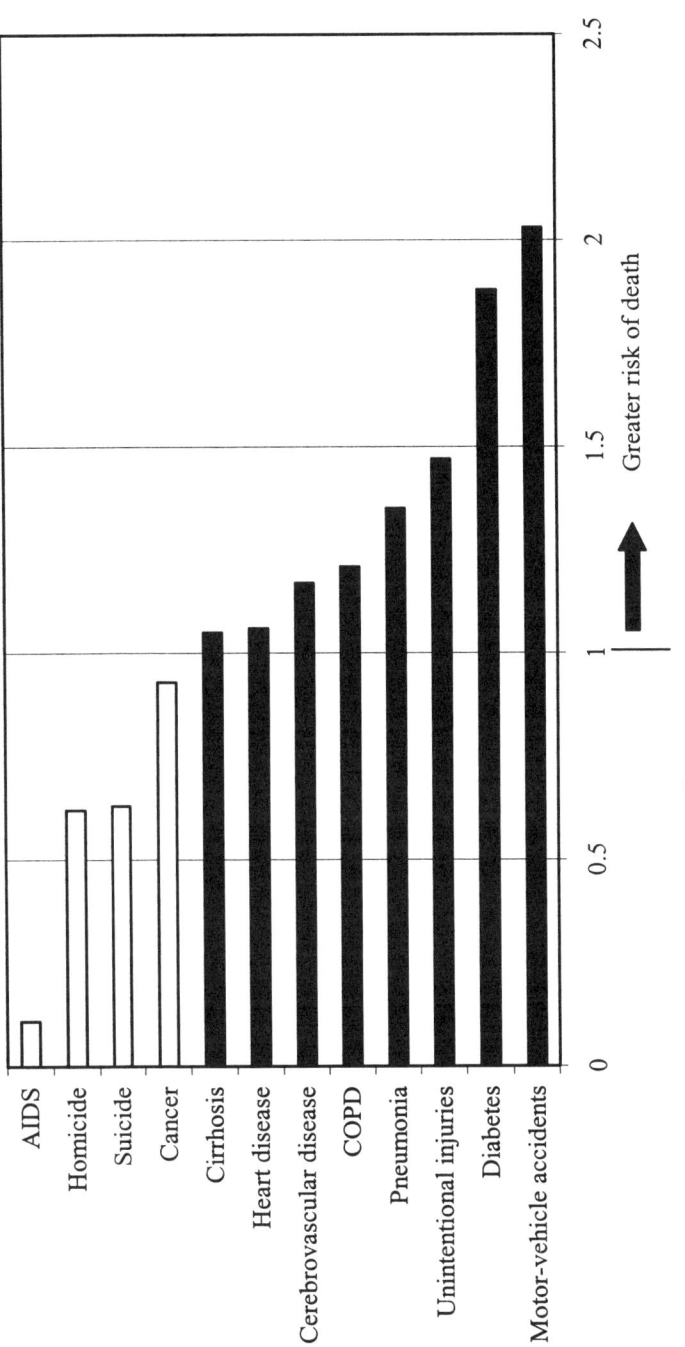

Source: Central Coast Environment Health Program, 2000.

Figure 6.7. Composition of Births and Division of U.S.-Born and Immigrant Latinas in California, 1998

U.S.-born Latinas 35.3%

Immigrant Latinas 64.7%

47.5%
1.1%
10.7%
6.8%
33.9%

- Latino
- Non-Latino White
- African American
- Asian and Pacific Islander
- Other

All Births

Latino Births

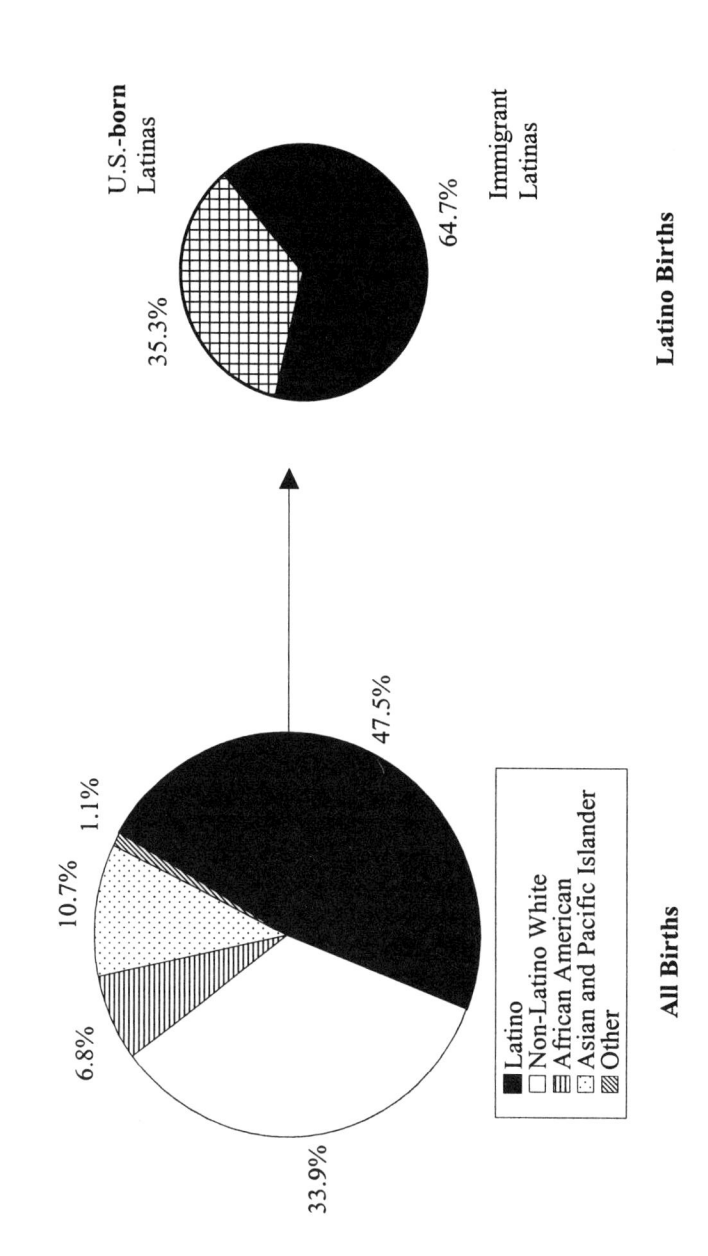

Source: California, Department of Health Services, Master Birth File, 1998.

by these birth outcomes. Data from the 1998 Master Birth File allow us to separate immigrant from U.S.-born Latina mothers.[7] The sheer numbers of Latino births (nearly a quarter of a million annually) ensure the robustness and stability of these patterns.

The 1998 data divide Latino mothers into two groups: immigrant Latinas, who were born outside the United States but are now residents; and U.S.-born Latinas. The pie chart in Figure 6.7 illustrates this division. Nearly two-thirds (64.7 percent) of Latina mothers in 1998 were immigrant Latinas, and over one-third (35.3 percent) were U.S.-born Latinas.

Not only is the average newborn in California a Latino, but the average Latino family in which that baby is raised consists of U.S.-born Latino children and immigrant Latino parents. The basic issues of child and adolescent development that any family confronts—a healthy infancy, motor skills such as walking, intellectual development such as speech, the adolescent passage, and the emergence into adulthood—take place in the context of immigrant Latino parents raising U.S.-born Latino children.

The dire pronouncements about the minority health-disparity might lead some to conclude that the average baby might not fare well in the future. Some data will help clarify the chances these babies have throughout their lives.

Education Level

Figure 6.8 shows an overview of the mothers' educational levels by race and ethnicity. Nearly all (90.2 percent) non-Latino white mothers had graduated from high school, as did Asian and Pacific-Islander mothers (86.2 percent). African-American mothers were only slightly less likely (79.5 percent) to graduate.

Latina mothers present a different picture. If all Latina mothers are grouped together, less than half (47.2 percent) graduated from high school. However, this grouping masks a very important dynamic. Immigrant Latina mothers have far lower educational levels than U.S.-born Latina mothers. Slightly over one-third of immigrant Latina mothers (36.9 percent) graduated from high school. On the other hand, over two-thirds of U.S.-born Latina mothers (68.6 percent)—nearly twice the percentage of immigrant Latina mothers—graduated from high school.

Low Birth-Weight

A low birth-weight baby weighs less than 2,500 grams at birth. Infant mortality occurs more often among low birth-weight babies than in normal birth-

---

[7]California Department of Health Services, *Master Birth File,* 1998.

Figure 6.8. Percentage of California Mothers Who Graduated from High School, 1998

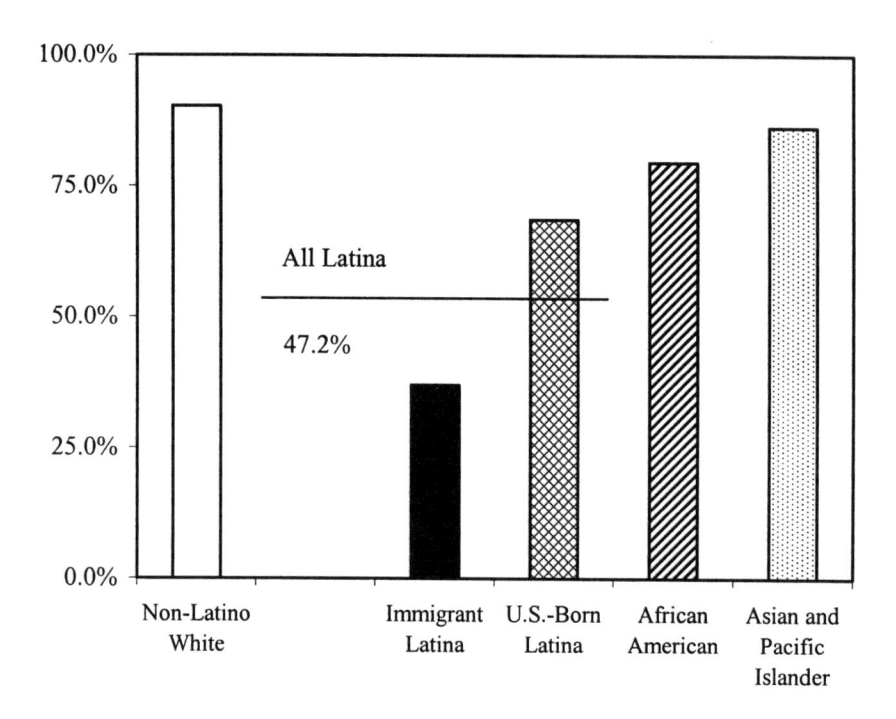

[Bar chart showing percentages by group: Non-Latino White (~87%), Immigrant Latina (~37%), U.S.-Born Latina (~65%), African American (~78%), Asian and Pacific Islander (~82%). A horizontal line labeled "All Latina 47.2%" crosses the chart.]

Source: California, Department of Health Services, Master Birth File, 1998.

weight babies (2,500 grams or more). Birth-weight serves as an important early indicator of a baby's chances of survival beyond the first year of life.

The first indicator that the race and ethnic health-disparity model might not describe the Latino situation well is provided by Figure 6.9, which displays the percentage of births that are low birth-weight. African-American babies do seem to fit the race and ethnic disparity model; over twice as many such babies (11.7 percent) are born of low birth-weight than non-Latino white babies (5.7 percent).

Latino babies show a marked departure from the race and ethnic disparity pattern. Combined, all Latino babies, from both immigrant and U.S.-born Latina mothers, have the same low percentage of low birth-weight babies as non-Latino whites—5.7 percent. The health-disparity model would lead us to look for a

Figure 6.9. Percentage of Low Birth-Weight Babies in California, 1998

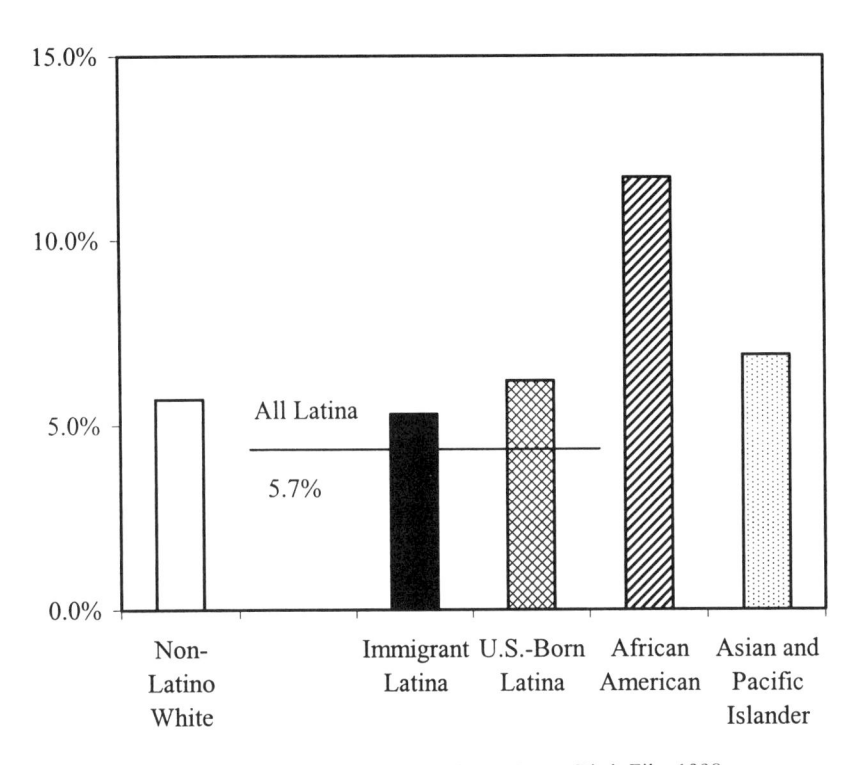

Source: California, Department of Health Services, Master Birth File, 1998.

higher percentage of low birth-weight babies, given that educational levels of the Latina mothers are far lower than those of African-American mothers.

Low birth-weight breaks even more sharply from the health-disparity model when Latina mothers are disaggregated into two groups by nativity. In fact, immigrant Latina mothers sharply contradict the health-disparity model. While they have far lower educational levels—only one-third graduated from high school—they have a lower percentage of low birth-weight babies (5.3 percent) than non-Latino white mothers (5.7 percent). U.S.-born Latina mothers have much higher educational levels than immigrant Latina mothers, yet they have a slightly higher percentage (6.2 percent) of low birth-weight babies than non-Latino white mothers.

The race and ethnic disparity model would posit that lower education leads to adverse birth outcomes, such as a higher percentage of low birth-weight babies. Yet immigrant Latina women, with far lower educational levels, are seven percent less likely than non-Latino white mothers and 15 percent less likely than U.S.-born Latina mothers to give birth to low birth-weight babies. And, confounding the health-disparity model, immigrant Latina mothers are 45 percent less likely than African-American mothers to give birth to low birth-weight babies.

Access to Prenatal Care

The Office of Minority Health (OMH) has decided that the first goal in its Race and Health Initiative is to eliminate the race and ethnic disparities in infant-mortality rates. OMH sees that a major step in eliminating the infant-mortality disparity is to increase access to prenatal care early in the pregnancy. According to the OMH's *Eliminating Racial and Ethnic Disparities in Health,* "There are substantial racial disparities in the timely receipt of prenatal care.... Eliminating these disparities requires the removal of financial, educational, social and logistical barriers to care."

Mirroring the nation in differential access to prenatal care, California's non-Latino whites access prenatal care during the all-important first trimester of pregnancy at rates far higher than any other ethnic group. Figure 6.10 shows that 88.2 percent of non-Latino white mothers received first-trimester care, compared to 78.1 percent for all Latina, 79.5 percent for African-American, and 84.9 percent for Asian and Pacific-Islander mothers. Immigrant Latina mothers are a little less (77.7 percent) likely to access first-trimester care than U.S.-born Latina mothers (79.0 percent), a difference that has been consistently observed for the past 10 years.

Access to prenatal care is important. A small percentage of pregnancies develop major problems. These should be detected as early as possible into the pregnancy for management and, eventually, to change potentially bad birth outcomes into good ones. The Office of Minority Health's *Eliminating Racial and Ethnic Disparities in Health* argues:

> Women who receive prenatal care in the first trimester have better pregnancy outcomes than women who receive little or no prenatal care. Infant death rates among blacks, American Indians and Alaska natives, and Hispanics in 1995 or 1996 were all above the national average.

Illness and Wellness: The Latino Paradox 173

Figure 6.10. Percentage of California Mothers Receiving Prenatal Care in First Trimester, 1998

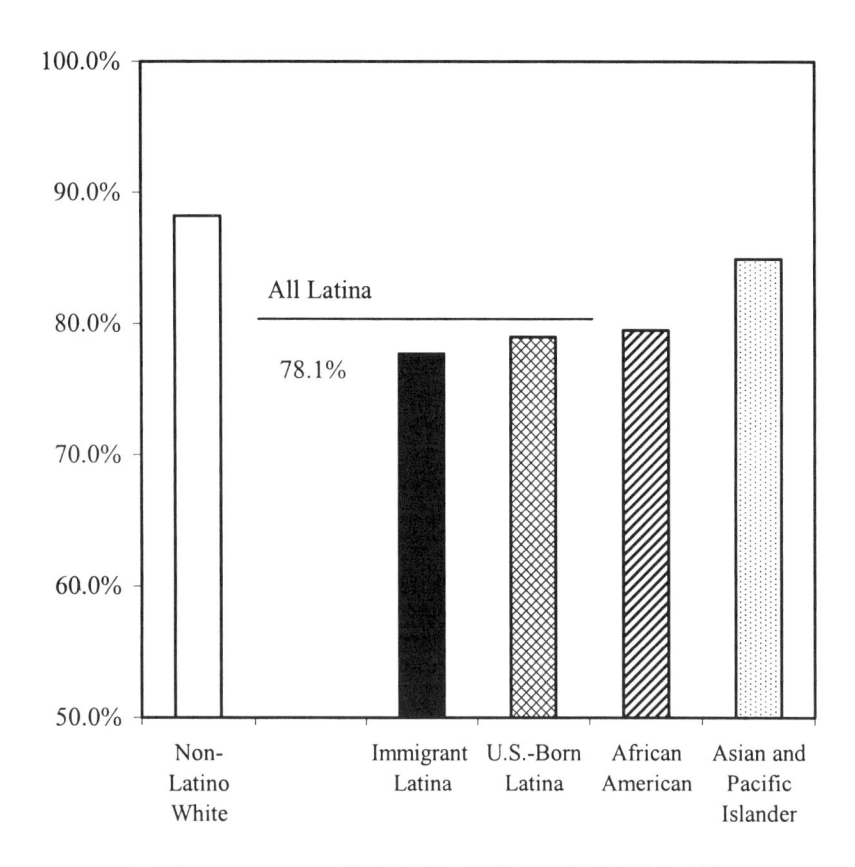

[Bar chart showing percentages: Non-Latino White ~88%; Immigrant Latina 78.1%; U.S.-Born Latina ~79%; African American ~79%; Asian and Pacific Islander ~85%. All Latina reference line at ~80%.]

Source: California, Department of Health Services, Master Birth File, 1998.

Infant Mortality

The race and ethnic disparity model seems to fit a comparison of the infant mortality of non-Latino whites and African Americans. A lower percentage of African-American women (84.9 percent) receive first-trimester care compared to non-Latino white women (88.2 percent). Correspondingly, African-American babies suffer an infant-mortality rate that is over twice that of non-Latino whites (13.2 compared to 5.4 deaths per 1,000 live births). See Figure 6.11.

Figure 6.11. Infant Mortality Rates per 1,000 Live Births in California, 1998

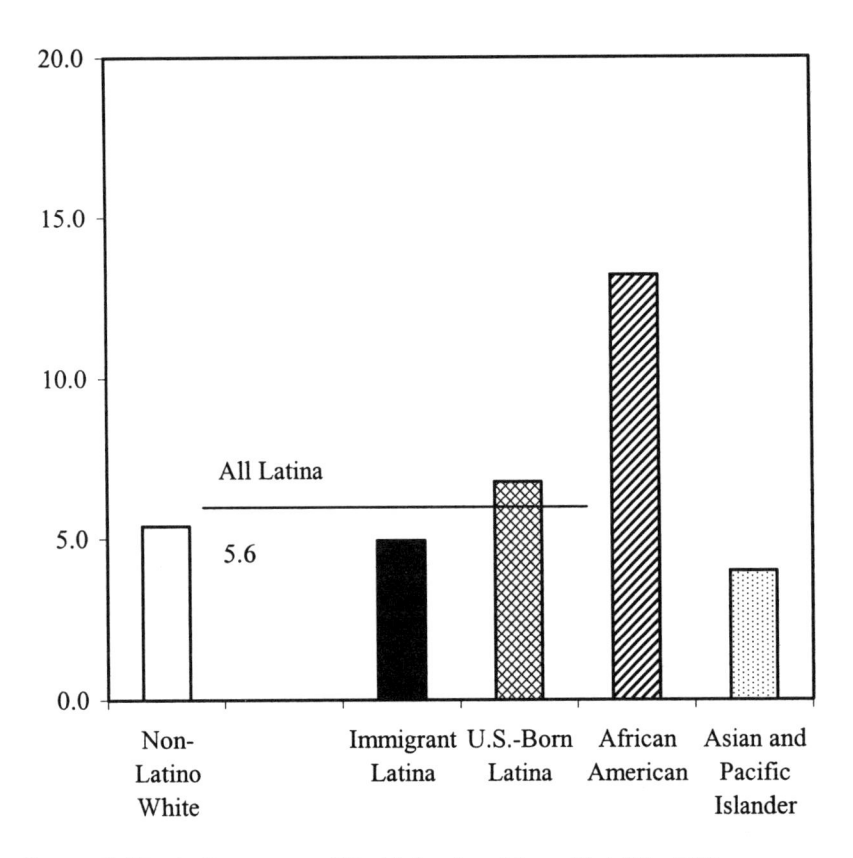

[Bar chart showing infant mortality rates: Non-Latino White ~5.4; Immigrant Latina 5.0; U.S.-Born Latina ~7; African American ~13; Asian and Pacific Islander ~4. All Latina line at 5.6.]

Source: California, Department of Health Services, Master Birth File, 1998.

The model breaks down when Latinas are compared to non-Latino whites. Despite Latinas' far lower educational levels and substantially lower prenatal-care access (not to mention lower income, covered in Chapter 2), the Latino infant mortality rate is only slightly higher than that of non-Latino whites (5.6 compared to 5.4 deaths per 1,000 live births). The race and ethnic disparity model would lead one to expect a far higher infant mortality rate for Latinos, as high as, or perhaps even exceeding, the rate for African Americans.

The model breaks down even further when Latina mothers are disaggregated by citizenship status. Immigrant Latina mothers, with far lower educational levels and prenatal access (and income), have lower infant-mortality rates than non-Latino whites (4.9 compared to 5.4 deaths per 1,000 live births). Curiously, U.S.-born Latina mothers, enjoying far higher educational levels and somewhat better access to care (and higher income), nonetheless experienced somewhat higher infant mortality rates (6.8 deaths per 1,000 live births) than their immigrant Latina or non-Latino white counterparts.

Hospital Utilization

The hospital utilization pattern of Latinos is distinct from that of non-Latinos. In general, Latinos use hospitals far less than non-Latinos, except for birth-related hospitalizations. Because of the lag in release of data, the following hospital discharge data are for 1994.[8]

All Age Groups
In general, 1,000 Latinos generated 95.6 hospital discharges—a lower rate than 1,000 non-Latinos, who generated 116.9 discharges. There are some significant age-group variations in this comparison.

Age 0–14
Reflecting the higher birth rate of Latinos, 1,000 Latinos age 0–14 generated a higher number of hospital discharges (106.9) than did 1,000 non-Latinos (97.3).

Age 15–24
Reflecting the higher birth rate and younger mothers, 1,000 Latinos age 15–24 generated more hospital discharges (97.2) than 1,000 non-Latinos (70.1).

Age 25–44
Among young adults, the hospital discharge rate falls considerably: 1,000 Latinos generated 73.6 discharges versus 83.4 discharges for 1,000 non-Latinos.

Age 45–64
In middle-aged adults, the Latino rate falls even lower than the non-Latino rate. One thousand Latinos generated 78.0 discharges, compared to the 99.5 for non-Latinos.

---

[8]D. E. Hayes-Bautista and P. Hsu, *Health of Latino California* (UCLA: Center for the Study of Latino Health, 1997).

Age 65+.
Among the elderly, the Latino discharge rate falls even lower: 224.5 discharges per 1,000, far lower than the 303.9 for the non-Latino elderly.

Patient Bed-Days
Even with the higher hospital discharge rate generated by the higher Latino birth rate, Latinos overall generated far fewer bed-days per 1,000 population (388.1) than non-Latinos (676.2).

Average Per Capita Hospital Charge
Reflecting the fact that Latino hospital utilization is largely driven by birth-related hospitalizations, while non-Latino usage tends to reflect more-serious interventions, the average Latino hospital charge per capita of $880 is nearly half the non-Latino average per-capita charge of $1,528.

Total Per Capita Public-Funded Hospital Charges
Both Medi-Cal and Medicare are public sources of funding for hospitalization. When viewed as total public charges, Latinos generated lower charges than non-Latinos ($607 compared to $947 of Medi-Cal and Medicare combined).

In general, Latino hospital utilization, except for birth-related causes, is quite a bit lower than that of non-Latinos. In all age groups past adolescence (25+), the Latino utilization rate is significantly lower. How much of this lower utilization is due to lack of access (see insurance coverage, below) and how much is simply driven by lower levels of illness (as indicated above by the lower mortality rates for heart, cancer, and stroke) is not known. However, it is clear that the Latino pattern of hospital utilization differs markedly from that of non-Latinos.

Insurance Coverage

Latino access to health insurance is covered in detail in Chapter 7. In general, Latinos have less access to health insurance than do non-Latinos, and the problem appears to be growing. It is useful to point out that from a 1997 survey of Latino elderly, 31 percent of immigrant Latina elderly were not enrolled in Medicare.[9] The many reasons for this are detailed in Chapter 7.

---

[9]D. E. Hayes-Bautista, et al., *Latino Elderly and Medicare Coverage* (UCLA: Center for the Study of Latino Health, 2001).4

Communicable Diseases

Latinos have an overall lower mortality profile for communicable diseases than non-Latinos. Other types of illnesses, however, point to the risk to which this population is exposed. Since counties pay for prevention and treatment through health education and publicly funded clinics and hospitals, communicable diseases are the responsibility of local health departments. These diseases, while rarely fatal these days, can be temporarily incapacitating. If left untended, they can spread over a large population very quickly.

Constant surveillance, constant effective public education, and rapid application of control measures can keep the incidence of communicable diseases down. The Latino population routinely suffers more than the non-Latino population from some communicable diseases, indicating that surveillance and control efforts leave room for improvement. In Figure 6.12, data from Los Angeles County for 1995 are used for this analysis, because they are the most recent large entity for which ethnic-specific cases are identified.[10]

Nonsexually Transmitted Diseases
Compared to the non-Latino population in Los Angeles, Latinos have a higher relative risk for mumps (1.99), hepatitis A (1.74), giardiasis (1.60), and pertussis (1.33). Latinos have the same relative risk for tuberculosis and salmonellosis. Latinos have a lower relative risk for hepatitis C (0.90), malaria (0.70), and hepatitis B (0.64).

Sexually Transmitted Diseases
Generally, Latinos have a lower relative risk for sexually transmitted diseases compared to the non-Latino population (see Figure 6.13). In Los Angeles County, the Latino lower relative risk was seen for HIV/AIDS (0.76), syphilis (1 and 2) (0.55), chlamydia (0.44), and gonorrhea (0.22). The Latino risk for latent syphilis and campylobacteriosis was virtually identical to the non-Latino risk.

Culture and Health

Paradox and Culture

The standard model for predicting the health profile of a population is based on the notion that the demographic risk factors—income, education, and access to care—correlate directly with a health profile. A low-income, less-educated,

---

[10] Los Angeles County Department of Health Services, *Communicable Diseases Morbidity Report*, Disease Control Programs, 1995.

Figure 6.12. Rate of Relative Risk for Communicable Diseases Among Latinos and Non-Latinos in Los Angeles County, 1995

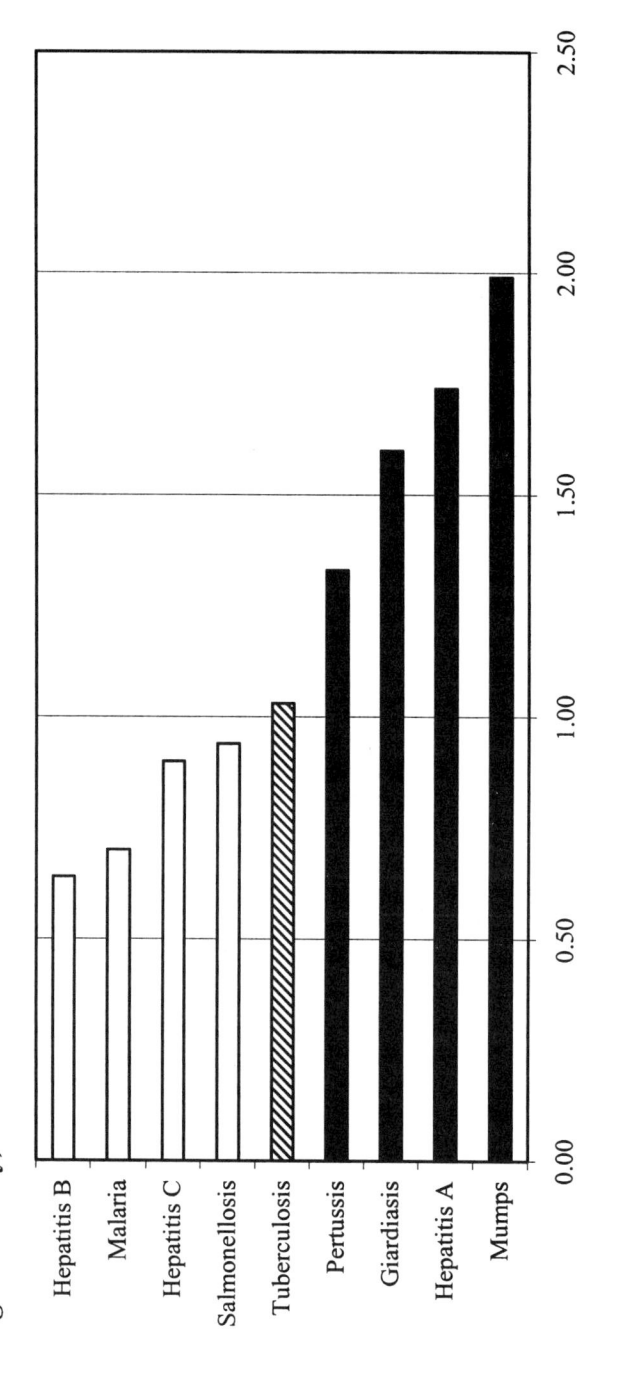

Source: Los Angeles County, Department of Health Services, 1995. *Communicable Disease Report*.

Illness and Wellness: The Latino Paradox 179

Figure 6.13. Rate of Relative Risk Among Latinos and Non-Latinos for Sexually Transmitted Diseases in Los Angeles County, 1995

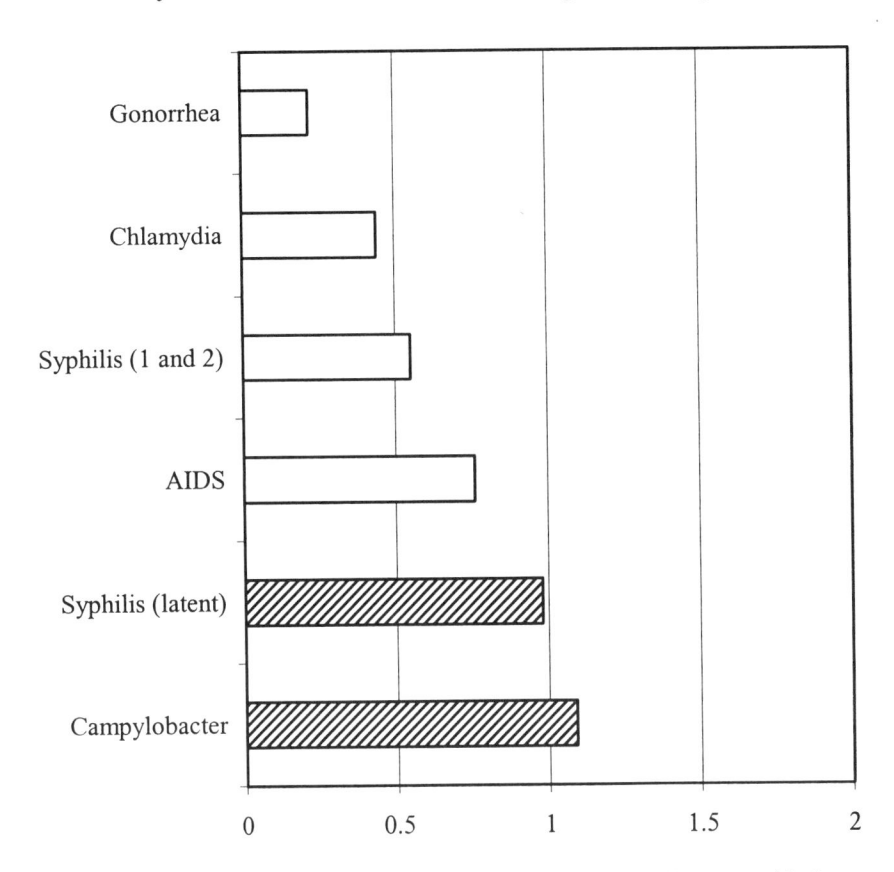

Source: Los Angeles County, Department of Health Services, 1995. *Communicable Disease Report.*

low-access group will have a lower health profile (e.g., greater mortality, adverse birth outcomes) than a high-income, highly educated, high-access group.

As we have seen, Latinos do not fit this pattern. While Latinos have higher demographic risk factors—lower income, lower educational levels, and less access to care—than non-Latinos, in general the Latino health profile is better. Thus, the so-called Latino epidemiological paradox emerges.

What causes this paradox? Current research suggests that, in some fashion, Latino culture plays a role, functioning as some sort of "protective factor" that holds at bay the otherwise deleterious effects of poverty, low education, and lack of access. Definitive testing has yet to be done, but the outside contours of this line of thought can be appreciated below.

Assimilation and Risk Behavior

The birth-outcome data suggest that the risk for Latinos is not so much in low income, level of education, or access to care, but assimilation. While the data are not conclusive, there is a strong pattern that suggests the following risks of Latino assimilation:
- U.S.-born Latinas are more likely to smoke than immigrant Latinas
- Second- and third-generation U.S.-born Latinas are less likely to abstain from drinking than immigrant Latinas
- U.S.-born Latinas are more likely to use drugs than immigrant mothers.[11]

With all the negative effects of assimilation on birth outcome, it must be noted that U.S.-born Latinas still have outcomes far different from those of African-American women, once again disproving the facile race and ethnic health-disparity model.

The Great Disparity: The Latino Physician Shortage

For the 10.4 million Latinos in California, the problem of access to care is compounded by issues of language and cultural competence. Even when Latinos have the good fortune to be covered by health insurance, they often encounter difficulty finding providers who can understand their illness experience and with whom they can communicate clearly and effectively. Anecdotally, patients in focus groups have complained of the difficulty in finding Spanish-speaking physicians. To date, there is no listing of Latino physicians because there has not been a comprehensive database of physicians in the state that identified their race or ethnicity.

The Center for the Study of Latino Health and Culture at UCLA has developed a methodology for identifying Latino physicians, by matching the listing of all 74,345 state-licensed physicians in 1999 against a set of characteristics highly correlated with Latino ethnicity. While this method has its strengths and

---

[11]H. Amaro, et al., *Acculturation and Marijuana and Cocaine Use,* Findings from HHANES 1982–1984, *American Journal of Public Health* 80 (Supplement 1990): 54–60.

weaknesses, it provides an initial look into the supply of Latino health-professionals.[12]

Underrepresentation of Latino Physicians

By means of this method, 3,578 physicians out of the total 74,345 were identified as Latino. In essence, 4.8 percent of all physicians were Latino. During the same year, 10.4 million Latinos were nearly one-third of the state's population—30.4 percent. Figure 6.14 shows the comparative Latino representation among physicians and among the state's general population.

Clearly, Latino physicians are underrepresented in the state. This underrepresentation should not be taken to mean that only Latino physicians can, or should, see Latino patients. However, it does serve as an indicator of the relative lack of Latino access to higher education and the medical profession. Many academic medical organizations, such as the American Association of Medical Colleges (AAMC) and the Council on Graduate Medical Education (COGME), have argued that the nation should move in the direction of parity between population representation and physician representation. Viewed in light of population parity, the California physician supply is critically lacking in Latino physicians.

Population-to-Physician Ratios

Another metric of the Latino physician supply is the population-to-physician ratio, which provides a rapid assessment of this disparity (see Figure 6.15). Using this ratio, there were 335 non-Latino patients for every non-Latino physician in the non-Latino population. The ratio was markedly worse for Latinos. There were 2,893 Latino patients for every Latino physician in the Latino population.

One way to comprehend this disparity in physician supply is to compare this ratio to those seen in Latin-American countries. California's Latino population of 10.4 million is equivalent to the population of a medium-sized Latin-American country, such as Chile or Cuba. While most Latin-American countries are considered to be less economically developed than California, some population-to-physician ratios are very close to that enjoyed by non-Latino California (335:1). For example, Cuba and Uruguay have better ratios (226:1 and 268:1, respectively), and the Argentine ratio of 364:1 is nearly identical to non-Latino

---

[12]D. E. Hayes-Bautista, P. Hsu, M. Hayes-Bautista, R. M. Stein, P. Dowling, R. Beltran, and J. Villagomez, "Latino Physician Supply in California: Sources, Locations and Projections." *Academic Medicine* 75(7), (2000): 727–36.

Figure 6.14. Latinos as Percentages of the California Physician and General Populations, 1999

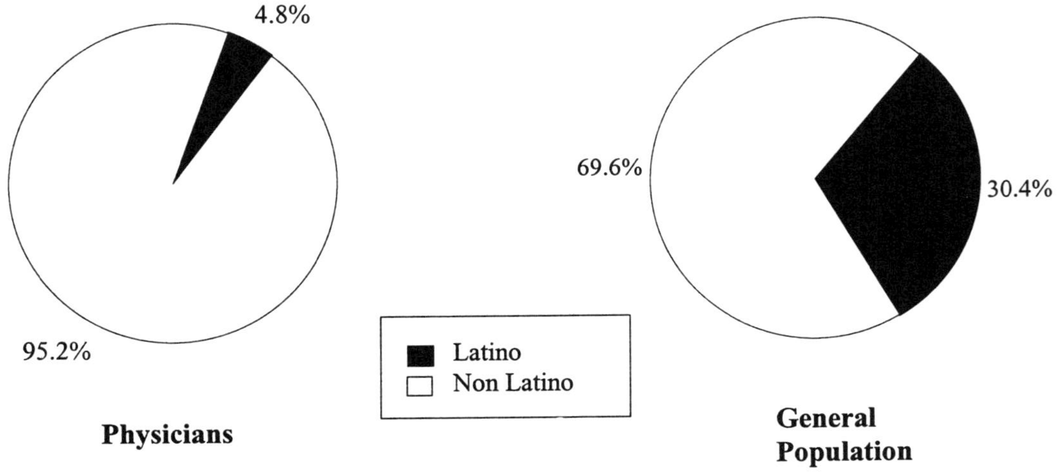

General Population: 30.4% Latino, 69.6% Non Latino

Physicians: 4.8% Latino, 95.2% Non Latino

Legend: ■ Latino □ Non Latino

Source: Latino Physician Supply in California, 2000.

Figure 6.15. California Population-to-Physician Ratios for Non-Latinos and Latinos, 1999

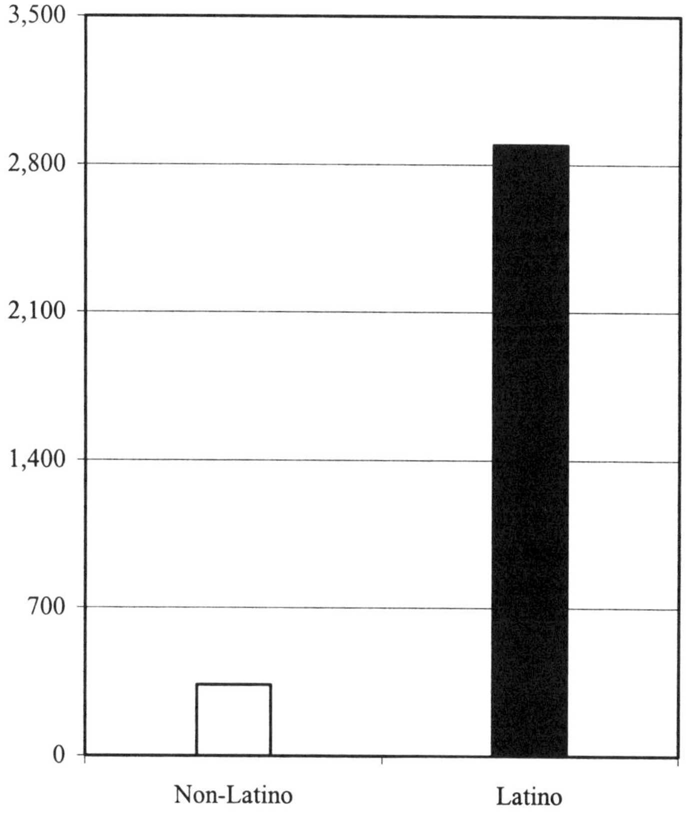

Source: Latino Physician Supply in California, 2000.

California. Mexico, for all its economic travails, has a ratio five times better than Latino California (593:1).

With its ratio of 2,893:1, Latino California has the dubious distinction of having a worse population-to-physician ratio than any country in Latin America, including severely underdeveloped countries such as Honduras (1,351:1), Bolivia (2,156:1), and Nicaragua (2,247:1).

Policy Implications

Identify and Document Latino Norms

For too long, Latino health research has been an afterthought, given attention only after the health of the non-Latino white and African-American populations were studied. At one point, when Latinos were a small minority, this oversight might have been understandable. However, Latino births now account for nearly half of all births in California, Texas, Arizona, and New Mexico. Yet, Latino norms have not been clearly established. Indeed, the fact of the Latino epidemiological paradox is still surprising to many health-services researchers and providers.

The basic epidemiological work of documenting Latino norms needs to occur in a number of areas:

Causes of Death
The preceding data on causes of death give only a glimpse into the uniqueness of Latino norms. These norms need to be tracked back several years, and established for states, counties, metropolitan areas, cities, and ZIP codes.

Birth Outcomes
Likewise, the Latino norms in birth outcomes need to be documented for past years, and broken out by the state, county, metropolitan area, city, and ZIP code.

Behavior
Latino behavioral patterns regarding smoking, drinking, drug use, exercise, seat-belt use, and similar behaviors, are not well established. There are contradictory data from a number of small area studies. Norms for these and related behaviors need to be established and documented.

Health-Services Access and Utilization
There are very few data on Latino health services utilization, including inpatient, outpatient, and physician's office visits. While some data on insurance coverage are available from the Current Population Survey, it is not sufficient to allow a fine-grained analysis of patterns of coverage. The private insurance and HMO world has very sparse Latino data because they have not had Latino identifiers on their records.

Identify Variations from Latino Norms

Once the norms for Latino populations are established, the variations from the norms can be identified, and the risk factors that cause these variations can then be sought. Some important variations that need to be understood include:

Gender
Generally, females of an ethnic group have a lower death rate than males. Latinas have a death rate that is 46 percent lower than Latino males (see Figure 6.3). However, for specific causes of death, this can vary. The Latino male death rate for firearm-related deaths is six times the Latina rate. But, for diabetes among California adults, the Latina death rate is virtually identical to the Latino male rate, instead of being over 40 percent lower, as is normally observed (see Figure 4). We need to understand the reasons for these gender variations so they can be addressed.

Latino Subgroup
As the data have demonstrated, there are subgroups within the overall Latino population whose health profiles need to be understood apart from the overall Latino norm. This applies particularly to adolescents, farmworkers, and adult males. These are but a few examples of intra-Latino variation from Latino norms. Rather than comparing Latino profiles to those of non-Latino whites or African Americans, it makes more sense to compare Latino subpopulations to overall Latino norms.

Develop Latino-Specific Theoretical Models

While it is common in health research to assume that the socio-economic-status model is applicable to Latino populations, generally it is not. More Latino-specific models need to be developed that can explain and predict the Latino epidemiological paradox and harness its dynamics for better health outcomes. The relation between culture and health needs to be understood, conceptualized, and operationalized. It may well be that the current socio-economic status-based models are but specific examples of larger, more comprehensive theoretical models that have not yet been developed.

Educational Models

Once the data have been collected and analyzed to develop basic theoretical models, the findings need to be worked into educational curricula, especially those of health providers. While the goal of "cultural competency" has often been held as an ideal, there is very little evidence-based research as to what exactly that means in medical practice. The recent book, *Healing Latinos: Realidad y Fantasia: The Art of Cultural Competence in Medicine*, is an initial attempt to provide guidance to physicians and other health providers.[13]

In matters of health, culture matters. This is especially important when dealing with Latino populations, as illustrated in the case of diabetes. Given the higher Latino death rate for diabetes, this is a priority disease for Latinos, health professionals, and policymakers.

Policy Models

Health policy at the national, state, and county or municipal level needs to be informed by Latino-specific data and findings. Most health policy today is based on assumptions about Latino norms and behavior and rarely on actual data.

Service Delivery

The design of delivery systems needs to be built up from Latino needs and desires regarding the provision of health services. One major need cited by Latino patients, especially immigrants, is for providers who speak Spanish. Recent work by the UCLA Center for the Study of Latino Health and Culture has validated this need.[14] The Latino physician shortage in California is of nearly disastrous proportions.

Conclusion

The guiding maxim in health-sciences research is: The science must be good, then all else follows. By following this principle, Latino health research can contribute to the scientific and intellectual foundations of Latino studies. Not only must Latinos be researched (hence identified in records and samples) for their own health benefit, but research on Latino culture, in all its heterogeneity,

---

[13] D. E. Hayes-Bautista, et al., *Healing Latinos: Realidad y Fantasia: The Art of Cultural Competence in Medicine* (Los Angeles, Calif.: Cedars-Sinai Health System, Center for the Study of Latino Health/UCLA, 1998).

[14] D. E. Hayes-Bautista, P. Hsu, M. Hayes-Bautista, R. M. Stein, P. Dowling, R. Beltran, and J. Villagomez. "Latino Physician Supply in California: Sources, Locations and Projections." *Academic Medicine*, 75(7), (2000): 727–36.

may well lead to a reduction of deaths from heart disease, cancer, and stroke in the population as a whole.

References

Amaro, H., et al. 1990. "Acculturation and Marijuana and Cocaine Use." Findings from HHANES 1982–1984. *American Journal of Public Health*, 80 (Supplement): 54–60.

American College of Physicians. 1997. "Inner City Health Care." *Annals of Internal Medicine* 15(126), (March): 485–90.

California, Department of Health Services, Master Birth File, 1998.

Division of Disadvantaged Assistance. 1990. *Health Status of the Disadvantaged Chartbook*. HHS: DHHS publication No. (HRSA) HRS-P-DV 90–01.

Environmental Defense Center. 2000. *The Central Coastal Environmental Health Project Baseline Assessment*. Ventura: EDC.

Hayes Bautista, D. E., et al. 1998. *Healing Latinos: Realidad y Fantasia: The Art of Cultural Competence in Medicine*. Los Angeles, Calif.: Cedars-Sinai Health System & Center for the Study of Latino Health/UCLA.

———. 2001. *Latino Elderly and Medicare Coverage*. UCLA: Center for the Study of Latino Health

Hayes-Bautista, D. E., and P. Hsu. 1997. *Health of Latino California: Chartbook 1997*. UCLA: Center for the Study of Latino Health.

Hayes-Bautista, D. E., P. Hsu, M. Hayes-Bautista, R. M. Stein, P. Dowling, R. Beltran, and J. Villagomez. 2000. "Latino Physician Supply in California: Sources, Locations and Projections." *Academic Medicine* 75(7): 727–36.

Health and Human Services Press Office. 1998. *White House Fact Sheet*. Feb. 21.

Los Angeles County Department of Health Services. 1995. *Communicable Diseases Morbidity Report*. Disease Control Programs.

U.S. Department of Health and Human Services Web site. Office of Minority Health. "Eliminating Racial and Ethnic Disparities in Health." 1998. Available at: http://raceandhealth.hhs.gov/sidebars/sbinitover.htm. Accessed August 17, 2000.

Chapter 7

Access to Illness Care and Health Insurance

R. Burciaga Valdez

Introduction

Despite reforms enacted over the last decade, the California illness-care environment is characterized by declining private health-insurance coverage, rising costs, and the inability of safety-net institutions to shift additional costs to those who are insured in order to provide care for the growing numbers of uninsured individuals. The state government's ability to provide an illness-care safety net rises and falls with California's roller coaster economy. In the late 1990s we saw several positive steps, particularly in the area of guaranteed medical care for the children of the working-poor population. With the precipitous decline in tax revenues in 2002, a real danger exists that recent advances may be dismantled. But whatever the short-run ups and downs, we can be certain that health coverage for California's working poor, who are disproportionately Latino, will continue to be a critical issue in the foreseeable future.

Latino vulnerability with respect to health-insurance coverage is easy enough to understand. For the working-aged population of the United States, health insurance continues to be employment-based, and it is optional for employers to provide coverage for their employees. Latino labor-force participation rates are high, but a large portion of Latino workers—the majority of immigrant workers—have low-paying jobs in small companies, often in marginal industries that do not include health insurance as a fringe benefit of employment. Undocumented workers and their families are particularly at risk because they are especially likely to fit that pattern, and they are usually in poor bargaining positions to boot. The result is that a very large proportion of Latino workers, especially immigrants, must find medical and dental attention through other public or private community-based health programs. At the best of times these services are underfunded and overcrowded, and these sorts of programs are the very ones most likely to face funding crises during periods of economic duress. This is precisely what was happening when this was being written (early 2002): state insurance programs are stagnating or being cut back at the same time as services for the uninsured are threatened with massive cutbacks.

In 1992, we estimated that 6.3 million Californians were without health insurance.[1] The ranks of the uninsured swelled to over seven million by the end of the decade.[2] In large part the growth in the uninsured population reflects the decline in the percentage of Californians who receive health insurance as a fringe benefit of employment. The voluntary employer-based health-insurance coverage arrangements that most Americans became accustomed to since the 1940s no longer appear to serve California (or the nation as a whole) because the state relies on a service-based economy, a sector that historically offers little to no fringe benefits. Latinos have been disproportionately affected by this trend; moreover, those voluntary arrangements have never served Latino communities well in California or elsewhere in the nation.

Illness-care costs continue to rise in California at about double the general rate of inflation. The recent leveling off in health-insurance premiums has given way once again to double-digit increases in annual premium costs. The last time we saw premium increases consistently in the double digits, many large businesses called for health care reforms and increased use of managed-care arrangements. Small firms largely decided they could not afford to offer their employees health-insurance coverage. We may once again see calls for major reforms, but this time they are likely to be calls that challenge the voluntary employment-based approach and even restructuring of service-delivery models.

As the cost of medical care services has continued to grow out of the financial reach of individuals and families, the state and federal governments have expanded coverage eligibility under title XIX (Medicaid, in California called Medi-Cal) and a new title XXI (child health insurance, in California called

---

[1] See, for example, E. R. Brown, R. B. Valdez, R. Wyn, H. Yu, and W. Cumberland, *Who Are California's Uninsured?* Policy Brief (UCLA School of Public Health, March 1994); and E. R. Brown, R. B. Valdez, H. Morgenstern, W. Cumberland, and C. Wang, *Californians Without Health Insurance in 1989* (California Policy Seminar, August 1991).

[2] H. Schauffler and E. R. Brown, *The State of Health Insurance in California, 1999* (Berkeley, Calif.: Regents of the University of California, January 2000).

Healthy Families) of the Social Security Act. Yet many Californians remain uninsured and ineligible for government-subsidized health-insurance coverage because of choices the state made in how to expand coverage and to whom to offer eligibility under these new federally subsidized efforts. Faced with huge budget deficits, the state's gains in coverage since the advent of Healthy Families and Medi-Cal expansions may be eroded.

These programs could form the foundation for a major public/private partnership in providing health-insurance coverage options to Californians, especially those employed in small firms. Reshaping Medi-Cal and Healthy Families into a single program that serves as a true health-insurance program for low-wage workers and their families, in addition to covering traditionally eligible categories of individuals such as the disabled and impoverished infants and mothers and poor elderly, the state could partner with small and medium-sized firms to provide health-insurance coverage to the vast majority of California's workforce and their dependents. Eliminating the stigma or misperception of Medi-Cal as a welfare program may require considerable investment in order to improve people's willingness to participate in a reformed coverage program.

California's uninsured families rely on a fragile network of safety-net organizations. Providing medical services to the uninsured is a major mission of community health centers and free clinics. County health departments also have a statutory responsibility to provide care for the uninsured as providers of last resort. Many Latinos in California rely on these safety-net providers for affordable primary medical care and preventive clinical services such as prenatal care and childhood immunizations. Many community health centers also provide population-based health promotion and disease prevention activities in their communities where official public health agencies may not exist as well as providing a source of economic stimulation for poor communities and job training and job opportunities for local residents. Reducing the financial uncertainty that safety-net organizations face annually must be part of a reformed health delivery system in California that better serves Latino communities and others in California.[3] Increasing coverage among uninsured families that rely upon these providers for primary care could stabilize this important but fragile network of providers.

---

[3] L. Wulsin, Jr., S. Djavaheri, J. Frates, and A. Shofet, *Clinics, Counties and the Uninsured: A Study of Six California Urban Counties* (February 1999).

Barriers to Illness Care for Latinos

Latinos face financial, structural, and institutional barriers to illness-care access in California that only multiple simultaneous strategies can overcome.[4] The financial barriers in large part reflect poor returns from employment. Despite significant and growing participation in the California workforce, Latinos do not receive adequate economic returns for their labor. Latino men and women are most often employed in low-paying jobs with few or no fringe benefits such as health insurance, pension plans, and life insurance. As a result, high labor-force participation rates have not translated into significant socio-economic gains for Latino communities. The greater concentration in service, blue-collar, and agricultural jobs has resulted in median income earnings for Latino men that are less than two-thirds of the median earnings of non-Latinos. Inadequate family incomes and the lack of health-insurance coverage limit Latino access to medical and dental care.

Many Latino elderly who enter the Medicare Program, the national health-insurance coverage program of the elderly, are unfamiliar with insurance programs and how best to use covered services. Some remain ineligible for Medicare because it too has ties to employment requiring the payment of social security taxes during 40 quarters of employment.

The American College of Physicians has recently compiled and summarized the consequences of not having health insurance.[5] The population of uninsured, compared to the insured population, is:

- less likely to have a regular source of care

---

[4] See, for example, R. B. Valdez, "Insuring Latinos Against the Costs of Illness," testimony before the U.S. House of Representatives Select Committee on Aging and the Congressional Hispanic Caucus, September 19, 1991, RAND, P-7750; R. B. Valdez, "Health Care for All in the Year 2000?" in *Latinos and Blacks in the Cities,* ed. H. D. Romo (Austin: Lyndon Baines Johnson Library and Lyndon B. Johnson School of Public Affairs, 1990); F. M. Treviño, M. E. Moyer, R. B. Valdez, and C. A. Stroup, "Health-Insurance Coverage and Utilization of Health Services by Mexican Americans, Mainland Puerto Ricans, and Cuban Americans," in *Health Policy and the Hispanic,* ed. A. Furino (Boulder, Colo.: Westview Press, 1992); R. B. Valdez, A. Giachello, H. Rodrigues-Trias, P. Gomez, C. de la Rocha, "Access to Health Care in Latino Communities," *Public Health Reports,* vol. 108, no. 5 (Sept.-Oct. 1993): 534–39; R. B. Valdez, H. Morgenstern, E. R. Brown, R. Wyn, C. Wang, W. Cumberland, "Insuring Latinos against the Costs of Illness," *JAMA* 269(7) (Feb. 17, 1993): 889–94; and R. B. Valdez, "Latino Health Access Issues in the Age of Managed Care," prepared for U.S. Department of Health and Human Services Assistant Secretary for Planning and Evaluation, March 1999.

[5] American College of Physicians—American Society of Internal Medicine, *No Health Insurance? It's Enough to Make You Sick—Scientific Research Linking the Lack of Health Coverage to Poor Health* (Philadelphia: American College of Physicians—American Society of Internal Medicine, 1999), 4–11.

- less likely to have had a recent physician visit
- up to 3.6 times more likely to delay seeking care
- less likely to use preventive services.

As a result, the uninsured population experiences poorer medical outcomes and health. The uninsured:

- are 1.5 times more likely to report fair or poor health
- experience higher mortality and higher in-hospital mortality
- experience adverse health outcomes three times more than privately insured individuals
- are found to be more likely than insured patients to require both avoidable hospitalizations and emergency hospital care (up to 2.8 times for diabetes, 2.4 times for hypertension, and 1.6 times for a bleeding ulcer).

In California, twice as many nonelderly Latinos as non-Latino whites have no usual source of care. Fourteen percent of Latino children and seven percent of non-Latino white children are without a usual source of care. Among adults, 31 percent of Latinos and 17 percent of non-Latino whites have no usual source of care. Focusing solely on the uninsured population, we find that 35 percent of Latino children and 25 percent of non-Latino white children have no usual source of care. Similarly, 57 percent of Latino adults and 48 percent of non-Latino white adults have no usual source of care.

Uninsured Latino children were twice as likely as insured Latino children not to have visited a physician in the last year (28 percent versus 13 percent). Lack of health insurance reduces the opportunities for preventive clinical services and childhood developmental services for Latino children.

Lack of health insurance also reduces access to physicians during illness. Among nonelderly Latinos in fair or poor health, 49 percent have no usual source of care, compared to eight percent among the insured population. In fact, 45 percent of the uninsured say that they have delayed care, compared to 11 percent of the insured. Almost 30 percent of the uninsured have not seen a physician for more than a year, compared to about 10 percent among the insured.

The numerous structural barriers to health care that Latinos face include problems in enrolling in and using the Medi-Cal program and other publicly sponsored insurance-coverage programs. Even when Latinos succeed in enrolling in these programs, they face difficulties in finding providers or arranging for appropriate care.[6] They face a largely fragmented delivery system that is ill-prepared to provide culturally sensitive services. Providers' inability to communicate effectively with their patients raises serious quality-of-care concerns. No challenge is greater for California medicine than the training of culturally competent providers to serve Californians in the 21st century.

Furthermore, the focus on the financing crisis for personal illness-care services draws us away from investments in public health. Many communities lack

---

[6]Valdez, "Latino Health Access Issues."

clean safe water, basic sanitation, adequate housing, and adequate markets for the purchase of fresh fruits and vegetables and other nutritious foods. Latino communities often pay higher prices for basic goods and services and often are the last to receive adequate infrastructure investments.

Last, Latinos face numerous institutional barriers. Latinos are largely excluded from leadership roles in health care decision making and policymaking in the current market. Without a clear role for Latino consumers to contribute to system reform, financial and nonfinancial barriers will persist.

Latino Health-Insurance Coverage

Latinos nationally and in California have the lowest health-insurance coverage of any ethnic group. Only 40 percent of California's Latino population had employment-based coverage in 1998. In contrast, among the non-Latino white population 70 percent had employment-based coverage (see Table 7.1). Despite what was, until recently, a rapidly growing economy, Latino health-insurance coverage rates have increased by only two percentage points since 1995.

The slight increase in employment-based coverage among the Latino population is partially offset by the loss in coverage provided by the Medi-Cal program. Medi-Cal covered about 17 percent of the Latino population in 1998, but Latinos have seen a dramatic drop in the protection afforded by the Medi-Cal program since 1995, when 22 percent of the population was covered under this program. The decline in Medi-Cal coverage contributed to an increase of two percentage points in the rate of the uninsured among Latinos from 1995 to 1998. In 1998, 40 percent of the Latino population was uninsured, compared to about 15 percent of the non-Latino white population. But even if the Latino rates converged on non-Latino white population uninsured rates, this level is still unacceptably high in terms of both financial burden and health risk. The 15 percent level is unacceptably high for any California population group and puts the state's economy and its people's health and welfare at risk.

Immigrants in California have seen their rates of health-insurance coverage decline from 1995 to 1998 (see Table 7.2). From 1995 to 1998, naturalized citizens experienced a four percentage-point rise in the proportion that is uninsured. Noncitizen residents experienced an increase of six percentage points over this same time period. Different dynamics appear to account for the increases in the uninsured in these two groups.

Disparities in insurance coverage based on citizenship status is found forb oth employment-based coverage and Medi-Cal coverage. U.S.-born citizens are more likely to be insured than naturalized citizens and noncitizen residents through both major mechanisms for health-insurance coverage available in California. About 63 percent of U.S.-born citizens were covered under employment-based health-insurance programs, whereas 59 percent of naturalized citizens and

Table 7.1. Health-Insurance Coverage of Latinos and Non-Latino Whites, 1995 and 1998

Insurance Coverage	1995 (%)	1998 (%)
Uninsured		
Latino	38	40
Non-Latino white	15	15
Employment-based coverage		
Latino	38	40
Non-Latino white	70	70
Privately purchased coverage		
Latino	1	2
Non-Latino white	7	7
Medi-Cal coverage		
Latino	22	17
Non-Latino white	7	6
Other coverage		
Latino	1	1
Non-Latino white	2	2

Source: Analysis of March 1996 and 1999 Current Population Surveys.

only 39 percent of noncitizen residents gained insurance coverage through employment-based programs.

It appears that the lower health-insurance coverage rates for naturalized citizens reflect a loss of eight percentage points in coverage through employment-based health insurance. No other group of residents appears to have experienced such a loss in insurance coverage during this period. In fact, the coverage rates of U.S.-born citizens and noncitizen residents remained largely unchanged from 1995 to 1998.

Changes in Medi-Cal coverage appear to play a role in the overall dynamics of the health-insurance coverage of Californians, particularly immigrant Californians. Naturalized citizens' coverage under the Medi-Cal program remained largely unchanged, but noncitizen residents experienced a loss of eight percentage points in health-insurance coverage from 1995 to 1998. In part, this loss in coverage reflects state and national changes in immigration law and social assistance programs, as well as the resulting confusion about eligibility. The

Table 7.2. Health-Insurance Coverage for California's U.S.-Born and Immigrant Communities, 1995 and 1998

Insurance Coverage	1995 (%)	1998 (%)
Uninsured		
U.S.-born citizen	17	19
Naturalized citizen	20	24
Noncitizen resident	44	50
Employment-based coverage		
U.S.-born citizen	62	63
Naturalized citizen	67	59
Noncitizen resident	34	36
Privately purchased coverage		
U.S.-born citizen	4	5
Naturalized citizen	7	7
Noncitizen resident	3	3
Medi-Cal coverage		
U.S.-born citizen	14	12
Naturalized citizen	5	7
Noncitizen resident	17	9
Other coverage		
U.S.-born citizen	2	2
Naturalized citizen	1	3
Noncitizen	1	1

Source: Analysis of March 1996 and 1999 Current Population Surveys.

anti-immigrant climate of the times in certain social and political circles also contributed to the loss in coverage.

Many eligible Latinos decline publicly sponsored health-insurance programs or do not even try to enroll for fear that they will have to pay back benefits or will be denied citizenship when it comes time to apply. Confusion about immigration policy and immigrant fears about a social or political backlash if they participate in the Children's Health Insurance Program (i.e., Healthy Families), Medi-Cal, Medicare, or other public programs discourage them from participation. Almost 40 percent of Latinos are not citizens so the overall impact of this confusion and fear is great in California. Recent immigration law changes

Table 7.3. Rates of Uninsured in California Counties and Regions, 1997–98

County or Region	Percent Uninsured	Range	Percent Latino in County or Region
Yuba, Sutter	36	29–43	18
Los Angeles	32	31–34	44
Tulare	31	24–37	46
Butte	30	22–37	10
Monterey	30	22–39	41
Santa Barbara	29	22–36	33
San Luis Obispo	27	19–35	17
Riverside, San Bernardino	23	20–25	33
Orange	23	20–26	29
Marin	23	20–26	10
Kern	23	18–29	35
San Francisco, San Mateo, San Joaquin	22	16–28	22
San Diego	22	19–24	26
Fresno	20	15–24	43
Merced	19	13–25	4
Ventura	18	13–23	33
Stanislaus	18	12–24	28
Santa Clara	17	14–20	26
Sonoma	16	9–23	14
Alameda, Contra Costa	15	12–17	17
Sacramento, El Dorado, Placer	14	11–17	14
Napa, Solana	11	7–16	17
Yolo	*	*	26
All other counties combined	13	6–19	*

*Unable to estimate from the data.
Note: Uninsured rates are estimated two-year average rates. The true rate is likely to fall between the estimated range with 95% confidence.
Source: Analysis of the March 1997 and 1998 Current Population Surveys.

have discouraged immigrants from using or participating in programs sponsored by the government.

The fiscal and medical burden resulting from lack of health insurance differs dramatically from county to county in the state (see Table 7.3). People living in Sutter, Yuba, Los Angeles, and Tulare counties are more likely to be uninsured than people living in Alameda, Contra Costa, Sacramento, and El Dorado counties. These disparities in insurance coverage reflect differences in the dynamics of health-insurance coverage (e.g., the relative mix of employment-based coverage and Medi-Cal coverage) in each county. As we will see, the employment-based coverage available reflects the mix in the size of businesses and dominant industries operating in each county. Among the 10 counties with the highest percentages of uninsured residents, five are in the Southern California region—Los Angeles, Orange, Riverside, San Bernardino, and Santa Barbara. These counties are demographically, economically, and politically diverse. One thing they have in common is that they are home to large Latino communities. The other counties in this group are rural counties that have increasingly become Latino communities over the 1990s.

This geographic variation in health-insurance coverage creates different levels of burden on counties, which have the ultimate responsibility for the illness care of their residents. Each county handles this obligation in its own way. Some provide direct medical services, others contract with community providers, while others contract with the state for certain public health services.

Despite a then booming economy and persistently high labor-force participation rates, four in 10 Latinos living in families with breadwinners who worked full-time for the entire year went without health-insurance coverage in both 1995 and 1998 (see Table 7.4). Employment-based coverage as well remained largely unchanged during this period, with about 44 percent receiving health insurance through this mechanism. In 1998, Medi-Cal provided coverage for about 14 percent of Latinos living in working families.

Disparities between Latinos and non-Latino whites in health-insurance coverage among individuals living in working families remain dramatic. In 1998, only 44 percent of Latinos in working families, compared to 75 percent of non-Latino whites, had employment-based coverage. Medi-Cal played a bigger role in providing coverage for Latinos (14 percent) in working families than it did for non-Latino whites (four percent) in 1998. The bigger role that Medi-Cal plays reflects the fact that many Latino working families have breadwinners who work in low-wage jobs but whose income is low enough that some family members (primarily children and pregnant women) qualify for the Medi-Cal program. These disparities in sources of coverage are reflected in the 26 percentage-point difference in the proportion of uninsured among Latinos (39 percent) and non-Latino whites (13 percent) in working families.

Working-age Latino men and women, the breadwinners of the family, are at great financial and health risk because they lack health-insurance coverage (see Table 7.5). Almost 50 percent of Latino men and women lack health-insurance coverage. Women in their child-bearing years can often rely on Medi-Cal to provide some coverage during pregnancies. But in general, adult Latino men and women often must go without health-insurance coverage of any kind. Latino

Table 7.4. Health-Insurance Coverage of Persons in California Working Families, 1995 and 1998

Insurance Coverage	1995 %	1998 %
Uninsured		
Latino	39	39
Non-Latino white	14	13
Employment-based coverage		
Latino	43	44
Non-Latino white	74	75
Privately purchased coverage		
Latino	1	2
Non-Latino white	7	6
Medi-Cal coverage		
Latino	16	14
Non-Latino white	4	4

Source: Analysis of March 1995 and 1999 Current Population Surveys.

Table 7.5. Lack of Health-Insurance Coverage for California Men and Women Ages 19–64, 1995 and 1998

Uninsured	1995 (%)	1998 (%)
Latino		
Men	49	48
Women	39	45
Non-Latino white		
Men	18	17
Women	14	15

Source: Analysis of March 1996 and 1999 Current Population Surveys.

Table 7.6. Health-Insurance Coverage for Los Angeles Elders 65 and Older, 2001

Coverage	Overall (%)	Non-Latino White (%)	Latino (%)
Medicare only	66	89	46
Medi-Cal only	5	0	10
Medicare and Medi-Cal	20	7	32
Other coverage	5	4	7
No coverage	4	0	5

Source: Analysis of Center for the Study of Latino Health and Culture, UCLA CDC Adult Immunization Study Data.

adults experience a disparity of about 30 percentage points compared to non-Latino whites in the proportion who are uninsured. In 1998, 48 percent of Latino men, in contrast with 17 percent of non-Latino white men, were uninsured. Similar disparities were found for Latino and non-Latino women.

Elders in Los Angeles appear to be less well-covered by health-insurance programs than national reports of coverage suggest (see Table 7.6). Among the elder non-Latino white population, about 96 percent report being covered by the Medicare program, with seven percent also reporting Medi-Cal coverage. Latino elders fare more poorly with regard to Medicare coverage, with only 78 percent reporting Medicare coverage. This is considerably below the national estimate of around 90 percent. Medi-Cal-only coverage provides protection to an additional 10 percent of Latino elders. No non-Latino white elderly person reported having only Medi-Cal coverage, but four percent reported other private health-insurance programs as their source of health-insurance coverage. Latino elders (seven percent) also report other coverage sources, primarily private health insurance. The nature or extent of coverage of these private insurance programs is unknown. Five percent of Latino elders report no health-insurance coverage, private or public.

Many Latino elders have a work history of reflecting both high levels of unemployment and high labor-force participation in low-wage jobs. Frequent and extended periods of unemployment not only create immediate financial hardship; they also can disqualify a worker from receiving pension benefits because of vesting requirements. For example, only 75 percent of Latino elders report receiving Social Security payments, compared to 91 percent of non-Latino white seniors. This vesting problem could also affect participation in the Medicare program

Medi-Cal's Role

In July 1998, California expanded children's income eligibility for Medi-Cal and created a new program called Healthy Families in response to federal legislation called the Children's Health-Insurance Program. This Medi-Cal expansion, along with stagnant employment-based coverage for children, has, over the last couple of years, raised the number of children under age 18 eligible for Medi-Cal coverage to almost 840,000 (see Table 7.7 for children's coverage rates). A child is Medi-Cal-eligible if he or she is a citizen or documented immigrant and meets the income requirements, which vary by age. Families with infants under age one have a family income limit of 200 percent of the federal poverty level (FPL). Children ages 1–5 may not have a family income in excess of 133 percent of FPL; those with children ages 6–18 may not have a family income that exceeds 100 percent of FPL. Children who meet these requirements qualify for no-share-of-cost Medi-Cal (i.e., the family pays no premium).

The Healthy Families Program offers another way to increase Latino health-insurance coverage, especially if it is expanded to include parents. In November 1999, the legislature expanded eligibility for children for the Healthy Families program, closing major gaps in coverage opportunities for children in California. A child is eligible for the Healthy Families program if he or she meets age and income requirements and is a citizen or documented immigrant who immigrated before August 22, 1996. Children under age one in families with incomes between 201 percent and 250 percent FPL are eligible for Healthy Families coverage; children ages 1–5 with family income between 134 percent and 250 percent FPL are eligible; and children ages 6–18 with family income between 101 percent and 250 percent FPL are eligible. The Healthy Families Program charges families modest premiums for health-insurance coverage.

Given the recent Medi-Cal and Healthy Families eligibility expansions, we estimate that about two-thirds of all Latino children qualify for either Medi-Cal or Healthy Families depending on age and family income. Because Latino families tend to be larger than non-Latino white families, it would not be unusual for family members to fall in and out of eligibility for these two separate programs as children grow older and family income fluctuates.

According to the UCLA Center for Health Policy Studies' analysis of the March 1999 Current Population Survey, 64 percent of uninsured children under age 18 are eligible for Medi-Cal or Healthy Families Program coverage under post-November 1999 policy, compared to 21 percent of non-Latino white children. A third of Latino uninsured children are likely to be left without coverage

Table 7.7. Children's Health-Insurance Coverage, 1998

Insurance Coverage	Percent
Uninsured	
Latino	32
Non-Latino white	12
Employment-based coverage	
Latino	36
Non-Latino white	71
Privately purchased coverage	
Latino	1
Non-Latino white	6
Medi-Cal coverage	
Latino	28
Non-Latino white	11

Source: Analysis of the March 1999 Current Population Survey.

from either one of these programs because they immigrated after August 22, 1996, or because their family incomes disqualify them from participating.

Medi-Cal Assistance with Medicare Costs

Most Medicare beneficiaries have some form of public or private supplemental insurance to help pay for benefits not covered by the program or cost-sharing requirements. Latino elders, however, are much less likely than their non-Latino white counterparts to have private supplemental coverage—either retiree health benefits or individually purchased Medicare supplemental insurance policies, referred to as "Medigap policies."

The most common type of supplemental coverage among Latinos nationally comes from Medicaid, the state-administered health-insurance program for low-income Americans. Across the nation, more than a quarter of Latinos rely on Medicaid to supplement Medicare. Given their disproportionately low incomes, many more Latino elders in California are likely to qualify for Medi-Cal assistance (i.e., Qualified Medical Beneficiary, Specified Low-Income Medicare Beneficiary, and Qualifying Individuals Programs) with the costs associated with the Medicare program. Most Latino elderly, however, are unaware that assistance to cover the cost of premiums and cost sharing is available through the Medi-Cal program for low-income elders.

Medi-Cal's Reliance on Managed Care

Managed care plays an important role in the Medi-Cal program. Because Medi-Cal is implemented at the county level, it is probably best to think of it as 58 separate programs with some common state and federal requirements and eligibility rules. Counties have chosen to implement managed care in their Medi-Cal programs in a variety of ways. Each approach affects access to care for the uninsured. Medi-Cal managed care has diverted funds from traditional safety-net providers to private and for-profit health plans and other providers. This diversion of funds reduces the availability of charity care for the uninsured.[7]

Managed-care systems can be complex and confusing. For patients who are unaccustomed to their new responsibilities and who lack understanding about how to use the system, access to care can be diminished even though they have an assigned and responsible "source of care." These barriers can be doubly difficult to overcome when assistance mechanisms available for monolingual Spanish-speaking patients in an English-dominant environment are inadequate. The state's use of contractual requirements rather than regulation to enhance the services delivery systems to provide adequate levels of service in non-English languages promised to help make the service environments patient-centered and friendly. How well these provisions have worked remains an unanswered question.

Other issues of cultural competency affect the care provided through managed care as well as fee-for-service organizational arrangements. For example, the increased reliance on managed care in Medi-Cal poses numerous problems for migrant farmworker families because programs are implemented at the local level and often rely on managed-care networks that are regionally limited. Portability of Medi-Cal coverage from county to county remains a hidden issue worthy of considerable attention, especially for migrant and seasonal agricultural working families but also other families that move frequently throughout the year.

Latinos have little or no experience with today's health-insurance mechanisms (see Table 7.8). Almost a third (31 percent) report never having been covered under a health-insurance program of any type. For another fifth of Latino adults (19 percent) it has been more than five years since they were covered by

---

[7]D. P. Andrulis, *The Public Sector in the Emerging Health Care Environment: Evolution or Dissolution?* (Washington, D.C.: The National Public Health and Hospital Institute, 1997).

Table 7.8. Percent of Adults Reporting Periods with No Health-Insurance Coverage, 1999

Ethnic Group	Period without Coverage			
	Less than One Year	One to Five Years	More than Five Years	Never Covered
Latino	21	28	19	31
Non-Latino white	35	30	28	6

Source: Schauffler and Zawicki, *The State of Health-Insurance Coverage in California, 1999.* Analysis of the California Behavioral Risk Factor Survey of 1999.

health insurance. This pattern of coverage is in stark contrast with coverage patterns for non-Latino white adults. Two-thirds (65 percent) have spells of health insurance-loss of less than five years, with a third being without health insurance for less than a year.

This pattern suggests that Latinos have little or no knowledge about how insurance-coverage systems work or how best to work these systems when they are lucky enough to gain coverage. The influence of nonfinancial barriers to care is clearly high, as is the need for patient education and adequate instructional materials to enhance appropriate service use, particularly preventive service use. The increased reliance on managed-care arrangements can also heighten confusion about how, where, and when services are available, because each program organizes and manages care differently.

Employment-Based Coverage

Much of the problem of health-insurance coverage in California stems from the very structure of the economy. California's economy is made up of many very small enterprises. More than three-quarters of all firms in the state employ fewer than 10 employees. Another fifth of the firms employ between 10 and 50 employees. About 35 percent of Latinos and 29 percent of non-Latino whites earn their income from work in firms with fewer than 25 employees. Small firms are the least likely to offer health-insurance coverage to their employees as a fringe benefit of employment.

These firms must look to the small-group health-insurance market for coverage. Among very small firms (3–9 employees), 41 percent offer some type of health-insurance coverage to their employees (see Table 7.9). Among small firms (10–50 employees), 62 percent reported that they offer a health-insurance plan to their employees. Unfortunately, the small-group market offers many inadequate health plans at considerable expense. Small firms that offer health insurance face the same fixed administrative costs for providing these benefits to their employees as larger firms as well as perhaps contributing a larger share of the premium for coverage.

Despite the inadequate plan offerings in the small-group market, employees generally accept the offer of health-insurance coverage from their employers. In fact, as Table 7.9 shows, there appears to be little or no difference in the proportion of employees who accept an employer's offer of health-insurance coverage regardless of the size of the firm. Employees obviously understand the financial and health protection that such coverage provides for them and their families.

Yet, Latinos are more likely (17 percent) than non-Latino whites (nine percent) to say they are uninsured because they were not offered employment-based health-insurance coverage.[8] The main reason the majority of both Latinos and non-Latino whites cite for why they do not have health insurance is that it is too expensive. If employers offer coverage, some employees, especially low-wage employees, may not be able to accept the offer of health insurance because of the share of the premium they are expected to contribute. If employers do not offer health-insurance coverage, people must look to the individual health-insurance market, where premiums are considerably higher than small- or large-group premiums.

Indeed, health insurance is costly, especially for low-wage workers in California. Data from the 1996 Medical Expenditure Panel Survey—Insurance Component show that in 1996, California employers who offered health insurance required employees to contribute an average of $1,461 (30.6 percent of the premium) to obtain family coverage or $299 (14.8 percent of the premium) for single coverage. A typical low-wage worker earning below 200 percent of the federal poverty level (FPL was $17,274 for a family of four in 1999) would be required to pay a substantial share of income to cover the family. About 60 percent of Latinos, compared to about 20 percent of non-Latino whites, earn incomes below 200 percent of the FPL in California.

The main reason reported by many small firms for not offering their employees health-insurance coverage is the cost of premiums for small-group plans (see Table 7.10). Employers, perhaps until recently, have not seen it as necessary to use fringe benefits as a way to attract or keep employees. Industries that rely on unskilled immigrant labor, especially undocumented immigrant labor,

---

[8]Schauffler and Brown, *The State of Health Insurance in California.*

Table 7.9. Employment-Based Health-Insurance Coverage by Size of Firm, 1999

Firm size (Number of Employees)	Firms Offering Coverage (%)	Eligible Employees Accepting Offer of Coverage (%)	Percentage of firms in State by Size (Number of Employees)
3–9	41	87	77.4
10–50	62	82	18.6
51–999	94	86	3.8
1,000 or more	94	87	0.2

Source: Kaiser/HRET/U.C. Berkeley California Employer Health Benefits Survey, 1999.

Table 7.10. Reasons Small Firms Cite for Not Offering Health-Insurance Coverage, 1999

Reason for Not Offering Coverage, Rated as Somewhat Important or Very Important	Percent of Firms with 3–9 Employees	Percent of Firms with 10–50 Employees
Premiums are too high	77	80
Turnover is too high	25	77
Can attract employees without offering	51	1
Administrative hassle	30	42
Employees covered elsewhere	59	39
Firm too new	6	24

Source: Kaiser/HRET/U.C. Berkeley California Employer Health Benefits Survey, 1999.

find it especially unnecessary, not because their workers do not need the coverage, but because they are not in a position to demand it.

The disparity in health-insurance coverage between Latinos and non-Latino whites persists regardless of the size of the firms in which earners work. Among those living in families in which the main breadwinner works for a firm with fewer than 100 employees, Latinos are about half as likely to have employment-based health insurance as non-Latino whites. Latinos are about two-thirds as likely as non-Latino whites to have health insurance when the firm has 100 to 499 employees and about 80 percent as likely when the firm has 500 or more employees.

Half of Latinos (49 percent) and about a third (37 percent) of non-Latino whites live in families supported by breadwinners who work in retail, service, construction, or agricultural jobs. Compensation in these industries has historically included few fringe benefits such as health-insurance coverage. Just as we have seen with regard to firm size, Latinos are less likely to receive health insurance as part of their employment compensation in all industries, compared to non-Latino whites. For example, in the nondurable-goods manufacturing industry, 85 percent of non-Latino whites have employment-based health-insurance coverage compared to only 45 percent of Latinos. In part, this reflects the types of low-paying jobs Latinos are relegated to performing across industries.

Community Health Care Resources

California's vast geography poses major challenges to ensuring that adequate medical and dental resources are within reach of all Californians. The maldistribution of illness-care resources reflects in part the economic resources available in local communities. A shortage of resources can be found in poor rural and urban communities throughout the state. Upper-income urban communities such as West Los Angeles have almost twice as many physicians on average as do rural and low-income urban areas.[9]

Patients must often travel for lengthy periods to gain access to appropriate medical services. Overcoming these geographical and distributional barriers requires a combination of approaches, including building community infrastructure that locates multiple medical and human services in a single site, innovative transportation or mobile resources, and increased use of telemedicine and other technological solutions.

In 1999, 20 percent of Latinos cited cost as a major barrier to seeking medical care they or their families needed. In contrast, nine percent of the non-Latino

---

[9] J. M. Coffman et al., *California Needs Better Medicine: Physician Supply and Medical Education in California* (San Francisco: California Primary Care Consortium and the Center for the Health Professions, 1997).

white population in California cited cost as a barrier to needed care. This should not be surprising because groups least likely to have health insurance are more likely to report that in the last year they did not seek services when they needed it, because of its high cost. Therefore, not only do many Latinos lack health insurance, but a substantial number are unlikely to seek medical care when they need it because of the high costs associated with care. Delay in seeking treatment for illnesses and injuries can lead to more serious and costly health problems.

Any strategy for protecting and improving the health of the Latino community must include policies and programs that ensure preventive clinical care services, and access to primary care for acute illnesses and injuries. Support for direct-service programs such as community health centers and migrant health centers should serve as the centerpiece of a strategy because these facilities play a major role in providing culturally sensitive medical care in Latino communities across the state. But this strategy must include increasing family health-insurance coverage so these facilities are financially stable. More than 50 percent of all patients seen by these service providers are Latino. These facilities are a major source of care for the uninsured in many California counties.

Latinos, whether insured or not, are more likely to report community health centers or public hospitals as their usual source of care. Forty percent of uninsured Latino children rely on community health centers or public hospitals for their care, compared to 11 percent of non-Latino white children. Among insured Latino children, about 15 percent report that these providers are their usual source of care, compared to about three percent of insured non-Latino white children. Similarly, among Latino uninsured adults, 30 percent rely on these providers for regular care, compared with eight percent of uninsured non-Latino whites. About eight percent of insured Latino adults and two percent of insured non-Latino whites report that these providers are their regular source of care.

In recent years, diminishing numbers of Medi-Cal patients, lower amounts of federal support, and diminishing county support for community health centers have endangered the capacity of these institutions to care for the uninsured.[10] Recent federal and state policies threaten the financial viability of these providers. Congress is phasing out cost-based reimbursement for federally qualified health centers (FQHCs). Other funding designed to compensate hospitals that serve disproportionate numbers of uninsured patients is also being phased out.

Both community health centers and county providers depend on unstable funding streams. Perhaps their most stable source of funds is a fragile Medi-Cal revenue stream. This stream has become increasingly unstable as Medicaid provisions of the 1997 Balanced Budget Act phase out FQHC funding and further

---

[10] T. Henderson and A. Markus, "Medicaid Managed Care: How Do Community Health Centers Fit?" *Health Care Financing Review* 17 (1996): 135–42.

restrict disproportionate share hospital (DSH) funding for uninsured care at many county hospitals.

This reduction in subsidies for safety-net providers and diversion of Medi-Cal funds to private providers challenges the fiscal integrity of the safety-net providers. The move to Medi-Cal managed care in some counties diverts patients away from these safety-net providers without evidence that access or illness improves. While county health departments have seen growth in realignment revenues for the uninsured and for public health, other revenue streams have declined. In fact, General Fund contributions to care for the uninsured have declined in most counties. Phase-down of FQHC, the decline in Medi-Cal revenues, and DSH funding present community health centers and county hospitals with an uncertain future.

Funding of California's care for the uninsured is a mix, and dynamic remix, of realignment, Proposition 99, county contributions, and Medi-Cal SB855 and SB1255 revenues.[11] This mix and the level of support are subject to annual state and local budgeting decisions. Creating a stable funding base in support of direct service programs would enhance the ability of the organizations providing care for the uninsured to plan and respond to the current crisis. Clearly a major investment in these organizations is called for given the decade-long decline in revenues they have experienced and the increased demand for their services.

The mixed financing sources and the level of those resources depend on each county's approach to meeting its obligations to care for its uninsured indigent residents. Meeting the increased demands for illness care in rural communities, in particular, requires a re-examination of how best to finance care for Californians in general. Reliance on annual distributions from the various revenue funds does not allow for investment in infrastructure or personnel.

Implications for Health and Social Policy

Increasing access to care requires at least a two-pronged strategy. Substantial reductions in financial barriers must accompany investments in the health-care safety net. A short-run goal as we move toward a more systematic response to the issue must be to stabilize community-based safety-net delivery systems' financial situations and improve their capacity to provide high-quality care. Reducing financial barriers requires integrating some public programs with each other and making publicly sponsored health-insurance programs consumer-friendly.

Changes in the medical care market over the last 20 years have significantly affected Latino communities and the providers who have traditionally served

---

[11] L. Wulsin, Jr., S. Djavaheri, J. Frates, and A. Shofet, "Clinics, Counties and the Uninsured: A Study of Six California Urban Counties" (February 1999).

these communities through safety-net institutions such as community health centers. Larger business interests, health professionals, and government regulators have played a significant role in shaping California's decision-making and policymaking environments. Consumers, especially Latino consumers, have had little voice in balancing the interests of other stakeholders. Thus, patients have little control over their own medical care and distribution of resources to address the wider community-health concerns of Latino communities.

The recent conversion of nonprofit health-care organizations to for-profit status has been unprecedented. Nonprofit hospitals provide significantly more community benefits such as charity care than do for-profit institutions.[12] But with the dominance of managed care organizations in California, for over a decade little attention has been paid to the community-benefits contributions of managed care organizations. While one might suspect that nonprofit HMOs provide greater community benefits than for-profit HMOs, the question remains open to debate. What should managed-care organizations operating in the California market contribute to increase the well-being of the state's people, many of whom remain uninsured?

Increasing the health-insurance coverage of Latinos can be achieved by increasing access to employment-based coverage and decreasing the cost of health insurance to employers and employees. Employment-based coverage can be made more affordable to low-wage employees through increased financial assistance provided by employers, government, or both.

The state could transform the Medi-Cal program and the Healthy Families Program into a single new health-insurance coverage program and extend coverage through a buy-in to employers and employees of small firms as well as the categorical groups it covers today. The state could identify individuals eligible for federal subsidies or matching funds (e.g., categorically covered groups) as part of the internal administrative process of arranging financing streams. Medi-Cal's fee-for-service and HMO coverage plans and commercial plans offered through Healthy Families could be offered to provide an array of choices. Providing employer buy-in to a health insurance scheme sponsored by the state, but operated as a single or multiple regional purchasing pools, could increase health-insurance coverage dramatically across the state, especially among Latinos, given that they are disproportionately employed by small employers.

One approach to reducing the cost to small firms would be to offer the buy-in to all employers and employees of firms with 50 or fewer employees. The state could provide these small employers with a tax subsidy if they contribute at least 50 percent of health-insurance premiums for plans. Employees earning incomes below 200 percent of the federal poverty level would receive a subsidy to assist them with paying for their share of the premium. Thus, the cost of in-

---

[12]G. Claxton et al., "Public Policy Issues in Nonprofit Conversions: An Overview," *Health Affairs* 16 (1997): 9–28.

suring the vast majority of the uninsured in California would be shared by the state, employers, and employees.

Health-insurance coverage programs sponsored by the state government that are designed to improve access to medical care services have not reached their intended audiences. Eligible Californians do not use current programs for a variety of reasons that reflect failure in implementation of public policies and inadequate marketing by state agencies. Public agencies are largely unaccustomed to marketing their programs, especially programs that have historically been part of the state's welfare system, in which financial incentives often discouraged the full use of these programs by the public. Unfortunately, the public sector has often assumed that if a program is developed, the customers will come, rather than recognizing that customers need to be cultivated through culturally appropriate and targeted marketing strategies.

For example, it is not uncommon for some members of a Latino family to have coverage while others do not. Yet work on this topic suggests that some Latino parents can be uncomfortable enrolling one qualified child in a public program while leaving other children—those who are older or not born in the United States—uninsured.[13] Parents tend to think about health care coverage in whole-family terms.

Latinos indicate language barriers exist when they attempt to enroll in publicly sponsored health-insurance programs. They say that enrollment officers speak poor Spanish, or that only one or two Spanish-speaking enrollment officers are there to process scores of applicants. Similar problems may exist in the private sector, where information about health plans may not be translated, or where companies do not have Spanish-speaking human resources personnel who can help Latino employees enroll in a health plan.

In a recent Kaiser Family Foundation survey regarding barriers to enrollment in Medicaid, it appears that there is a group of families that have never received public assistance despite their eligibility for Medi-Cal coverage.[14] This group tends to be less informed about public programs and health-insurance options in general because they have limited or no experience with the public-

---

[13]See, for example, M. Perry, S. Kannel, and R. B. Valdez, *Speaking Out: What Beneficiaries Say about the Medi-Cal Program* (The Medi-Cal Policy Institute, January 2000); N. Halfon, D. L. Wood, R. B. Valdez, M. Pereyra, and N. Duan, "Medicaid Enrollment and Utilization of Appropriate Health Services by Latino Children in Inner City Los Angeles," *JAMA* 227(8) (February 1997): 636–41; and M. Perry, E. Stark, and R. B. Valdez, *Barriers to Medi-Cal Enrollment and Ideas for Improving Enrollment: Findings from Eight Focus Groups in California with Parents of Potentially Eligible Children* (The Henry J. Kaiser Family Foundation, September 1998).

[14]M. Perry, S. Kannel, R. B. Valdez, *Medicaid and Children: Overcoming Barriers to Enrollment, Findings from a National Survey* (The Henry J. Kaiser Family Foundation, January 2000).

assistance system and do not use the health system regularly. Furthermore, they may lack peers or other family members who participate in public-assistance programs and could assist them.

Almost three in 10 uninsured Latino children are eligible for Medi-Cal but not enrolled.[15] In fact, about two-thirds of the Medi-Cal–eligible but uninsured children are Latino. Expanding and targeting outreach to immigrant Latino communities would be helpful in enrolling more children.

The Child Health and Disability Prevention (CHDP) program—the state's version of the Medicaid Early, Periodic, Screening, Diagnosis, and Treatment program and a state-funded component for children not eligible for federal Medicaid dollars—remains largely unused. For example, in the San Joaquin Valley fewer than a third of the eligible low-income children received CHDP screening and treatment for medical and dental problems in 1994.[16] Fewer than one in 10 high-risk children were screened for lead poisoning.

The federal welfare-reform law delinks welfare (i.e., cash assistance) from Medi-Cal eligibility.[17] Despite this delinking in policy, these programs remain linked administratively and in the public mind. In combination with immigration-law changes, these legal reforms may discourage some people from seeking participation, particularly immigrants who may fear deportation or other immigration-related actions. Yet the passage of the federal Child Health Insurance Program creates a financial incentive to increase program participation.

Unfortunately, it is often the case that people simply do not know about available services and programs. A wide array of public and private programs exists throughout California. The programs are highly fragmented, focus on specific populations or offer only particular services, and often rely on categorical funding streams. Integrating human-services programs remains one of the largest challenges in California in a governance structure that relies on counties and localities to play the central role in the medical care and health of its population.

A final word on a problem that is certain to get much attention in the future: the dilemma of immigrant seniors. Medicare has often been seen as a platform upon which health-insurance coverage for other Americans could be built. In fact, Medicare expansions to working persons ages 55–64 have been suggested as an incremental step toward universal health-insurance coverage. Yet, even before such expansions are considered it should be noted that some American

---

[15] See, for example, Medi-Cal Policy Institute, 2000; and R. B. Valdez, M. Hochstein, and N. Halfon, *Declining California Spending for Medicaid Services* (UCLA Center for Healthier Children, Families and Communities, 1999).

[16] J. Diringer, C. Ziolkowski, and N. Paramo, *Hurting the Heartland: Access to Health Care in the San Joaquin Valley* (Rural Health Advocacy Institute and California Rural Legal Assistance Foundation, 1996).

[17] D. Super and S. Parrott, et al., *The New Welfare Law* (Center on Budget and Priorities, August 1996).

seniors are left out of the program as it is currently designed. Evidence suggests that the program is not covering Latino elders adequately: In Los Angeles only about 78 percent of Latino elders reported Medicare coverage. Almost a quarter of the Latino elders in Los Angeles appear to be without the financial security and access that Medicare coverage provides. As the Latino senior population grows in size in other parts of the country, the universality of Medicare may be further threatened unless swift action is taken to include those now excluded.

References

American College of Physicians—American Society of Internal Medicine. 1999. *No Health Insurance? It's Enough to Make You Sick—Scientific Research Linking the Lack of Health Coverage to Poor Health.* Philadelphia: American College of Physicians—American Society of Internal Medicine, 4–11.

Andrulis, D. P. 1997. *The Public Sector in the Emerging Health Care Environment: Evolution or Dissolution?* The National Public Health and Hospital Institute, Washington, D.C.

Brown, E. R., R. B. Valdez, H. Morgenstern, W. Cumberland, and C. Wang. 1991. *Californians Without Health Insurance in 1989.* California Policy Seminar, August.

Brown, E. R., R. B. Valdez, R. Wyn, H. Yu, and W. Cumberland. 1994. *Who Are California's Uninsured?* Policy Brief, UCLA School of Public Health, March.

———. 1994. *Medi-Cal Offsets Declining Private Job-Based Insurance Coverage.* UCLA School of Public Health, March.

Coffman J. M., J. Q. Young, et al. 1997. *California Needs Better Medicine: Physician Supply and Medical Education in California.* A joint publication of the California Primary Care Consortium and the Center for the Health Professions, San Francisco, Calif.

Claxton G., J. Feder, et al. 1997. "Public Policy Issues in Nonprofit Conversions: An Overview." *Health Affairs* 16(9): 9–28.

Diringer J., C. Ziolkowski, and N. Paramo. 1996. *Hurting the Heartland: Access to Health Care in the San Joaquin Valley.* Rural Health Advocacy Institute and California Rural Legal Assistance Foundation.

Halfon, N., D. L. Wood, R. B. Valdez, M. Pereyra, and N. Duan. 1997. "Medicaid Enrollment and Utilization of Appropriate Health Services by Latino Children in Inner City Los Angeles." *JAMA* 227(8): 636–41.

Hayes-Bautista, David E., Paul Hsu, Maria Hayes-Bautista, and Delmy Iñiguez. 2001. *Latino Elderly and Medicare Coverage.* Center for the Study of Latino Health and Culture, UCLA.

Henderson T., and A. Markus. 1996. "Medicaid Managed Care: How Do Community Health Centers Fit?" *Health Care Financing Review* 17: 135–42.

Perry, M., S. Kannel, and R. B. Valdez. 2000. *Medicaid and Children: Overcoming Barriers to Enrollment, Findings from a National Survey.* The Henry J. Kaiser Family Foundation, January.

———. 2000. *Speaking Out: What Beneficiaries Say about the Medi-Cal Program.* The Medi-Cal Policy Institute, January.

Perry, M., E. Stark, and R. B. Valdez. 1998. *Barriers to Medi-Cal Enrollment and Ideas for Improving Enrollment: Findings from Eight Focus Groups in*

California with Parents of Potentially Eligible Children. The Henry J. Kaiser Family Foundation, September.

Schauffler, H., and E. R. Brown. 2000. *The State of Health Insurance in California, 1999.* Berkeley, Calif.: Regents of the University of California, January.

Schauffler, H., and Zawicki. 1999. *The State of Health-Insurance Coverage in California, Analysis of the California Behavioral Risk Factor Survey of 1999.* Berkeley, Calif.: Regents of the University of California.

Super D., S. Parrott, et al. 1996. *The New Welfare Law.* Center on Budget and Priorities. Washington, D.C., August.

Treviño, F. M., M. E. Moyer, R. B. Valdez, and C. A. Stroup. 1992. "Health-Insurance Coverage and Utilization of Health Services by Mexican Americans, Mainland Puerto Ricans, and Cuban Americans." In *Health Policy and the Hispanic,* ed. A. Furino. Boulder, Colo.: Westview Press.

Valdez, R. B. 1999. "Latino Health Access Issues in the Age of Managed Care." Prepared for U.S. Department of Health and Human Services Assistant Secretary for Planning and Evaluation, March.

———. 1991. "Insuring Latinos Against the Costs of Illness." Testimony before the U.S. House of Representatives Select Committee on Aging and the Congressional Hispanic Caucus, September 19, 1991, RAND, P-7750.

———. 1990. "Health Care for All in the Year 2000?" In *Latinos and Blacks in the Cities,* ed. H. D. Romo. Austin: Lyndon Baines Johnson Library and Lyndon B. Johnson School of Public Affairs.

Valdez, R. B., A. Giachello, H. Rodrigues-Trias, P. Gomez, and C. de la Rocha. 1993. "Access to Health Care in Latino Communities." *Public Health Reports* 108, no. 5 (Sept.–Oct.): 534–39.

Valdez, R. B., M. Hochstein, and N. Halfon. 1999. "Declining California Spending for Medicaid Services." UCLA Center for Healthier Children, Families and Communities.

Valdez, R. B., H. Morgenstern, E. R. Brown, R. Wyn, C. Wang, and W. Cumberland. 1993. "Insuring Latinos against the Costs of Illness." *JAMA* 269(7) (Feb. 17): 889–94.

Wulsin, L., Jr., S. Djavaheri, J. Frates, and A. Shofet. 1999. *Clinics, Counties, and the Uninsured: A Study of Six California Urban Counties.* February.

Wyn R., E. R. Brown, R. B. Valdez, H. Yu, W. Cumberland, H. Morgenstern, C. Halfner-Eaton, and C. Wang. 1993. *Health-Insurance Coverage of California's Latino Population and Their Use of Health Services.* Berkeley: California Policy Seminar, University of California.

Chapter 8

Latino Mental Health in California: Implications for Policy

Kurt C. Organista and Lonnie Snowden

Until about 20 years ago, almost nothing conclusive could be said about Latino mental health. The knowledge base until then consisted of sporadic local-community studies, employing a variety of research methods, on different Latino subgroups displaying different mental-health problems. The purpose of this chapter is to convey what we have learned in the last two decades about Latino mental health in California and to offer policy recommendations that are based on that information.

Fortunately, Mexican Americans, who constitute 80 percent of California's nearly eight million Latinos, were included in the largest psychiatric prevalence study of mental health in America during the 1980s. They were also the sole focus of an epidemiological survey in the 1990s. Data from these studies are supplemented by a limited state and county database that needs further development. Thus, for the majority of California Latinos, informative data on patterns of mental-health problems and treatment are beginning to emerge and can be used to inform policy.

Non-Mexican-American Latinos in California are a small and heterogeneous group. Central Americans collectively constitute the second-largest group of

Latinos at 8.4 percent, while South Americans make up another 4.5 percent.[1] There have been only a handful of community studies of Central Americans, but their consistent findings provide a useful sketch of this group's mental-health needs.

The mental health of Latinos is an especially timely issue. The U.S. Surgeon General issued a report in August 2001 on mental health, culture, race, and ethnicity.[2] Chapter six of the report is entitled "Mental Health Care for Hispanic Americans." An overarching message of the report is worthwhile to restate: "culture counts." This report reaffirms important conclusions from the original report it supplements. It notes that mental illnesses are legitimate and troubling conditions and that the efficacy of various available treatments is well documented. Because mental-health care is more decentralized in California than in any other state, California is home to a natural experiment in mental-health service delivery to its Latino populations.

Many Latinos are struggling to gain a foothold in society, and mental illness such as depression—an increasingly widespread problem—can markedly hinder their efforts. For example, a careful study of depression found that the impaired functioning uniquely associated with depressive symptoms, with or without a diagnosis of major depressive disorder, was generally worse than the dysfunction associated with eight major chronic medical conditions (including hypertension, diabetes, current advanced coronary artery disease, and arthritis).[3] The only medical condition that proved comparable to depression in terms of functional impairment was heart disease. Further, this study found that the combined effects of depression and medical conditions on functioning were additive. For example, heart disease plus depression resulted in twice the dysfunction than either condition alone. As the surgeon general's report discusses, efficacious treatments for depression have been shown capable of reducing such dysfunction. Connecting vulnerable Latinos to available and effective mental-health services must be a focus of California health and mental-health policies.

---

[1] J. Stiles, J. Cohen, Z. Elkins, and F. Gey, *California Latino Demographic Databook* (Berkeley: California Policy Seminar, University of California, 1998).

[2] U.S. Department of Health and Human Services, *Mental Health: Culture, Race, and Ethnicity—A Supplement to Mental Health: A Report of the Surgeon General* (Rockville, Md.: U.S. Department of Health and Human Services, Substance Abuse and Mental Health Administration, Center for Mental Health Services, 2001).

[3] K. B. Wells, A. Stewart, R. D. Hays, A. Burnam, W. Rogers, M. Daniels, S. Berry, S. Greenfield, and J. Ware, "The Functioning and Well-Being of Depressed Patients: Results from the Medical Outcomes Study," *Journal of the American Medical Association* 262 (1989): 914–19.

Mental Illness Among California's Latinos

The two surveys reviewed below are similar with respect to epidemiological survey methods. They established diagnoses based on the *Diagnostic and Statistical Manual of Mental Disorders* (DSM) of the American Psychiatric Association; they used large representative samples of Mexican Americans and careful translations and adaptations of instruments; and they included acculturation measures. These two surveys represent a relatively sophisticated pair of mental-health studies in comparison to previous research.

The Epidemiologic Catchment Areas (ECA) Study

Most of what we know about the prevalence of mental disorders in American has come from the ECA study sponsored by the National Institute of Mental Health during the 1980s.[4] The ECA, which was conducted with population-based probability sampling from catchment areas in five major Americans cities, assessed DSM III–based[5] diagnoses.

Reports comparing the mental health of Mexican Americans and non-Latino whites are based on the Los Angeles ECA (LA-ECA) site, where the study was conducted in 1983–1984 with a primary focus on Mexican Americans (N = 1,244). Reports from the LA-ECA reveal comparable lifetime and six-month prevalence rates of mental disorder in Mexican Americans (33 percent and 20 percent, respectively) and their white counterparts (32 percent and 19 percent, respectively).[6]

However, Burnam et al. examined the relation between acculturation and mental illness in the Mexican-American sample and found that immigrant Mexican Americans had lower lifetime prevalence than both non-Latino whites (i.e., lower rates of major depression, obsessive-compulsive disorder, and drug abuse and dependence) and U.S.-born Mexican Americans (i.e., lower rates of alcohol

---

[4]L. N. Robins and D. A. Regier, eds., *Psychiatric Disorders in America: The Epidemiologic Catchment Areas Study* (N.Y.: The Free Press, 1991).

[5]American Psychiatric Association, *Diagnostic and Statistical Manual of Mental Disorders,* 3d ed. (Washington, D.C.: American Psychiatric Association, 1980).

[6]See, for example, M. Karno, R. L. Hough, M. A. Burnam, J. I. Escobar, D. M. Timbers, F. Santana, and J. H. Boyd, "Lifetime Prevalence of Specific Psychiatric Disorders among Mexican Americans and Non-Hispanic Whites in Los Angeles," *Archives of General Psychiatry* 44 (1987): 695–701; and M. A. Burnam, R. L. Hough, J. I. Escobar, M. Karno, D. M. Timbers, C. A. Telles, and B. Z. Locke, "Six-Month Prevalence of Specific Psychiatric Disorders among Mexican Americans and Non-Hispanic Whites in Los Angeles," *Archives of General Psychiatry* 44 (1987): 687–94.

abuse and dependence, dysthymia, and phobia).[7] Further, results revealed that acculturation was positively associated with higher lifetime prevalence of several mental disorders (i.e., alcohol abuse and dependence, substance abuse and dependence, and phobia), even after controlling for age, sex, and marital status. More specifically, U.S.-born Mexican Americans (who had higher acculturation scores) had higher rates on all of the above disorders, with the addition of major depression disorder and dysthymia.

The fact that immigrant Mexican Americans have far better mental health than their U.S.-born counterparts is intriguing, given the former group's generally lower socio-economic status and supposed stress from migration. One popular explanation for this finding is the *selective-migration hypothesis,* which holds that perhaps Mexicans who immigrate to America are especially healthy as compared to Mexicans who do not emigrate. A better explanation is the *social-stress hypothesis,* which holds that the poorer mental health of native-born Mexican Americans has to do with their especially stressful experience in America as a devalued and discriminated ethnic-minority group. This latter hypothesis is more consistent with the study by Vega et al. reviewed below. Before a discussion of that survey, a brief mention of the National Comorbidity Survey (NCS) is in order.

National Comorbidity Survey (NCS)

The NCS is the first mental-health prevalence study based on a national probability sample of adults ($N = 8,098$) that included representative percentages of Latinos (9.7 percent) and African Americans (11.5 percent) in addition to non-Latino whites (75.3 percent). DSM III-R–based[8] diagnoses were assessed. Results published by Kessler et al. revealed generally comparable mental-health profiles across ethnic groups, although Latinos had significantly higher levels of current affective disorders and "comorbidity," which refers to simultaneous diagnoses of three or more mental disorders.[9] Unfortunately, the NCS represents a giant step backward with regard to understanding Latino mental health and its relation to acculturation: The NCS lumped Latinos of various national-origin backgrounds together and interviewed only English-speaking Latinos. The fact

---

[7] M. A. Burnam, R. L. Hough, M. Karno, J. I. Escobar, and C. A. Telles, "Acculturation and Lifetime Prevalence of Psychiatric Disorders among Mexican Americans in Los Angeles," *Journal of Health and Social Behavior* 28 (1987): 89–102.

[8] American Psychiatric Association, *Diagnostic and Statistical Manual of Mental Disorders,* 3d ed., revised (Washington, D.C.: American Psychiatric Association, 1987).

[9] R. C. Kessler, K. A. McGonagle, S. Zhao, C. B. Nelson, M. Hughes, S. Eshleman, H. Wittchen, and K. S. Kendler, "Lifetime and 12-Month Prevalence of DSM-III-R Psychiatric Disorders in the United States," *Archives of General Psychiatry* 51 (1994): 8–19.

that about half of Latinos participating in prevalence studies elect to do the interview in Spanish underscores the enormity of this omission.

Mexican American Prevalence and Services Survey (MAPSS)

Fortunately, the prevalence study on Mexican-American mental health by Vega et al. continues to advance our understanding of the relation between acculturation and Latino mental health.[10] Vega et al. surveyed a stratified random sample of 3,012 noninstitutionalized adults of Mexican background in Fresno County, California. As in the NCS, DSM III-R–based diagnoses were made. To better understand the relation between acculturation and mental health, Vega et al. compared U.S.-born Mexican Americans to short-term (less than 13 years in United States) and long-term (13 years or more in United States) immigrants. Further, findings from the MAPSS were compared to those of the NCS and to those of a Mexico City prevalence study. Thus, this study is extremely helpful in expanding upon the prevalence studies reviewed above.

Like the NCS, initial analysis from the MAPSS suggests comparable mental-health prevalence rates between Mexican Americans and the general U.S. population (i.e., a lifetime prevalence rate of nearly 50 percent for any disorder assessed). However, further analyses of MAPSS data reveal comparable prevalence rates only for U.S.-born Mexican Americans. In contrast, immigrant Mexican Americans had only half of the general prevalence of U.S.-born Mexican Americans, a rate comparable to results of the Mexico City survey. Table 8.1 shows the dramatic positive relation between acculturation and mental disorder by comparing short- and long-term immigrants and U.S.-born Mexican Americans across virtually all major mental disorders assessed.

With regard to understanding the relation between acculturation and Mexican-American mental health, Vega et al. conclude that their findings do not support the selective-migration hypothesis, given the comparable prevalence rates for immigrants in the MAPSS and Mexicans in the Mexico City study. Instead these researchers conclude that "Mexican immigrants share the lower risk status of their national origin, but acculturation has deleterious effects on many aspects of their health at the population level" (p. 777).

The MAPSS included a subsample of 500 male and 501 female migrant farmworkers. Results revealed that male and female farmworkers had similarly high lifetime-prevalence rates of mood disorders (7.2 percent and 6.7 percent, respectively) and anxiety disorders (15.1 percent and 12.9 percent, respec-

---

[10] W. A. Vega, B. Kolody, S. Aguilar-Gaxiola, E. Alderete, R. Catalano, and J. Caraveo-Anduaga, "Lifetime Prevalence of DSM-III-R Psychiatric Disorders among Urban and Rural Mexican Americans in California," *Archives of General Psychiatry* 55 (1998): 771–82.

Table 8.1. Lifetime Prevalence of Mental Disorders in the MAPSS, Mexico City, and NCS Surveys

	MAPSS Immigrants <13 Years	MAPSS Immigrants >13 Years	MAPSS U.S. Born	Mexico City	NCS Latinos	NCS Total
Number of participants	884	851	1,145	1,733	305	5,384
Major depression	3.2	7.9	14.4	7.8	18.3	17.2
Manic depression	1.3	1.6	2.7	1.3	0.5	0.4
Dysthymia	1.6	1.6	5.2	1.5	8.6	6.8
Any affective disorder	5.9	10.8	18.5	9.0	20.4	19.5
Panic disorder	1.0	2.6	1.8	0.4	1.8	3.5
Agoraphobia without history of panic	3.0	7.5	11.8	3.8	6.8	5.0
Social phobia	3.8	5.7	11.8	2.2	19.0	13.4
Simple phobia	2.6	7.9	12.0	3.0	16.4	11.1
Generalized anxiety disorder	0.0	0.0	0.0	1.1	6.2	5.4
Any anxiety disorder	7.6	17.1	24.1	8.3	28.0	25.0
Alcohol abuse	0.5	2.2	5.2	3.1	6.6	9.9
Alcohol dependency	8.6	10.4	18.0	8.2	14.2	15.1
Substance abuse	0.0	1.8	3.4	0.3	3.3	4.7
Substance dependency	3.0	5.3	13.8	0.8	7.0	7.9
Any abuse/dependency	9.7	14.3	29.3	11.8	24.7	28.2
Any mental disorder	18.4	32.3	48.7	23.4	51.4	48.6

Note: MAPSS = Mexican-American Prevalence and Services Survey; NCS = National Comorbidity Survey. A rate of 0.0 indicates that there were no cases in this category.
Source: W. A. Vega, B. Kolody, S. Aguilar-Gaxiola, E. Alderete, R. Catalano, and J. Caraveo-Anduaga, "Lifetime Prevalence of DSM-III-R Psychiatric Disorders among Urban and Rural Mexican Americans in California," *Archives of General Psychiatry* 55 (1998): 771–82.

tively).[11] Interestingly, this unusual gender pattern of results contradicts general-population studies, which consistently show greater mood and anxiety disorders in women than in men. Results further revealed that nine percent of men had a lifetime-prevalence rate of alcohol dependence, and a 12 percent lifetime prevalence of any substance abuse/dependency disorder. Taken together, results of the MAPSS data on farmworkers suggest a pattern of serious mental-health problems most likely related to the considerable loneliness, isolation, and insecurities associated with what is now America's most dangerous occupation.[12] It should also be noted that an estimated 50 percent of farmworkers in the United States are undocumented and thus lack entitlements to the health and mental-health services that they need.[13]

Underutilization of Mental-Health Services by Latinos

Do Latinos in California who suffer from mental-health problems receive needed treatment? There is good reason to believe that for the most part they do not. Results from the Los Angeles ECA indicated that among persons suffering from major depression during the previous six months, only 11 percent of Mexican Americans received specialty mental-health treatment as compared to 22 percent of non-Latino whites.[14] Sue et al. also documented the underutilization of Los Angeles County mental-health services, by Latinos and Asians, in a review of 12,000 charts over a five-year period.[15] As Table 8.2 shows, Latinos composed 26 percent of the county mental-health records, yet constituted 34 percent of the population of Los Angeles County. From the MAPPS, Vega et al. reported that only about 12 percent of Mexican Americans born in the United States, and five percent of those born in Mexico, had been treated by a mental-

---

[11]E. Alderete, W. A. Vega, B. Kolody, and S. Aguilar-Gaxiola, "Lifetime Prevalence of Risk Factors for Psychiatric Disorders among Mexican Migrant Farmworkers in California," *American Journal of Public Health* 90(4) (2000): 608–14.

[12]G. S. Rust, "Health Status of Migrants Farmworkers: A Literature Review and Commentary," *American Journal of Public Health* 80 (1990): 1213–17.

[13]U.S. Department of Labor, *Findings from the National Agricultural Workers Survey (NAWS): A Demographic and Employment Profile of United States Farmworkers* (Washington, D.C.: U.S. Department of Labor, 1998).

[14]R. L. Hough, J. A. Landsverk, M. Karno, M. A. Burnam, D. M. Timbers, J. I. Escobar, and D. A. Regier, "Utilization of Health and Mental Health Services by Los Angeles Mexican Americans and Non-Hispanic Whites," *Archives of General Psychiatry* 44 (1987): 702–09.

[15]S. Sue, D. C. Fujino, L. Hu, D. T. Takeuchi, and N. W. S. Zane, "Community Mental Health Services for Ethnic Minority Groups: A Test of the Cultural Responsiveness Hypothesis," *Journal of Consulting and Clinical Psychology* 59 (1991): 533–40.

Table 8.2. Mental-Health Service-Utilization Patterns for Los Angeles County by Major Ethnic/Racial Groups (N = 1,200)

Group	Percent of County Population	Percent of County Patient Population
Latino Americans ($N = 3,000$)	34	26
Asian Americans ($N = 3,000$)	9	3
Anglo Americans ($N = 3,000$)	43	44
African Americans ($N = 3,000$)	13	21

Source: S. Sue, D. C. Fujino, L. Hu, D. T. Takeuchi, and N. W. S. Zane, "Community Mental Health Services for Ethnic Minority Groups: A Test of the Cultural Responsiveness Hypothesis," *Journal of Consulting and Clinical Psychology* 59 (1991): 533–40.

health specialist.[16] It should also be noted that Mexican Americans with mental-health problems were more likely to have received care in the primary care and general medical sector, consistent with past research.[17]

Indeed, Latinos suffering from mental-health problems may receive needed care less than Latinos with physical-health problems receive general medical care. Another study from the Los Angeles ECA compared Mexican Americans and whites in receiving health and mental-health care.[18] Data indicated that during the previous six months, high-acculturated Mexican Americans were about .73 times as likely as whites, and low-acculturated Mexican Americans were about .65 times as likely, to have made an outpatient medical visit. Mental-health care-related disparities were even more pronounced: High-acculturated Mexican Americans were only .54 times as likely, and low-acculturated Mexican Americans were only .14 times as likely, to have been treated.

---

[16] W. A. Vega, B. Kolody, S. Aguilar-Gaxiola, and R. Catalano, "Gaps in Service Utilization by Mexican Americans with Mental Health Problems," *American Journal of Psychiatry* 156 (1999): 928–34.

[17] A. M. Padilla, M. L. Carlos, and S. E. Keefe, "Mental Health Service Utilization by Mexican Americans," in *Psychotherapy with the Spanish Speaking: Issues in Research and Services Delivery* (Monograph #3), ed. M. R. Miranda (Los Angeles: Spanish Speaking Mental Health Research Center, University of California, 1976).

[18] K. B. Wells, R. L. Hough, J. M. Golding, M. A. Burnam, and M. Karno, "Which Mexican Americans Underutilize Health Services?" *American Journal of Psychiatry* 144 (1987): 918–22.

The undertreatment of Latinos was a primary consideration leading the surgeon general to conclude that among minorities, the "burden" of mental illness was especially great. Burden was established by reference to the high rates of untreated mental illness among minorities and the marked degree of functional disability suffered by the mentally ill.

Ethnic and linguistic matching of therapist and client makes a difference in improving access to care and treatment outcome. Sue et al. studied the impact of linguistic and ethnic matching of therapists and clients by reviewing the mental-health charts of 12,000 Los Angeles County mental-health patients.[19] They examined the charts of 3,000 Latino, 3,000 Asian, 3,000 African-American, and 3,000 non-Latino white mental-health patients. Results revealed that linguistic and/or ethnic matching was associated with improved treatment outcome, decreased drop-out from therapy, and increased total number of therapy sessions, but *only* for Latinos and Asians who were low in acculturation (i.e., recent immigrants, less likely to speak English, and less familiar with the mental-health system). Thus, the presence of bilingual and/or bicultural mental-health professionals is imperative for the huge numbers of Latinos low in acculturation that have special language and adaptational needs.

Latinos in the California Public Mental-Health System

Lacking health insurance and living in poverty, many Mexican Americans are dependent on the public mental-health system for specialty mental-health care. In California, public mental-health care has been decentralized since enactment of "program-realignment" legislation in 1991. Program realignment removed restrictions on use of state funds and consolidated them into a single source, thereby delegating responsibility to the counties and granting them autonomy and control.[20] California counties designed differing mental-health programs and documented those differences in preparing plans during the transition to managed care. In preparation for managed care, the two existing systems providing specialty mental-health services to Medi-Cal eligibles—the fee-for-service system and the county "Short Doyle" system—were merged. In fiscal year 1994–1995, inpatient mental-health services were combined in what is known as "inpatient consolidation." In fiscal year 1997–1998, the same occurred for outpatient mental-health services through "outpatient consolidation." As a result, all

---

[19] S. Sue, D. C. Fujino, L. Hu, D. T. Takeuchi, and N. W. S. Zane, "Community Mental Health Services for Ethnic Minority Groups: A Test of the Cultural Responsiveness Hypothesis," *Journal of Consulting and Clinical Psychology* 59 (1991): 533–40.

[20] A. Zhang, R. Scheffler, and L. R. Snowden, "The Effects of Program Realignment on Severely Mental Ill Persons in California's Community-Based Mental Health System," *Psychiatric Services* 51 (2000): 1103–06.

Medi-Cal eligibles were required to obtain needed specialty mental-health care through one of 59 county public mental-health plans. County plans now receive state general fund monies, which were previously spent on fee-for-service care, to fund services for their new clients.

Underutilization Among Medi-Cal–Eligible Latinos

An important challenge for county mental-health plans has been the provision of culturally appropriate services to an increasingly diverse clientele. In the 1997–1998 fiscal year, Latinos were found to be dramatically underrepresented among mental-health service users: Latinos made up 43 percent of Medi-Cal eligibles but only 13 percent of those using mental-health services.[21] Further, comparable levels of underrepresentation did not occur among African Americans and Asian Americans. Thus, the medical penetration rate (the rate of mental-health service use by persons on Medi-Cal) for Latinos was only 1.1 percent, lower by at least half than that for any other group considered.

In California and elsewhere, Medicaid recipients enrolled in managed behavioral-health care plans are protected by "quality assurance rules" set forth in the Balanced Budget Act of 1997 that have focused attention on cultural responsiveness and other special needs.[22] To facilitate the development of culturally competent mental-health services, consolidation required each county plan to develop a cultural-competency plan and to examine the ethnic makeup of its client population. County plans were also required to evaluate outcomes for various ethnic groups and for other vulnerable populations, such as children and the elderly, who may experience barriers to care. Led by the Department of Mental Health Office of Multicultural Services, efforts are under way to understand the character and scope of response by county mental-health plans to the low Latino rates of participation in services. Such understanding will need to consider the mental-illness prevalence and service underutilization detailed above, as well as a few salient cultural factors such as those discussed below.

---

[21] I.D.E.A. Consulting, *California's Medi-Cal Mental Health Service Delivery System: Assuring Access, Quality and Cost Effectiveness, Volume I. Statewide Data.* Prepared for the California Department of Mental Health, Independent Assessment, HCFA 1915b Waiver, August (Sacramento: Department of Mental Health, 1999).

[22] National Association of State Mental Health Program Directors (NASMHPD), "Summary and Analysis of the Balanced Budget Act of 1997 (H.R. 2015)," 2000. www.nasmhpd.org.

Cultural Factors

Preference for Health Versus Mental-Health Providers
According to the MAPSS, a significant number of mentally ill Mexican Americans are seen by physicians and others during health-care visits. Mexican Americans with mental-health problems may seek assistance for mental problems from health-care providers to a greater extent than others.

A preference for health-care providers appears to reflect lack of access to appropriate mental-health care, stigma associated with treatment, and a tendency to express mental-health–related suffering as somatic concerns. Thus, attention to mental illness during health-care calls is needed to build adequate health-care safety nets.[23] For Mexican Americans and other low-income groups, much health care is provided by public hospitals, community health centers, rural health clinics, and programs provided by local health departments. The impact of such screening and referral, or treatment of mental-health problems, remains largely unknown but appears promising. For example, Miranda et al. conducted a county general hospital-based randomized clinical trial comparing cognitive behavioral therapy (CBT), with and without social-work clinical case management (CCM), in the treatment of low-income primary-care patients suffering from major depression disorder.[24] Forty percent of participants were Latinos who received services in Spanish from Latino clinicians. All of the participants were recruited by aggressive outreach in collaboration with medical providers who were trained to screen for depression and to refer to the hospital-based clinic. Results revealed less drop-out from the CBT-plus-CCM condition. The CBT-plus-CCM condition was also more effective than CBT alone in decreasing depression and improving functioning, but *only* for the Latino clients. This is most likely due to the special linguistic and acculturation-related needs of the Latino clients.

Somatization
There is empirical support for the widespread belief that Latinos and other traditionally oriented groups tend to express emotional problems through their bodies (somatization) and thus seek help from medical as opposed to mental-health providers for such somatic distress.[25] The tendency for Latinos to somati-

---

[23]Institute of Medicine, *America's Health Care Safety Net: Intact But Endangered* (Washington, D.C.: National Academy Press, 2000).

[24]J. Miranda, F. Azocar, K. C. Organista, E. Dwyer, and P. Arean, "Treatment of Depression among Impoverished Primary Care Patients from Ethnic Minority Groups," *Psychiatric Services* 54 (2) (2003): 219–25.

[25]M.Carlos, A. Padilla, and S. Keefe, "Mental Health Service Utilization by Mexican Americans," in *Psychotherapy with the Spanish Speaking: Issues in Research and Services*

cize is especially true for the less acculturated and for females. For example, Escobar et al. used the Los Angeles ECA data to compare somatization disorder in Mexican Americans ($N = 1{,}242$) and non-Hispanic whites ($N = 1{,}309$) and found that while men did not differ, Mexican-American women over 40 were more highly represented than their non-Latino white counterparts.[26] Somatization in Mexican-American women was also found to be positively correlated with age and negatively correlated with level of acculturation. Further, looking just at women who met diagnostic criteria for major depression or dysthymia, Escobar et al. also found that about 50 percent of Mexican-American women also met criteria for somatization disorder as compared to 20 percent of non-Latino white women.

It should be noted that the diagnosis of somatization disorder is extremely rare (e.g., prevalence of 0.1 percent in the ECA study) partly because of the complex criteria required in the DSM. Thus, to better capture somatic symptoms in Latinos and the broader community, Escobar et al. developed a less strict abridged index of the most common somatic symptoms. Using the abridged index, they were able to diagnose a prevalence of 4.4 percent in the Los Angeles ECA and to derive the above findings on Mexican-American women. Such a measure should be standard in Latino community settings.

Use of Folk Doctors

The Latino mental-health literature insists that we consider the importance of folk healers and practices such as *curanderismo* in the case of Mexican people.[27] While more research is needed, that which has been conducted fails to support the notion of widespread use of folk healers by Mexican Americans and clearly does not support its use to the exclusion of conventional services. For example, Padilla, Carlos, and Keefe's early survey of 666 Chicanos from Los Angeles, discussed in "Mental-Health Service Utilization by Mexican Americans," found that only two percent had consulted a *curandero* for emotional problems during the past year, and that only eight percent had ever done so in their entire lives. Furthermore, when asked the first place recommended to someone with an emotional problem, zero percent indicated a *curandero* as opposed to a doctor (25 percent), relative/compadre (20 percent), priest (17 percent), friend (14 percent), mental-health clinic (14 percent), or psychiatrist/counselor (9 percent).

Delivery (Monograph #3), ed. M. R. Miranda (Los Angeles: Spanish Speaking Mental Health Research Center, University of California, 1976).

[26] J. I. Escobar, J. M. Golding, R. L. Hough, M. Karno, M. A. Burnam, and K. B. Wells, "Somatization in the Community: Relationship to Disability and Use of Services," *American Journal of Public Health* 77 (1987): 837–40.

[27] *Curanderismo* is a term for folk-healing practice in Mexico. *Curandero* is a native-language term meaning folk doctor.

A sample of 3,623 Mexican Americans from the Southwest similarly showed that only 4.2 percent reported consulting a *curandero,* herbalist, or other folk practitioner during the past year.[28] Interestingly, folk-doctor use by this small percentage was predicted by low income and dissatisfaction with modern medical services recently received, indicating use of *curanderos* as a last resort. Thus, it appears that California Latinos would be better served by policy designed to enhance the accessibility and cultural competence of needed mental-health services.

Conclusions

Vega et al. end "Lifetime Prevalence of DSM-III-R Psychiatric Disorders among Urban and Rural Mexican Americans in California" with a series of questions, including two that will be entertained here. The first question is: Why does socialization into American culture and society increase susceptibility to psychiatric disorders so markedly, what are the risk factors, and is this process generalizable to other ethnic groups? Obviously this is a complex question requiring long and qualified answers based on new and improved research. However, one short answer is that acculturation histories of different Latino groups in America predispose them to varying degrees of adaptational stress and, consequently, varying degrees of risk for mental disorders, health impairment, and other social problems.

Acculturation and Mental Health

Application of acculturation theory to U.S. Latino groups appears to be supported by several reports from the Hispanic Health and Nutrition Examination Survey (H-HANES), which was the first major prevalence study of Latino health in America. The H-HANES was conducted by the National Center for Health Statistics between 1982 and 1984 and included the following large samples of Latinos: 7,462 Mexican Americans in the five southwestern states, 2,834 Puerto Ricans in the New York area, and 1,357 Cubans in Miami, Florida. As Table 8.3 shows, reports indicate highest risk for mental disorders in Puerto Ricans, and lowest risk in Cuban Americans, for disorders such as major depression, heavy drinking, and related chronic medical conditions. Mexican Americans are closer to Puerto Ricans in this database. Such a pattern of results is not only consistent with the different poverty levels of these three Latino groups, but

---

[28] J. C. Higginbotham, F. M. Trevino, and L. A. Ray, "Utilization of Curanderos by Mexican Americans: Prevalence and Predictors: Findings from HHANES 1982–84," *American Journal of Public Health* 80 (supplement) (1990): 32–35.

Table 8.3. Mental-Health Comparisons of the Three Major U.S. Latino Groups on H-HANES

	Mainland Puerto Rican	Mexican American	Cuban American
Prevalence of Major Depression Disorder (percent)			
Lifetime	8.9	4.2	3.9
Six-month	5.8	2.3	2.4
One-month	4.8	1.8	1.4
Rates of Past Heavy Drinking (percent)			
Male	35	36	17
Female	17	15	0.5

Sources: See, for example, E. K. Moscicki, D. S. Rae, D. A. Regier, and B. Z. Locke, "The Hispanic Health and Nutrition Survey: Depression among Mexican Americans, Cuban Americans, and Puerto Ricans," in *Research Agenda for Hispanics*, ed. M. Garcia and Arana (Chicago: University of Illinois Press, 1987), 145–59; and D. J. Lee, K. S. Markides, and L. A. Ray, "Epidemiology of Self-Reported Past Heavy Drinking in Hispanic Adults," *Ethnicity and Health* 2 (1997): 77–88.

also with their different acculturation histories, which similarly vary in degree of acculturative stress.

With regard to Vega et al.'s second question—What components of Mexican culture are protective against mental-health problems, and can these be conserved?—much has been written about healthy and protective aspects of traditional Mexican culture such as close and supportive extended-family systems. As a core characteristic of Latino culture, familism is likely to buffer acculturative stress and the effects of poverty but is probably also weakened by such challenging processes and situations. For example, Sabogal et al. studied the effects of acculturation on familism in a mixed sample of 452 Latinos and 227 non-Latino whites.[29] They found that perceptions of the family as highly supportive remained constant across Latinos of varying levels of acculturation and that

---

[29] F. Sabogal, G. Marin, R. Otero-Sabogal, B. VanOss Marin, and E. J. Perez-Stable, "Hispanic Familism and Acculturation: What Changes and What Doesn't?" *Hispanic Journal of Behavioral Sciences* 9 (1987): 397–412.

even the most acculturated Latinos were more familistic than their non-Latino white counterparts. On the other hand, other dimensions of familism, such as sense of family obligation and use of family as behavioral and attitudinal referents, did decrease with acculturation.

Interestingly, the idea of slowly diminishing protective Latino cultural factors may help to explain why U.S.-born Mexican Americans and Puerto Ricans do not have overall prevalence rates that greatly exceed the general U.S. population. That is, considering the much higher poverty rates of island Puerto Ricans (60 percent), mainland Puerto Ricans (40 percent), and Mexican Americans (25 percent), as compared to non-Latino whites (7 percent), it is amazing that their mental-health profiles are roughly comparable to non-Latino whites with regard to prevalence at the population level.

Central-American Mental Health

Given that California is one of the major receiving states for Central-American refugees, a brief sketch of their mental-health needs is in order. There is consensus in the literature that the majority of Central Americans in the United States fled their countries of origin under war-related duress,[30] yet their adaptation to the United States has been hampered by a general denial of refugee status (including entitlements to social services) due to limited ability to prove direct political persecution.[31] The historical denial of political asylum leads to inhibited social and community life, mistrust, and perceptions of the U.S. government as supportive of repressive governments in Latin America.[32]

The Central-American predicament is unfortunate because community studies report elevated symptom levels of depression, anxiety, somatization, and interpersonal sensitivity as compared to American norms.[33] In addition, Central

---

[30] See, for example, R. Cordova, "Undocumented El Salvadorans in the San Francisco Bay Area: Migration and Adaptation Dynamic," *Journal of La Raza Studies* 1 (1979): 9–35; and L. A. Leslie and M. L. Lietch, "A Demographic Profile of Recent Central American Immigrants: Clinical and Service Implications," *Hispanic Journal of Behavioral Sciences* 11 (1989): 315–29.

[31] E. G. Ferris, *The Central American Refugees* (New York: Praeger, 1987).

[32] P. J. Farias, "Emotional Distress and Its Socio-Political Correlates in Salvadoran Refugees: Analysis of a Clinical Sample," *Culture, Medicine, and Psychiatry* 15 (1991): 167–92.

[33] T. G. Plante, G. M. Manuel, A. V. Menendez, and D. Marcotte, "Coping with Stress among Salvadoran Immigrants," *Hispanic Journal of Behavioral Sciences* 17 (1995): 471–79.

Americans are higher than Mexican immigrants in symptoms of depression and migration-related stress,[34] as well as post-traumatic stress disorder (PTSD).[35]

Policy Recommendations

At the outset, it is important to acknowledge that we continue to lack important information about Latino mental health in California. Nevertheless, MAPSS and other epidemiological studies have provided sufficient evidence to support a cogent set of policy recommendations responsive to the mental-health needs of California's Latino population. These recommendations will be further refined as ongoing research efforts teach us more about Latino mental health.

In particular, we recommend two areas of new inquiry in the field of Latino mental health. First, we await systematic documentation of how managed-care plans guide provision of public mental-health care in California counties, and the response to the special needs of the Latino population they represent. Because coverage and access vary significantly across counties, these county programs should be evaluated with regard to their effectiveness.

Second, the role of general health-care programs and service providers must be better understood. The complex set of arrangements comprising the health-care safety-net plays an especially prominent role in light of Latino poverty and lack of heath insurance, and the greater likelihood that Latinos with mental-health problems will seek assistance from general medical providers. At present, we know little about the response of affected providers to mental-health problems that are brought to them.

Based on the current data and analysis reviewed in this chapter, we have identified eight areas for public-policy development and implementation to improve mental-health services for Latinos:

- Develop policy approaches to increase the bilingual/bicultural capabilities of mental-health professionals in California in order to meet the needs of Latinos and other language minorities. Senate Bill 1451 (2000) provided an approach to achieving this objective.

Latino clients in the public mental-health system treated by Latino clinicians received more care, and showed more improvement, than other Latino

---

[34] V. N. Salgado de Snyder, R. C. Cervantes, and A. M. Padilla, "Gender and Ethnic Differences in Psychosocial Stress and Generalized Distress among Hispanics," *Sex Roles* 22 (1990): 441–53.

[35] R. C. Cervantes, V. N. Salgado de Snyder, and A. M. Padilla, "Post Traumatic Stress Disorder among Immigrants from Central America and Mexico," *Hospital and Community Psychiatry* 40 (1989): 615–19.

clients.[36] The beneficial impact was restricted to less-acculturated Latinos. The knowledge and skills producing a favorable response in Latino clients cannot yet be fully explained. Nevertheless, it appears that when treating some Latino clients, Latino clinicians enjoy a relative advantage over non-Latino clinicians.

Professional Latino mental-health practitioners are in short supply. There are only 29 Latino professional mental-health practitioners per 100,000 Latinos in the United States versus 173 per 100,000 whites.[37] Recruitment and training of professional Latino clinicians appears to be an important step toward improving the quality of care for Latino clients.

In the spring of 2000, California Senator Liz Figueroa introduced SB 1451 to create a loan-forgiveness program whereby the state would pay a portion of loans incurred by graduate students preparing to become psychologists, social workers, or marriage, family, and child counselors. The program was intended for students who agreed to provide counseling and therapy services for at least two consecutive years for a public or nonprofit agency serving a large population of low-income clients in a language other than English. Although the legislature passed the bill, Governor Gray Davis returned the legislation unsigned. This was unfortunate, given that loan-forgiveness programs have been used with success in areas such as education.[38]

- Develop and integrate hospital- and health-clinic–based mental-health outreach, screening, and services into general-health settings. This is needed because of the tendency for Latinos to overutilize general-health services for emotional and mental-health problems.

Preliminary mental-health outcome research (as Miranda et al. discuss in "Treatment of Depression in Disadvantaged Medical Patients") indicates that coordinating hospital-based mental-health services with primary care and gen-

---

[36] S. Sue, D. C. Fujino, L. Hu, D. T. Takeuchi, and N. W. S. Zane, "Community Mental Health Services for Ethnic Minority Groups: A Test of the Cultural Responsiveness Hypothesis," *Journal of Consulting and Clinical Psychology* 59 (1991): 533–40.

[37] U.S. Department of Health and Human Services, *Mental Health: Culture, Race, and Ethnicity—A Supplement to Mental Health: A Report of the Surgeon General* (Rockville, Md.: U.S. Department of Health and Human Services, Substance Abuse and Mental Health Administration, Center for Mental Health Services, 2001).

[38] One example is the Assumption Program of Loans for Education (APLE), established in 1983 with the enactment of SB 813. APLE serves the dual purpose of: (1) encouraging outstanding postsecondary students to enter the teaching field; and (2) providing successful teaching candidates with loan-repayment assistance upon completion of a credential program and fulfillment of a required teaching service commitment. Since the inception of APLE, over 5,300 participants have obtained teaching credentials and nearly 80 percent have completed three consecutive years of teaching service. Teaching in low-income schools constitutes 40 percent of teaching service commitments, while teaching in subject shortage areas (e.g., bilingual education, math, and science) constitutes the remaining 60 percent.

eral medicine is a winning strategy for "intercepting" and treating Latinos in need of mental-health services for serious but treatable problems such as major depression.[39]

- Provide effective health-care coverage for immigrant laborers in general and farmworkers in particular, including the population lacking legal-immigration status. Effective coverage is also needed for especially vulnerable Latino subgroups such as the children of shorter-term immigrants and the undocumented. Both the federal and state governments can play a role in providing coverage and reforming immigration law in ways to allow access to mental-health care for the immigrant population.

California's massive and lucrative service sector and agricultural industry are highly dependent on immigrant-Latino labor, which includes many undocumented workers. For example, 50 percent of migrant farmworkers are undocumented and frequently in need of basic family health as well as specialized mental-health services (such as treatment for drug/alcohol dependence and for major depression).[40] Considering immigrants' contribution to the California economy (e.g., agricultural business produces $27 billion annually in profits), access to a range of health services is a benefit to both the immigrant population and society as a whole. In California, community medical clinics provide most of the health services to undocumented immigrants, who are currently not eligible for a number of state programs. One solution at the federal level is to adopt legislation that would allow for the regularization of long-term immigrants without legal status.

- Support bilateral approaches to health and mental-health care such as the newly established California-Mexico Health Initiative funded by the California Endowment and spearheaded by the University of California.

The MAPPS study provided a rare look at the mental health of migrant farmworkers. It revealed significant levels of mental illness, especially alcoholism and substance abuse. Although MAPPS investigators did not assess whether their respondents possessed documents, there is reason to believe that, like migrant farmworkers overall, many lacked legal papers.

Undocumented agricultural workers sometimes cross the U.S.-Mexico border and return home to Mexico, where they reside for a significant part of the year. Thus, mental-health problems affecting this population occur both in the United States and Mexico, and the two countries have a stake in formulating a cooperative response.

---

[39] J. Miranda, F. Azocar, K. C. Organista, E. Dwyer, and P. Arean, "Treatment of Depression among Impoverished Primary Care Patients from Ethnic Minority Groups," *Psychiatric Services* 54 (2) (2003): 219–25.

[40] U.S. Department of Labor, *Findings from the National Agricultural Workers Survey (NAWS): A Demographic and Employment Profile of United States Farmworkers* (Washington, D.C.: U.S. Department of Labor, 1998).

Dr. Guido Belsasso, Mexico's national commissioner against drug addiction and for mental health, discussed the need for U.S.-Mexico collaboration in his keynote address to the UC Berkeley Institute of Governmental Studies conference "Coping with Mental Illness and Crafting Public Policy." He outlined the respective responsibilities of the two countries; noting that each ought to provide treatment on respective sides of the border.[41]

Others observed that preliminary steps are under way; that California members of Congress have discussed cooperative efforts and that Health and Human Services Secretary Tommy Thompson has met with Mexico counterpart Dr. Julio Frenk several times, recognizing shared problems and working to develop better health care for both nations. Dr. Belsasso's remarks stressed the importance of considering mental health as these efforts go forward.

Policies that promote binational tracking of mental-health needs, service-utilization rates, and outcome, as well as cost sharing, would help to build upon this historical initiative between the U.S. and Mexican governments, with California playing a central role to promote this binational effort.

- Encourage safety-net health-care providers and others serving Latino populations to conduct outreach and screen their patients for mental-health problems, and to treat the mentally ill, or make referrals for treatment to mental-health specialists. Cutting-edge developments in integrating behavioral medicine with primary care should be encouraged for use with Latino populations.[42]

Latinos, particularly Mexican Americans, seek care for mental-health problems from general health-care providers. Research suggests various reasons: inadequate access to mental-health care; a perceived stigma for treatment of mental health; and a tendency for Latinos to somaticize. Health care is sought from public hospitals, community health centers, rural health clinics, and local health-department programs. Providers at such safety-net health-care organizations are well-situated to detect treatable mental-health disorders and refer patients to mental-health specialists.

- Develop policies to promote fuller utilization of existing culturally competent services for Latinos (i.e., from community-based Latino mental-health agencies that offer alternatives to traditional mental-health services). Encourage county mental-health plans to contract with existing Latino-focused culturally competent mental-health service providers.

---

[41]"Symposium Keynote Guido Belsasso praises cross-border efforts," University of California, Institute of Government Studies, *Public Affairs Report* 43(1) (2002): 14–15.

[42]W. Katon, M. Von Korff, E. Lin, E. Walker, G. E. Simon, T. Bush, P. Robinson, and J. Russo, "Collaborative Management to Achieve Treatment Guideline: Impact of Depression in Primary Care," *Journal of the American Medical Association* 273 (1995): 1026–31.

Latinos are dramatically underrepresented as users of mental-health services. Neither African Americans nor Asian Americans have comparable low levels of participation in mental-health services.
- Examine financing methods to determine whether they provide appropriate incentives for inclusion of Latinos.

As an example, capitation rates might need to be adjusted for the sociocultural needs of Latinos (e.g., higher reimbursements for subgroups evidencing greater need, such as U.S.-born Latinos whose needs are comparable to the general U.S. population; Latinos at risk for comorbid mental disorders; Central Americans at higher risk for PTSD and major depression; and migrant farmworkers at higher risk for substance dependence and major depression).
- Facilitate and support additional mental-health research on the prevalence of mental illness in Latino communities, with special attention to the roles of acculturation, social stress, and protective cultural factors, and to barriers and facilitators to mental-health service utilization. This research should address the national-origin, generational, and socioeconomic diversity within this population, including the special needs of recent immigrants, U.S.-born Latinos, Central-American refugees, and migrant farmworkers.

The literature reveals that declining mental health accompanies increasing levels of acculturation to the United States for Latinos. The literature also reveals elevated psychiatric symptoms levels for Central Americans, especially high rates of depression and alcohol/substance dependence for migrant farmworkers, and widespread underutilization of both health and mental-health services on the part of Latinos, including those with Medi-Cal eligibility.

References

Alderete, E., W. A. Vega, B. Kolody, and S. Aguilar-Gaxiola. 2000. "Lifetime Prevalence of Risk Factors for Psychiatric Disorders among Mexican Migrant Farmworkers in California." *American Journal of Public Health* 90(4): 608–14.

American Psychiatric Association. 1980. *Diagnostic and Statistical Manual of Mental Disorders,* 3d ed. Washington, D.C.: American Psychiatric Association.

———. *Diagnostic and Statistical Manual of Mental Disorders,* 3d ed., Revised. Washington, D.C.: American Psychiatric Association.

Burnam, M. A., R. L. Hough, J. I. Escobar, M. Karno, D. M. Timbers, C. A. Telles, and B. Z. Locke. 1987a. "Six-Month Prevalence of Specific Psychiatric Disorders among Mexican Americans and Non-Hispanic Whites in Los Angeles." *Archives of General Psychiatry* 44: 687–94.

———. 1987b. "Acculturation and Lifetime Prevalence of Psychiatric Disorders among Mexican Americans in Los Angeles." *Journal of Health and Social Behavior* 28: 89–102.

Cervantes, R. C., V. N. Salgado de Snyder, and A. M. Padilla. 1989. "Post Traumatic Stress Disorder among Immigrants from Central America and Mexico." *Hospital and Community Psychiatry* 40: 615–19.

Cordova, R. 1979. "Undocumented El Salvadorans in the San Francisco Bay Area: Migration and Adaptation Dynamic." *Journal of La Raza Studies* 1: 9–35.

Escobar, J. I., J. M. Golding, R. L. Hough, M. Karno, M. A. Burnam, and K. B. Wells. 1987. "Somatization in the Community: Relationship to Disability and Use of Services." *American Journal of Public Health* 77: 837–40.

Farias, P. J. 1991. "Emotional Distress and its Socio-Political Correlates in Salvadoran Refugees: Analysis of a Clinical Sample." *Culture, Medicine, and Psychiatry* 15: 167–92.

Ferris, E. G. 1987. *The Central American Refugees.* New York: Praeger.

Higginbotham, J. C., F. M. Trevino, and L. A. Ray. 1990. "Utilization of Curanderos by Mexican Americans: Prevalence and Predictors: Findings from HHANES 1982–84." *American Journal of Public Health* 80 (supplement): 32–35.

Hough, R. L., J. A. Landsverk, M. Karno, M. A. Burnam, D. M. Timbers, J. I. Escobar, and D. A. Regier. 1987. "Utilization of Health and Mental Health Services by Los Angeles Mexican Americans and Non-Hispanic Whites." *Archives of General Psychiatry* 44: 702–09.

I.D.E.A. Consulting. 1999. *California's Medi-Cal Mental Health Service Delivery System: Assuring Access, Quality and Cost Effectiveness, Volume I.* Statewide Data. Prepared for the California Department of Mental Health,

Independent Assessment, HCFA 1915b Waiver, August. Sacramento: Department of Mental Health.
Institute of Medicine. 2000. *America's Health Care Safety Net: Intact but Endangered.* Washington, D.C.: National Academy Press.
Karno, M., R. L. Hough, M. A. Burnam, J. I. Escobar, D. M. Timbers, F. Santana, and J. H. Boyd. 1987. "Lifetime Prevalence of Specific Psychiatric Disorders among Mexican Americans and Non-Hispanic Whites in Los Angeles." *Archives of General Psychiatry* 44: 695–701.
Katon, W., M. Von Korff, E. Lin, E. Walker, G. E. Simon, T. Bush, P. Robinson, and J. Russo. 1995. "Collaborative Management to Achieve Treatment Guideline: Impact of Depression in Primary Care." *Journal of the American Medical Association* 273: 1026–31.
Kessler, R. C., K. A. McGonagle, S. Zhao, C. B. Nelson, M. Hughes, S. Eshleman, H. Wittchen, and K. S. Kendler. 1994. "Lifetime and 12-Month Prevalence of DSM-III-R Psychiatric Disorders in the United States." *Archives of General Psychiatry* 51: 8–19.
Lee, D. J., K. S. Markides, and L. A. Ray. 1997. "Epidemiology of Self-Reported Past Heavy Drinking in Hispanic Adults." *Ethnicity and Health* 2(½): 77–88.
Leslie, L. A., and M. L. Lietch. 1989. "A Demographic Profile of Recent Central American Immigrants: Clinical and Service Implications." *Hispanic Journal of Behavioral Sciences* 11(4): 315–29.
Miranda, J., F. Azocar, K. C. Organista, E. Dwyer, and P. Arean. 2003. "Treatment of Depression among Impoverished Primary Care Patients from Ethnic Minority Groups," *Psychiatric Services* 54 (2): 219–25.
Moscicki, E. K., D. S. Rae, D. A. Regier, and B. Z. Locke. 1987. "The Hispanic Health and Nutrition Survey: Depression among Mexican Americans, Cuban Americans, and Puerto Ricans." In *Research Agenda for Hispanics,* ed. M. Garcia and Arana. Chicago: University of Illinois Press, 145–59.
NASMPHD. 2000. Summary and Analysis of the Balanced Budget Act of 1997 (H.R. 2015). http://www.nasmhpd.org.
Padilla, A., M. Carlos, and S. Keefe. 1976. "Mental Health Service Utilization by Mexican Americans." In *Psychotherapy with the Spanish Speaking: Issues in Research and Services Delivery* (Monograph #3), ed. M. R. Miranda. Los Angeles: Spanish Speaking Mental Health Research Center, University of California.
Plante, T. G., G. M. Manuel, A. V. Menendez, and D. Marcotte. 1995. "Coping with Stress among Salvadoran Immigrants." *Hispanic Journal of Behavioral Sciences* 17(4): 471–79.
Robins, L. N., and D. A. Regier, eds. 1991. *Psychiatric Disorders in America: The Epidemiologic Catchment Areas Study.* N.Y.: The Free Press.
Rust, G. S. 1990. "Health Status of Migrants Farmworkers: A Literature Review and Commentary." *American Journal of Public Health* 80(10): 1213–17.

Sabogal, F., G. Marin, R. Otero-Sabogal, B. VanOss Marin, and E. J. Perez-Stable. 1987. "Hispanic Familism and Acculturation: What Changes and What Doesn't?" *Hispanic Journal of Behavioral Sciences* 9(4): 397–412.

Salgado de Snyder, V. N., R. C. Cervantes, and A. M. Padilla. 1990. "Gender and Ethnic Differences in Psychosocial Stress and Generalized Distress among Hispanics." *Sex Roles* 22(7/8): 441–53.

Sue, S., D. C. Fujino, L. Hu, D. T. Takeuchi, and N. W. S. Zane. 1991. "Community Mental Health Services for Ethnic Minority Groups: A Test of the Cultural Responsiveness Hypothesis. *Journal of Consulting and Clinical Psychology* 59: 533–40.

Stiles, J., J. Cohen, Z. Elkins, and F. Gey. 1998. *California Latino Demographic Databook*. Berkeley, Calif.: California Policy Seminar, University of California.

"Symposium Keynote Guido Belsasso Praises Cross-Border Efforts." 2002. Berkeley: University of California, Institute of Government Studies, *Public Affairs Reports* 43(1): 14–15.

U.S. Department of Labor. 1998. Findings from the National Agricultural Workers Survey (NAWS): A Demographic and Employment Profile of United States Farmworkers. Washington, D.C.: U.S. Department of Labor.

U.S. Department of Health and Human Services. 2001. *Mental Health: Culture, Race, and Ethnicity—A Supplement to Mental Health: A Report of the Surgeon General*. Rockville, Md.: U.S. Department of Health and Human Services, Substance Abuse and Mental Health Administration, Center for Mental Health Services.

Vega, W. A., B. Kolody, S. Aguilar-Gaxiola, E. Alderete, R. Catalano, and J. Caraveo-Anduaga. 1998. "Lifetime Prevalence of DSM-III-R Psychiatric Disorders among Urban and Rural Mexican Americans in California." *Archives of General Psychiatry* 55: 771–82.

Vega, W.A., B. Kolody, S. Aguilar-Gaxiola, and R. Catalano. 1999. "Gaps in Service Utilization by Mexican Americans with Mental Health Problems." *American Journal of Psychiatry* 156: 928–34.

Wells, K. B., R. L. Hough, J. M. Golding, M. A. Burnam, M. Karno. 1987. "Which Mexican Americans Underutilize Health Services?" *American Journal of Psychiatry* 144: 918–22.

Wells, K. B., A. Stewart, R. D. Hays, A. Burnam, W. Rogers, M. Daniels, S. Berry, S. Greenfield, J. Ware. 1989. "The Functioning and Well-Being of Depressed Patients: Results from the Medical Outcomes Study." *Journal of the American Medical Association* 262: 914–19.

Zhang, A., R. Scheffler, and L. R. Snowden. 2000. "The Effects of Program Realignment on Severely Mental Ill Persons in California's Community-Based Mental Health System." *Psychiatric Services* 51: 1103–06.

Chapter 9

Crime and Justice:
Developments in the Last Twenty Years and Priorities for the Next Twenty

José A. Canela-Cacho

Introduction

The importance of issues relating to crime and justice will increase for California Latinos in the years ahead. Since the early 1990s, Latinos have reached relative-majority status in all criminal-justice confinement institutions at the state and local levels, accounting by the end of 1998 for 38.1 percent of all Californians under some form of criminal-justice custody. The situation is more extreme for juveniles, as Latinos already account for 48 percent of all juveniles in custody.[1]

On the flip side of Latino punishment—Latino victimization—the trends cannot be gauged as precisely with current data-collection practices. To the extent that we can gauge it, however, the victimization picture that emerges mirrors that of punishment. Since 1989, Latinos have systematically accounted for

---

[1] Estimates were computed by the author from various official publications. See the Appendix for a description of data sources.

the largest share of total homicide victims in the state, averaging a historical peak of 45 percent from 1994 to 1998—ironically the period during which the overall homicide rate in the state saw its steepest decline since at least 1952.[2]

Though cross-tabulations of robbery victims by ethnicity are not available for California, an extrapolation from National Crime Victimization Survey (NCVS) estimates shows that Latinos account for the largest share of robbery victims in California—close to 40 percent for 1998.[3] The high vulnerability of Latinos to robbery is not a recent development. Reviewing the NCVS data for the period 1979–1986, the Bureau of Justice Statistics concluded that the robbery victimization rate for Latinos nationwide was 1.5 times that for non-Latinos. During the period 1985–1987, the Latino robbery victimization rate was slightly higher than that for African Americans.[4]

This review of leading punishment and victimization statistics reveals the extent to which crime and justice issues will constitute a policy and political priority for California Latinos in the first decade of the 21st century. It also reveals the difficult challenge that lies ahead for all Californians if both safety and sanctioning levels are to improve measurably from the standpoint of the Latino community. Absent a comprehensive strategy to reduce Latino victimization and incarceration rates simultaneously, criminal-justice policy will inexorably become ever more polarized along a racial and ethnic divide. This could not only compromise the ability of the state to fund other important state functions, it could undermine the legitimacy of public institutions and democratic governance.

This chapter attempts to contribute to the formulation of a successful Latino agenda along the lines of "more safety and less punishment" by providing an empirical analysis of the factors that have put Latinos in the position of being the leading contributors to the debit (victims) and credit (offenders) entries of the criminal-justice ledger. The specific focus of the chapter is the 18-year period beginning in 1980, the turning point in imprisonment policies in California and indeed in the nation as a whole. The change during this period moved in the direction of more certain and harsher punishments for virtually all forms of

---

[2]*Homicide in California, 1998,* California Department of Justice, 1999.

[3]Extrapolated from national victimization data reported in U.S. Department of Justice, *National Crime Victimization Survey for 1997, Criminal Victimization in the United States, 1998 Statistical Tables,* NCJ181585, Bureau of Justice Statistics, May 2000.

[4]See U.S. Department of Justice, *Special Report: Hispanic Victims,* Bureau of Justice Statistics, January 1990, NCJ-120507. It should also be pointed out that the robbery victimization rate for African Americans averaged 9.5 per 100,000 residents, for the period 1985–1987. Possibly then Latinos had the highest robbery victimization among all ethnic groups, and thus the conclusion by the Bureau of Justice Statistics that "compared to other groups, Hispanics [Latinos] are victimized particularly for robbery."

criminal behavior,[5] leading to a colossal escalation of the state's incarceration rate since 1980, as depicted in Figure 9.1.

The Populations under Criminal-Justice Supervision

The criminal-justice system includes various populations under the control of state and local authorities at varying levels of supervision. By year-end 1998, approximately 700,000 individuals were under criminal-justice control in California, of whom only about one-third were confined in state prisons, county jails, and state and county juvenile facilities. The remaining two-thirds were offenders on probation—convicted for a crime but not serving an incarceration term—and parolees who, having served their sentences, were released subject to a period of supervision of up to three years.

Ideally, one should include every one of these components in any study of participation by a group in crime and its control. Regrettably, this is not possible because the county-level criminal-justice institutions have yet to develop rigorous accounting systems that describe the stocks and flows of the respective populations, appropriately broken down by attributes such as race, age, and offense. This omission is especially noteworthy for the probation population, which accounts for 46 percent of the total population under criminal-justice supervision. This population is of particular concern because one of the main feeding lines of the prison population consists of probationers who violate the terms of their conditionally suspended sentences and are sent to prison.

Of the confined population, one-third is under the control of county authorities—county jails for adults and juvenile detention centers for the underage. The vast majority of the remaining two-thirds are adult state prisoners under the control of the California Department of Corrections (CDC). This group includes the offenders who have committed the most serious crimes and who serve the longest sentences.

In addition, the state has a juvenile system, the California Youth Authority (CYA), for the custody of minors who have committed serious offenses and are in custody for periods longer than one year. California law allows the state to retain juvenile offenders in custody up to age 25. Since 1980 the CYA has had a population with an average age above 18 and gradually increasing to its cur-

---

[5]See, for example, Franklin Zimring and Gordon Hawkins, *Prison Population and Criminal Justice Policy in California* (Berkeley, Calif.: Institute of Governmental Studies Press, University of California, 1992); and Jacqueline Cohen and José A. Canela-Cacho, "Incarceration and Violent Crime," in *Understanding and Preventing Violence, Consequences and Control*, Vol. IV, ed. A. Reiss and J. F. Roth (Washington, D.C.: National Academy Press, 1994), 296–388.

Figure 9.1. Adult Incarceration Rate, California 1960–1998

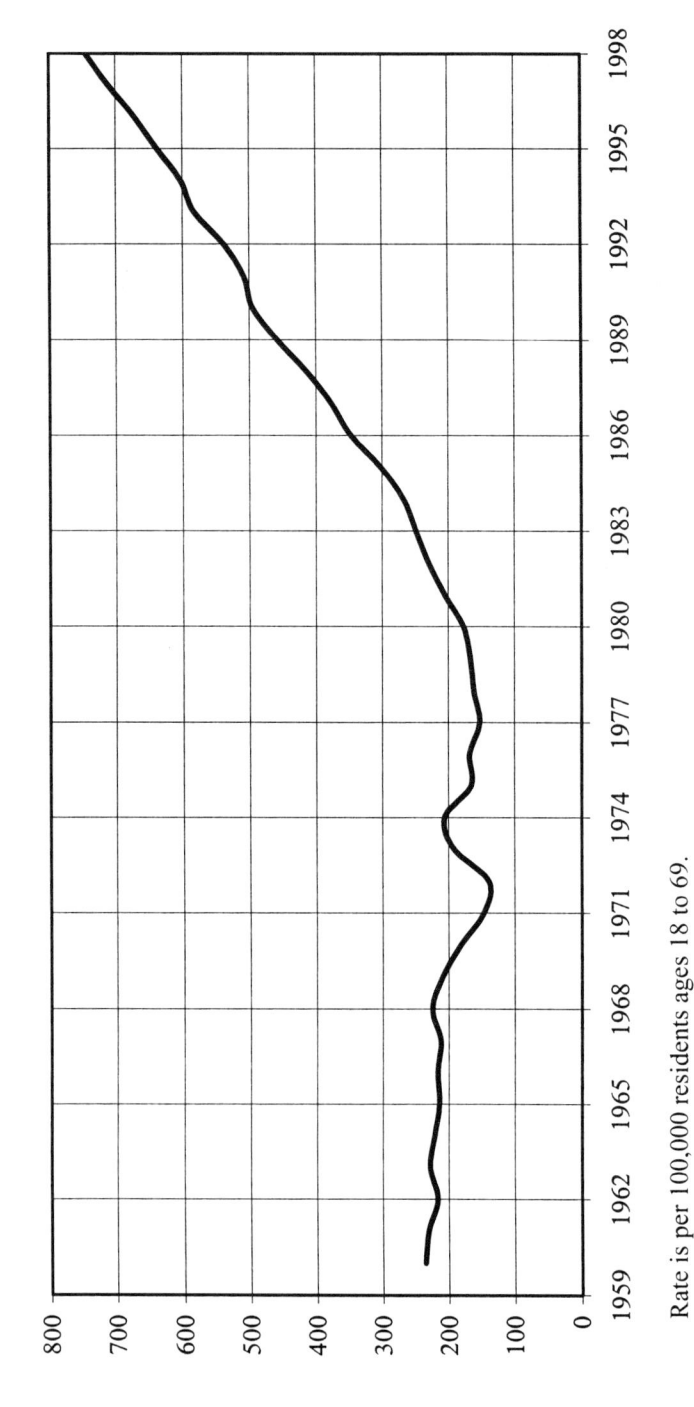

Rate is per 100,000 residents ages 18 to 69.
Source: *Crime and Delinquency Report*, 1998, California Department of Justice, 1999.

rent average of 19.2. By 1999, roughly only one in four CYA wards was under-age.

The analysis presented in this chapter is limited to CDC- and CYA-incarcerated populations. Since at least the early 1960s, both of these institutions have published detailed annual reports that permit systematic tracking of the number of offenders and their crimes. CDC also provided the author with breakdowns of offenders classified by race, crime type, and gender, making possible the calculation of race-, crime-, and gender-specific incarceration rates for the period 1980–1998. A comprehensive examination of such disaggregate rates does not seem to be available for California prior to preparation of this chapter. On a national level, in 1999 Blumstein and Beck published an analysis of all state and federal prisoners that in part compares Latinos to non-Latino whites and non-Latino blacks.[6] Examinations of this type are recent; traditionally, race studies have compared blacks and nonblacks or Latinos and non-Latinos. For the first time we are beginning to separate Latinos from non-Latino whites and non-Latino blacks.

To study relationships between arrests and incarceration rates, this chapter relies on arrest statistics disaggregated by gender, race, crime, and age, published annually by the California Department of Justice in the series *Crime and Delinquency in California*. At least since 1980 the state has published these statistics in a more or less consistent manner, making it possible for the author to compile disaggregated arrest time series of the type needed for this study. Annual estimates of California population by age, gender, and ethnicity—based on the censuses for 1980 and 1990, respectively—were obtained from the U.S. Census Bureau and updated by means of the current population surveys. By and large, the population figures from this data set are highly consistent with the aggregated population estimates of the California Department of Finance, which are generally used in state publications in the computation of arrest and incarceration rates.

A Snapshot of Latinos' Representation in California Crime and Justice Statistics

Latinos have reached relative-majority status in all California criminal-justice statistics (see Table 9.1). In part, this has resulted from the dynamic growth of

---

[6] Alfred Blumstein and Allen J. Beck, "Factors Contributing to the Growth in U.S. Population," in *Prisons, Crime and Justice: A Review of Research*, vol. 26, ed. Michael Tonry and Joan Petersilia (Chicago: University of Chicago Press, 1999), 17–61.

Table 9.1. Latinos in Crime and Justice Statistics, California, 1998

	Total	% Latino	Proportionality Index
Population under State and Local Supervision			
Under State Supervision			
Juvenile Wards	8,297	48.0%	1.25
Juvenile Parolees	6,049	49.3%	1.29
Prison Inmates	160,093	33.9%	1.25
Prison Parolees	112,564	39.7%	1.46
Under Local Supervision			
Juveniles in Custody	12,963	44.4%	1.16
Jail Inmates	81,274	NA	NA
Probationers	324,427	NA	NA
All	**705,667**	**NA**	**NA**
Felony Arrestees			
Homicide			
Ages 10 to 17	308	56.8%	1.48
18 and Above	1,809	44.9%	1.66
Robbery			
Ages 10 to 17	6,821	40.2%	1.05
18 and Above	14,686	39.7%	1.46
Other Violent Offenses			
Ages 10 to 17	12,662	43.1%	1.12
18 and Above	107,947	38.6%	1.42
Property Offenses			
Ages 10 to 17	38,308	40.0%	1.04
18 and Above	106,720	33.7%	1.24
Drug Offenses			
Ages 10 to 17	7,392	43.8%	1.14
18 and Above	134,356	32.5%	1.20
Sex Offenses			
Ages 10 to 17	1,664	40.4%	1.05
18 and Above	7,377	39.5%	1.46
Driving Offenses			
Ages 10 to 17	203	43.8%	1.14
18 and Above	6,674	43.8%	1.61
All	**431,009**	**37.5%**	**1.21**

Victims			
Homicide	2,170	44.7%	1.58
Robbery	120,619	39.1%	1.38
Household Burglary	444,270	29.0%	1.12
State Population (thousands)			
Under age 10	5,262	43.1%	-
10 to 17	3,649	38.4%	-
18 and above	23,755	27.1%	-
All	**32,667**	**31.0%**	-
State Households (thousands)			
All	**11,080**	**25.9%**	-

Source: Calculated by the author based on data sources described in the Appendix.

the Latino population, which increased at an annualized rate of 4.5 percent over the last 20 years. It is also a result of the overrepresentation of Latinos on both sides of the criminal-justice ledger—as victims and offenders—relative to their representation in the overall population, as shown in Table 9.1. This is indicated by the fact that the proportionality index in Table 9.1 is always greater than one. This index results from dividing the percent of Latinos in the respective category over the percent of Latinos in the population.

The overrepresentation of Latinos among arrestees varies substantially by crime type and age group. Latinos are most overrepresented among adult arrestees for homicide and robbery (1.7 and 1.5 times their representation in the overall population, respectively), and least overrepresented among juveniles arrested for property offenses (only 1.05 times their representation in the overall population). On the victims' side, publicly available information is substantially more limited than it is with respect to offenders, but available data show the same pattern of Latino overrepresentation as in the case of arrestees, the most for homicide and the least for residential burglary.

Trends in Punishment, 1980–98

Adult Prisoners

The dramatic increase in adult incarceration rates for the period 1980–1998 is displayed in Table 9.2. No group or gender was spared in what has been de-

Table 9.2. Institution Population by Gender and Race, California Department of Corrections, 1980 and 1998

	Number of Prison Inmates			Imprisonment Rate per 1000,000 Adults Ages 18-69		
	1980	1998	Percent Increase	1980	1998	Percent Increase
Total	24,559	159,563	550	156	764	390
Male	23,253	148,078	537	296	1,364	361
White	8,976	43,683	387	165	770	367
Black	8,139	45,756	462	1,469	6,574	348
Latino	5,674	51,383	806	411	1,566	281
Other	465	7,256	1,460	97	604	523
Female	1,316	11,485	773	17	111	553
White	575	4,295	647	10	77	670
Black	446	3,847	762	76	536	605
Latina	249	2,722	994	19	99	421
Other	46	620	1,246	9	48	433

Source: For imprisonment data, *Historical Series 1977–1997*, California Department of Corrections, and *Characteristics of Population in California State Prisons by Institution, June 1999*, California Department of Corrections. See the Appendix for a discussion of the population data sources used to estimate imprisonment rates.

scribed as one of the largest changes in the scale of imprisonment in a western democracy in peacetime.[7]

A noticeable observation from Table 9.2 is that while males continue to represent the vast majority of prison inmates, the number of female inmates grew substantially faster than that of males, eightfold versus sixfold, respectively. This is a national trend reflecting a larger growth in female arrest rates *vis-à-vis* males, in particular for drug offenses, the reasons for which are as yet not fully explained.[8]

---

[7]Franklin Zimring and Gordon Hawkins, *The Scale of Imprisonment* (Chicago: University of Chicago Press, 1991).

[8]Kathleen Daly, "Gender, Crime, and Criminology." in *The Handbook of Crime and Punishment*, ed. Michael Tonry (New York: Oxford University Press, 1998), 85, 110.

The increase in the absolute number of Latino and "other" (mostly Asian American, Native American, and Pacific Islander) prison inmates is particularly striking, and in large part the result of the dramatic shift in the size and composition of the state population. California added roughly 10 million residents between 1980 and 1998 from a base of 22 million. Latinos and Asian Americans experienced the largest growth, with annualized rates for that 18-year period of 4.5 percent and 5.3 percent, respectively. In contrast, white non-Latinos increased at an annualized rate of 0.4 percent and blacks at 1.3 percent. Moreover, for teens and young adults, the age groups with the highest crime-participation rates, the differences in growth rates among ethnic groups were even more striking. For example, between 1980 and 1988 the 20–29 age cohort for Latinos and Asian Americans increased by 78 percent and 99 percent, respectively, whereas the same cohort for whites and blacks decreased by 34 percent and 12 percent, respectively. Latinos and Asian Americans currently constitute 51 percent of the total population in the 10–29 age groups.

As we look at the increase in the incarceration rates as opposed to the absolute number of prisoners (last column in Table 9.1), we observe that, controlling for population size, Latinos experienced the lowest percentage increase in incarceration rates from 1980 to 1998 for both men and women. This finding is indeed surprising. Moreover, it apparently does not hold for the nation as a whole. Blumstein and Beck estimated that for the period 1980–1996, Latinos as a group had the largest growth in incarceration rate relative to blacks and whites. This, however, does not mean that California Latinos did better than Latinos elsewhere. They did not. The growth in the Latino incarceration rate for 1980–1996 was 235 percent for the nation as a whole, whereas the comparable figure for California was 294 percent. The rankings in California are reversed because the other ethnic groups did substantially worse here than in the rest of the nation.

We should not, however, overlook the fact that the incarceration rate for Latinos remains appreciably higher than that of whites. Still, as Figure 9.2 indicates, as the scale of incarceration expanded, Latinos fared relatively better than the other groups for most of the period. Figure 9.2 plots the ratio of the Latino incarceration rate to the incarceration rate of each of the other three ethnic groups that serve as comparisons. An exception is the case of blacks, where the ratio has been reversed since the black incarceration rate is substantially larger than the Latino rate. In 1980 the incarceration rate for Latinos was 2.1 times the rate for whites, and 3.9 times the rate for "others." On the other hand, in 1980 the incarceration rate for blacks was 3.8 times the rate for Latinos. Over the next 18 years, while all groups experienced increases in their incarceration rate as documented in Table 9.2, the increase for Latinos generally lagged behind the increase for other groups. Thus, by the end of the period of analysis in 1988, the incarceration rate for blacks was almost 4.5 times the rate for Latinos, whereas

Figure 9.2. Ratio of Incarceration Rates, Adult Male Correctional Institution Population California, 1980–1998

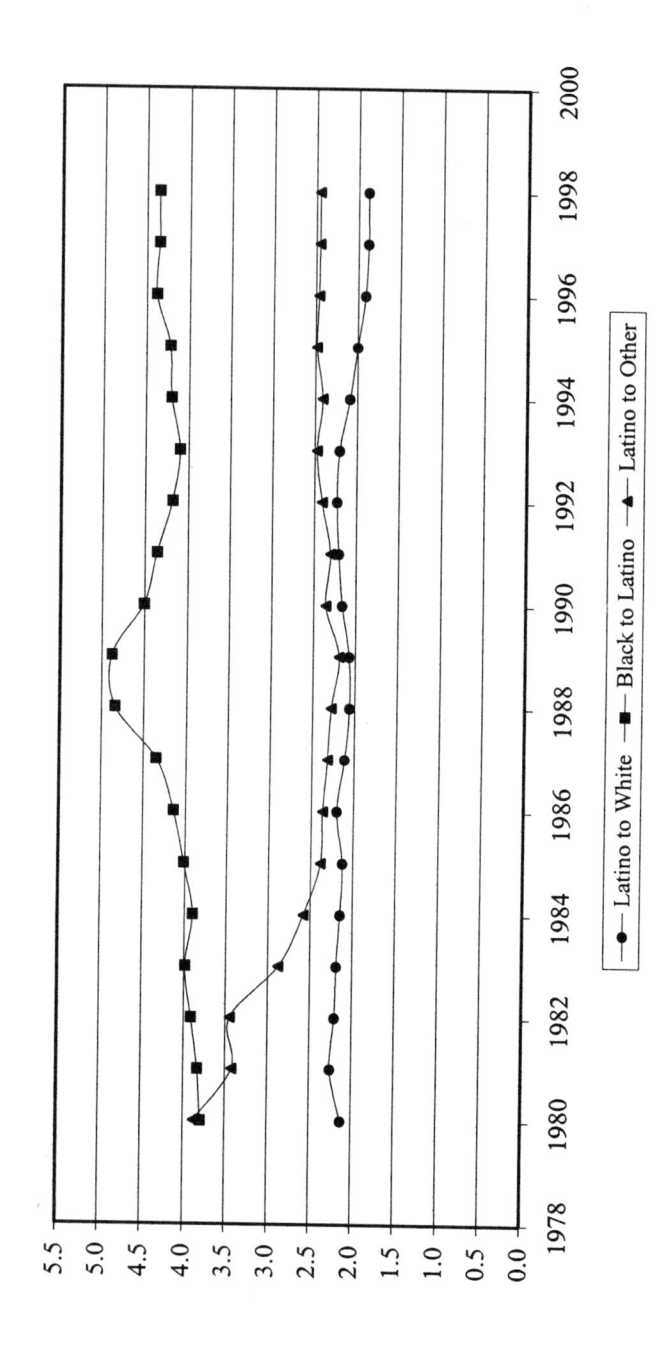

─●─ Latino to White ─■─ Black to Latino ─▲─ Latino to Other

Source: Calculated by the author from data sources described in the Appendix.

the Latino incarceration rate was 2.1 times the rate for the "others," compared to 3.9 times in 1980. The gap in the Latino incarceration rate *vis-à-vis* that of whites began a slight but steady decline as of 1993, coinciding with the dramatic drop in crime rates that has since occurred in California.

The trends for women largely track those just described for men, except that they are more pronounced. Since 1984 the gap in the incarceration rates between Latinas and white women has been closing; by the end of 1998 the incarceration rate for Latinas was 1.3 times the rate for white women. Thus, whatever factors are behind the differences in incarceration rates between Latinos and whites, they are clearly not identical across gender.

Trends in Incarceration Rates Disaggregated by Crime Type

The trends in incarceration rates by crime type vary appreciably from the overall trends discussed previously. In the case of burglary, the ratio of the incarceration rate of Latino males to both white and black males remained fairly constant from 1980 to 1991, with Latinos doing considerably better than these other two groups from 1992 onward (see Figure 9.3). For instance, the Latino incarceration rate for burglary was 2.8 times the rate for whites in 1980, but only 1.6 times in 1998. On the other hand, blacks had a burglary incarceration rate almost three times the rate for Latinos in 1980 and almost five times in 1998.

In contrast, in the case of robbery, a more serious crime than burglary because it is a violent offense, Figure 9.4 shows a marked deterioration for Latinos—certainly after 1989, when the Latino incarceration rate grew at a faster rate relative to both whites and blacks.

The so-called War on Drugs, which substantially toughened criminal sanctions for the possession and sale of drugs, was a major factor fueling expansion in the national prison population, both state and federal. California was no exception, and whereas in 1980 only one inmate in 14 was imprisoned for drug offenses, by 1998 one of every four cells was occupied by a drug offender. The dramatic nature of this reversal in the composition of the prison population can be more fully appreciated by noting that in 1998 there were 31,000 inmates for robbery and burglary combined, compared to almost 39,000 for drugs. In contrast, the number of drug inmates in 1980 was not even one-fifth of the number of burglars and robbers in prison.

Figure 9.5 explores how the dramatic build-up in the use of incarceration for drug offenses has affected each of the ethnic groups. The black-to-Latino ratio displays the enormous effect that the War on Drugs had on the incarceration rate for blacks, which more than doubled *vis-à-vis* Latinos between 1984 and 1989. Implicitly, Figure 9.5 shows that by 1989 the incarceration rate of

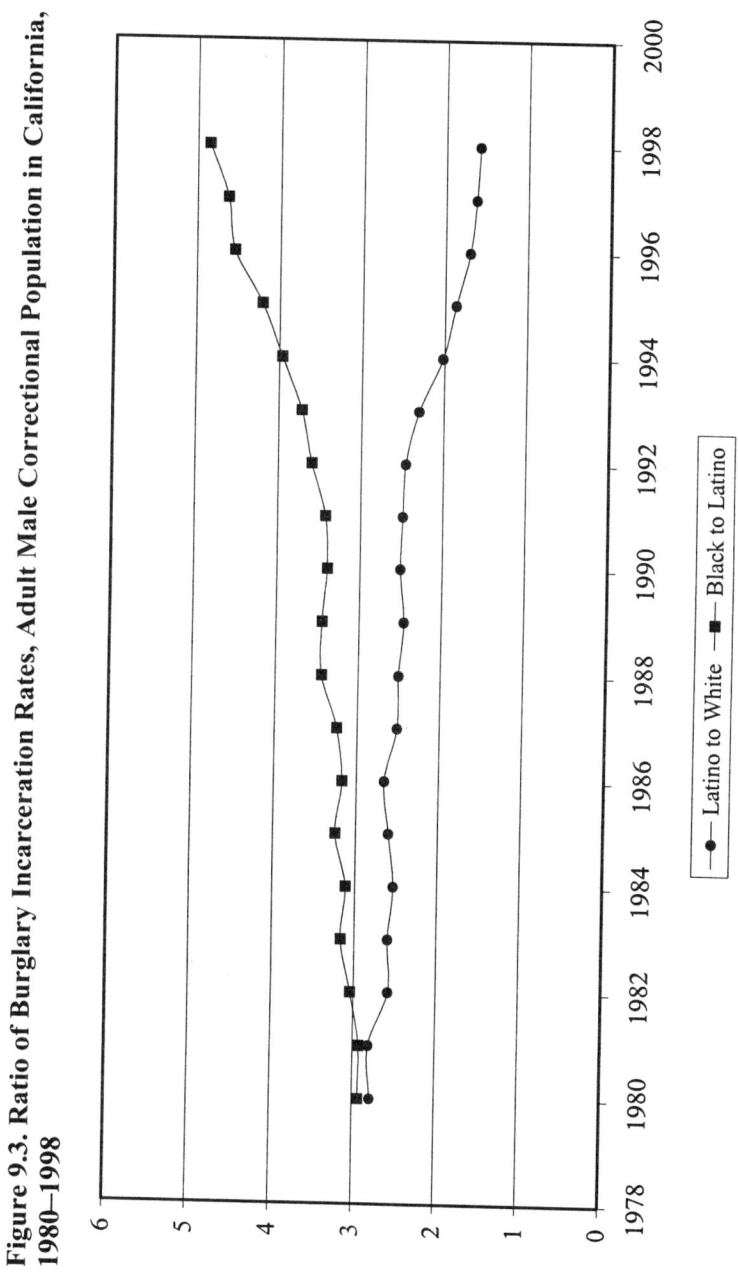

Figure 9.3. Ratio of Burglary Incarceration Rates, Adult Male Correctional Population in California, 1980–1998

Source: Calculated by the author based on data sources described in the Appendix.

Figure 9.4. Ratio of Robbery Incarceration Rates, Adult Male Correctional Population, California, 1980–1998

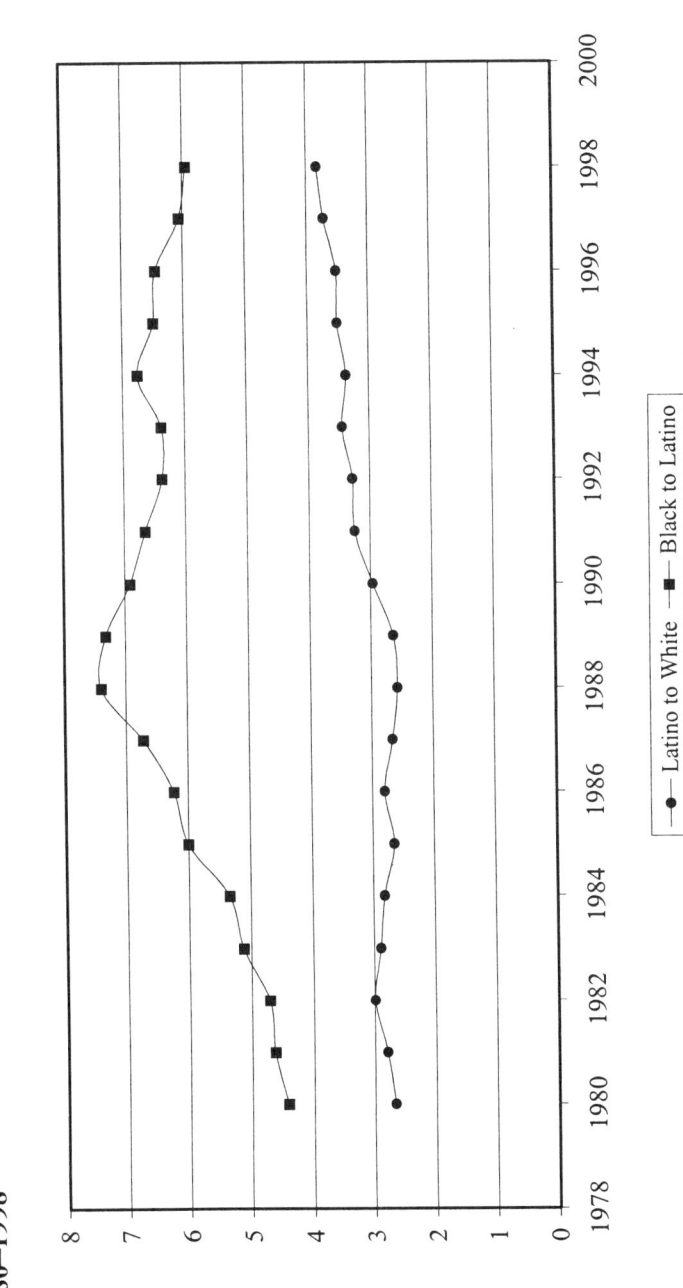

── Latino to White ── Black to Latino

Source: Calculated by the author from data sources described in the Appendix.

Figure 9.5. Ratio of Drug Incarceration Rates, Adult Male Correctional Population, California, 1980–1998

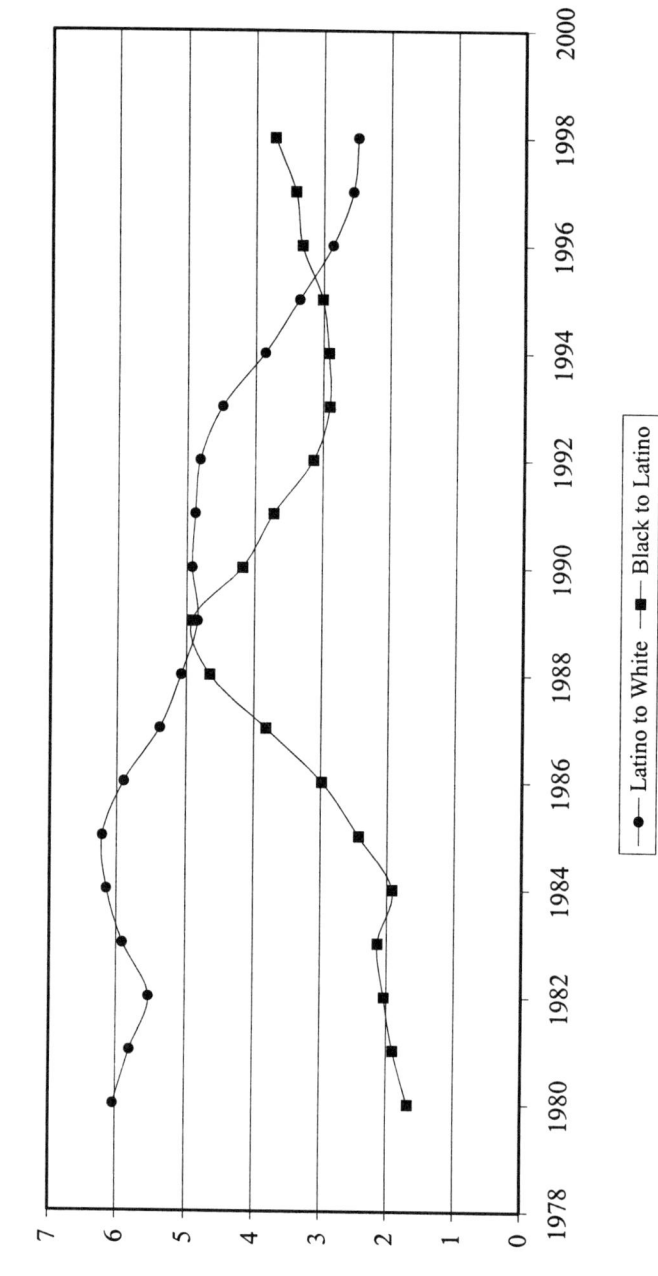

Source: Calculated by the author from data sources described in the Appendix.

blacks was almost 24 times that of whites. Even though the black-to-white ratio of incarceration rates had declined to a value of roughly nine by 1998, these overwhelmingly disproportionate effects on a single group have led scholars to seriously question the fairness of the sanctioning schemes that have accompanied the War on Drugs.[9]

However, Figure 9.5 indicates that Latinos were the least affected by the War on Drugs, *relative to the other groups*. This is an important insight that again underscores how demographic, punitive, and criminality effects, plus potential disparate enforcement practices, can all combine to generate unsuspected outcomes. Latinos were considerably affected by the policies of the War on Drugs: The Latino incarceration rate for drugs showed an annualized increase of 13.2 percent over the period 1980–1998. Nevertheless, this compares favorably to the corresponding annualized rates for whites and blacks, which reached nearly 19 percent in both cases. Moreover, as of 1985 the growth in the Latino incarceration rate for drug offenses was always below the growth of the drug incarceration rate for whites, thus the downward trajectory for the Latino-to-white ratio of incarceration rates displayed in Figure 9.5.

Juvenile Wards

The contrast between the adult and the juvenile systems could hardly be more pronounced. Table 9.3 shows that in comparison to the adult system, the juvenile confinement rate, despite growing by 37 percent in the intervening 18 years of this study, could easily be described as stationary in that it is not even one-tenth the growth in the adult incarceration rate. Unlike the situation for adults, the gender differences don't show systematic patterns by race. This is no doubt due, in large part, to the very small size of the female juvenile institutionalized population. For this reason, no further analysis will be pursued for female institutionalized juveniles.

The most striking observation about Table 9.3 is that, in the case of males, the CYA is overwhelmingly populated by minorities; Latinos, blacks, and "other" (mostly Asian Americans) now constitute 84 percent of the total number of wards. This is a result of both an increase in the confinement rate of all minority groups and a decrease in the rate for whites.

The approach described earlier can be used to track the evolution of the confinement rate for Latino juvenile wards relative to that of the other groups. Two distinct patterns emerge. From 1980 to 1989, changes in the Latino juvenile

---

[9]Michael Tonry, *Malign Neglect: Race, Crime and Punishment in America* (New York: Oxford University Press, 1995).

Table 9.3. Institution Population by Gender and Race, California Youth Authority, 1980 and 1998

	Number of Wards 1980	1998	Percent Increase	Number of Wards per 100,000 Youths Ages 10–19 1980	1998	Percent Increase
Total	5,043	8,297	65	132	181	37
Male	4,857	7,982	64	251	343	37
White	1,569	1,102	−30	136	113	−17
Black	1,710	2,331	36	953	1,321	39
Latino	1,467	3,871	164	312	433	39
Other	112	678	507	84	242	188
Female	186	315	69	13	18	38
White	75	88	17	9	12	34
Black	53	95	79	39	70	78
Latina	50	106	112	14	17	17
Other	8	26	223	8	12	42

Source: For institutionalized juveniles, *A Comparison of the Youth Authority's Institution and Parole Population*, February 1990 and August 1998; and *Characteristics of CYA Population*, June 30, 1999. California Youth Authority. For population figures, *Population Estimates for States by Age, Sex, Race, and Hispanic Origin: July 1, 1998*, U.S. Census Bureau Internet Release date September 15, 1999. First released as (ST-98-31). Tables renumbered effective October 6, 1999.

confinement rate were substantially smaller than those for blacks, as well as for "other." Over that period the Latino-to-white ratio of the confinement rates of juvenile wards showed a slight downward trend, whereas the growth in the rates for blacks and "other" substantially outpaced the growth in the Latino rate. Since 1989, however, Latinos have fared substantially worse than both white and black juveniles.

Criminality and Punitiveness, 1980–98

In the last two sections, the evolution of incarceration rates by ethnic group was considered in the context of the expansion in the overall institutionalized population, and differences and similarities across groups in the confinement trends were identified. This section focuses on two of the important factors behind the expansion in confinement rates, after removing the demographic effects. These two factors are criminality (involvement in crime) and punitiveness (criminal sanctions as they actually materialize).

There is ample documentation of the various ways in which the criminal-justice system became more punitive. In California, as elsewhere in the country, sentences became longer, and for those arrested and charged with a crime, incarceration became more certain. Surprisingly, despite the heavy emphasis on policing over the last decade, the likelihood of arrest did not change appreciably, if at all. For all violent crimes in California, the ratio of arrests to crimes reported between 1980 and 1993 remained strikingly constant at around 40 percent. Thereafter, there was a slight upturn affecting little, if at all, the arrest risk for the more serious crimes such as homicide and robbery, and affecting more the arrest risk for property crimes like burglary.[10]

Ironically, it was in relation to some property offenses, which generally raise less serious concerns among the population, that the probability of arrest showed an upward trend in the 1980s. For instance, the arrest-to-crime ratio for burglary increased from about .16 to .20, or 25 percent, during the 1980s.[10] Still, changes of this magnitude pale by comparison to the severalfold increases in the incarceration rates during the 1980s, discussed earlier. Thus, this section studies both how incarceration into prisons or the CYA has changed after controlling for arrests, and how long individuals are confined following commitment. Of course, the main interest is to inquire whether there is any relationship between changes for either commitment rates or length of incarceration when the data are broken down by ethnicity. Unfortunately, examining arrest data is the only way to gauge changes in criminality, with the exception of homicide. This cancels the possibility of studying biases in the arrest process, which remains a critical issue addressed in the last section of this chapter.

---

[10]Calculated from the author based on data from the report *Crime and Delinquency in California* published annually by the California Department of Justice, issues for 1980, 1990, and 1993.

Adult Prisoners: From Arrest to Prison

The flow from arrest to imprisonment is considered for three crime types: robbery, burglary, and drug offenses. The analysis is limited to males from three ethnic groups: Latinos, non-Latino whites, and non-Latino blacks.

The ratio of new prison commitments to adult arrests is calculated for each ethnic group, crime type, and year. These ratios can be treated as probabilities describing the likelihood of incarceration given arrest, and since crime type is controlled for, one would expect in principle that for any given year these ratios would be of roughly the same magnitude for the three groups. In addition, in accordance with the earlier discussion about changes in punitiveness, an upward trend in these ratios over time is anticipated.

Figure 9.6a displays the prison commitments-to-arrest ratios for robbery by ethnic group. An important observation from Figure 9.6a is that the ratios for all three groups hang together relatively closely, and the anticipated upward trend is unambiguous for the three ethnic groups. Interestingly, prior to 1989 the prison commitments-to-arrest ratios for whites tend to be above those for Hispanics and blacks, whereas the situation reverses after 1990.

Figure 9.6b presents a comparable analysis for burglary. Again, the upward trend in punitiveness is striking, but in contrast to 6a, a difference in trends appears to exist between blacks on the one hand and Latinos and whites on the other. In the early years all three groups show prisons commitment-to-arrest ratio values around .10. However, as the years progress, the rate of growth in the ratio for blacks increases consistently at a faster pace, so that by the end of the period that ratio reaches values of around .27, compared to around .20 for Latinos and whites.

The analysis for drug offenses, shown in Figure 9.6c, displays a substantially different situation from that of the prior two crime types, although this is based only on data from 1990 to 1998. For drug offenses, the prison-to-arrest ratios for Latinos and blacks are substantially higher than those for whites over the entire observation period, in some instances differing by a factor of two.[11]

It should be acknowledged that the data in Figures 9.6a-c do not prove that groups were treated differently in the process from arrest to incarceration. A first point is that legitimate factors might explain the observed differences across ethnic groups. For instance, in the case of the burglary analysis, the data limitations precluded separating first- and second-degree burglary, despite the fact

---

[11] A probit analysis of the data presented in Figure 9.6, shows that the identified differences in trends are statistically significant for the three crime types included in this chapter. The probit analysis uses the empirically observed prison commitments-to-arrest ratios to estimate the probability of incarceration given arrest as a function of time and ethnic group. The probit results are available from the author upon request.

Figure 9.6a. Ratio of Prison Commitments to Arrests by Ethnicity and Crime Type, California, 1980–1998

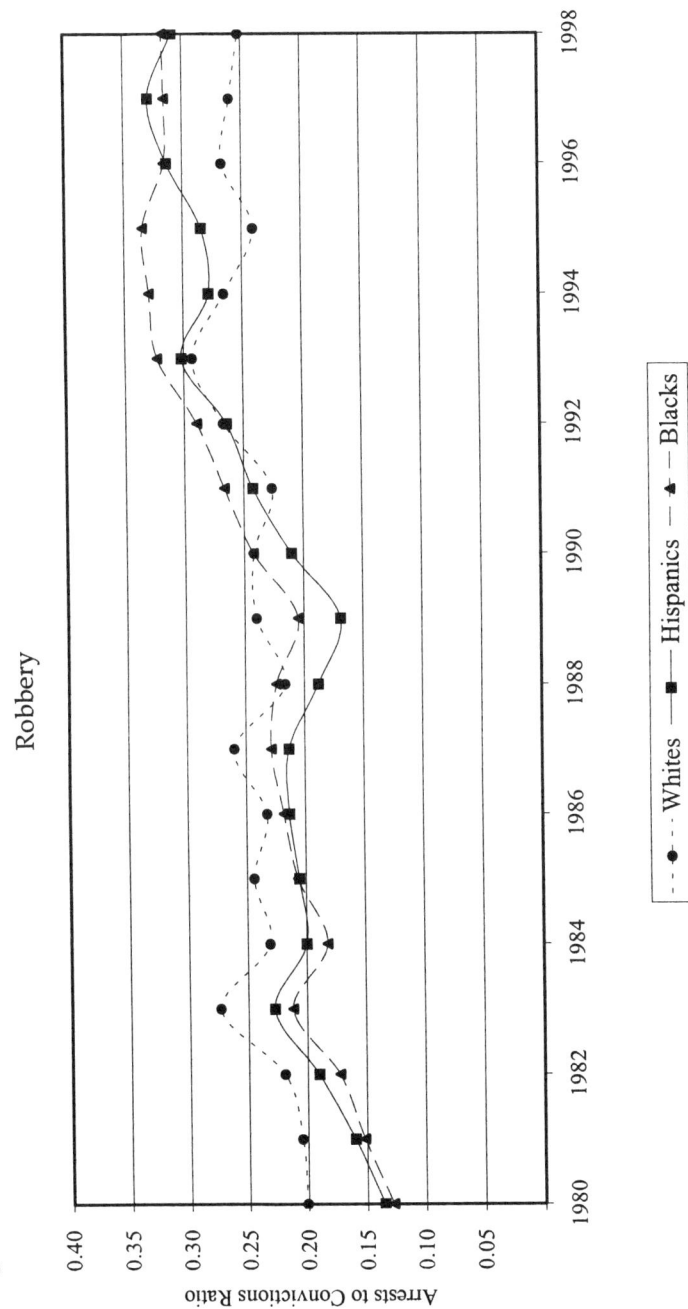

Robbery

- - ◆ - - Whites —■— Hispanics — ▲ — Blacks

Source: Calculated by the author from data sources described in the Appendix.

Figure 9.6b. Ratio of Prison Commitments to Arrests by Ethnicity and Crime Type, California, 1980–1998

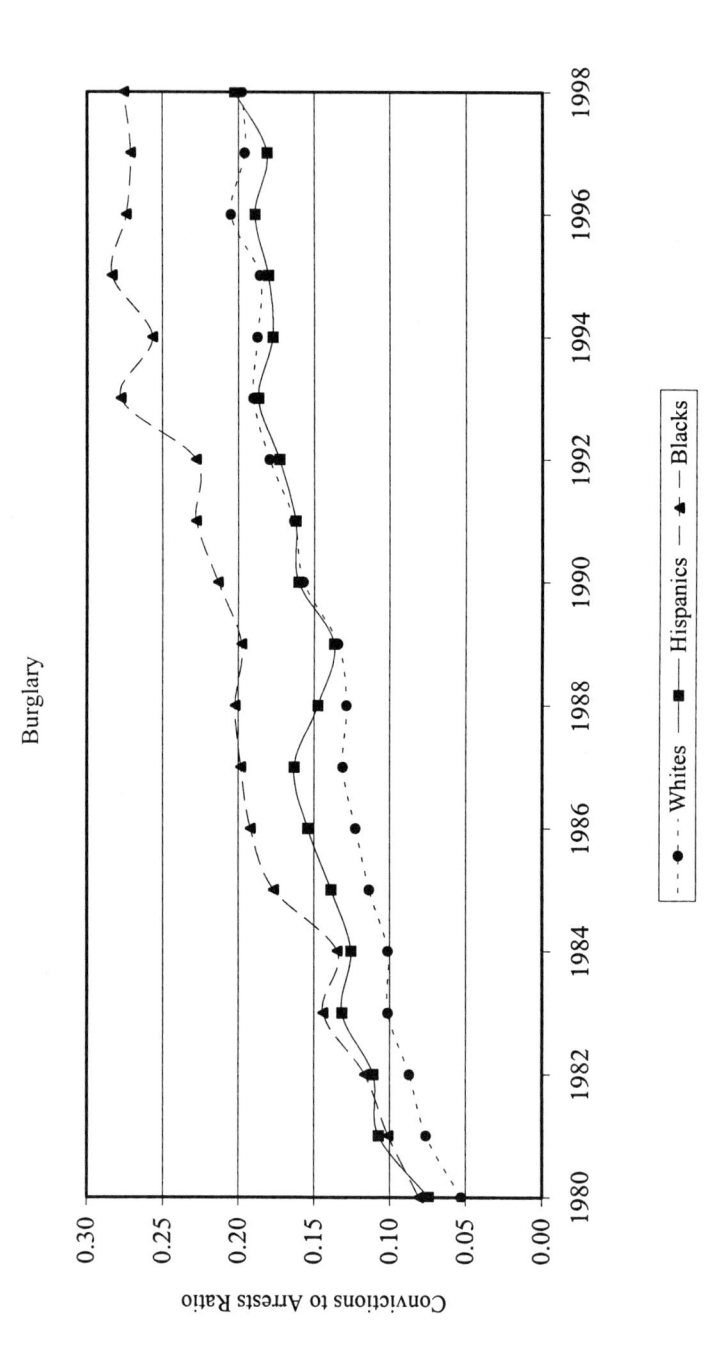

Burglary

Source: Calculated by the author from data sources described in the Appendix.

Figure 9.6c. Ratio of Prison Commitments to Arrests by Ethnicity and Crime Type, California, 1980–1998

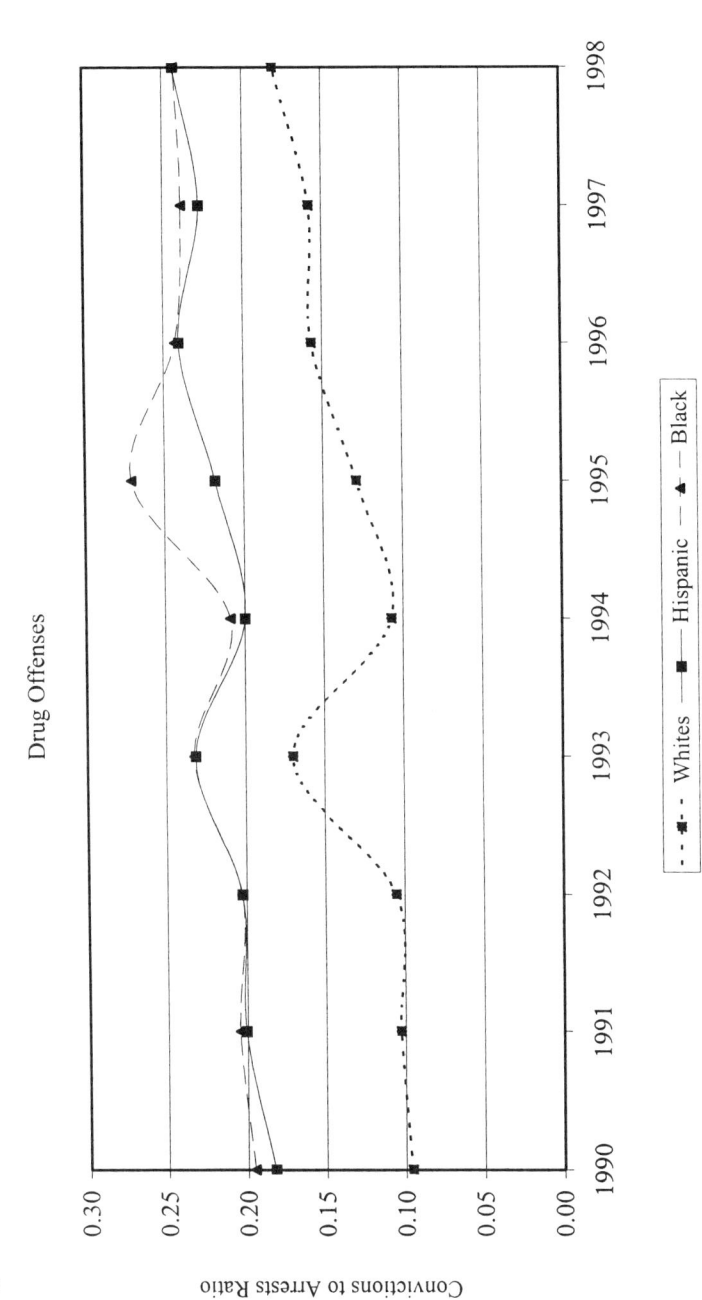

Drug Offenses

Source: Calculated by the author from data sources described in the Appendix.

that first-degree burglary is a more serious offense—sometimes treated as a violent offense. The group with the highest incarceration-to-arrest ratio may have participated to a larger extent in first-degree burglary. Similarly, in the case of robbery, it is important to know if and the extent to which the victim was harmed as a result of the robbery. The ethnic groups with higher incarceration-to-arrest ratios may have participated in more violent forms of robbery.

From a policy standpoint, the important point is that this type of data is or could easily be collected and systematically analyzed to guard against inequitable outcomes in criminal-justice processing. It is remarkable that this is not done, given the importance of the issue. Thus, as we look into the future and implement an agenda toward improved Latino equality, it is important to make a priority the timely and continuous compilation and publication of data bases designed with the specific purpose of ascertaining whether the criminal-justice system treats all groups equitably.

Collectively, the three portions of Figure 9.6 make another important point: Disparate treatment is not a problem that generically affects one ethnic group *vis-à-vis* others. Clearly, the crime type and the period of analysis matter. Identified treatment differences across ethnic groups were not of the same magnitude for the three crime types considered.

Time Served

From CDC records it is possible to estimate the actual amount of time served by exiting prison inmates. Within each crime type, prison inmates released to parole for the first time were distinguished from prison inmates previously paroled and recommitted to prison with a new sentence before the end of their parole. This distinction is important because, generally, recommitment to prison for a new offense while on parole results in longer prison terms.

Across all crime types, as shown in Figure 9.7, time served increased over the study period only for recommitted parolees, roughly by 50 percent in the case of first-degree burglary and robbery. In the case of drug offenses, before 1985 there was a decrease in average time served but this trend reversed in the late 1980s.

In sharp contrast to the data in the previous section, Figure 9.7 also shows that differences in time served by ethnicity are generally very small and are almost nonexistent for first-degree burglary and drug possession. In the two cases where differences do occur—drug dealing and robbery—the ethnic group with the highest time served varies. White robbery inmates on average almost always served slightly longer terms than either Latino or black robbery inmates. However, Latinos and blacks exhibited a somewhat larger average time served for

Crime and Justice 263

Figure 9.7. Time Served by Crime Type, Ethnic Group, and Prison Status, California State Prisoners, 1980–1998

First Time Parolees, Robbery

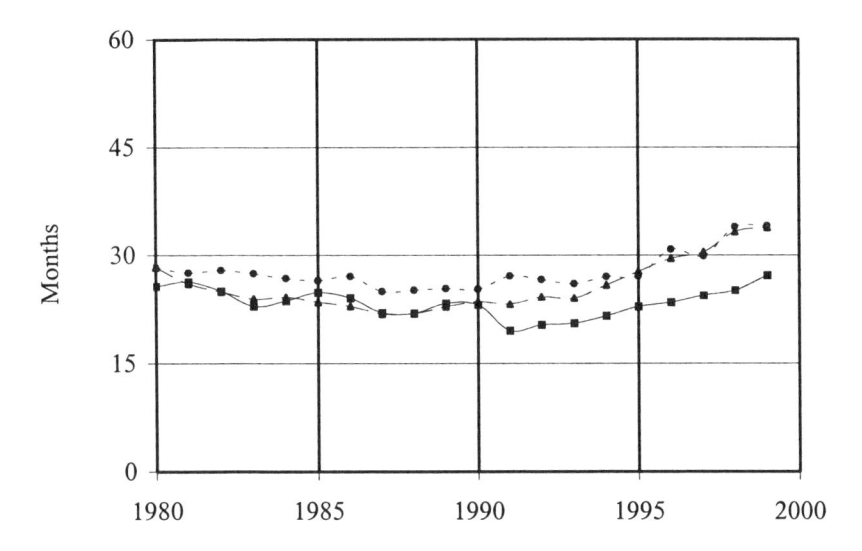

Parolees Recommitted with New Robbery Offense

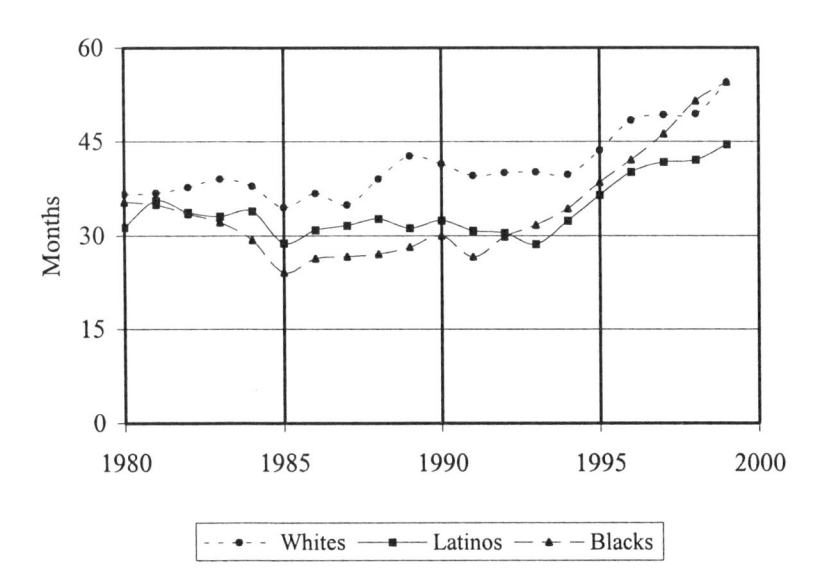

- - ◆ - - Whites —■— Latinos — ▲ — Blacks

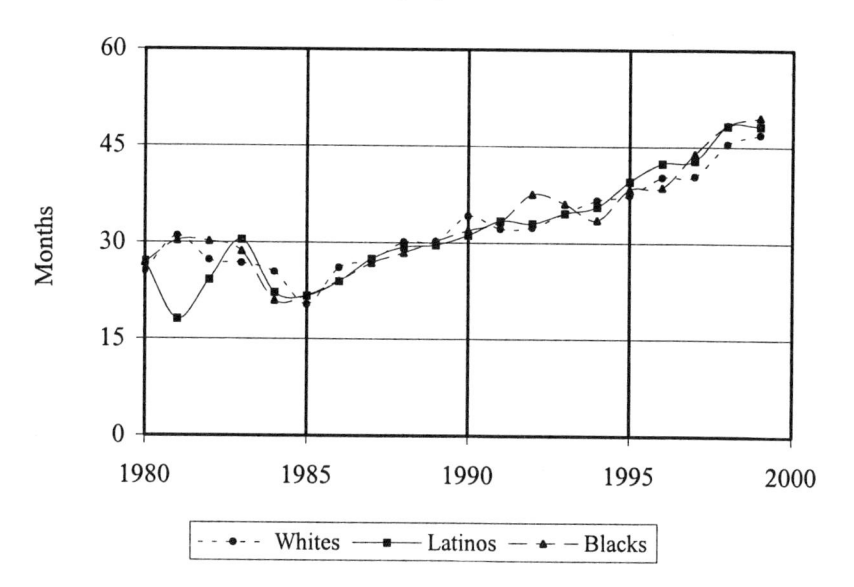

Figure 9.7. Continued.

First Time Parolees, Burglary 1st

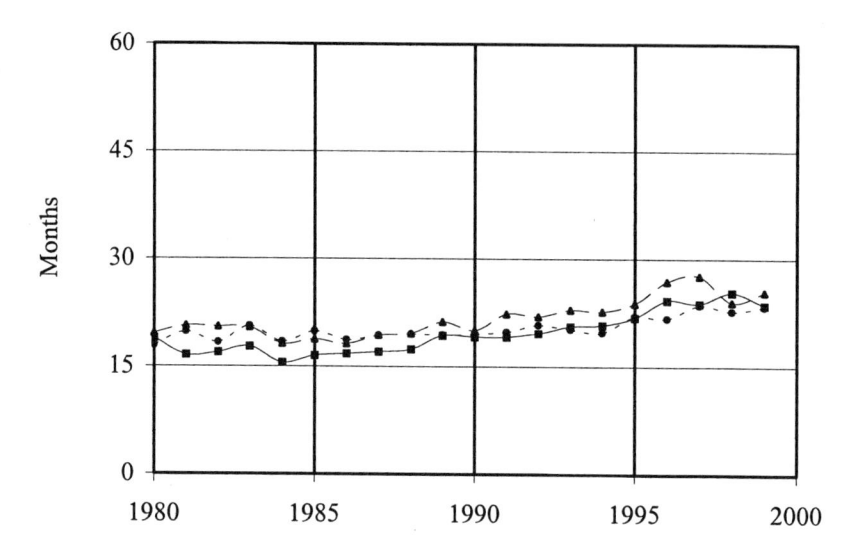

Parolees Recommitted with New Burglary 1st Offense

- - •- - Whites —■— Latinos — ▲ — Blacks

Figure 9.7. Continued.
First Time Parolees, Drug Sales

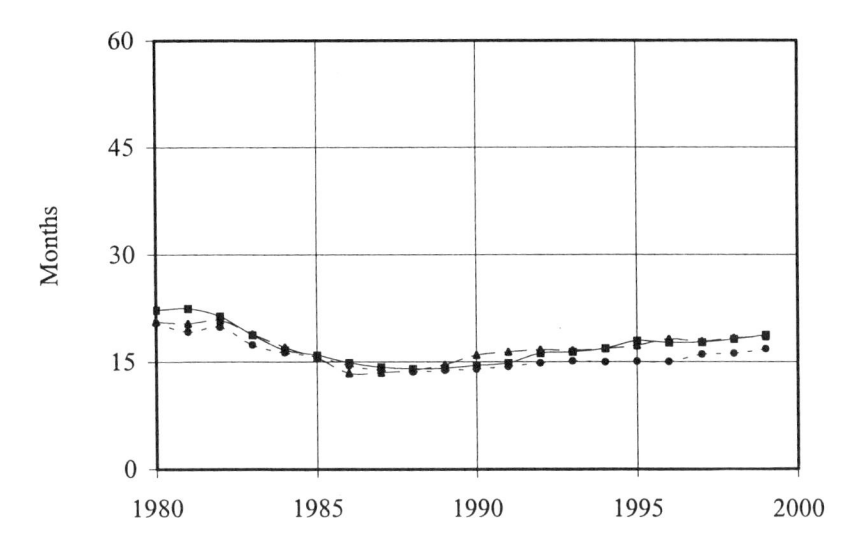

Parolees Recommitted with New Drug Sales Offense

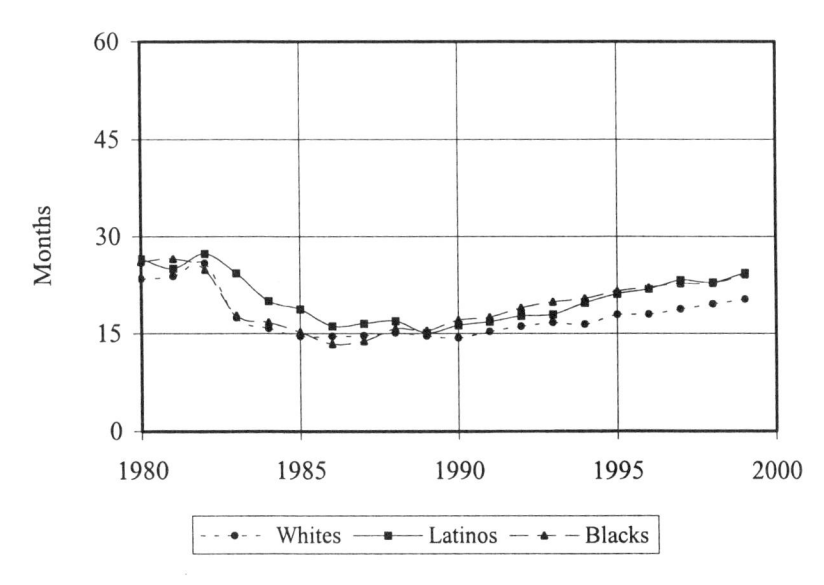

- - • - - Whites —■— Latinos — ▲ — Blacks

Source: Calculated by the author from data sources described in the Appendix

drug dealing, but only after 1990. Most of the published research in the area of disparate treatment by the criminal-justice system approaches the issue from the standpoint of time served. By and large, the findings reported here are consistent with major studies that find little or no difference in time served by ethnicity when all appropriate factors are controlled for.[12]

Two additional observations are in order. The documentation for time served, since it involves only one governmental agency, is much more carefully and reliably done. The simple facts that time served is measured and that the resulting data are promptly published may lead to better institutional performance. In addition, the policy change toward determinate sentencing in California in the late 1970s was in part implemented to eliminate unwarranted differences in time served. Whatever one thinks of this policy change—and the criticisms are many—the objective of equal time served for equal offenses seems to have been largely met, at least from the perspective of ethnic-group comparisons.

Juvenile Wards

In the case of the juvenile sector, the overall system was relatively stable, but the overwhelming increase in the relative participation of minorities is striking and unsettling. A comparable analysis to that done for the adult population—separate analyses for time served and for the flow of arrestees into prison inmates—isn't possible because counts of the CYA population broken down by both crime type and ethnicity don't seem to be available for the period 1980–1998.

To determine the extent to which the trends in the resident CYA population reflect changes in arrests for juveniles, we employed an approach originally used by Blumstein.[13] This approach, since then applied elsewhere,[14] is somewhat lim-

---

[12]See, for example, Joan Petersilia, *Racial Disparities in Criminal Justice Systems* (Santa Monica, Calif.: RAND Corporation, 1983); S. Klein, J. Petersilia, and S. Turner, "Race and Imprisonment Decisions in California," *Science* 247 (February 1990): 812–816; and Martha A. Myers and S. Talarico, *The Social Context of Criminal Sentencing* (New York: Springer-Verlag, 1997).

[13]Alfred Blumstein, "On the Racial Disproportionality of United States Prison Populations," *Journal of Criminal Law & Criminology* (1982): 1259.

[14]See, for example, Patrick A. Langan, "Racism on Trial: New Evidence to Explain the Racial Composition of Prisons in the United States," *Journal of Criminal Law and Criminology* 76(3), (1995): 666–83; R. D. Crutchfield, G. S. Bridges, and S. R. Pitchford, "Analytical and Aggregation Biases in Analysis of Imprisonment: Reconciling Discrepancies in Studies of Racial Disparity," *Journal of Research in Crime and Delinquency* 31(2), (1994): 166–82.

ited but has the major advantage of requiring only disaggregated arrest data by ethnicity and crime type, and the total count of wards for each ethnic group.

The following example, taken from actual data, illustrates the statistical underpinnings of the approach. In 1990, 4,022 wards were institutionalized for violent offenses. In that same year, white males constituted 18 percent, Latino males 41 percent, black males 33 percent, and "other" 8 percent of all juvenile arrestees for violent offenses. Under the assumption that all juveniles arrested for a violent crime face the same risk of institutionalization, independent of ethnicity, one would expect that the 4,022 wards would be distributed among the various ethnic groups in proportion to their representation among arrestees. That is, we would expect about 724 of them to be white, 649 Latino, 1327 black, and the remaining 322 to be "other."

For each group and crime type, similar expected values are generated and then aggregated across ethnicity to yield an expected total number of wards for each ethnic group, shown in Figure 9.8. These charts compare the numbers actually observed to the values expected from the described statistical approach. The results strongly show that the substantial reduction in white wards observed since 1990 was not to be expected given the observed arrest trends and assuming comparable risks of institutionalization by ethnic group. For instance, by 1994 white wards had declined to 1,252—42 percent below expectations. In contrast, for each year since 1990, the number of institutionalized African Americans was between 30 percent and 40 percent above expectations. Only in the case of Latinos were the observed and expected populations very close.

While these results could be interpreted as saying that Latinos are equitably represented in the juvenile institutionalized population (when arrests are controlled for), the truth is that a critical equity issue remains, given the underrepresentation of whites. In 1997 the ratio of the actual confinement rate for juvenile Latinos relative to juvenile whites was 3.7, whereas, using the expectations generated for the respective ethnic groups, the ratio should have been 1.9. Relative to blacks, however, Latinos were underrepresented. Clearly, these disparities among ethnic groups raise the specter of discriminatory treatment, absent the identification of other factors that legally and ethically should result in differential treatment.

Victimization, 1980–1998

Our ability to track changes in victimization by ethnic group within California is seriously hampered by the inadequacy of current data-collection practices. Since

Figure 9.8. Observed Versus Expected CYA Resident Population Based on Arrest Rates, 1990–1997

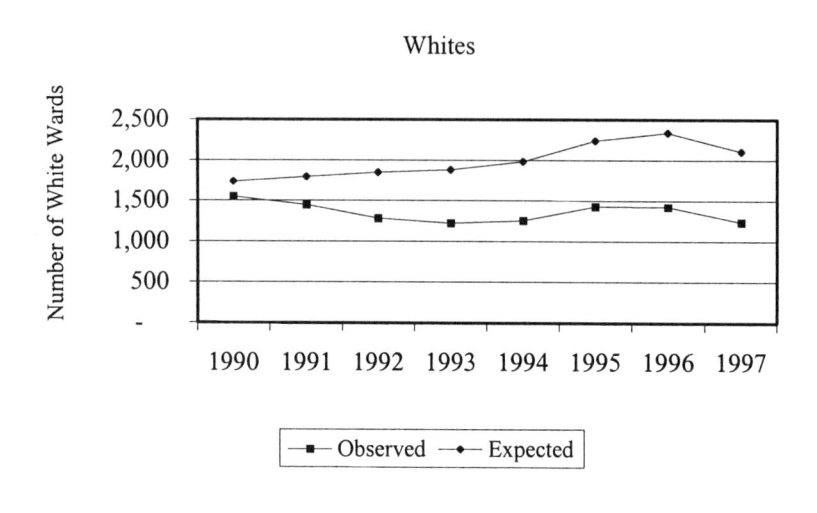

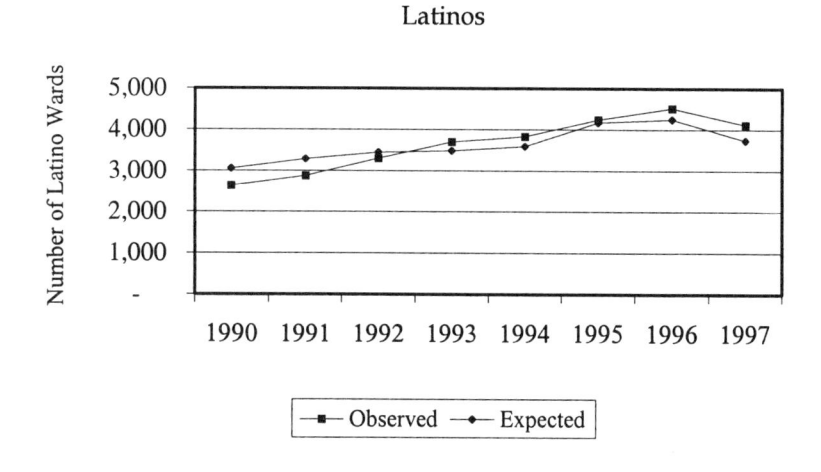

Whites

Latinos

Figure 9.8. Continued.

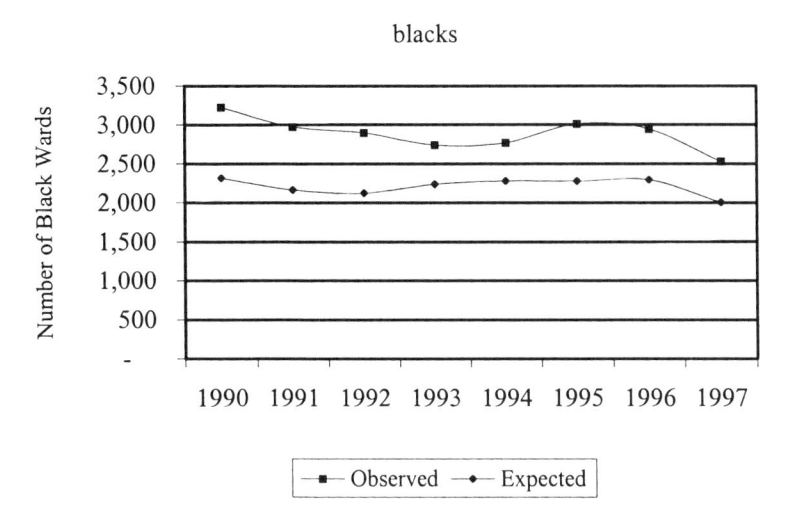

blacks

[Chart: Number of Black Wards, 1990–1997, Observed and Expected series]

Source: Calculated by the author from data sources described in the Appendix.

1973 the federal government's National Crime Victimization Survey (NCVS) has provided valuable information about victimization risk, but only at the national level. The one statewide victimization survey for California known to the author was conducted by the federal government in the late 1970s and published in 1981.[15] Furthermore, while NCVS data compare victimization rates for Hispanics to non-Hispanics, it does not allow for comparisons between Hispanics and white non-Hispanics, and between Hispanics and black non-Hispanics.

As part of the recent emphasis on community policing and public perceptions of safety, the federal government has again undertaken victimization surveys in 12 cities, including Los Angeles and San Diego.[16] Whether this will become a permanent effort that serves the needs of Californians remains to be seen.

---

[15] U.S. Department of Justice, *Criminal Victimization of California Residents, A National Crime Survey Report,* NCS-S-2, NCJ-70944, Bureau of Justice Statistics, March 1981.

[16] U.S. Department of Justice, *Criminal Victimization and Perceptions of Community Safety in 12 Cities, 1998,* NCJ 173940, Bureau of Justice Statistics, May 1999.

A victimization survey is a complex and costly enterprise, so it is not entirely surprising that the state hasn't undertaken its own. However, it is startling that with the exception of homicide, the data on victims routinely collected by police departments when crimes are reported are not systematically tabulated and published for analysis by public agencies, scholars, and the community at large. Advocating the publication of victimization statistics, by ethnic group, from crimes reported to the police ought to be a priority for Latinos and other minorities.

Homicide Victimization, 1980–1998

Since 1989 the state of California has published a detailed report on homicide victims, making possible the computation of Latino homicide victimization rates as distinguished from non-Latino-white and non-Latino-black victimization rates. Based on the work of Sorenson et al.[17] with coroner files, it is possible to generate Latino homicide victimization rates going back to the early 1970s for comparison with the other groups.

Figure 9.9 depicts the long-term trends of Latinos relative to whites and the victimization rate of blacks relative to Latinos. Throughout the 1980s, the Latino-to-white ratio of homicide victimization rates remained fairly constant at about 2.5. In 1989, when the most recent upswing in the California homicide rate occurred, the disparity between Latinos and whites changed substantially, putting the ratio of rates at 3.7 by 1991. It increased to a historical peak value of 3.9 in 1995, suggesting that as the overall homicide rate came down, it did so at a slower rate for Latinos than for whites. Its current value of 3.2 provides a sense of the improvements in safety that Latinos have yet to achieve.

The trend in the ratio of victimization rates for blacks relative to Latinos decreased over the period, suggesting that the relative improvement in homicide victimization rates for blacks was greater than for Latinos. Using 1989 as a point of comparison, the victimization risk for Latinos increased by about 40 percent in relation to both blacks and whites.

Given the robust correlation between robbery and homicide rates in California and elsewhere, it is likely that the trends in Latino robbery victimization rates mirror those for homicide.

---

[17]Susan B. Sorenson and Haikang Shen, "Homicide Risk among Immigrants in California, 1970 through 1992." *American Journal of Public Health* 86(1), (1996): 97–100; and Lawrence D. Chu and Susan B. Sorensen, "Trends in California Homicide, 1970 to 1993," *Western Journal of Medicine* (1996): 165, 119–25.

Figure 9.9. Ratio of Homicide Victimization Rates, Hispanics Relative to Other Race and Ethnicity Groups, California, 1970–1998

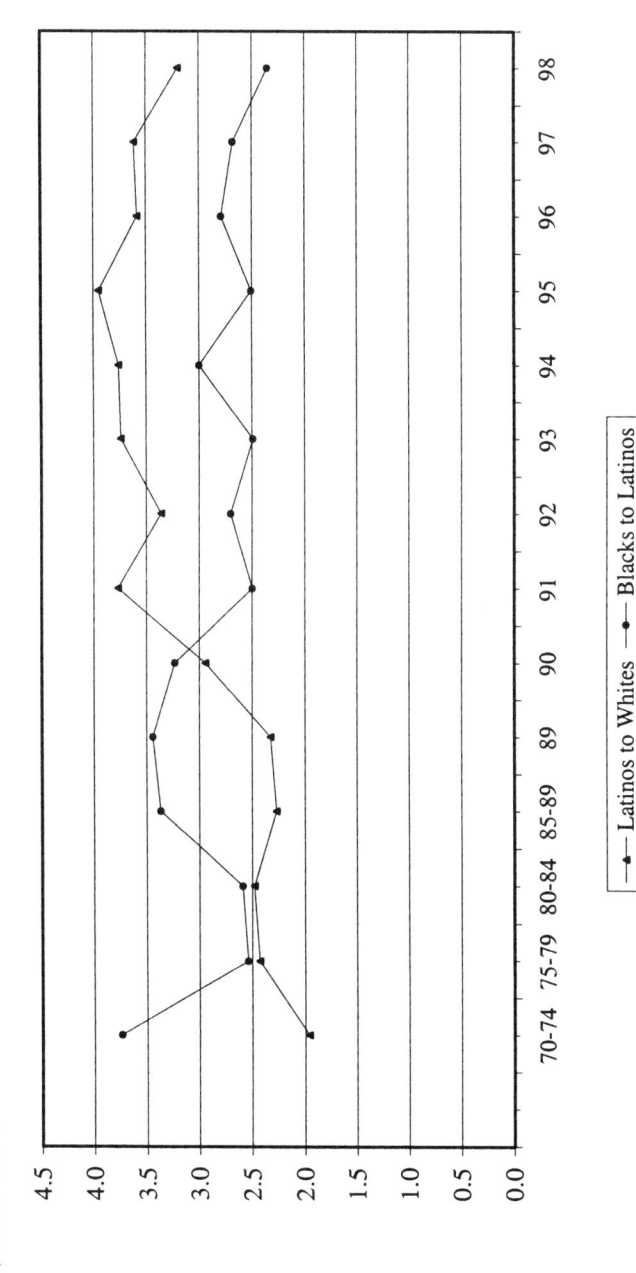

Ratio of Homicide Rates

— Latinos to Whites   — Blacks to Latinos

Source: For 1970–1987: Lawrence D. Chu and Susan B. Sorensen, "Trends in California Homicide, 1970 to 1993." *Western Journal of Medicine* 165 (1996): 119–25. For 1988 and later: *Homicide in California, 1998*, California Department of Justice, 1999.

Discussion

This chapter has reviewed California's crime and justice experiences over the last 20 years, focusing on how Latinos fared relative to other ethnic groups. Simply because of demographics, Latino males reached relative-majority status in practically all domains of the criminal-justice system, even though overall Latino confinement rates grew at a slower rate than those of other ethnic groups.

A particularly important finding is that for Latinos the long-term trends in violent offenses are discouraging, in terms of both victims and offenders. Latino overrepresentation for homicide and robbery worsened substantially over the period 1978–1995, with some minimal improvement since then.

It is important to account for the overrepresentation of Latinos at all levels of the criminal-justice system because of the concern that overrepresentation in some measure may result from disparate—in the worst case, discriminatory—treatment, by the criminal-justice system. A limited amount of scholarly work is directly on point; most of the overrepresentation studies have focused on blacks versus nonblacks because, historically, blacks have experienced the most extreme cases of overrepresentation.

The crucial issue is to separate the overrepresentation that results from differential involvement in crime from overrepresentation attributable to disparate treatment. At the present time, data are available to compare time served in prison by ethnic group, controlling for offense. For example, data presented in this chapter allow for comparison of time served by Latinos and non-Latino whites imprisoned for various offenses. No measurable differences in time served by ethnic group were identified, a result that in large part can be attributed to the adoption of determinate sentencing policies in the late 1970s that essentially removed administrative discretion in the parole process. In all other areas of the criminal-justice process, data-collection practices remain utterly inadequate for assessing comparable treatment for all groups. This is particularly the case for processes occurring at the county level, such as prosecutorial decisions and revocation of probationary status.

Over the last decade the legitimacy of the criminal-justice system has improved measurably, despite infamous cases of police abuse such as the Rodney King beating. While the majority of all ethnic groups agree in national surveys that they are not at risk of being arrested when they are completely innocent, Latinos express fear of unwarranted arrest at 2.4 times the rate of non-Latino whites.[18]

---

[18] "Public attitudes toward crime and criminal justice-related topics," table 2.30 in *Sourcebook of Criminal Justice Statistics 2000,* ed. Kathleen Maguire and Ann L. Pastore (Washington, D.C.: Bureau of Justice Statistics, 2001).

Recent surveys of California residents have indicated that on a scale of one to four (lowest to highest fairness), all ethnic groups consider their interactions with the police and with the court system to have an average fairness score of at least three. Still, an important ethnic gap remains: Latinos and blacks rank fairness at 3.1, whereas whites report a score of 3.4. Such findings suggest that Latinos and other minorities implicitly acknowledge that differences in outcomes across ethnic groups result from legitimate factors, but that concerns over discriminatory treatment are still prevalent.[19]

In the end, what Latinos demand and expect from the criminal-justice system is no different from the expectations of other ethnic groups: reduction in the victimization risk, fair and equitable treatment in the enforcement of criminal laws, and containment of criminal-justice expenditures to a reasonable level lest other important social needs and priorities go unmet.

---

[19]Yuen J. Huo and Tom R. Tyler, *How Different Ethnic Groups React to Legal Authority* (San Francisco, Calif.: Public Policy Institute of California, 2000).

Appendix
Data Sources

The data were collected from various sources. The total number of prison inmates, prison parolees, jail inmates, and probationers were obtained from Table 43 of the *Crime and Delinquency in California* report for 1998. The Latino percentage among prison inmates and parolees was calculated from actual 1996 and 1997 percentages, as reported in Table 2 of *Historical Trends, Institution and Parole Population 1977–1997*, and in Table 58 of *California Prisoners and Parolees, 1995 & 1996*, respectively.

The ethnic breakdown for jail inmates and probationers is not available. Nationwide, in 1998 Latinos accounted for 15.5 percent (Table 7, *Bureau of Justice Statistics at Midyear 1999*, April 2000, NCJ 181643) of all inmates in local jails. Extrapolating from that basis to California, Latinos would be expected to represent 45.2 percent of jail inmates, an overestimate because the imprisonment rate for Latinos is lower than the national average, whereas for whites and African Americans the reverse is true. (Compare estimates in Blumstein and Beck,[20] with estimates provided in this chapter.)

The data for juvenile wards and juvenile parolees—and their ethnic breakdown—were taken from Tables 1 and 4 of *A Comparison of the Youth's Authority's Institution and Parole Populations*, State of California, Department of the Youth Authority, August 1998. The number of juveniles under local custody was estimated from the results of the Census of Juveniles in Residential Placement conducted by the Bureau of Justice Statistics, as published in Howard Snyder and Melissa Sickmund, *Juvenile Offenders and Victims: 1999 National Report*, National Center for Juvenile Justice, September 1999, p. 189. In 1997 California had 19,888 juveniles in residential facilities. The census estimates the juveniles in custody under age 21 and includes juveniles under that age institutionalized at the CYA, which according to CYA amounts to 86.5 percent of the resident population.[21] We therefore deducted from this total the number of CYA wards who are under 21, equal to 6,936. Therefore, the number of juveniles (under age 21) in county facilities is equal to 19,888 minus 6,936, or 12,952.

Data for felony arrests were taken from Table 33 of *the Crime and Delinquency Report 1998*.

Population figures were obtained from two sources, the Statistical Abstract of the United States 1999, Table 34 of Population section; and (ST-98-40) Popu-

---

[20] Alfred Blumstein and Allen J. Beck, "Factors Contributing to the Growth in U.S. Population," in *Prisons, Crime and Justice: A Review of Research*, vol. 26, ed. Michael Tonry and Joan Petersilia (Chicago: University of Chicago Press, 1999), 17–61.

[21] See Table 3 in *Comparison of the Youth's Authority's Institution and Parole Populations*, State of California, Department of the Youth Authority, June 1999.

lation Estimates for States by Age, Sex, Race, and Hispanic Origin: July 1, 1998, U.S. Census Bureau Internet Release date September 15, 1999. First released as (ST-98-31). Tables renumbered effective October 6, 1999.

References

Blumstein, Alfred. 1982. "On The Racial Disproportionality of United States Prison Populations." *Journal of Criminal Law & Criminology,* 1259.

Blumstein Alfred, and Allen J. Beck. 1999. "Factors Contributing to the Growth in U.S. Population." In *Prisons, Crime and Justice: A Review of Research,* ed. Michael Tonry and Joan Petersilia. Chicago: University of Chicago Press, 17–61.

California Department of Justice. 1999. *Homicide in California, 1998.* California Department of Justice.

Chu, Lawrence D., and Susan B. Sorensen. 1996. "Trends in California Homicide, 1970 to 1993." *Western Journal of Medicine* 165:119–125.

Cohen, Jacqueline, and José A. Canela-Cacho. 1994. "Incarceration and Violent Crime." In *Understanding and Preventing Violence, Consequences and Control IV,* ed. A. Reiss and J. F. Roth. Washington, D.C.: National Academy Press, 296–388.

Crutchfield, R. D., G. S. Bridges, and S. R. Pitchford. 1994. "Analytical and Aggregation Biases in Analysis of Imprisonment: Reconciling Discrepancies in Studies of Racial Disparity." *Journal of Research in Crime and Delinquency* 31(2): 166–82.

Daly, Kathleen. 1998. "Gender, Crime, and Criminology." In *The Handbook of Crime and Punishment,* ed. Michael Tonry. New York: Oxford University Press, 85, 110.

Huo, Yuen J., and Tom R. Tyler. 2000. *How Different Ethnic Groups React to Legal Authority.* San Francisco, Calif.: Public Policy Institute of California.

Klein S., J. Petersilia, and S. Turner. 1990. "Race and Imprisonment Decisions in California." *Science* 247 (February): 812–16.

Langan, Patrick A. 1995. "Racism on Trial: New Evidence to Explain the Racial Composition of Prisons in the United States." *Journal of Criminal Law and Criminology* 76(3): 666–83.

Myers, Martha A., and S. Talarico. 1997. *The Social Context of Criminal Sentencing.* New York: Springer-Verlag.

Pastore, Ann L., and Kathleen Maguire, eds. 2001. *Sourcebook of Criminal Justice Statistics 2000.* Washington, D.C.: Bureau of Justice Statistics.

Petersilia, Joan. 1983. *Racial Disparities in Criminal Justice Systems.* Santa Monica, Calif.: Rand Corporation.

Sorenson, Susan B., and Haikang Shen. 1996. "Homicide Risk among Immigrants in California, 1970 through 1992." *American Journal of Public Health* 86(1) (January): 97–100.

State of California. 1999. *Comparison of the Youth's Authority's Institution and Parole Populations.* State of California, Department of the Youth Authority, June.
Tonry, Michael, and Malign Neglect. 1995. *Race, Crime and Punishment in America.* New York: Oxford University Press.
U.S. Department of Justice. 1981. Criminal Victimization of California Residents, A National Crime Survey Report. NCS-S-2, NCJ-70944. Bureau of Justice Statistics, March.
———. 1990. *Special Report: Hispanic Victims,* Bureau of Justice Statistics, NCJ-120507, January.
———. 1999. *Criminal Victimization and Perceptions of Community Safety in 12 Cities, 1998.* NCJ 173940, Bureau of Justice Statistics, May.
———. 2000. *National Crime Victimization Survey for 1997, Criminal Victimization in the United States, 1998 Statistical Tables,* NCJ181585, Bureau of Justice Statistics, May 2000.
Zimring, Franklin, and Gordon Hawkins. 1991. *The Scale of Imprisonment.* Chicago: University of Chicago Press.
———. 1992. *Prison Population and Criminal Justice Policy in California.* Berkeley, Calif.: Institute of Governmental Studies Press, University of California.

Chapter 10

Housing:
Crisis or Opportunity?

Dowell Myers[1]

Introduction

California's rapid population growth is not being met with adequate construction of housing. The housing shortage, which is on the order of 500,000 units, is especially a problem for Latinos, who are expected to constitute 62 percent of the state's population growth from 2000 to 2010.[2] The housing shortages have undesirable consequences for housing affordability, overcrowding of housing, and opportunities for homeownership, not only among Latinos but for all of the state's residents.

---

[1]The author gratefully acknowledges the outstanding research assistance provided by Angelica Herrera, as well as the many useful comments offered by the editors and other contributors to this volume.

[2]California Department of Finance, *Race/Ethnic Population with Age and Sex Detail, 1970–2040* (Sacramento: Demographic Research Unit, Department of Finance, 1998).

Importance of Housing

Housing contributes significantly to the well-being of families and individuals. The rented apartment or mortgaged house is typically the most important single part of a family's budget, often consuming more than one-fourth of gross income. Among lower-income renters, housing expenses can exceed half of the family's income; among low-income homeowners, the housing investment is the major source of family wealth and savings.

Beyond these financial considerations, housing has special importance because the place of residence serves as the staging ground for daily life. Children and parents return to the home after days spent at school or work, and they embark from the home on fresh adventures each day. When families choose a home to occupy, they choose a place of residence, a neighborhood, and a location in the region.

The quality and affordability of housing in the state varies enormously by region and locality, and across neighborhoods. Dense, high-demand areas such as San Francisco and the west side of Los Angeles are characterized by apartments renting for over $2,000 per month, while their suburbs contain heavily landscaped neighborhoods of single-family homes selling for over $1 million. Lower-income residents are forced to less-desirable districts that often border industrial zones with environmental hazards. The cheapest housing of all is provided for farmworkers in the Central Valley, but even at $200 per month those quarters may exceed the rent-paying ability of these lowest-income workers.

The spatial variation in housing availability has several major consequences. Because of zoning practices that require similar types, and therefore prices, of housing within each neighborhood, economic-class segregation is effectively enforced throughout urban areas. As a result of their generally lower incomes and limited housing-payment ability, Latinos are often separated from middle- and higher-income groups. An additional element of racial and ethnic clustering leads to segregation of Latinos from non-Latino whites and other groups.[3] Given that schools are funded from local property taxes and have attendance based largely on residential proximity, Latino children are funneled into some of the least-advantaged schools in the state. Initial disadvantages incurred in elementary education compound themselves in higher education and in subsequent labor-market experiences. This pattern is somewhat self-perpetuating: The children of lower-income parents grow up without the ability to afford residence in higher-income neighborhoods for their own children. At the root of this cumulative disadvantagement lies the distribution of housing opportunities.

---

[3] Philip J. Ethington, *Segregated Diversity: Race-Ethnicity, Space, and Political Fragmentation in Los Angeles County, 1940–1994,* final report to The John Randolph Haynes and Dora Haynes Foundation, University of Southern California, Department of History, 2000.

Particular Challenges for Latinos

Latinos in California face several challenges in their quest for adequate housing. The first challenge is that Latino family structures generally are larger and require more housing space. Latino households in 1990 were more likely to be headed by married couples: 59.1 percent versus 52.7 percent for non-Latino white households.[4] They were much more likely to have children present: 55.9 percent versus 27.3 percent for non-Latino white households. The presence of children leads directly to larger households. In 1990, 54.5 percent of all California households contained only one or two persons. Among Latinos, roughly half as many households (27.1 percent) were that small. Instead, 35.9 percent of Latino households contained at least five persons (versus 7.6 percent of non-Latino white households).

A second challenge faced by Latinos is that they live in California, a state with one of the highest costs of housing in the nation. According to a recent report, "There is no denying that rents in California are high; in 1990, two states had median rent levels that were greater than $600—Hawaii and California (with median rent levels of $650 and $620 respectively). In fact, only three other states had rent levels within 10 percent of California."[5]

The third challenge is that many Latinos have lower family incomes, as previous chapters have discussed. Living in larger households, without benefit of higher incomes, poses an urgent economic problem when housing costs are as high as they are in California. Income constraints often force Latinos to occupy smaller units that would be judged as overcrowded, and/or lower-quality units that are more affordable. Latinos are also less likely to be able to afford homeownership, although their achievement of homeownership in this regard may be surprising.

Finally, Latinos constitute the majority of population growth in the state, but that growth is not being met with adequate construction of housing. These serious shortages fall most heavily on Latinos, not only because of their prominence in the growing population, but because their lower incomes make them less able to withstand the resulting increases in rents and prices.

---

[4]These data are taken from the 1990 census, Public Use Microdata Sample (PUMS) file, a five percent sample of all households and individuals in California. The same data source is used throughout, with some exceptions, as noted. Data more recent than the 1990 census are available, but the Current Population Survey and American Housing Survey both contain samples too small to be sufficient for the detailed analysis conducted here.

[5]California Department of Housing and Community Development, *The State of California's Housing Markets: 1990–1997* (Sacramento: Department of Housing and Community Development, 1999).

Scope of This Chapter

A diversity of housing experiences faces Latinos in different parts of the state, as media reports on the Silicon Valley and the Central Valley highlight. For purposes of statewide policymaking, it is useful to understand experiences with housing in the state as a whole. Rather than focus on different cities in the state, this analysis will emphasize differences within the Latino population and comparisons with non-Latinos. Accordingly, in the discussion that follows, several major subgroups of Latinos will be assessed. First compared are all Latinos and non-Latino whites, next U.S.-born and foreign-born Latinos, and finally new immigrant arrivals versus the longer-settled foreign-born Latinos.

From among the many dimensions of the housing dilemma we have chosen four major topic areas of special importance for Latinos. First, the mounting shortages of housing construction in the state amount to a great housing collapse, and Latinos are much more affected than others by this crisis. Second is the housing-payment burden carried by renters and owners. Third is the issue of residential density, including both overcrowded housing and neighborhood density. The fourth topic is the attainment of homeownership, often proclaimed as the American dream and gateway to the middle class.

The housing situation of Latinos could be judged in some respects as a problem of crisis proportions. Yet, at the same time, elements of Latinos' adaptation to a difficult situation suggest the opportunity for more favorable conditions ahead. This juxtaposition of crisis and opportunity is woven through the analysis that follows.

The Great Housing Collapse

The 1990s were extremely hard on Californians from a housing point of view. Even after the economic recovery in most parts of the state, housing construction continued to fall far short of requirements to meet population growth. The vigorous rebound of construction that has followed every recovery from recession since World War II failed to materialize. So great is the enormity of the construction shortfall displayed in Figure 10.1 that we term it the Great Housing Collapse. Figure 10.1 shows steady construction in each of the last three decades until the 1990s, coupled with steady increases in population each decade.

Construction for the 1990s fell to half the level recorded in the 1980s (1.105 million versus 2.066 million units), with multifamily housing especially hard hit. Whereas multifamily housing maintained a 45–49 percent share of all construction in each of the preceding three decades, during the 1990s its share of an already-diminished production fell to 25 percent. Failure to produce needed multifamily housing places the burden of California's housing shortages squarely on

Figure 10.1. The Great Housing Collapse

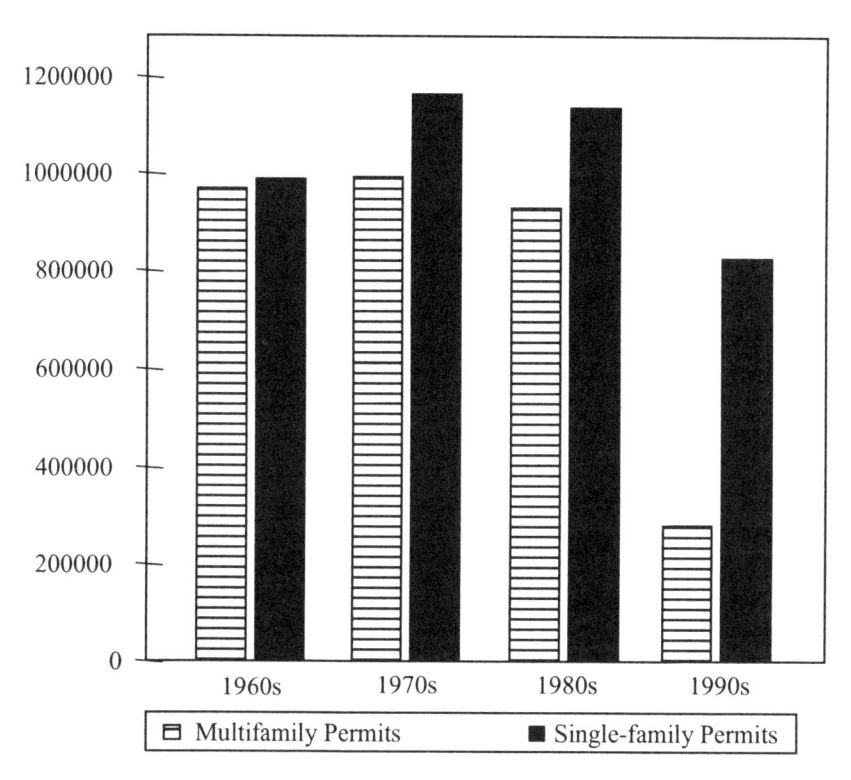

[Bar chart showing Multifamily Permits and Single-family Permits by decade (1960s, 1970s, 1980s, 1990s), with values ranging from 0 to 1,200,000]

Source: U.S. Census Bureau

the shoulders of renters and low-income would-be owners, precisely the segment of the population that has grown most rapidly. The Great Housing Collapse particularly impacts Latinos, because they are more likely to be renters and to be residents in multifamily housing.

Affordability Problems

The high cost of housing in California poses major affordability problems, especially for Latinos and other groups that have generally larger households that require larger-sized units. Families with relatively low incomes may be particularly hard-pressed. The standard assumption of state and federal housing policy is that households should pay no more than 30 percent of their total income for

Figure 10.2. Housing Payment Burdens Relative to Income Among Latino Households in California, 1990

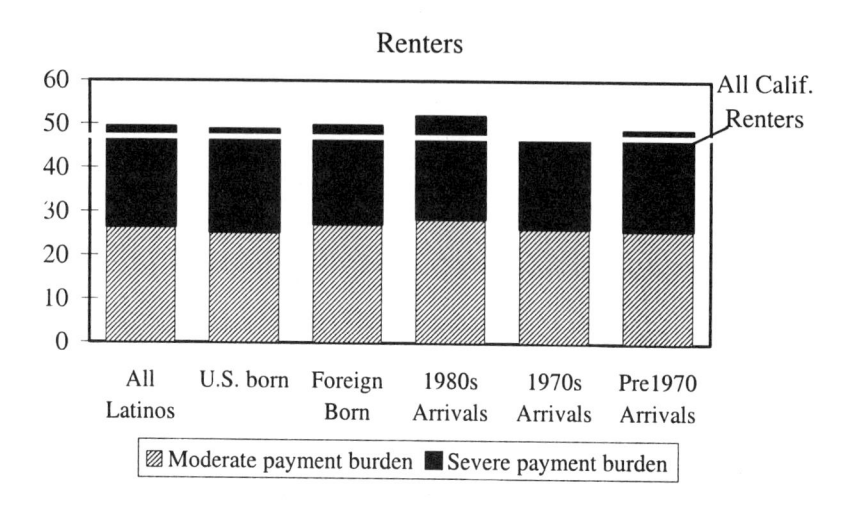

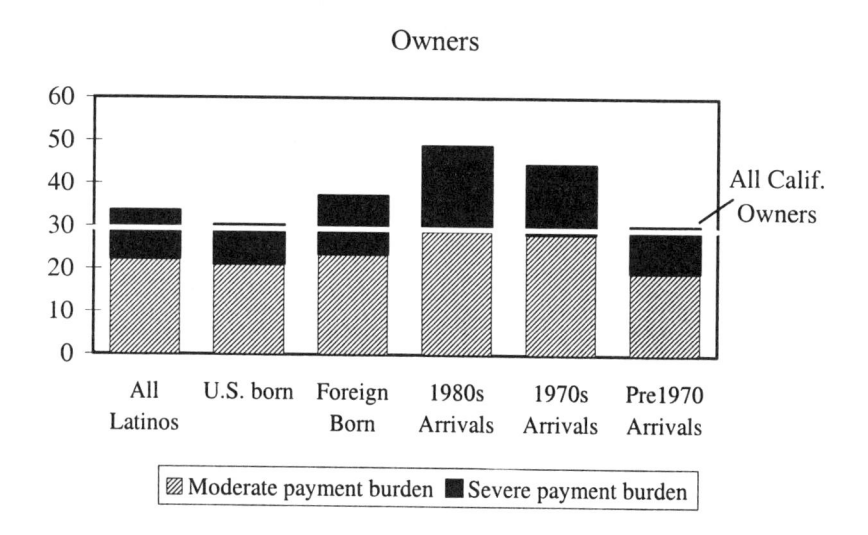

Renters

Owners

Moderate payment burden ■ Severe payment burden

rent, mortgage, and other housing expenses. Households paying more than 30 percent of income for housing carry an excessive payment burden.

Among all California households, renters have a substantially greater likelihood of carrying excessive payment burdens. This reflects the generally lower incomes of renters, on the one hand, and the generally lower mortgage payments of homeowners who have lived in their homes a number of years, on the other. Among all Californians in 1990, 47.3 percent of renters and 29.5 percent of owners were paying more than 30 percent of income for housing. Once the economic findings of the 2000 census become known, we can learn how much worse the affordability crisis has grown in response to the Great Housing Collapse.

Surprisingly, despite their larger household sizes, most Latino renters carry payment burdens very close to those of all Californians. Only recent immigrants have significantly higher likelihood of excessive payment burdens (see Figure 10.2). Apparently, Latinos have found ways to economize on housing costs, one of which is to rent smaller units and another of which is to occupy older housing. The savings they achieve in this way can be better invested in other family needs.

Among Latino homeowners, in contrast, the incidence of overpayment is substantially greater for recent immigrant arrivals, but lower for U.S.-born citizens (see Figure 10.2). This reflects the fact that newcomers by definition must have purchased homes more recently, whereas immigrants who arrived before 1970, or those who are native-born and older, are likely to have purchased homes in the past that now carry lower mortgages. While immigrant homebuyers' payment burdens are high, they reflect the desire to stretch their resources to secure this important investment for their families. High payments by homeowners today create an opportunity for future wealth accumulation by their families.

It is somewhat surprising that Latino households do not carry heavier payment burdens than they do. Given their large household sizes and often low incomes, and the high cost of housing in the state, there is no question that they experience major affordability problems. They cope in ways other than paying a higher fraction of their income for housing. The most prevalent solution is higher-density living.

Density of Residence

Density of residence is an area of policy interest in which Latinos stand out from the average Californian. The topic is addressed here from two vantage points: density within the home (often termed overcrowding) and density in neighborhoods. Although the two aspects overlap, they lead to very different policy interpretations.

Overcrowded Housing

Overcrowded housing has been one of the most contentious urban policy issues involving Latinos. As reviewed elsewhere,[6] overcrowding had been in sharp decline, both in California and the nation, since the Great Depression. After 1980, however, a dramatic resurgence of the problem occurred, more so in California than in any other state.[7] In both state and federal policy, overcrowding is defined as housing units occupied by more than one person per room (including kitchens and living rooms, but not bathrooms, hallways, closets, or porches). Among renters, overcrowding in California increased between 1980 and 1990 from 11.2 percent to 19.6 percent. In some cities, like Santa Ana, overcrowding increased to extremely high levels (49 percent of renters) in a short time.[8]

The effort to restrict occupancy so that units would not be overcrowded made this problem controversial. City officials in Santa Ana were among the leaders in this effort. The stated rationale was threefold: first, that overcrowded housing was bad for the health and welfare of the occupants; second, that overcrowded housing posed a public-safety hazard; and third, that overcrowded housing created excess demands on public services and infrastructure. Regarding the welfare of the occupants, little evidence has been produced to make any definitive claims. (See the review by Myers et al.) With respect to the public-safety issue, overcrowded units were assumed to be stuffed also with mattresses and other possessions that fire officials believed made the units more combustible and more difficult to escape from in the event of fire. The Santa Ana Fire Department even carried out a public test of this thesis, but, contrary to what one might expect, the results did not lead to the conclusion that overcrowded units would burn faster than others. A far greater hazard than overcrowding is the installation of security grates to keep burglars out, a response to crime that endangers occupants needing a rapid escape during a fire.

More justified as a perceived cost of overcrowding is the burden imposed by growing density on public services and infrastructure. Typically, residential neighborhoods are planned and developed with infrastructure adequate to sup-

---

[6]Dowell Myers, William C. Baer, and Seong-Youn Choi, "The Changing Problem of Overcrowded Housing," *Journal of the American Planning Association* (Winter 1996): 66–84.

[7]Bureau of the Census, *Housing: Then and Now: 50 Years Of Decennial Censuses,* 1999 (www.census.gov/hhes/www/housing/census/histcensushsg.html).

[8]These figures are from the 1990 census, summary tape file 1.

port a population size derived from a presumed average occupancy per unit. When that occupancy level increases dramatically, it can place strain on such installed physical infrastructure as available parking places, water and sewer connections, and school facilities. Major municipal services such as garbage collection, fire protection, and police protection may need to be increased as the population density grows, but those adjustments are made more easily and rapidly than improvements in infrastructure.

The heart of the controversy over overcrowding lies less with rational assessment of increased service loads and more with political reactions to change. Longtime residents often object strenuously when population change in the neighborhood brings newcomers who live in large household groups. The oldtimers, who are usually members of the long-established white or black populations, typically are older and live alone or with one other person. Understandably, they view the arrival of large households as jarring to the peace and quiet to which they are accustomed in their neighborhood. Thus, even though overcrowding may be benign within the home, it creates social friction in the neighborhood. Because the high cost of housing makes it difficult to find housing, many Latinos, especially the foreign-born, view overcrowding as a solution, not a problem.

Not all Latinos are equally likely to live in overcrowded housing. Those with the least income or the largest household sizes are the most at risk. As a group, in 1990 38.9 percent of all Latino householders occupied homes with more than one person per room, and 24.8 percent occupied homes with more than 1.5 persons per room, a level deemed severe overcrowding. The overall incidence of overcrowding among Latinos is roughly three times greater than for all California households and 10 times greater than for non-Latino white households. However, as Figure 10.3 shows, the rate of overcrowding among U.S.-born Latino householders is very low, only slightly exceeding the level of all California households. In contrast, among households of the foreign-born, fully 55.7 percent are overcrowded, and over half are living at severely overcrowded levels. This incidence is highest for the most recent immigrant arrivals: In total, 69 percent are overcrowded, and 49.6 percent are severely overcrowded. The likelihood of living in overcrowded housing drops markedly for immigrants who have lived in the U.S. since before 1970, at least in part because these are older persons whose children are more likely to have grown and left home. Given the spectacular growth of the Latino immigrant population since 1990, we can be certain that these disparities are at least as great today, and have probably increased.

In sum, foreign-born Latinos exhibit much greater likelihood of living in overcrowded housing. Judged by the middle-class norms of state and federal housing policy, they live in substandard housing conditions. However, it is much less clear that the occupants themselves perceive this problem. Even at higher

Figure 10.3. Incidence (%) of Overcrowded Housing Among Latino Households in California, 1990

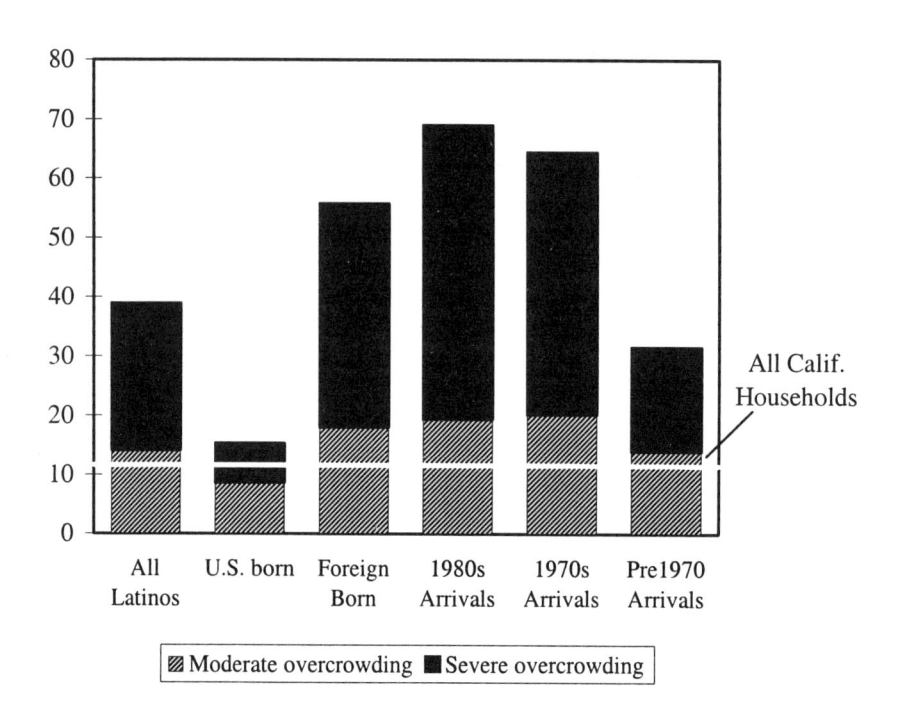

[Bar chart showing incidence of overcrowded housing. Categories along x-axis: All Latinos (~39%), U.S. born (~15%), Foreign Born (~56%), 1980s Arrivals (~69%), 1970s Arrivals (~64%), Pre1970 Arrivals (~31%). Each bar divided into moderate overcrowding (hatched, lower) and severe overcrowding (black, upper). A reference line labeled "All Calif. Households" is indicated.]

☒ Moderate overcrowding ■ Severe overcrowding

income levels, Latinos (and Asian Americans) are much more likely to live in housing deemed overcrowded than are members of white or black households, the vast majority of whom are U.S.-born. This suggests that cultural preferences and family structure—not simply poverty and inability to afford suitable housing—are important determinants of overcrowding.

Neighborhood Density and Compact Cities

Neighborhoods with rising proportions of overcrowded housing units are likely to grow more densely populated. As was discussed above, from the viewpoint of longtime residents, the growing density leads to undesirable increases in congestion and noise. Hence, political friction surrounds the overcrowding issue in areas where foreign-born Latinos are replacing U.S.-born residents.

Stepping back from the issue, we see that more than overcrowding within the housing unit is involved. The density of housing structures is also important, and the consequences in some respects can be viewed with favor. The Latino population generally lives at higher densities and in more compact form than other population segments in California. This is a model that urban planners would like to have more Californians follow, though no evidence exists that Latinos do so by choice.

Residential densities are generated at two basic levels: the number of people in each dwelling unit and the density of dwelling units per acre.[9] More specifically, population density in a land area is a mathematical product of persons per room (the overcrowding measure), rooms per unit, units per structure, and structures per acre. A series of these density factors is depicted in Table 10.1. On average, Latino households have more people per unit than non-Latino white households (4.01 versus 2.43, respectively). Even though Latinos occupy an average of one fewer room per unit, they place more people in each room. This is especially pronounced among immigrant arrivals with less than 10 years in the United States, who have the fewest average rooms (2.99) and the highest ratio of persons per room (1.60).

Not only are Latino-occupied units smaller than others, but they are also more likely to be located in multi-unit structures. Whereas 31.5 percent of California housing units are part of multi-unit structures (also called multifamily housing), that is true of 38.3 percent of all Latino-occupied housing (see Table 10.1). Among foreign-born Latinos, the prevalence of multi-unit housing is much higher, reaching 64.3 percent for the newest immigrant arrivals.

The net result is that total population per acre is much greater among Latinos, reflecting both the larger household sizes and the greater density of units in structures. Assuming that multi-unit structures have an average of 20 units per gross acre, while single-family units average six units per gross acre, we can calculate a statewide average population density per acre for the different population subgroups. (Obviously, this density level could prove much greater in some cities than in others.) As the last column of Table 10.1 shows, overall population density is estimated to vary from 25.9 persons per acre for non-Latinos to 32.7 persons per acre for U.S.-born Latinos. Density is much higher (55.8 persons per acre) for the foreign-born and is highest for new immigrant arrivals (71.6 persons per acre).

A little-recognized benefit of this high population density is that fewer acres of land are consumed by population growth in more compact cities. This has urgent significance in California because the Department of Finance has forecast

---

[9]Walter F. Abbott, "The Decomposition of Intra-Urban Gross Density: Unit-Level and Unit-Contextual Determinants," *Social Forces* 61 (1982): 587–99.

Table 10.1. Selected Measures of Residential Density in California, 1990

	Persons per Unit	Rooms per Unit	Persons per Room	% in Multi-Unit Structures	Population per acre[1]
Total Households	2.79	4.88	0.57	31.5	29.0
Non-Latino Households	2.54	5.05	0.50	30.0	25.9
All Latino Households	4.01	4.07	0.99	38.3	45.6
U.S. Born	3.22	4.72	0.68	29.7	32.7
Foreign Born	4.57	3.61	1.27	44.4	55.8
1980s Arrivals	4.77	2.99	1.60	64.3	71.6
1970s Arrivals	4.97	3.48	1.43	42.6	59.5
Pre1970 Arrivals	3.89	4.42	0.88	25.5	37.2

Source: 1990 Census (PUMS file, household records).
[1]Estimated by assuming an average density of 20 units per acre for units in multi-unit structures and six units per acre for single-unit structures.

an increase of 15 million new residents, a 50 percent increase in population, between 1990 and 2020.[10] Urban planners in California are at a loss to explain how so many new residents can be accommodated. If the newcomers will "take up space" to the same degree as each of the 1990 residents, that would imply a 50 percent expansion in all services and facilities. As the state is already one-third of the way through this period, California clearly will not achieve such an expansion.

One favored solution is to encourage more efficient and sustainable land use by building more compact developments—ones that house more people per unit at a higher density of units per acre. This solution goes hand-in-hand with increased emphasis on public transit, primarily buses, in urban areas across the state. The dilemma is that these changes may make sense in the aggregate as a solution to the problem of 15 million new residents; individually, however, residents appear unwilling to give up their low-density, car-dependent life styles.

---

[10]The latest forecast was prepared by the Demographic Research Unit in December 1998 and is due for revision after the results of the 2000 census have been processed, most likely in 2003. Details of the population forecast by race, Hispanic origin, age, and gender for each county in California can be found at www.dof.ca.gov/html/Demograp/druhpar.htm.

The Latino population provides a model that more of the state's population may need to follow. Even if others are unwilling to live in larger household groups, a higher density of units per acre is surely in store for the average Californian.

Homeownership Attainment

By most accounts, the primary measure of housing achievement in the U.S. is attainment of homeownership. Indeed, this is widely ascribed as an integral part of the American dream. Ownership of a home is both a goal in its own right and proof that one can get ahead by hard work in this country. Some have also posited that attainment of homeownership represents entry into the middle class in California.[11] This notion has some merit, especially for retired Californians living on reduced incomes, because homeownership represents their accumulated lifetime status better than their current income. The following analysis follows the standard convention of measuring homeownership rates by the percentage of all households that own their homes, either with a mortgage or free-and-clear. Consistently with leading national studies, we find that Latinos have substantially lower rates of homeownership and that this property constitutes the great majority of family wealth.[12]

Lower Homeownership in California

California has become a low-homeownership state in recent decades. In 1950, the ownership rate in the state (54.3 percent) nearly matched the nation's (55.0 percent). However, in the ensuing two decades of booming growth, California's homeownership rate failed to rise, while that of the nation increased to 62.9 percent in 1970, rising further to 64.2 percent by 1990. In contrast, the ownership rate in California remained at only 55.6 percent in 1990, with lower rates found only in New York, Hawaii, and Nevada. Recent survey data provide fragmentary evidence that California's homeownership rate may have risen 2.2 percentage points between 1990 and 1999, but this barely kept pace with the national increase of 2.4 percentage points.[13] Explanations for the low rate of homeownership in California include the high cost of home purchase in the state. Those high prices stem, in turn, from the scarcity of supply created by a

---

[11]Gregory Rodriguez, *The Emerging Latino Middle Class* (Malibu, Calif.: Pepperdine University, 1996).

[12]Harvard Joint Center for Housing Studies, *The State of the Nation's Housing: 2000* (Cambridge, Mass.: Joint Center for Housing Studies of Harvard University, 2000).

[13]Bureau of the Census, *Housing Vacancies and Homeownership Annual Statistics: 1998* (www.census.gov/hhes/www/housing/hvs/annual98/ann98t13.html), 1999b.

very low rate of housing production in comparison to the state's employment and population growth.

Previous studies have emphasized that Latinos acquire homeownership at much lower rates than other Californians.[14] However, it also has been reported that Latino immigrants achieve higher rates of homeownership than would be expected in light of their generally low incomes and occupation statuses.[15] Whereas Asian immigrants enter homeownership very quickly after arrival in the U.S., which reflects their ready access to capital, Latino immigrants move steadily upward toward homeownership for two or three decades after arrival, reflecting the accumulated rewards of hard work. In this respect, Latino immigrants have been said to follow the old model of assimilation based on European immigrants more closely than do recent Asian arrivals.

Table 10.2 gives a summary of homeownership status achievement. For reasons discussed below, a longer-term perspective is required to understand homeownership differences. Here we track homeownership rates from 1970 to 1990, using the same subgroups of the population as above. Overall, California's homeownership rate has held fairly steady in recent years, with the highest rate recorded in 1980 (56.4 percent). Non-Latino white households have consistently held higher homeownership rates than Latinos, and the gap has grown in recent years as their homeownership rates have risen slightly while those of Latinos have declined (from 43.9 percent in 1970 to 40.1 percent in 1990). This decline is likely due to growing numbers of immigrant Latinos, because the homeownership rate of native-born Latinos has held steady and even increased slightly. Indeed, a recent study in Los Angeles County shows that, given equivalent education, income, and nativity attributes, Latinos achieve the same level of homeownership as non-Latino whites.[16]

Among foreign-born Latinos, homeownership rates have trended downward, from 36.7 percent in 1970 to 33.1 percent in 1990. This reflects two factors: first, the growing numbers of recent arrivals among all foreign-born residents and, second, a falling homeownership rate for the recent arrivals (17.7 percent in 1970, 16.3 percent in 1980, and 9.9 percent in 1990). The lower homeownership of more recent arrivals is probably due to the higher housing prices encountered by newcomers in recent years. Meanwhile, the long-settled immigrants who arrived before 1960 have achieved even higher homeownership rates than those of the native-born. Over time, the 1960s arrivals have similarly rapidly increased their homeownership rate (from 17.7 percent in 1970 to 42.5

---

[14]William A. V. Clark, *The California Cauldron* (New York: Guilford Press, 1998).

[15]Dowell Myers and Seong Woo Lee, "Immigrant Trajectories into Homeownership: A Temporal Analysis of Residential Assimilation," *International Migration Review* 32 (Fall 1998): 593–625.

[16]Gary Painter, Stuart Gabriel, and Dowell Myers, "Race, Immigrant Status, and Housing Tenure Choice," *Journal of Urban Economics* 49 (2001): 150–67.

Table 10.2. Percentage of Homeowners in California

	1970	1980	1990
Total Households	54.9	56.4	55.6
Non-Latino Households	56.0	58.5	58.8
All Latino Households	43.9	42.9	40.1
U.S. Born	48.3	49.5	49.8
Foreign Born	36.7	35.8	33.1
1980s Arrivals	--	--	9.9
1970s Arrivals	--	16.3	32.5
1960s Arrivals	17.7	42.5	53.0
Pre1960 Arrivals	50.4	59.8	66.7

Source: 1970, 1980, and 1990 Census (PUMS file, household records).

percent in 1980, and to 53.0 percent in 1990). These results, however, are not controlled for age, and so comparisons of long-settled (largely older) immigrants cannot be made fairly with the native-born, who are largely younger.

Trajectories of Different Generations

Several factors make homeownership more challenging to assess than other aspects of socio-economic achievement. Comparisons at a single point in time can be misleading. On the one hand, young adults (age 25–34) and new immigrants have not had time to achieve their ultimate level of homeownership. On the other hand, long-established homeowners often achieved their status decades earlier under much more favorable conditions. Thus we need to follow the life-cycle trajectories of different generations and pay particular attention to the newest housing-market entrants, either young adults (age 25–34) who are native-born or newly arrived immigrants.[17] In essence, homeownership is a cumu-

---

[17] The generational quality of homeownership has led housing demographers to develop new analytic techniques emphasizing birth cohorts (see John R. Pitkin and Dowell Myers, "The Specification of Demographic Effects on Housing Demand: Avoiding the Age-Cohort Fallacy," *Journal of Housing Economics* 3 [September 1994]: 240–50.) and immigration cohorts (see Dowell Myers and Seong Woo Lee, "Immigrant Trajectories into Homeownership: A Temporal Analysis of Residential Assimilation," *International*

lative status: Once they achieve it, few households return to renting. These dynamics require that we treat homeownership more as a career endeavor than as a status achieved at a single point in time.

The best means of representing the housing-career achievement of homeownership is through cohort trajectories that track the upward sweep of homeownership achievement as people grow older (and live longer in the United States). For this purpose we can link observations made in the censuses of 1970, 1980, and 1990. Figure 10.4 displays the progress into homeownership of native-born Latinos in California. Most of the cohorts follow the same general upward trajectory (the "expected" line). One exception is the cohorts over age 45 in 1970, who had substantially lower ownership rates than the younger cohorts to follow. The other exception is the cohorts under age 45 in 1990 (the black dots in Figure 10.4), whose ownership rates fell markedly below those observed at comparable ages in 1980 or 1970. A key question to be addressed with new data from the 2000 census will be the degree to which these younger cohorts have gotten back on track or whether they are locked into permanently lower trajectories.

Latino immigrants have much lower trajectories of homeownership, but this depends on how long they have lived in the U.S. and how old they were when they arrived. Immigrants of the 1960s had achieved much higher rates of homeownership by 1990 than had immigrants who arrived in the 1970s (see Figure 10.5). In fact, the two youngest cohorts of 1960s arrivals are on very similar paths to those expected of U.S.-born Latinos. Indeed, the young immigrants are achieving homeownership at higher rates than those observed in 1990 for young native-born Latinos.

The outstanding feature of both the 1960s and 1970s immigrant arrivals is how rapidly their rates of homeownership track upward as they grow 10 years older and reside in the U.S. 10 years longer. The older cohorts, who will have shorter eventual careers in the U.S., will never reach the homeownership levels of the native-born or the youngest immigrants (i.e., age 25–34 in 1990). Nevertheless, their upward movement into homeownership—doubling in the first 10 years—is impressive. Unfortunately, the record of strong progress into homeownership appears to be faltering.

One point of concern is that the rate of immigrant progress into homeownership has been decelerating in recent decades. As Table 10.2 shows, the 1960s arrivals advanced from 17.7 percent ownership to 42.5 percent ownership after an additional decade of U.S. residence. In contrast, the 1970s arrivals advanced from 16.3 percent ownership to only 32.5 percent ownership after a decade. The upward trajectories appear most stunted among 1970s arrivals for cohorts under age 45 (see Figure 10.5). We now await evidence from the 2000 census on the

---

Migration Review 32 [Fall 1998]: 593–625.). Those techniques are now finding application in other topic areas of immigrant advancement.

Figure 10.4. Trajectories of Homeownership Attainment by Native-Born Latinos in California
(Percent Homeownership in 1970, 1980, and 1990, Linked as Cohorts Grow Older)

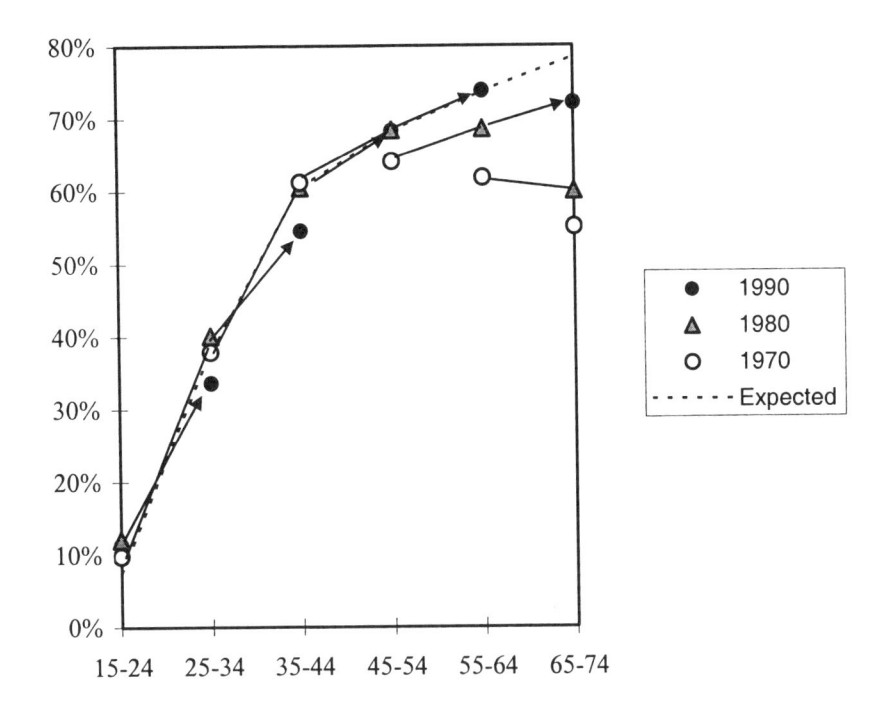

outcome of 1980s arrivals who started at only 9.9 percent ownership. Current information indicates that we face a crisis of collapsing homeownership opportunity for new immigrant Latinos, even as earlier immigrants continue to advance upward in achievement.

The crisis centers on the lagging progress of newcomers. Not only new immigrants, but also new, young adults (age 25–34) who are native-born are facing diminished opportunity. The ownership rates of younger native-born Latinos (age 25–34) are falling short of those achieved by their predecessors who occupied the same age group 10 or 20 years earlier. Those who had passed age 45 by 1990 appear much more successful than their successors, probably because they had opportunity to purchase homes in the great homeownership run-up of the latter 1970s and before the price escalation of the 1980s.

Figure 10.5. Trajectories of Homeownership Attainment by Latino Immigrants in California
(Percent Homeowners in 1970, 1980, and 1990, Compared to Trajectory of US-Born Latinos)

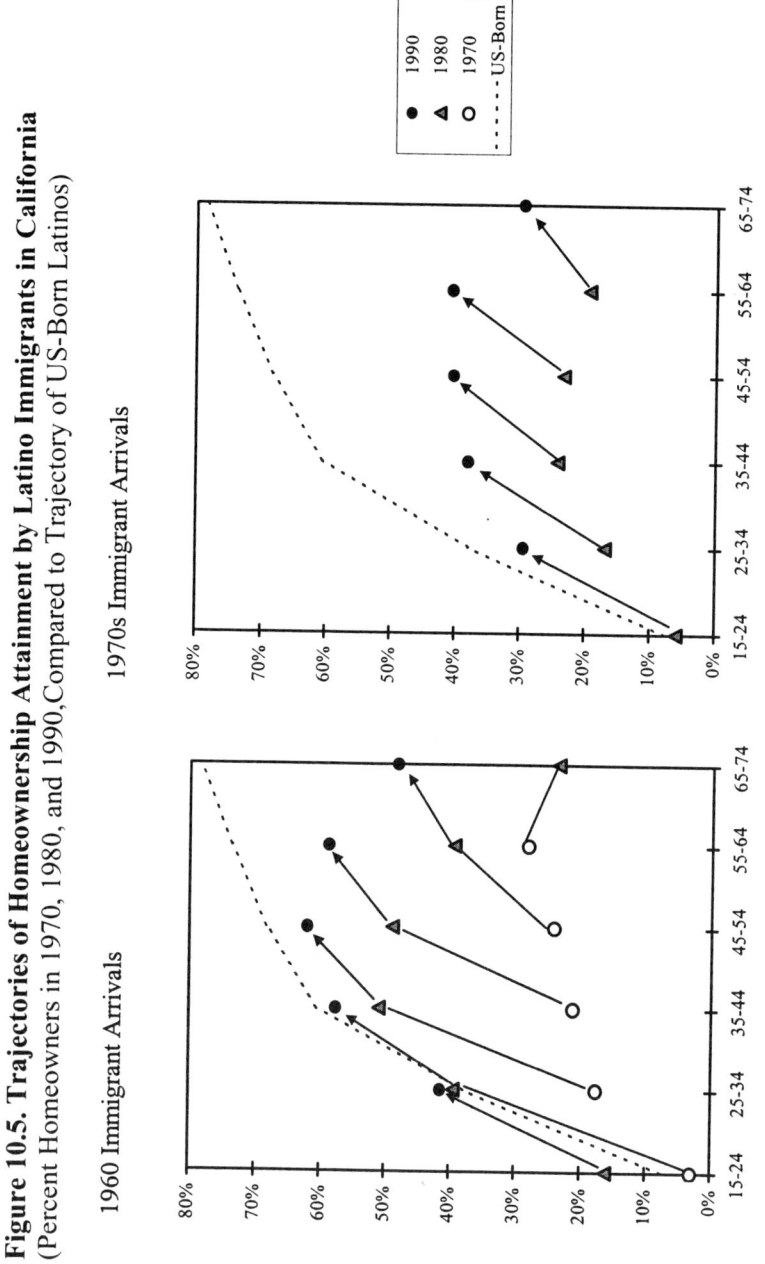

Source: 1970, 1980, and 1990 Censuses (PUMS file).

Policy Initiatives

In the past few years, California's housing prices and rents have soared even above their previous high levels. The extreme shortfall in housing production contributes to these increasing costs by making housing scarce for the growing population. With the exception of a few areas in the Central Valley, the struggle to secure adequate housing has reached crisis proportions, leading to a broad consensus on the need for change.[18] How disproportionately this housing crisis bears on Latinos may be less widely understood.

Latinos are at special risk in this unfavorable housing market. The kinds of housing most likely to be occupied by Latinos are the ones being least produced, even though the Latino population accounts for well over half of all population growth. In addition, doubling up in smaller units is less of a solution now than in the past because Latinos already exercised that solution to survive in the housing market of the 1990s. To double up still further would exacerbate the problems of overcrowding to levels far beyond those decried by a number of city officials.

Solutions to assist Latinos have the advantage that they would be of benefit to most Californians. The following three policy initiatives are of greatest importance.

Restarting Multifamily Construction

Most important is to restart multifamily housing construction in California, as well as boost construction of single-family homes. Increased supply will help to forestall further increases in rents and prices. To achieve this goal, the state legislature needs to strengthen the teeth of existing state housing-needs programs that supervise local planning processes. Localities need to plan for a fair share of the state's rental housing needs to match their share of job growth and other factors. Of further assistance would be reduction of the fiscal disincentives for local housing construction. At present only commercial construction returns net tax benefits to localities. Residents of housing are viewed as a liability because they consume costly services. To nullify this disincentive, retail sales taxes and other funds collected by the state can be rebated to localities in proportion to their resident populations, with an extra bonus to those localities that

---

[18]See, for example, California Senate Office of Research, *The Right Home in the Right Place at the Right Price* (Sacramento: Senate Office of Research, 1999); and California Department of Housing and Community Development, *Raising the Roof* (Sacramento: Department of Housing and Community Development, 2000).

supply new multifamily housing units. These changes would benefit all Californians by reducing housing shortages.

Larger Apartments

Of particular benefit to Latinos would be incentives to include a sizable share of three-bedroom apartments among multifamily construction. The 1990 census showed that 11 percent of all apartments had three or more bedrooms (down from 17 percent in 1980). With their larger household sizes, Latinos would benefit from more bedrooms, and the growth in Latino population suggests that the construction trend needs to be reversed, from smaller to larger apartments. Local government can give density bonuses for projects that incorporate large shares of three or four-bedroom units (e.g., more than 20 percent). State government can establish financial subsidies for such projects.

Greater Access to Homeownership

A crisis is mounting for newcomers to California's housing market that affects new immigrant arrivals and young native-born Latinos in their 20s and 30s alike. Expanded subsidies for first-time homebuyers are needed if young adults are to approach the homeownership achievement levels of the preceding generation. Recognizing that the previous level of homeownership fell well below that of the nation, it is especially important that California not fall further behind. Without hope for homeownership in this state, California will increasingly lose its middle class to states offering better opportunities.

Conclusion

As a group, Latinos are unusually disadvantaged in the high-priced California housing market. Not only do Latinos live in larger families, they tend to have lower incomes. The very group that requires the most housing is the one least able to pay for it. Failure to build the housing required by population growth, especially multifamily housing, has a severe impact on the residential well-being of Latinos and other Californians.

The higher-density residential pattern of Latinos is a source of both problems and of solutions. The pattern of high-density living can be a source of social friction with longer-established residents in neighborhoods. At the same time, it is a solution Latinos employ to cope with overpriced housing that is built with too few bedrooms. Higher residential densities also can be viewed as an opportunity for planning a more livable state. Urban planners are increasingly emphasizing the desirability of building more compact cities so that less land will be consumed by future population growth. The burgeoning "smart growth" movement can take advantage of the compact lifestyles pioneered by Latino residents in California.

In the case of homeownership, we have found evidence of both crisis and opportunity. Although recent immigrants appear to have very low homeownership rates, over time they progress rapidly into homeownership. The greatest success is enjoyed by immigrants of the 1960s who arrived as young children and who are now middle-aged. Such rapid progress suggests the American dream is alive and well for Latino immigrants.

At the same time, a crisis is unfolding for newcomers to California's housing market. This crisis affects two major groups. First, the newest immigrant arrivals are achieving homeownership at much lower rates shortly after arrival, suggesting that their upward trajectories may be much weaker than for previous immigrant arrivals. The second group facing crisis comprises young native-born Latinos in their 20s and 30s. The most recent cohorts of young adults are falling below the homeownership achievement levels of the preceding generation. Evidence shows that this group is also falling behind the progress of the immigrant children who have now matured into adulthood.

The overall conclusion is that finding adequate housing in California is a struggle that is becoming more difficult each decade. This struggle is rooted in the high cost of housing, which in turn is derived from the extremely low housing-construction levels in the state. Solving the problems of the Latino population will go a long way toward solving the problems of all Californians.

Chapter 11

Latino Political Incorporation in California, 1990–2000

Luis Ricardo Fraga and Ricardo Ramírez

The increased presence of Latinos in the politics of California is undisputed. Major newspapers, important news journals focusing on statewide politics, and scholarly analyses suggest that the most significant change in the politics of California since 1990 has been the importance of Latinos in their roles as residents, voters, and elected officials.[1] Latinos are now estimated to make up 32

---

[1] See, for example, the range of issues covered by the following articles in *The California Journal:* James Carroll, "Courting California: Both Parties Lust after Those Golden Electoral Votes," *California Journal,* vol. 23, no. 9 (September 1992): 433–36; Dale Maharidge, "Did 1992 Herald the Dawn of Latino Political Power?" *California Journal,* vol. 24, no. 1 (January 1993): 15–18; Elizabeth López, and Eric Wahlgren, "The Latino Vote: The Lure of Four Million Ballots" *California Journal,* vol. 25, no. 11 (November 1994): 29–31; and Sherry Bebitch Jeffe, "Year of the Latino?" *California Journal,* vol. 27, no. 10 (October 1996): 20. See also: Byran O. Jackson and Michael B. Preston, eds., *Racial and Ethnic Politics in California* (Berkeley: Institute of Governmental Studies, University of California, Berkeley, 1991); Aníbal Yáñez-Chávez, ed., *Latino Politics in California* (San Diego: Center for U.S.-Mexican Studies at the University of California, San Diego, 1996); Michael Preston, Bruce E. Cain, and Sandra Bass, eds., *Racial and Ethnic Politics in California* (Berkeley: Institute of Governmental Studies,

percent of the California population,[2] and the Census Bureau estimates that they will be the largest ethnic and racial group in the state by 2014.[3] Exit polls conducted by the Cable News Network (CNN) estimate that Latinos constitute 14 percent of all Californians who voted in 2000, twice the percentage of African-American voters.[4] Latino elected officials currently constitute 25 percent of all members of the state Assembly and 18 percent of the state Senate. The current lieutenant governor, Cruz Bustamante, is Latino. Until recently, Antonio Villaraigosa was the second Latino Speaker of the California State Assembly. These accomplishments are dramatic.

The changing nature of Latino politics in California gives rise to a number of important questions. Does the increased Latino presence reflect a fundamental shift in the distribution of political influence in California? What is the likelihood that the almost three-to-one disparity between population percentage and voter turnout in Latino communities will continue into the next decade? Has Latino nonelectoral civic participation increased at rates similar to increases in the likelihood of Latinos to vote? More Latinos are elected to state and local offices than ever before. How likely is it that this increased presence in state and local governments will translate into public policy that will serve the identified interests of Latino communities?

These questions have been the focus of much attention from journalists and scholars. Interestingly, both sets of analysts have reached similar conclusions regarding the electoral influence, representation, and policy benefits attained by Latinos during the period 1990–2000. Our review of major findings reveals the following:

- Latinos will continue to grow in their share of the California population.
- It is likely that this increased population growth, in combination with a sizeable increase within the next decade in the portion of the Latino population above age 18, will lead to Latinos continuing to grow as a major segment of the statewide electorate.
- Latinos are still substantially underregistered when compared to African American and non-Latino white voters.

University of California, Berkeley, 1998); and especially Harry P. Pachón, "Latino Politics in the Golden State: Ready for the 21st Century?" In *Racial and Ethnic Politics in California, Volume Two,* ed. Michael B. Preston, Bruce E. Cain, and Sandra Bass (Berkeley: Institute of Governmental Studies, University of California, Berkeley, 1998), 411–38.

[2] State of California, Department of Finance, Demographic Research Unit (www.dof.ca.gov/HTML/DEMOGRAP/Druhpar.htm, last visited 10/25/00).

[3] Hans P. Johnson, "How Many Californians? A Review of Population Projections for the State," *California Counts, Population Trends and Profiles,* vol. 1, no. 1, October (San Francisco: Public Policy Institute of California, 1999), 7–8.

[4] Cable News Network, Voter News Service, Exit Poll Data, 2000.

- Despite some contrary public comment, Latinos' propensity to register and vote as Democrats has grown since 1994.
- Of 11 statewide races for president, U.S. senator, and governor from 1990–2000, Democrats have won nine. In seven of these races (78 percent) the racial and ethnic vote was the margin of victory. In three of nine races (33 percent), the Latino vote alone was the margin of victory.
- The increased presence of Latinos from 1990 to 2000 in both houses and major parties of the state legislature has been consistent.
- Although Latinos now exercise a greater level of electoral and legislative influence than at any time in the history of the state, it is unclear whether public policies have been enacted that directly benefit Latino communities.

These findings suggest a number of strategies that should be pursued by those interested in increasing the political incorporation of Latinos in California:

- Campaigns must be conducted to encourage noncitizen Latinos to naturalize as soon as they are eligible.
- Every effort must be made to encourage Latinos over age 18 to register and vote.
- Youth between the ages of 14 and 17 are an extremely important subset of the California Latino population that should be the focus of much political socialization. By 2015, this segment of the Latino population is likely to represent the largest percentage increase in the Latino electorate ever.
- Latino legislators must continue to maximize their influence within their respective parties. Such influence may be key to developing the necessary coalition support to enact legislation favorable to Latino communities.
- The magnitude of Latino legislative influence at state levels must be used to leverage state resources to better serve local governments and to leverage collaborative relationships with major holders of private capital at both state and local levels.

To examine systematically the available literature on Latino politics in the last decade, we organize this chapter into three parts. First, we outline a multidimensional model of political incorporation that distinguishes among electoral influence, representation, and policy benefit. In this model we use the analytical dimensions of access, opportunity, and institutionalization to examine the evolution and current state of Latino political incorporation. Second, we review published research, essays presented at major academic conferences, and original data to determine the empirical evidence of the increased presence of Latinos in California politics. We are able to assess the current state of knowledge regarding Latino politics. We find some major omissions in our understanding of Latino politics in the state. Primary among them is the linkage of increased political incorporation to the enactment of public policy favorable to Latino communities. Third, we suggest areas of future research and possible strategies to further enhance the political incorporation of Latinos in the state.

Conceptualizing Political Incorporation

Before summarizing major findings and conclusions, we develop a multidimensional conceptualization of political incorporation to serve as a guide in assessing the changing nature of Latino politics in California. This conceptual framework provides a way of deepening our understanding of the progress made by Latinos over the past 10 years.

Political incorporation can be defined as the extent to which self-identified group interests are articulated, represented, and met in public policymaking.[5] Political incorporation has three *descriptive* dimensions: electoral, representational, and policy-based. The electoral dimension captures the presence and potential influence of Latinos in affecting politics through their increased proportion of the general population, of U.S. citizens, of registered voters, of voters who turn out, and of bloc voters. The representational dimension, by comparison, focuses on the presence of Latinos in elected positions in state and local governments, their presence within majority and minority legislative delegations, and their presence in positions of formal policymaking, such as Assembly speaker, committee chairs, and partisan leadership. The policy dimension refers to the extent to which Latinos receive specified benefits from public policy. Although the policy dimension can be understood largely in procedural terms, such as policies giving greater access to educational or job opportunities, we suggest that this dimension must also include indicators of material condition such as median income, poverty rates, educational levels, and homeownership rates.[6]

Analytically, it is necessary to know the precise sources of increases in electoral influence. For example, increased presence in the population can lead to increased voter registration. This direct relationship, however, very much depends upon whether the population increase is due to immigration or birth of native citizens. If it is due to immigration, the increased presence in the population will translate into increased voter registration only as mediated through the processes of naturalization. Relatedly, even if most of the population increase is due to native births, it is important to know when substantial numbers of youth are likely to be age 18 and thus eligible to register and vote.

Similar questions can be posed regarding the increased representation of Latinos in legislative arenas. Although numbers have increased dramatically, are

---

[5]This definition is based upon Rufus P. Browning, Dales Rogers Marshall, and David H. Tabb, *Protest Is Not Enough: The Struggle of Blacks and Hispanics for Equality in Urban Politics* (Berkeley: University of California Press, 1984), 25. They state, "The concept of political incorporation concerns the extent to which group interests are effectively represented in policy making."

[6]For a more extended discussion of policy responsiveness, see Luis Ricardo Fraga, "Racial and Ethnic Politics in a Multicultural Society," Charles E. Gilbert Lecture, Swarthmore College, Swarthmore, Pennsylvania, November 16, 2000.

these representatives members of the majority party in legislatures? Have these Latino elected officials been chosen from districts where Latinos comprise majorities of the population or the electorate? Are more of these public officials male or female?

Specifying increases in electoral influence and representation is, in and of itself, important. It is even more important, however, to know if such increases have translated into policy benefits for Latino communities. Has the increased presence of state legislators led to the making of public policy favorable to Latino communities at state levels? Has the increased presence of city councilmembers and members of school boards led to policy that serves the self-identified interests of Latino communities? Understanding policy benefits is an analytical task fraught with challenges. Which policy areas should be examined? How should the analyst distinguish among potential benefits in issue articulation, agenda setting, and gains in laws and ordinances that are formally enacted? How does one distinguish analytically between policy benefits in legislatures and benefits made though the statewide referendum process?

To address these and related questions we specify three distinct *analytical* dimensions of political incorporation in each of the arenas of electoral influence, representation, and policy benefit. The three analytical dimensions are access, opportunity, and institutionalization.[7] In electoral influence, access refers to the extent to which Latinos are a potential component of the electorate. This potential can be driven by population growth and by naturalization of immigrants. A low level of access would occur when the population growth of the native-born is small or declining, or when naturalization rates are low. High levels of access would be obtained through high birth rates of the native-born and high naturalization rates among immigrants. Opportunity, by contrast, is more directly related to acquisition of the franchise. High levels of opportunity to influence the electoral process occur when the percentages of Latinos eligible to register are high or when actual registration rates grow substantially. The most important indicator of high electoral opportunity exists when Latinos constitute sizeable portions of the statewide electorate. Institutionalization at the electoral level occurs when Latinos vote together as a sizeable bloc for successful candidates and positions on statewide referenda. High rates of population growth, naturalization, registration, and voting do not necessarily translate into increased elec-

---

[7]This analytical framework builds upon Hero's concept of "two-tiered pluralism." See Rodney E. Hero, *Latinos and the U.S. Political System* (Philadelphia: Temple University Press, 1992). Hero distinguishes between political gains and material gains. Our framework more precisely specifies the nature of political gains and material gains. We suggest that it is important to distinguish the precise levels of gain in each of the three descriptive dimensions of electoral, legislative, and policy influence. These three dimensions can be mutually reinforcing. They can, however, also be quite independent of one another.

toral influence if Latino voters do not vote as a sizeable bloc that is able to influence the outcome of elections at state and local levels. Among the primary determinants of the influence of the Latino vote is the extent to which other major segments, especially non-Latino whites,[8] vote as a bloc in opposition to Latino preferences. High levels of electoral institutionalization occur when Latino voters vote as a bloc, vote for winning candidates and issues, and do both with consistency over time.

Representation can also be understood in terms of the three analytical dimensions. Access occurs to the extent that there are open or competitive seats in state and local government that Latino candidates have a reasonable chance of winning. High levels of opportunity exist when Latinos win elective office in substantial percentages relative to the number of other candidates. These high levels of opportunity are especially apparent when these officials are elected from constituencies where Latinos constitute a sizeable component, if not majority, of the population and/or electorate and cast most of their votes for the victorious candidate. Legislative institutionalization occurs when Latinos constitute a sizeable portion of a legislature, when they constitute a sizeable portion of the majority party, and when they hold influential positions in the larger legislative process such as Assembly speaker, committee chairs, and party positions.

Policy benefit can also be understood in terms of access, opportunity, and institutionalization. Greater access in policy gains occurs when issues of concern to Latino communities are addressed with greater frequency and consistency in legislative arenas. This articulation of issues is most likely to come from newly elected Latino officials whose electoral constituencies include sizeable numbers of Latino voters. Policy opportunity exists to the extent that laws and ordinances are enacted that seriously consider the needs and interests of Latino communities. These laws and ordinances can deal with any of a number of issues ranging from employment to education to health care. Such legislation need not target Latinos explicitly. A broad program to increase access to health care for all uninsured Californians, for example, can especially help Latinos, who constitute a very large percentage of the uninsured in the state. Policy institutionalization occurs to the extent that Latinos experience an improvement in their material well-being as a result of enacted policies. These gains must not be temporary, and the policies that directly contribute to these gains must have a high likelihood of not being removed by subsequent legislatures.

Our model of political incorporation suggests that electoral influence, representation, and policy benefit can exist in a direct positive relationship. A gain in the first dimension can lead to gains in the other two. However, the model does not require that this be the case and is designed, in fact, to allow us to identify

---

[8]Non-Latino whites refers to voters who choose to identify themselves as non-Latino whites. Throughout the remainder of this essay, "white" will be used to refer to non-Latino whites.

various patterns of clustering among the three dimensions. Although electoral influence may be considerable, the election of public officials who are the first-choice candidates of Latino voters may not result. Gains in legislative representation, by contrast, can occur without a sizeable increase in Latino voters. This can happen, for example, as a result of changes in the boundaries of representational districts. Latino candidates might also be more competitive in open seats created by term limits. Similarly, increases in electoral influence and representation need not lead to policy benefits. Increased representation can lead to the development of diverse coalitions of popular and legislative support for a specific proposal. The key to such support, however, is likely to be the identification of mutual self-interest more than legislative influence alone. What, then, are the patterns of electoral influence, representation, and policy benefit for Latinos from 1990 to 2000?

The Growing Presence of Latinos in California Politics

The academic research devoted to the growing presence of Latinos in California politics is not extensive. In this work, emphasis is placed on systematically examining population growth, naturalization, voter registration, and turnout. Most work focuses on Latino political influence at the statewide level. Only a few studies examine their presence in local governments. No research systematically examines the influence that Latino legislators have on enacting public policy at any level.

Electoral Influence

The substantial population growth of Latinos is often noted as one of the major changes in California over the last 10 years. As Figure 11.1 demonstrates, the California Department of Finance estimates that the Latino population grew from 26 percent of the state's population in 1990 to 31.6 percent in 1999. By comparison, the Asian population grew from 9 percent to 12.2 percent over the same time period and the African-American population remained a consistent 7–7.5 percent throughout the decade. Of special note, the white population declined from 57 percent of the population in 1990 to an estimated 49.9 percent in 1999. Over the period 1990–1999, Latinos experienced the largest growth in the California population of any major racial and ethnic group.

Alvarez and Butterfield, using estimates of the State of California, Department of Finance, specify that the net increase in the Latino population from

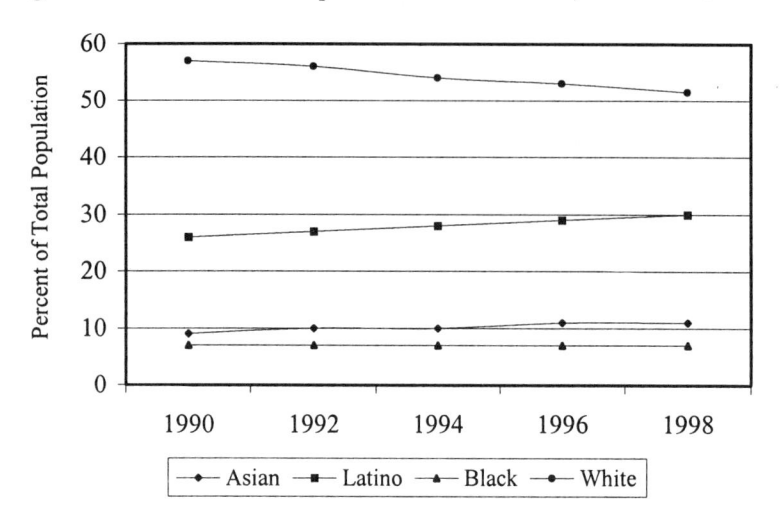

Figure 11.1. California Population Distribution, 1990–1998

Source: State of California, Department of Finance.

1990 to 1995 (i.e., natural births plus migration, minus deaths) was 1,414,112.[9] Of this number, however, 1,228,026 were from births, and only 186,086 were from migration or immigration. Alvarez and Butterfield state:

> Clearly the population of Latinos is increasing dramatically; and most of this increase can be attributed to births, not immigration. Simply, the net natural increase of Latinos is six times greater than their net migration (p. 5).

The implications for the California electorate are clear. When these younger Latino Californians reach age 18, they could represent a sizeable increase in the voting-age population. Alvarez and Butterfield suggest that a key year may be 2015, when many of these youth will reach voting age (p. 5).

Regarding voter registration and turnout, Alvarez and Butterfield use the method of generalized bounds with county-level data to estimate statewide and regional patterns for Latinos. This method, they argue, is less likely to overestimate registration and turnout as compared to postelection surveys or oversam-

---

[9]Michael Alvarez and Tara L. Butterfield, "Citizenship and Political Representation in Contemporary California," Social Science Working Paper 1041, California Institute of Technology, Pasadena, July 1998. The calculations were made from data provided in the Appendix, Table A1, State Level Population Estimates by Ethnicity (1990–1995).

pling in high-concentration areas (p. 6).[10] Figures 11.2 and 11.3 specify their statewide estimates of Latino registration and voting. Latino registration shows a variable pattern and an overall increase from 1990 to 1996 (Figure 11.2). Latino voter registration of those eligible, i.e., citizens over age 18, was 52 percent in 1990 and increased to 67 percent in 1996. Alvarez and Butterfield note that an increase in white voter registration also occurred, from 79 percent in 1990 to 86 percent in 1996. They state: "When these voter registration estimates are compared, we see that the registration rate is 18 percent higher for whites than it is for Latinos but that the increase in Latino participation is more than twice that for whites" (p. 10).

A recent study by the Field Institute estimates that as of May 2000, 16 percent of all registered voters in California were Latinos.[11] This represents an increase of about one million Latino registered voters in California since 1990. This increase accounts for just over 90 percent of all newly registered voters in the last 10 years, an astonishing figure. During the same period of time there was a net decrease in white non-Hispanic registered voters of about 100,000. In 2000 whites constituted 72 percent of the state's registered voters, down from 79 percent in 1990. The Field Institute estimates that African Americans have experienced an absolute decline of about 50,000 voters and now constitute six percent of the registered voters in the state. Asian Americans and others have grown by 300,000 voters since 1990 and they now constitute six percent, up from four percent in 1990, of the registered voters in the state.

The Field Institute study presents several additional findings regarding Latinos in California. The study estimates that in 2000 there were 6,025,641 Latino adults in California. Of these, 4,518,628 (75 percent) were citizens. Latino registered voters totaled 2,350,000 (52 percent) of all adult Latino citizens. If all Latino adult citizens registered to vote, they could constitute as much as 31 percent of all registered voters in the state. Notably, 1,084,615 Latinos, 46 percent of all Latino voters in the state, registered between 1994 and 2000. Of these more recently registered voters, 50 percent were under the age of 30, 44 percent were born outside of the United States, 42 percent resided in Los Angeles County, 38 percent had less than a high-school education, and 34 percent had incomes of less than $20,000 per year. Perhaps most significantly, 59 percent of these recently registered voters registered as Democrats, and only 18 percent registered as Republicans. This pattern is similar to that of Latinos who registered prior to 1994, of whom 61 percent are currently registered as Democrats and 24 percent as Republicans. In 2000, 60 percent of all registered Latinos are registered as

---

[10]Generalized bounds is a method that uses row marginals to estimate the values for groups in individual cells. It is a statistical method that some scholars believe provides accurate estimates when individual responses are suspect.

[11]"California's Expanding Latino Electorate," California Opinion Index, Volume 1, 2000. The calculations in this paragraph are derived from estimates in Table 1, p. 2.

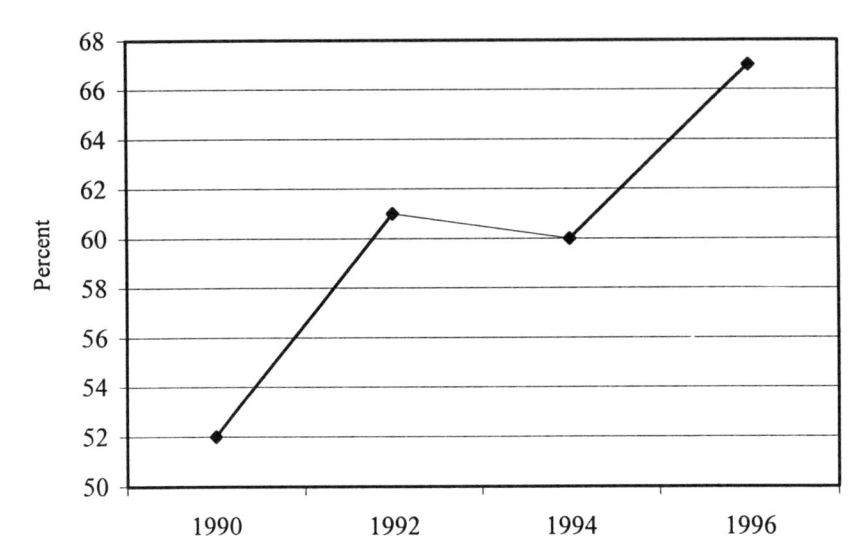

Figure 11.2. Latino Voter Registration, 1990–1996

Source: Alvarez and Butterfield, 1999.
*Latino voter registration is the number of Latinos registered to vote divided by the total number of Latinos eligible to vote.

Democrats and 22 percent as Republicans. This is in contrast to the overall California population; in 2000, 42 percent of the state's electorate was registered as Democrat and 39 percent as Republican.

Figure 11.3 provides estimates for Latino voter turnout from 1990 to 1996. Alvarez and Butterfield, in "Citizenship and Political Representation in Contemporary California," estimate that Latino turnout (as a percentage of those eligible) almost doubled from 29 percent in 1990 to 57 percent in 1992. Latino turnout was 43 percent in 1994 and 52 percent in 1996 (p. 11). Over the same time period, white voter turnout was more varied. It was 73 percent in 1990, 85 percent in 1992, 81 percent in 1994, and 76 percent in 1996. Latino voter turnout, although still 24 percent lower than white turnout, doubled between 1990 and 1996 (p. 11). Regional variations are suggestive. Alvarez and Butterfield note that the "largest increases [in voter turnout] occurred in Southern California, the Bay Area, and the Central Valley, where Latino voter turnout increased by approximately 25 percent" (p. 12). In Los Angeles County, these authors note that "the turnout rates of whites and Latinos increased between 1990 and 1996, the white turnout rate increasing 4 percent and the Latino turnout rate increasing

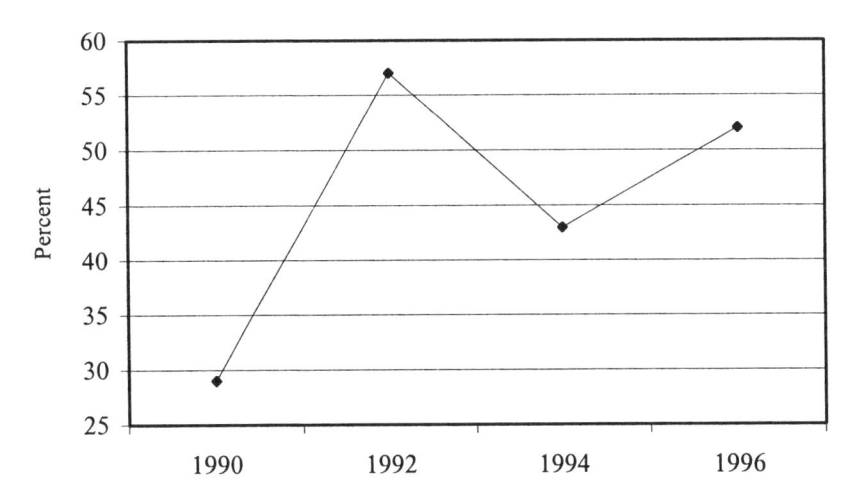

Latino Political Incorporation in California, 1990–2000 311

Figure 11.3. Latino Voter Turnout, 1990–1996*

Source: Alvarez and Butterfield, 1999
*Latino voter turnout is calculated by dividing the total number of Latinos who voted by the total number of eligible Latino citizens.

15 percent (nearly four times the rate of increase for whites)" (p. 12). There is, however, still a 25 percent higher rate of participation for whites than for Latinos.

What is the percentage of the overall electorate in California represented by Latino voters? These data are critical for understanding the types of growth for 1990–1998 that are based on a variety of exit polls, including those of the Voter Research Service, the *Los Angeles Times,* CNN, and a special poll (ANPRG) of five Assembly districts conducted for the California Secretary of State. According to Alvarez and Nagler, the Latino share of the California electorate varied from 5 percent in 1990 to 14 percent in 1998. Using the estimates based on exit polls conducted by the *Los Angeles Times* and CNN, Figure 11.4 provides estimates for 1992 to 2000. Latino voters doubled their percentage of the California electorate from 7 percent in 1992 to 14 percent in 2000. It is apparent that this trend has been gradual and consistent. The trend for African-American voters is distinct. They have remained relatively stable at 6–8 percent of the California electorate from 1992 to 2000. Asian-American voters have increased their percentage of the statewide electorate. They were 3 percent of the statewide electorate in 1992 and were estimated at 4 percent in 1994–1998, and 6 percent in 2000. These changes are mirrored by a sizeable decrease in the presence

Figure 11.4. Share of California Electorate, 1992–2000

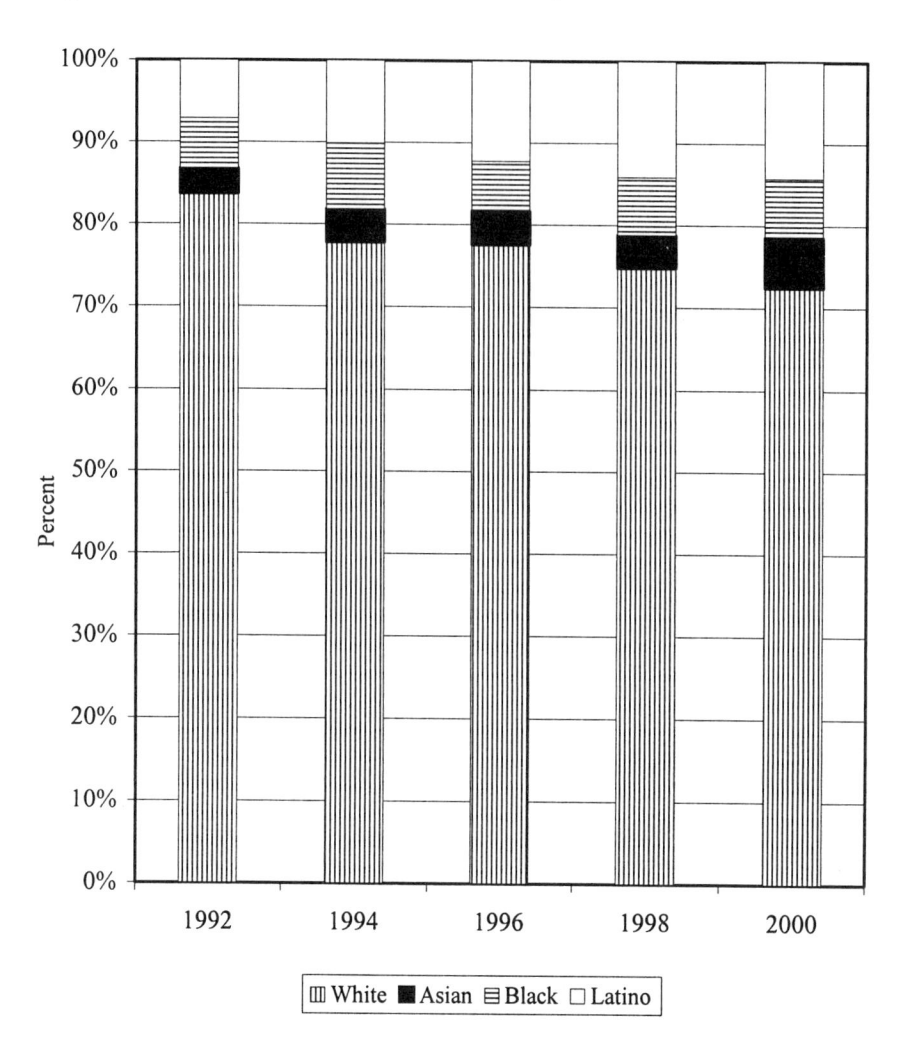

□ White ■ Asian ☰ Black □ Latino

Source: *Los Angeles Times* Exit Polls 1992 and CNN Exit Polls 1994–2000.

of the white electorate over the same period. In 1992, they constituted 82 percent of the California statewide electorate. In 2000, they represented 71 percent, a decrease of 11 percent. This decrease has been gradual and sustained.

Despite the claims made by some Latino advocates and some pundits regarding variable partisan loyalty of Latino voters, every survey conducted between 1990 and the 1998 primary has found that a clear majority of Latinos identify with the Democratic, rather than the Republican, party. In 1990, 64 percent of Latinos identified as Democratic partisans. According to Alvarez and Nagler, in 1992, 1994, 1996, and 1998, 68 percent, 66 percent, 62 percent, and 74 percent, respectively, identified as Democrats.[12]

The growth in the Latino population is significant and is likely to increase. Similarly, there is a consistent trend of Latinos registering to vote. This trend contributed to the fact that Latinos constituted a larger share of the California electorate in the last election than ever before. Does this suggest that Latinos have become an increasingly significant vote in determining the outcome of statewide elections?

In 1996, Guerra and Fraga developed a model of the "conditions for an effective statewide Latino electorate."[13] These authors argued that the influence of the Latino electorate would be enhanced to the extent that a set of contextual and strategic conditions were met. Contextual conditions referred to circumstances that were not in the direct control of Latino voters and leaders. Among these conditions were competitive elections, the minimization of backlash, opportunities to elect Latino candidates, and the presence of ballot issues of particular concern to Latino voters (pp. 132–33). Strategic conditions are much more in the control of Latino voters and their leaders. These conditions are subdivided into those that are voter-focused and those that are elite-focused. Voter-focused conditions include voting as a bloc and effective voter-mobilization strategies on election day. Elite-focused conditions include voter registration and naturalization drives, substantive advocacy for Latino interests during campaign strategy sessions, "unity and intensity of endorsement by Latino political elites, organizations, and media," and community-based "organizational development and coordination" (pp. 134–37).[14]

---

[12]The surveys in 1990–1998 were conducted by the Voter Research Service, a consortium of media groups. According to Alvarez and Nagler in "Is the Sleeping Giant Awakening? Latinos and California Politics in the 1990s," the results reported for 1998 are from exit polls conducted by the *Los Angeles Times*.

[13]Fernando Guerra and Luis Ricardo Fraga, "Theory, Reality, and Perpetual Potential: Latinos in the 1992 California Elections," in *Ethnic Ironies: Latino Politics in the 1992 Elections,* ed. Rodolfo O. de la Garza and Louis DeSipio (Boulder, Colo: Westview Press, 1996), 132.

[14]Guerra reclassifies a number of these conditions as external and internal in Fernando Guerra, "Latino Politics in California: The Necessary Conditions for Success," in

The data in Figure 11.5 show the varying role Latinos have had in affecting major elections for president, U.S. senator, and governor from 1990 to 2000. These data specify the percentage of the statewide vote represented by each racial and ethnic partisan voting block. This method combines the size of a group of voters in the statewide electorate with the extent to which that vote is cast as a bloc for each candidate. How often were Latinos an effective statewide electorate from 1990 to 2000?

Latinos were critical in determining the outcome of one senatorial election in 1992. They were not significant, however, in affecting the outcome of the presidential race, nor were they critical in the other senatorial race. Barbara Boxer, the Democratic candidate, lost the white vote to her opponent. She would not have been elected senator in 1992 if it were not for the vote provided by Latino, African-American, and Asian-American voters. In the cases of both Bill Clinton and Diane Feinstein, they each received such an overwhelming share of the white vote that the votes of communities of color was insignificant in determining the outcome of their respective elections.

This same situation appeared in the gubernatorial election in 1994. In his re-election campaign, Governor Pete Wilson received a clear majority of the statewide vote. White voters comprised the vast majority of his total support. Whites comprised nine tenths of Wilson's 53 percent statewide majority. His opponent, Kathleen Brown, received the support of only 42 percent of the statewide electorate. Voters of color, including Latinos, provided Brown with 36.1 percent of her statewide vote. The situation was very different for Senator Feinstein in her 1994 re-election campaign. As can be seen in Figure 11.5, in this race the white vote split in favor of her opponent. Voters of color represented 31.4 percent of her statewide total. This election was the first time that Latinos represented the largest segment of the minority vote received by a winning Democratic candidate. Latinos comprised 13.9 percent of Feinstein's statewide support; African Americans comprised 13.3 percent; and Asian Americans comprised 4.3 percent. Feinstein would not have won her re-election without the support of Latino voters.

This pattern of Latino voters representing the largest bloc of voters of color for successful Democratic candidates appears in the presidential election of 1996 and in both the gubernatorial and senatorial elections of 1998. Because of the split in the white vote, Clinton would not have won California in 1996 without the support of communities of color, including Latinos. Latino voters provided President Clinton with 18.7 percent of his statewide vote; African Americans provided him with 10.8 percent; and Asian Americans provided 4.4 percent. By comparison, white voters provided him with 66.2 percent of his vote. By

---

Racial and Ethnic Politics in California, Volume Two, ed. Michael B. Preston, Bruce E. Cain, and Sandra Bass, eds. (Berkeley: Institute of Governmental Studies, University of California, Berkeley, 1998), 439–52.

Figure 11.5. Electoral Influence in California Races, 1990–2000

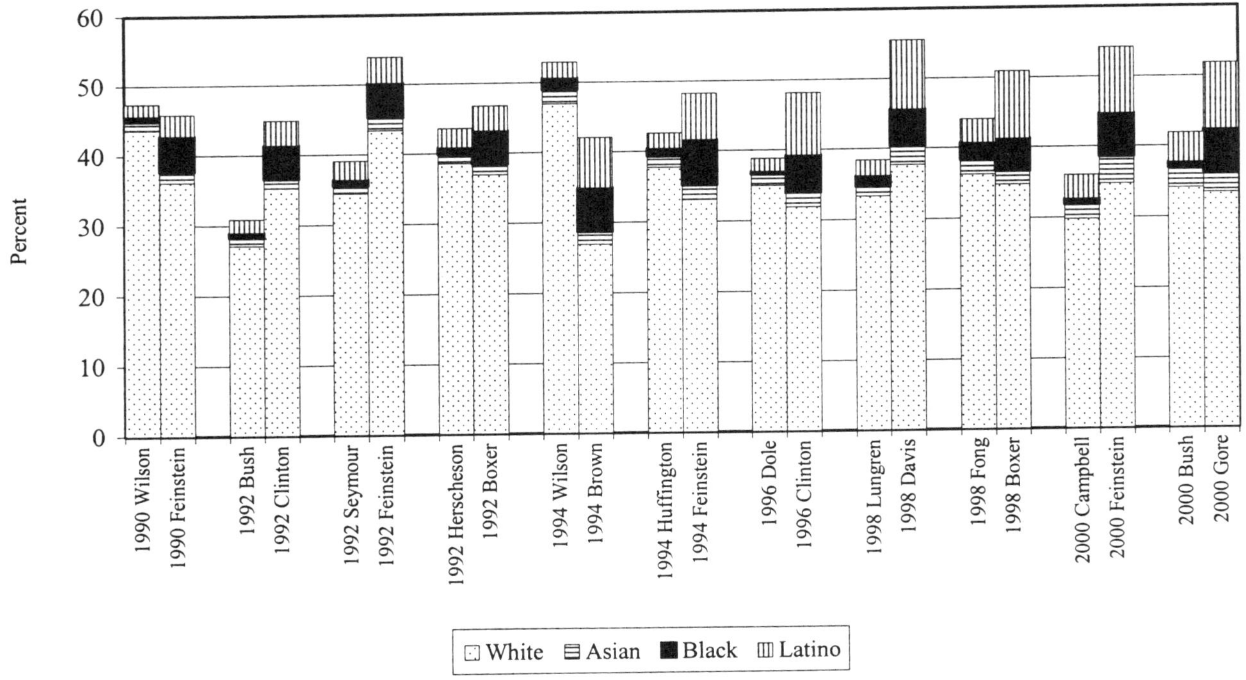

Source: *Los Angeles Times* Exit Poll 1992–1998 and CNN Exit Polls 1994–2000.

contrast, whites provided Bob Dole with 90.2 percent of his statewide vote. Similarly, in 1998, voters of color provided gubernatorial candidate Gray Davis and incumbent Senator Barbara Boxer with important components of their margins of victory. Davis won a majority of the votes of all racial and ethnic segments of the California electorate, but would have lost the election without the support from communities of color. Latinos provided him with a full 17.8 percent of his statewide vote. Senator Boxer did not receive a majority of the white vote in her election. However, she did receive 19 percent of her winning vote from Latinos, 8.8 percent from African Americans, and 3.7 percent from Asian Americans.

The pattern of Latinos comprising the largest portions of the votes from communities of color for successful Democratic candidates statewide was again evident in 2000. Senator Feinstein won re-election in 2000, and again it was the votes she received from communities of color that allowed her to defeat her Republican opponent. Latinos contributed 17.4 percent of her statewide vote; African Americans contributed 11.3 percent; Asian Americans contributed 7 percent. The votes of communities of color were even more critical to Al Gore's margin of victory in the presidential race. As stated earlier, Gore did not receive a majority of the votes cast by whites, but he did receive a majority of the votes cast by Asians, African Americans, and Latinos. Of these groups, Latinos comprised the largest percentage of the statewide total: a full 18.3 percent.

From 1990 to 2000, 11 elections were held for governor, U.S. senator, and president. Democrats have won nine of these races. In seven of these nine (78 percent) Latino voters were significant contributors to the winning Democratic candidates. Three of these nine successful Democratic candidates (i.e., one-third) would not have won without the Latino vote. Figure 11.5 demonstrates that in the 1990s Latino voters utilized their growing percentage of the California electorate to vote consistently as a majority bloc in favor of Democratic candidates. The recent report by the Field Institute confirms these findings. They estimate that the "net edge Latinos gave Democrats in overall vote" grew from +0.3 percent of the overall statewide vote in 1990 to +8.5 percent in the 1998 gubernatorial election.[15]

A summary of major research findings regarding access, opportunity, and institutionalization of electoral influence will synthesize our argument. Latinos steadily increased their electoral influence from 1990 to 2000. Population growth continued, and although immigration and migration continue to be important factors contributing to population growth, most of the increase in the Latino population between 1990 and 2000 was also due to native births. This fact bodes well for the Latino electorate. Younger Latinos, already citizens, can constitute a sizeable portion of the statewide electorate. These Latinos will not have to go through the complex processes of naturalization. Access by Latinos

---

[15]"California's Expanding Latino Electorate," Field Institute, Volume 1, 2000, p. 6.

to electoral influence has grown over this 10-year period. In a similar fashion, the number of Latinos who are eligible to vote, who register, and who vote has increased considerably. Nonetheless, only half of eligible Latino citizens are registered to vote. Although Latino eligibility, registration, and turnout rates are still below those of whites, the magnitude of the difference has decreased significantly. Opportunity to influence elections, therefore, has increased substantially. Last, the institutionalization of electoral influence, when understood as the propensity of Latino registered voters not only to turn out, but to vote as a bloc, is increasingly critical to statewide Democratic margins of victory. Despite the increasing diversity within the Latino community represented by differences in country of origin, naturalization compared to native birth, and growing numbers of Latinos becoming more educated and middle-class, Latinos still vote for major Democratic candidates in substantial numbers. For some of these candidates, Latino voters represent the largest portion of the margin of victory received from communities of color.

The growing institutionalization of Latino statewide electoral influence, however, has had its limits. A consistent white bloc vote against the preferences of overwhelming majorities of Latino voters was the primary reason that Proposition 187 was approved in 1994, as were Propositions 209 in 1996 and Proposition 227 in 1998. Each of these propositions affected Latino communities directly.[16] The data in Table 11.1 demonstrate the support ethnic and racial subgroups of the California electorate provided for these propositions. Figure 11.6 displays the way in which the combination of the size and preferences of the white vote led to the enactment of each proposition. Interestingly, the ethnic and racial vote distribution on these propositions is very similar to the distribution that gave Pete Wilson his gubernatorial re-election victory in 1994.[17] Tolbert and Hero, in "Race/Ethnicity and Direct Democracy: An Analysis of California's Illegal Immigration Initiative," point to the importance of an ethnic and racial context at the county level in understanding the magnitude of white

---

[16]Proposition 187 limited the access that undocumented workers had to public education, social services, and health care. It also imposed state penalties for the use, forging, and distribution of false residency documents. Proposition 209 severely limited the use of affirmative-action programs. It outlawed the use of race and ethnicity in admissions to state colleges and universities, as well as in the awarding of contracts by state agencies and substate governments. Proposition 227 effectively eliminated the use of bilingual instruction in California public schools. Under this law, bilingual instruction was limited to one year for all students, regardless of language ability. Parents could petition for exceptions.

[17]Tolbert and Hero report that the correlation between county-level support for Proposition 187 and vote for Governor Pete Wilson was .85 (Caroline J. Tolbert and Rodney E. Hero, "Race/Ethnicity and Direct Democracy: An Analysis of California's Illegal Immigration Initiative," *The Journal of Politics*, vol. 58, no. 3 (August 1996): 806–18.

Table 11.1. Support for Statewide Propositions, 1992–98

	Proposition 187 Yes	Proposition 187 No	Proposition 209 Yes	Proposition 209 No	Proposition 227 Yes	Proposition 227 No
Latinos	23	77	24	76	37	63
Black	47	53	26	74	48	52
Asian	47	53	39	61	57	43
White	63	37	63	37	67	33
All	57	43	54	44	61	39

Source: *Los Angeles Times* poll 1994–98.

support for Proposition 187. Ramírez improves upon this contextual analysis by focusing at the level of Assembly districts in his examination of voting on Proposition 209.[18] These contextual factors enrich our understanding of how a consistent white bloc vote limited the statewide electoral influence of Latinos.

Unfortunately, research examining the electoral influence of Latinos in local elections is scant. Although it is well-known that more Latinos serve in city councils, county boards of supervisors, and schools boards than ever before,[19] no one study has examined systematically the longitudinal patterns of voting, and resulting legislative representation, in substate levels of government. This is a glaring omission in the scholarly and other analytical literature.

Representation

The legislative reapportionment and related redistricting that followed the 1990 U.S. Census provided new opportunities for Latinos to elect representatives to Congress, the state Senate, and the state Assembly. Guerra and Fraga in "Theory, Reality, and Perpetual Potential: Latinos in the 1992 California Elections," note that throughout the 1980s, Latinos were able to elect three members

---

[18] Ricardo Ramírez, "Race, Social Context, and Referendum Voting," prepared for delivery at the annual meeting of the American Political Science Association, Washington, D.C., August 31–September 3, 2000.

[19] Fernando Guerra, "Latino Politics in California: The Necessary Conditions for Success," in *Racial and Ethnic Politics in California, Volume Two* (Berkeley: Institute of Governmental Studies, University of California, Berkeley, 1998), 442–43.

Figure 11.6. Latino Electoral Influence in Statewide Ballot Propositions, 1992–1998

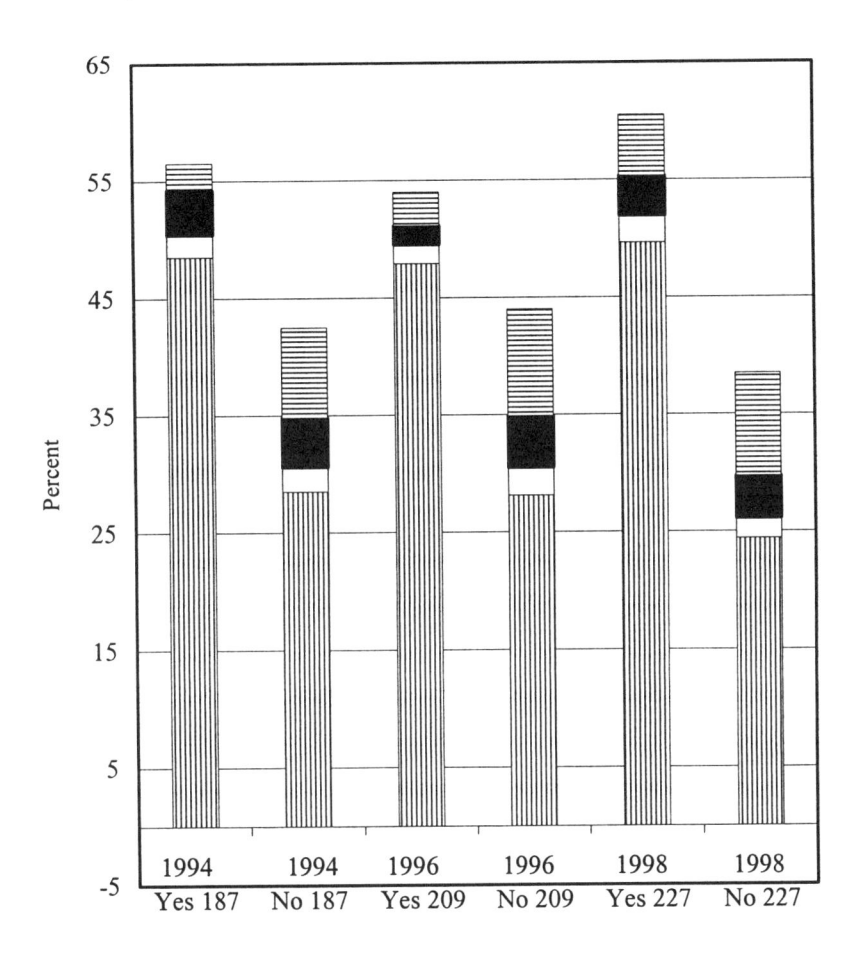

☐ White ☐ Asian ■ Black ☰ Latino

Source: *Los Angeles Times* exit polls 1992 and CNN exit polls 1994–1998.

of the U.S. Congress, three state senators, and four members of the state Assembly (p. 139). In 1992, however, one additional majority Latino population congressional district was drawn. Although Latinos constituted 61 percent of the population in the district, it was estimated that they constituted only 34 percent of the registered voters (p. 140). This was similar to the three previous districts that were majority Latino, where estimated Latino voter registration ranged from 42 percent to 48 percent (p. 140). Since 1991, four Latinos have been elected to the U.S. House of Representatives.

Guerra and Fraga indicate that the reapportionment of the state legislature in 1992 left three majority Latino population seats in the state Senate. However, three new majority Latino population districts were created in the state Assembly. Because two of the three successful congressional candidates had been members of the state Assembly, there were now five open majority Latino state Assembly seats. Not surprisingly, these five seats proved to be hotly contested between two major factions within the Latino political elite, especially in Los Angeles County. In each of these five seats, Latinos represented from 35 percent to 55 percent of the registered voters (pp. 141–43).

Examination of Figure 11.7 reveals that the number of Latinos in the state Senate increased to four in 1996, and seven in 2000. At present, Latinos comprise 18 percent of the state Senate, with the largest percentage increase occurring between 1996 and 1998.

The increases in the number of Latino representatives in the state Assembly have been even greater throughout the 1990s. As indicated in Figure 11.7, four Latinos were elected to the state Assembly in 1990, seven in 1992, 10 in 1994, 14 in 1996, 17 in 1998, and 20 in 2000.[20] Latinos now comprise 25 percent of the members of the state Assembly. This represents a five-fold increase in the presence of Latinos in the state Assembly. How likely is it that this level of Latino representation in the Assembly will be maintained?

This question is partly answered by examining levels of Latino voter registration in all 80 Assembly districts in 1992, 1994, 1996, and 1998. Figure 11.8 displays the number of districts with percentages of Latino voter registration at 40 percent and above of all registered voters in the district, between 20–39 percent, and those districts with less than 19 percent Latino registered voters. The vast majority of Assembly districts have fewer than 19 percent Latino registered voters. Not surprisingly, a Latino member of the assembly was elected from all four districts in 1992 and 1994 that had 40 percent and above Latino regi-

---

[20]In a special election held March 6, 2001, Assemblywoman Gloria Romero was elected to the state Senate seat formerly held by Hilda Solis, who won election to the U.S. Congress in 2000. It is likely that a Latino will be elected from Romero's former Assembly district. This would maintain the number of Latinos in the Assembly at 20 or 25 percent.

Figure 11.7 Latinos in the State Legislature, 1990–1998

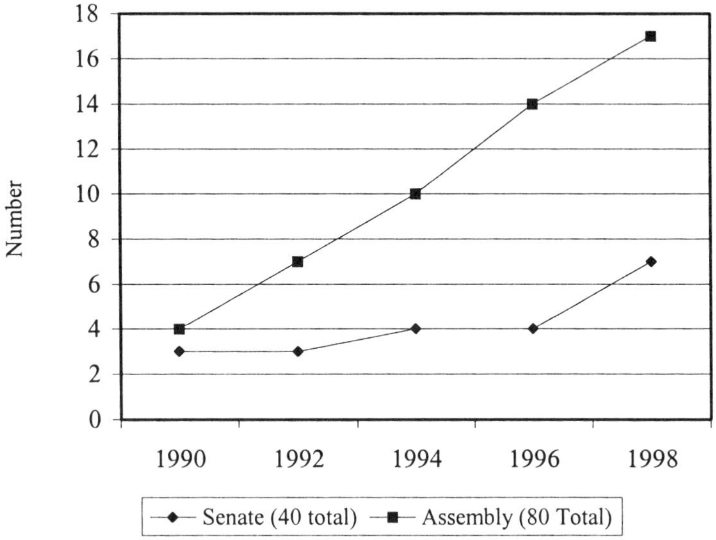

Source: California Secretary of State, Elections Division.

stration. A similar pattern appears in 1996 where all eight 40 percent and above districts elected a Latino, as did all nine such districts in 1998. All of these members of the Assembly have been Democrats. Attaining overall Latino registration percentages at 40 percent and above has led to the institutionalization of Latino representation.

In the 13 Assembly districts with 20–39 percent Latino voter registration from 1992 to 1994 and the 12 such districts in 1996–1998, a number of Latinos have been elected. The number elected from such districts, however, has varied. Three Latinos were elected from these districts in 1992. Although five Latinos were elected from such districts in 1994, the number of Latino representatives from such districts dropped to two in 1996, and increased again to five in 1998. One of the four in 1998 was a Republican; all the others were Democrats. The pattern in Assembly districts with under 19 percent Latino registration is distinct. No Latinos were elected from such districts in 1992, and only one was elected in 1994. However, four were elected from such districts in 1996; of these three were Democrats and one was a Republican. In 1998, only three Latinos were elected from such districts and all of them were Republicans.

Figure 11.8. Latino Registration and Representation in Assembly Districts, 1992–1998

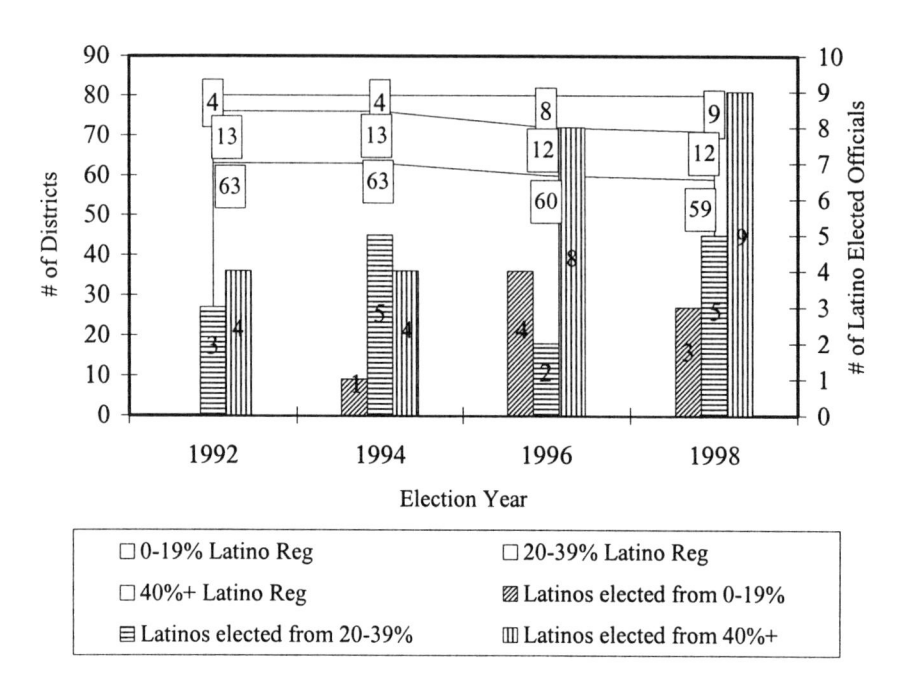

[Chart showing # of Districts and # of Latino Elected Officials by Election Year 1992, 1994, 1996, 1998.

Values shown on chart:
- 1992: 63, 13, 4; elected 3, 4
- 1994: 63, 13, 4; elected 1, 5, 4
- 1996: 60, 12, 8; elected 2, 4, 8
- 1998: 59, 12, 9; elected 3, 5, 9

Legend:
☐ 0-19% Latino Reg   ☐ 20-39% Latino Reg
☐ 40%+ Latino Reg   ▨ Latinos elected from 0-19%
☰ Latinos elected from 20-39%   ▥ Latinos elected from 40%+]

The patterns of registration and representation displayed in Figure 11.8 suggest that 40 percent and above Latino registration in an Assembly district guarantees the election of a Latino to office; institutionalization of Latino representation follows. Latinos can get elected from districts with noticeably lower rates of Latino registration, but it is unclear if such districts will continue to elect Latinos to the Assembly. Districts with Latino registration rates between 20–39 percent do seem fertile for the election of Latinos. Only time will allow us to determine if these representational gains can be maintained once incumbents are required to leave office due to term limits.

These above described patterns reveal that Latinas have been elected in increasing numbers as well. In 1992, of all seven Latinos in the Assembly, four were Latinas. Five of 10, seven of 14, and six of 17 were Latinas in 1994, 1996, and 1998 respectively. In 2000, although only six of 20 Latinos in the Assembly were women, four of seven Senate members were Latinas. Stated differently, in 2000, 30 percent of all Latinos in the Assembly and 57 percent of all Latinos in the Senate were women. By comparison, 30 percent of all members of the Assembly were women in 2000; the percentage of women in the Senate was 23 percent. The increased presence of Latinas within the state legislative delegation may suggest that issues of special significance to Latino youth, increases in the feminization of poverty, and concerns regarding spousal abuse, especially as it relates to immigrant women, may have a greater voice in the legislature than ever before. Unfortunately, there is no systematic study of the role of Latinas in the legislature. A careful examination of the career paths, policy agendas, committee assignments, and participation within the Latino Caucus of the state legislature would be most revealing.

As stated previously, most Latinos elected to the Assembly and the Senate have been Democrats. This has provided them the opportunity to exercise considerable influence in the selection of party leaders. For example, the 13 Latino Democrat members of the Assembly in 1996 comprised 60 percent of the 22 votes then needed to select party leaders. Democrats held 43 of the 80 seats in the Assembly. This helped Latinos be elected to the positions of Speaker of the Assembly, Majority Leader of the Assembly, and numerous committee chairs (Guerra, 1998, pp. 446–47). The pattern of Latino representational institutionalization was again apparent in 1998. Latino Democrats constituted 54 percent (13 of 24)[21] of the majority necessary to select party leaders in the Assembly and 54 percent (7 of 13)[22] of the majority necessary to select party leaders in the Senate. This undoubtedly helped elect Rep. Antonio Villaraigosa as the second Latino Speaker of the Assembly. In 2000, Latinos comprised 64 percent (16 of 25) of the majority needed to elect party leaders, and 54 percent (7 of 13) of the majority necessary in the Senate.[23]

Our findings with regard to representation demonstrate that considerable gains in access, opportunity, and institutionalization have been made in the 1990s. Access was enhanced through the drawing of majority Latino population districts at congressional and state Assembly levels as a result of the 1990 census. Majority-minority population districts have directly helped expand the number of Latino representatives. Due to the increased registration and turnout rates among Latinos, the number of Latino representatives from nonmajority Latino districts has increased as well. Opportunity for enhancing legislative influence has similarly increased with the election of increasing numbers of Latinos to these seats. This has occurred despite most of these districts not having a majority of registered voters who are Latino. In many state Assembly districts, however, Latinos are the plurality of registered voters. It is in the area of institu-

---

[21] There was a total of 47 Democrats in the House in 1998.

[22] There was a total of 25 Democrats in the Senate in 1998.

[23] In 2000, there were 49 Democrats in the Assembly and 25 Democrats in the Senate. Additionally, it will not be surprising if Latino Republicans are also provided opportunities to hold important positions should the Assembly have Republicans as the majority party in the future. This, of course, depends upon Latino Republicans continuing to get elected to these offices. No Latino Republicans have ever been elected to the Senate.

tionalization of legislative influence where, somewhat counter-intuitively, Latinos have made the greatest gains. They represent sizeable portions of the majority party in both the state Senate and the state Assembly. They have gained the powerful position of Speaker of the Assembly for two successive terms. A Latino currently serves as lieutenant governor. Much less is known about the patterns of access, opportunity, and institutionalization of Latino representation in cities, counties, and other substate levels of government. Guerra estimates that as of 1997 there were 300 Latino city councilmembers in the state (p. 442) with over 100 in the 88 incorporated municipalities in Los Angeles County. In 17 of these, Latinos are in the majority (p. 442). There is much less representation at the county level, and "there [was] not a single Latino elected district attorney or sheriff in the 58 counties of California [in 1997]" (p. 443). There is no systematic study of Latino representation on school boards. Although more Latino representatives are serving in substate levels than ever before, no data exist on the patterns of representation over time. It is, therefore, difficult to assess whether representation at the substate level can be characterized as attaining access, opportunity, or institutionalization.

Policy Benefit

It seems reasonable to expect that the purpose of increasing electoral influence and representation is to serve Latino communities better through the enactment of public policies that serve their interests. Unfortunately, we found no existing study of policy accomplishments by Latino legislators, whether in terms of interest articulation, agenda setting, or legislative enactment. The scholarly community has not enhanced our understanding of whether increases in access, opportunity, and institutionalization in electoral influence and representation have led to any policy benefit for Latino communities.[24]

Although it may be unwise for scholars and other analysts to stray into the world of policy influence, the absence of such research should not inhibit them from pushing their research to directly inform policy proposals. It will be unfortunate if scholars and analysts of Latino politics criticize public officials for not serving more successfully the constituents who helped put many of them in office. Although such critiques can be useful, it is important that these scholars and analysts hold their own scholarship to the same standards, relative to en-

---

[24] The only study of Latino state legislative influence we found was an analysis of Chicano legislators in Texas during the 67th session (1981) of the legislature. This excellent study deserves updating and replication across a number of states. See Tatcho Mindiola, Jr., and Armando Gutiérrez, "Chicanos and the Legislative Process: Reality and Illusion in the Politics of Change," in *Latinos and the Political System,* ed. F. Chris Garcia (Notre Dame, Ind.: University of Notre Dame Press, 1988), 349–62.

hancing policy gain, to which they hold public officials.[25] In this area of Latino politics, opportunities for information sharing should be maximized. Such sharing could increase the range of strategies to increase the policy benefits received by Latinos in the state.

Fraga suggests that the future attainment of policy gains by Latino communities could rest upon the capacity of Latino elected officials to link the interests of Latino communities to the broader public interest.[26] He terms the strategy to attain such linkages as the need for Latino public officials and their supporters to attain an *informed public interest*. Among the dimensions of this informed public interest are contingent color consciousness, opportunity and resource enhancement, self-determination, consensus building through the identification of mutual self-interest across diverse sets of legislative and popular stakeholders, and the acknowledgement of strategic roles.[27] Fraga's theory could be applied within the context of Latino policy benefit in California.

Interestingly, several journalists have noted that a number of Latino legislators in California prefer to limit the extent to which they are known primarily as advocates for Latino interests. They see themselves as not just Latino politicians. In "Did 1992 Herald the Dawn of Latino Political Power," Maharidge states, "They [several newly elected Latino legislators] are a diverse group, but among those interviewed, one commonality emerged: All strove to distance themselves from being seen strictly as Latino politicians" (p. 17). Maharidge quotes newly elected State Assemblyman Louis Caldera as saying, "'I do not see myself as a Latino politician in that this is the only community I represent. You're only going to be relevant if you address issues of all Californians, not just one community'" (p. 17). State Assemblywoman Martha Escutia stated:

> I came from a very conservative family. My family always told me, "You're not Chicana, you're not Mexican American. If you have to identify yourself as something, don't hyphenate yourself: You're either American or you're Mexican but you can't be both." So I never related to the so-called Chicano move-

---

[25] See for example: David Hayes-Bautista and Gregory Rodríguez, "Winning More Political Offices But Still No Agenda" (www.med.ucla.edu/cesla/oped/2-11-96.htm, last visited 5/24/00), 1996; and Dion Nissenbaum, "Assembly Speakers Set State for Power," *San Jose Mercury News*, April 10, 2000, A1.

[26] Luis Ricardo Fraga, "Self-Determination, Cultural Pluralism, and Politics," *The National Political Science Review*, vol. 3: (1992a): 132–36; Luis Ricardo Fraga, "Latino Political Incorporation and the Voting Rights Act," in *Controversies in Minority Voting: The Voting Rights Act in Perspective*, ed. Bernard Grofman and Chandler Davidson (Washington, D.C.: The Brookings Institution, 1992b), 278–82.

[27] Fraga's "Racial and Ethnic Politics in a Multicultural Society" and Luis Ricardo Fraga and Jorge Ruiz-de-Velasco, "Civil Rights in a Multicultural Society," in *Legacies of the 1964 Civil Rights Act*, ed. Bernard Grofman (Charlottesville: University Press of Virginia, 2000), 190–209.

ment, the *Movimiento*. When I was in college I was frankly too busy trying to do well academically and hold down 45 hours worth of jobs. I just had a different agenda. The agenda was I had to build the foundation in order to be successful, and after that I could become an activist (p. 18).

In April 2000, Assembly Speaker Villaraigosa resigned his position in order to run for mayor of Los Angeles. In reflecting upon the transfer of legislative power to incoming Speaker Bob Hertzberg, both Villaraigosa and Lieutenant Governor Bustamante commented on their strategy of integrating Latino interests with those of the entire state. Nissenbaum, in "Assembly Speakers Set State for Power," quotes Villaraigosa, "I think that the strength of my leadership is I've transcended the issue of race and ethnicity. It doesn't mean I don't fight—of course I fight for those [Latino] issues. But there are very few that are uniquely ethnic."

Nissenbaum also quotes a similar statement from Bustamante:

I'm an advocate on behalf of the Latino community. But for us to be leaders of an entire category, or of an entire state, or of an entire region, you have to be a leader of all people, not just a few.

As an example of the recent pursuit of legislation that served many Latinos in California, but was not presented as a "Latino" program, some point to the "Healthy Families Initiative" that provided access to health care for many of California's poorest children. Nissenbaum quotes Villaraigosa:

I knew going in that 50 percent of the 7 million uninsured were Latinos. But I would have been the author of Healthy Families if all 7 million had been white. It is one example where public policy was for everyone, but it particularly impacted Latinos.

Villaraigosa pursued a similar approach in supporting more minority outreach programs at the University of California after the passage of Proposition 209. According to Nissenbaum in "Assembly Speakers Set State for Power," he also pushed for a portion of a recently enacted $2 billion parks bond to be targeted for building playgrounds in poorer urban areas.

Areas of Future Research

There are several additional areas of future research where scholars and other analysts can contribute to a more comprehensive understanding of the current state of political incorporation of Latinos in California politics. One that should be explored is nonelectoral organizational participation, which has often been an area where communities of color have gained initial training and experience that can later be transferred to electoral politics. It is apparent that an increasing number of Latino community-based organizations have developed in several urban centers. Among the most prominent are those designed to serve the needs of immigrants, especially regarding the protection of their legal rights. Another is the activities of a variety of labor unions to better organize Latino citizen and immigrant workers. How successful are these organizations in serving Latino communities? Are there major differences in their membership and leadership across distinct Latino subgroups? What types of relationships do such organizations have to Latino elected officials? Do these organizations exercise any explicit influence in electoral politics?

A second area in need of research is bureaucratic representation. As we stated previously, Latinos have made great inroads in increasing their numbers in the state legislature and in a number of local governments. Has this increase led to the appointment, especially at more senior levels, of an increased number of Latinos in administrative positions? It is well known in the social sciences that those responsible for implementing public policy are often the most critical actors in determining the street-level consequences of legislative goals. It is also the case that they often outlive the terms of office of elected officials. This can be the case especially in California, where legislative term limits are prevalent.

A third area that needs further study is the selection of two successive Latinos to serve as Speaker of the California State Assembly and the election of Cruz Bustamante as lieutenant governor. The former was a major accomplishment, given that the speakership is one of the most powerful positions in the state legislative process. Despite the symbolic significance of the selection of Bustamante as the first Latino Assembly speaker in 1996, there is no scholarly examination of his attainment of this position or of his accomplishments in office. The selection of Antonio Villaraigosa as the second Latino Assembly Speaker has also not been studied by scholars. In 1998, Bustamante was the first Latino candidate to win statewide office. What was the process whereby he became the strongest Democratic candidate for this position? How distinctive was his vote distribution as compared to other successful statewide candidates? Answers to these questions would contribute greatly to our understanding of the likelihood that these accomplishments can be replicated in the future.

Latino Political Incorporation beyond 2000

We began this chapter by developing a model of political incorporation. Three distinct dimensions of political incorporation were specified: electoral influence, representation, and policy benefit. We can now return to the model to assess how much progress Latinos have made from 1990 to 2000. Figure 11.9 diagrams the evolution of this progress.

Our review suggests that the only substantial gains made by Latinos from 1990 to 1994 occurred in representation. Although gradual increases in naturalization, registration, and voting appeared, they were not substantial. The reelection of Pete Wilson as governor and the passage of Proposition 187 clearly signaled how much progress Latinos still had to make in exercising electoral influence. They were, however, a critical component of the winning coalition that put Diane Feinstein back in the U.S. Senate. By 1994, Latinos were winning seats in both the state Assembly and the state Senate with regularity. These representatives now had new opportunities to advocate on behalf of their constituents.

In 1996, substantial gains occurred in both electoral influence and representation. Latino registration went up considerably in that year, and as a result Latinos represented 12 percent of the statewide electorate. Latinos, in combination with African Americans, were critical components of the winning coalition that gave California's 54 electoral votes to President Bill Clinton. In 1996, Latinos maintained their considerable presence in the state Senate and increased their representation in the Assembly. After the 1996 the Assembly chose its first Latino speaker and elected Latinos to other influential positions in the majority Democratic legislature.

In 1998, Latinos built upon the gains described above. Registration and, especially, turnout rates increased, and Latinos continued to vote overwhelmingly Democratic. They were important components of the winning coalition of Governor Gray Davis and were critical players in the electoral majority that returned Barbara Boxer to the U.S. Senate. Cruz Bustamante was elected lieutenant governor, he is the first Latino elected to statewide office in well over 100 years. Positions in the state legislature were further maintained and institutionalized. As a result of this election there were now more Latinos in the state Assembly and Senate than ever before. They were influential components of the Democratic majority in both chambers. Four Latino Republicans were also now in the state Assembly. As Figure 11.9 demonstrates, these gains in electoral influence and representation grew even further in the 2000 election. Latino voters were the largest bloc of ethnic voters who guaranteed that Al Gore would receive California's 54 electoral votes.

Despite these gains, however, it is still the case that only 52 percent of otherwise qualified Latino adult citizens in California are registered to vote. Targeted naturalization and voter-registration campaigns are still necessary. Other efforts to increase registration should be considered as well. It is likely, for example, that same-day registration would increase the number of Latinos registered to vote. Including instructions in civic participation, and especially the responsibilities of citizenship, as part of the standard curriculum of adult-education classes, might socialize Latinos further in the importance of participating in politics. Such instruction could be included more explicitly in history and government classes for youth in high school as well. Because a higher per-

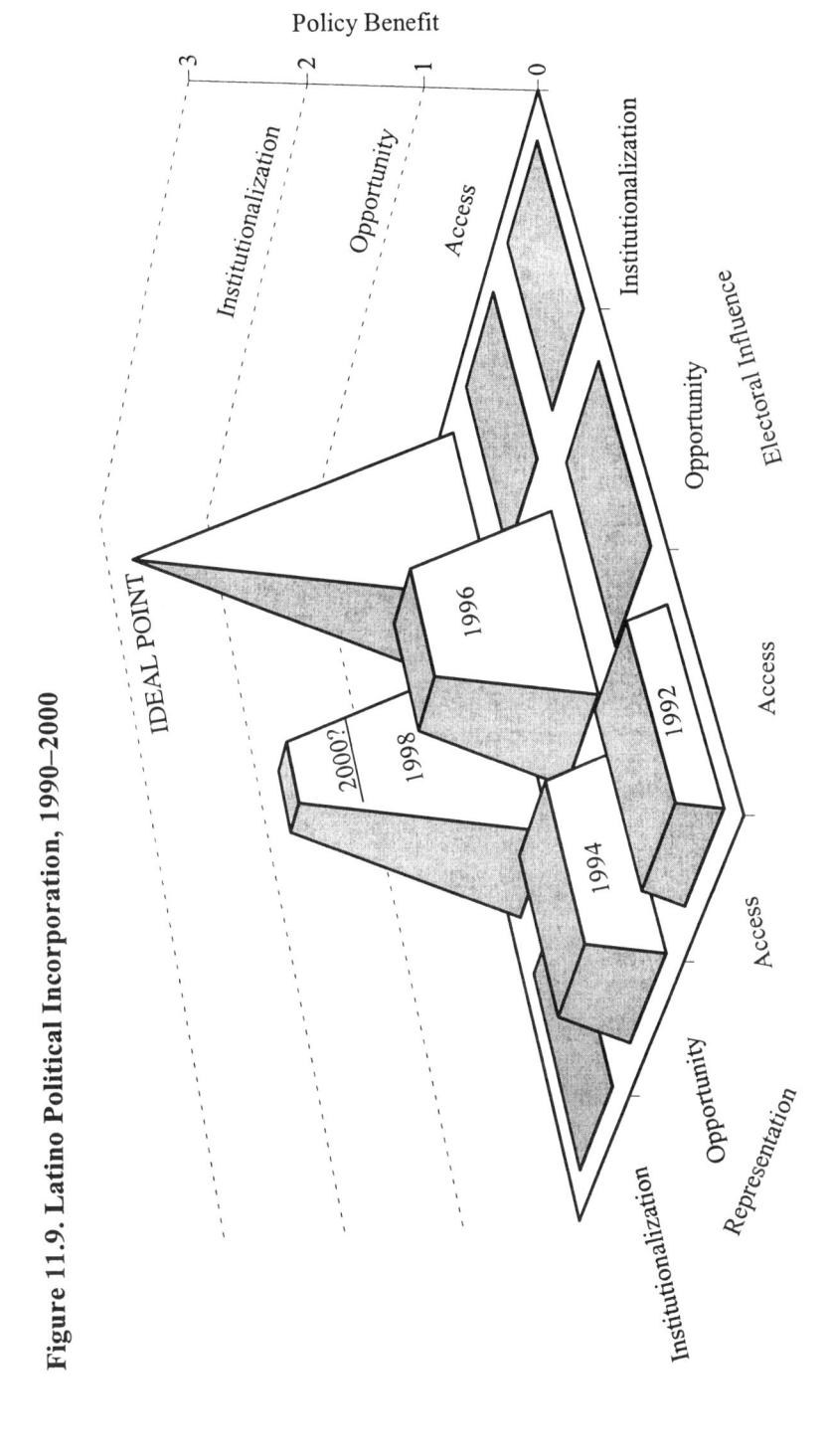

Figure 11.9. Latino Political Incorporation, 1990–2000

centage of Latinos are under the age of 18 compared to other subgroups, these youth could constitute a sizeable component of the future Latino electorate. Latino electoral influence could increase if noncitizens were allowed to vote in certain local elections. Although this has been limited to school-board elections, one can imagine the growth in Latino electoral influence that would occur if permanent residents were allowed to vote for some local officials. This would be the case especially in major urban areas where noncitizen, permanent residents are concentrated. Aspects of Los Angeles politics could be very different if noncitizens were allowed to vote in local elections, for example.

The key to Latinos continuing to exercise considerable influence in statewide elections rests upon both a sizeable turnout and consistent bloc voting. Latinos demonstrated their capacity to do this in 1996, 1998, and 2000. It is important to recognize, however, that this propensity of Latinos to support Democratic candidates can have costs. A consistent and predictable Latino bloc vote can be taken for granted by the Democratic Party. However, to the extent that Latinos split their votes between Democrats and Republicans, the likelihood of their influencing the outcome of an election decreases. This conundrum in which Latino voters find themselves rests, of course, upon the recent pattern of whites splitting their votes evenly between Democratic and Republican candidates. Whites still represent at least 74 percent of the voters on election day. An overwhelming white vote for a candidate, as occurred in the 1994 gubernatorial election of Pete Wilson, can still overshadow any competing Latino vote. This suggests that any efforts to rally Latino voters cannot come at the expense of alienating a sizeable segment of the white electorate.

In 1992, Bruce Cain noted this vulnerability of Latinos to a white bloc vote in statewide referenda.[28] In assessing the ways in which the Voting Rights Act allowed for the assessment of majoritarian electoral institutions to make sure that they treated ethnic and racial voters equally, he noted that "this effort may be undercut by the majoritarian techniques of new populism" (p. 275). He was referring specifically to the possibility that the referendum process in California could be used as a way to limit the increased success Latinos and other ethnic groups might have in electing their first-choice candidates to public office as a result of the effective enforcement of the Voting Rights Act. The votes on Propositions 187, 209, and 227 reflected this vulnerability of Latinos to a white bloc vote very clearly.

Increasing the representation of Latinos can occur along two dimensions. One, the reapportionment that will occur as a result of the 2000 census, will largely determine both the incumbency advantages for current Latino elected

---

[28] Bruce E. Cain, "Voting Rights and Democratic Theory: Toward a Color-Blind Society?" in *Controversies in Minority Voting: The Voting Rights Act in Perspective*, ed. Bernard Grofman and Chandler Davidson (Washington, D.C.: The Brookings Institution, 1992), 261–77.

officials and the likelihood that more Latinos will get elected to Congress, the state legislature, and local governments from districts where Latinos represent a sizeable segment of respective constituencies. A Democratic governor, Assembly, and Senate Democratic majorities should serve Latino interests well. If more Latino Democrats are elected to the state legislature as a result of reapportionment, the influence of Latinos within the Democratic Party should be substantial. Reapportionment enhances access and opportunity for Latinos in a variety of legislative arenas. Institutionalization should continue to occur to the extent that greater inroads are made to positions of party leadership.

Recent changes in the Supreme Court's view of the role that race and ethnicity should play in reapportionment and redistricting could prove challenging to Latino interests. In *Shaw v. Reno* (1993) the Court severely questioned the constitutionality of using race to draw district boundaries designed to increase the representation of minority interests. In subsequent decisions the Court also outlawed the use of race when it could be identified as the "predominant factor" in drawing districts. These rulings could limit the capacity of Latinos to receive a substantial increase in the number of majority or plurality (influence) districts. It is likely that litigation will resolve these issues in the future. It certainly behooves Latinos to pursue a variety of both legal and political strategies to maximize their interests in reapportionment, and thus increase the institutionalization of Latino representation. Among ideas to consider in developing such strategies are: (1) demonstrating that current Latino officials who represent majority or plurality Latino districts do not represent only Latino concerns, (2) using criteria other than race or ethnicity, such as sociodemographic criteria like education and income, to draw district boundaries, and (3) minimizing the extent to which Latino interests are seen as competitive to the interests of African Americans and Asians.

As Figure 11.9 demonstrates, the least progress has been made in approaching the ideal point to which Latino political incorporation should strive—the receipt of policy benefit. The current practice of a number of Latino elected officials to present themselves as representatives of both Latino interests and, at the same time, the larger public interest of the state, may be most critical to benefit being attained. Even though Latinos may become the majority population in the state within the next 20 years, it is very unlikely that they will possess the quantities of private investment capital that many business firms, and whites, generally enjoy. Coalition-building across diverse interests may be the key to future Latino policy benefits.

Let us assume that Latinos become the largest segment of the California population and electorate. Let us also assume that they hold a majority of seats in both the Assembly and the state Senate. Let us further assume that there is a Latino governor and a Latino Assembly speaker. Last, let us assume that these public officials have as one of their concerns the enhancement of policy benefits, such as greater educational attainment and material well being, for their

Latino constituents. Despite the apparent institutionalization of electoral influence and representation, the attainment of policy benefit over the long term will very much depend upon the successful negotiation of the mutual self-interest of Latinos with that of holders of major private capital. Economic growth and the resulting benefits of an expanded tax base rest squarely upon the propensity of holders of private capital to invest in California. Institutionalizing policy benefit for Latinos may rest, in large part, on the effectiveness of Latino elected officials in using public authority to serve a variety of the interests that comprise California.

The primary task of governance is the development of policy consensus, across a variety of issue areas, that can be maintained over the long term. That task is the same whether Latinos or others hold the reins of public power. With full political incorporation comes a great deal of responsibility to those who put one in office, and to building a larger informed public interest. This 10-year review of Latinos as voters, elected representatives, and policy decision makers suggests that they will continue to have the chance to undertake this most important task in California's future.

References

Alvarez, Michael, and Tara L. Butterfield. 1998. "Citizenship and Political Representation in Contemporary California." Social Science Working Paper 1041. California Institute of Technology, Pasadena, Calif., July.

Alvarez, Michael, and Jonathan Nagler. 1999. "Is the Sleeping Giant Awakening? Latinos and California Politics in the 1990s." Paper presented at the annual meeting of the Midwest Political Science Association, Chicago, Ill., April.

Berg, Larry. 1995. "California, Progress or. . . ." *California Journal*. vol. 26, no. 1 (January): 51–52.

Browning, Rufus P., Dales Rogers Marshall, and David H. Tabb. 1984. *Protest is Not Enough: The Struggle of Blacks and Hispanics for Equality in Urban Politics*. Berkeley: University of California Press.

Cain, Bruce E. 1992. "Voting Rights and Democratic Theory: Toward a Color-Blind Society?" In *Controversies in Minority Voting: The Voting Rights Act in Perspective,* ed. Bernard Grofman and Chandler Davidson. Washington, D.C.: The Brookings Institution, 261–77.

California Department of Finance, Demographic Research Unit. http://www.dof.ca.gov/HTML/DEMOGRAP/Druhpar.htm), last visited 10/25/00.

California Public Sector, 1991–1995 Directories. California Public Sector Publications, Sacramento California.

California Secretary of State, Elections Division Homepage, (http://www.ss.ca.gov/elections/elections.htm), last visited 10/25/00.

Carroll, James. 1992. "Courting California: Both Parties Lust After Those Golden Electoral Votes." *California Journal,* vol. 23, no. 9 (September): 433–36.

Fraga, Luis Ricardo. 1992a. "Self-Determination, Cultural Pluralism, and Politics." *The National Political Science Review*. vol. 3: 132–36.

———. 1992b. "Latino Political Incorporation and the Voting Rights Act." In *Controversies in Minority Voting: The Voting Rights Act in Perspective,* ed. Bernard Grofman and Chandler Davidson. Washington, D.C.: The Brookings Institution, 278–82.

———. 2000. "Racial and Ethnic Politics in a Multicultural Society." Charles E. Gilbert Lecture, Swarthmore College, Swarthmore, Pennsylvania. November 16.

Fraga, Luis Ricardo, and Jorge Ruiz-de-Velasco. 2000. "Civil Rights in a Multicultural Society." In *Legacies of the 1964 Civil Rights Act,* ed. Bernard Grofman. Charlottesville: University Press of Virginia, 190–209.

Guerra, Fernando. 1998. "Latino Politics in California: The Necessary Conditions for Success." In *Racial and Ethnic Politics in California, Volume Two,* ed. Michael B. Preston, Bruce E. Cain, and Sandra Bass. Berkeley, Calif.:

Institute of Governmental Studies, University of California, Berkeley, 439–52.

Guerra, Fernando, and Luis Ricardo Fraga. 1996. "Theory, Reality, and Perpetual Potential: Latinos in the 1992 California Elections." In *Ethnic Ironies: Latino Politics in the 1992 Elections,* ed. Rodolfo O. de la Garza and Louis DeSipio. Boulder, Colo.: Westview Press, 131–45.

Hayes-Bautista, David, and Gregory Rodríguez. 1996. "Winning More Political Offices But Still No Agenda." http://www.med.ucla.edu/cesla/oped/2-11-96.htm, last visited 5/24/00.

Hero, Rodney E. 1992. *Latinos and the U.S. Political System.* Philadelphia: Temple University Press.

Jackson, Byran O., and Michael B. Preston, eds. 1991. *Racial and Ethnic Politics in California.* Berkeley, Calif.: Institute of Governmental Studies, University of California, Berkeley.

Jeffe, Sherry Bebitch. 1996. "Year of the Latino?" *California Journal,* vol. 27, no. 10 (October): 20.

Johnson, Hans P. 1999. "How Many Californians? A Review of Population Projections for the State." *California Counts, Population Trends and Profiles.* vol. 1, no. 1 (October). San Francisco, Calif.: Public Policy Institute of California.

López, Elizabeth, and Eric Wahlgren. 1994. "The Latino Vote: The Lure of Four Million Ballots." *California Journal,* vol. 25, no. 11 (November): 29–31.

Maharidge, Dale. 1993. "Did 1992 Herald the Dawn of Latino Political Power." *California Journal,* vol. 24, no. 1 (January): 15–18.

Mindiola, Tatcho, Jr., and Armando Gutiérrez. 1988. "Chicanos and the Legislative Process: Reality and Illusion in the Politics of Change." In *Latinos and the Political System,* ed. F. Chris García. Notre Dame, Ind.: University of Notre Dame Press, 349–62.

Nissenbaum, Dion. 2000. "Assembly Speakers Set State for Power." *San Jose Mercury News,* April 10, A1.

Pachón, Harry P. 1998. "Latino Politics in the Golden State: Ready for the 21st Century?" In *Racial and Ethnic Politics in California, Volume Two,* ed. Michael B. Preston, Bruce E. Cain, and Sandra Bass. Berkeley, Calif.: Institute of Governmental Studies, University of California, Berkeley, 411–38.

Preston, Michael, Bruce E. Cain, and Sandra Bass, eds. 1998. *Racial and Ethnic Politics in California.* Berkeley, Calif.: Institute of Governmental Studies, University of California, Berkeley.

Ramírez, Ricardo. 2000. "Race, Social Context and Referendum Voting." Prepared for delivery at the annual meeting of the American Political Science Association, Washington, D.C., August 31–September 3.

Rodríguez, Gregory. 1998. "Antonio Villaraigosa: The Assembly's New Leader May Have an Historic Opportunity to Become an Ethnic Politician Who

Transcends Ethnicity." *California Government and Politics Annual 1998–1999*, 34–35.

Scott, Steve. 1997. "New Legislature: The Assembly's First Latino Speaker Confronts a Caucus Full of Rookies, a Lame-Duck Governor, and an Ascendant State Senate, All with One Eye on the Term-Limit Clock." *California Journal*, vol. 28, no. 1 (January): 6–11.

———— 1998. "Reality Votes: California's Political Demographics Are Slowly Growing More in Sync with its Overall Demographics. How Will This Change Affect the Way Elections Are Run—and Won—in 1998 and Beyond?" *California Journal*, vol. 29, no. 1 (January): 24–30.

Starkey, Danielle. 1993. "Immigrant-Bashing: Good Policy or Good Politics?" *California Journal*, vol. 24, no. 10 (October): 15–20.

Statewide Database, UC Berkeley Institute of Governmental Studies (swdb.berkeley.edu/.), last visited 10/25/00.

Tolbert, Caroline J., and Rodney E. Hero. 1996. "Race/Ethnicity and Direct Democracy: An Analysis of California's Illegal Immigration Initiative." *The Journal of Politics*, vol. 58, no. 3 (August): 806–18.

Yáñez-Chávez, Aníbal, ed. 1996. *Latino Politics in California*. San Diego, Calif.: Center for U.S.-Mexican Studies at the University of California, San Diego.

York, Anthony. 1999. "Latino Politics." *California Journal*, vol. 30, no. 2 (April) : 26–34.

Conclusion

Latinos and Public Policy in California:
An Agenda for Opportunity

David López

The foregoing chapters explore policy issues facing California's leaders and electorate that have special relevance to the state's Latino population, and more broadly to the needs of the state's low- and moderate-income populations. In these concluding observations, we call attention to the central cross-cutting issues raised in this volume and highlight the agenda for opportunity that emerges from the chapters. In particular, we discuss the challenges of improving immigrant integration and enhancing opportunities for California's school-age population, more than 40 percent of whom are Latino.

Educational Achievement and Social Mobility

Whatever the future of immigration, a key component of California's population growth will be the "second generation," the children of immigrants—and, as time goes by, their children as well. Over half of the state's school children in the early elementary grades are Latino, presaging an inevitable majority of K–12 enrollment within a few years. Most of them, including children of recent immigrants, are native-born. However, it is not only recently arrived Latino immigrants and their minor children who merit specific attention. A significant proportion of the state's nonimmigrant Latino youth, many with family roots in early 20th century immigration or earlier, face considerable obstacles in achieving academic success. It is worth recalling that the Chicano civil rights movement of the late 1960s arose in East Los Angeles among U.S.-born, English-speaking youth who were protesting inadequate schools, as well as police brutality and neglected neighborhoods.

It is clear that they had something to protest about: Research from the 1960s to the present has documented that second- and third-generation Mexican Americans did not and still do not experience the same degree of intergenerational mobility that groups of European origin did, either in the middle of the 20th century or today. All research that systematically addresses limited mobility emphasizes that low levels of academic achievement are at the core of the problem today—precisely as they were over 30 years ago when they triggered school walkouts.

The inequities experienced by earlier Mexican-American second generations, as well as the continuing inequities experienced by third-generation Mexican Americans today, are significant for two reasons. First, they serve as reminders that Latino issues are not exclusively related to immigration; second, and perhaps more importantly, they underscore the nature of the difficulties and diminished prospects facing Latino children today. These difficulties are not just temporary phenomena that will disappear with time.

If previous Mexican-American generations had joined the American mainstream in the "conventional" (i.e., Euro-American) three generations, it would be tempting to conclude that time (if a rather long time) and intergenerational changes will solve the glaring disparities in upward mobility between Latinos and non-Latino whites as well as Asians. But the experience of earlier generations of Mexican Americans suggests that inequalities will persist. The evidence of past and continuing problems of earlier generations of Latinos in California, and the well-documented disadvantages of the current second generation, illustrate that without significant policy and programmatic innovation, the educational achievement and economic advancement of Latinos reaching adulthood in the next several decades will continue to lag far behind those of other groups. As Latinos become the new demographic majority, such inequality could undermine the entire state's social and economic well-being.

Of course, the foundation for Latino educational achievement relies on effective public-school strategies to address the unique educational needs of this population. The state's educational crisis is rooted in the inability of a large swath of the population to take advantage of the strengths of California public education. California's K–12 public educational system serves middle-class children (including a considerable number of immigrant families) quite well. For example, when school children are divided into economically disadvantaged and other groups, the latter score well above average on such standardized tests as the Stanford Nine, and the former score quite low. When children are divided between those who are English-proficient and "English-language learners," the differences are even more dramatic. The politically uncomfortable truth is that California's public schools perform quite well for middle- and higher-income students, who include the majority of non-Hispanic white and Asian students, and poorly for low-income populations, which include a majority of Latinos and a substantial portion of African Americans.

Conflicting interpretations and explanations of these disparities in achievement remain unsettled, particularly the relative importance of the "cultural capital" that children bring with them to school and the uneven distribution of quality education from community to community. Faced with the enormous differences in school outcomes based on socioeconomic status, English-language ability, and ethnicity, it is tempting to conclude that "input," not the quality of schools, is what determines outcomes.

Certainly, what children bring to school has an enormous effect on what they get out of it. If they were all attending schools of the same quality, it might be logical to conclude that children's characteristics, not the school, are the decisive factors in educational achievement. But of course this is not the case. Long-standing residential patterns based on income and ethnicity have created significant disparities in the quality of public education. Suburban schools are able to attract the best teachers and create environments that are most conducive to learning. Most urban districts seem to be short of everything but students, and their pockets of excellence are usually found in magnet schools that serve largely to retain the district's middle-class and mostly non-Hispanic white and Asian students. Good schools and children who are fluent in English, or are from middle-class and upper-income homes, are a winning combination, and it is largely these children who go on to graduate from college and have much greater lifetime earning power. Before assigning the cause of the poor performance of African-American and Latino students to student "quality," students at risk of failure should, at a minimum, be provided an instructional program whose quality is at least the equivalent to that provided in suburban schools. Policymakers and public-interest groups are currently taking actions to address these inequities.

Any approach to reverse the low achievement of Latino students needs to begin with this fundamental fact: two-thirds of all Latino children, and the vast majority of the children of Latino immigrants, either come from low-income homes or enter school unable to speak sufficient English to understand what is going on in the classroom. There is nothing new about this. The same was true for Italian and Polish children (who also had their difficulties with public schooling) 80 years ago. The important point is that the sociolinguistic factor is enormous. Many immigrants from Asia, Latin America, and elsewhere are primarily from non-English-speaking homes, which nonetheless produce students who become fine scholars. The difference is that these are typically middle- or upper-income homes with parents who have completed some level of college education. It is not language itself, but rather the conjunction of English-language deficit and poverty, that puts immigrant children at risk. Educational reform has to begin with that crucial fact.

The Challenge of Immigrant Integration

Another cross-cutting issue in this volume is the importance of immigrant integration for improving educational, employment, and civic outcomes for a sizable portion of the state's Latino community. Large-scale immigration has fundamentally changed California in the past three decades, and will continue to affect public policy for decades to come. In 1970, immigrants constituted 7 percent of the state's workforce and 9 percent of the total population of 20 million. In 2000, immigrants represented more than 26 percent of California's 34 million people and now constitute more than one-third of the labor force, about three-quarters of whom are from Mexico and Central America.

As a barometer for the future, more than half of the state's public school children are recent arrivals and three-quarters of this population are from Spanish-speaking immigrant households. The growth rate of the state's immigrant population demonstrates that immigrants and their children will constitute a major component of the population for the foreseeable future—necessitating effective strategies for immigrant integration, including quality education for adults as well as children, job training, access to health care, and professional certification. Making it a public-policy priority to improve opportunities for this important segment of the population in a variety of settings will foster immigrants' readiness to seize those opportunities and benefit the state as a whole.

Thus, if educational achievement is the number-one issue for California's Latino community, the integration of immigrant workers and families is a close second. It would be a mistake to ignore the generation of immigrants themselves and not cultivate in them a sense of belonging, assuming that not much can be done for them and that they are content to be here in any case. We tend to forget the obvious: Most immigrants will not only spend the rest of their lives in California, but will also provide homes for children struggling to grow up in this state. Poverty is by far the greatest contributor to poor performance in school. Moreover, even if the children of immigrants are able to escape poverty, their parents may remain in precarious economic straits for the rest of their lives, especially when they join the ranks of the elderly.

In June 2002, the state's Little Hoover Commission issued *We the People: Helping Newcomers Become Californians*, a report that summarizes current knowledge and recommends policy and community approaches to achieve greater levels of immigrant integration. It also addresses a delicate and controversial issue that disproportionately affects Latinos: the plight of the poorest and least-protected segment of the state's population, at the core of which are families headed by undocumented immigrants. No one knows with certainty how many undocumented immigrants are in California. The commission report uses the 1996 Census Bureau estimate of around 2 million, but recent estimates based on the 2000 Census suggest there were 50 percent more undocumented immigrants in 2000 than previous INS or Census Bureau estimates—as many as 9 to 10 million nationwide, and possibly 3 million in California.

Clearly, a large proportion of California's immigrant workers suffer from legal marginality, in addition to their already substantial socioeconomic disadvantages. These numbers continue to be a topic of lively controversy, but more important than the absolute numbers is the commission report's emphasis that "illegal immigrants" are a caste apart only in the minds of anti-immigrant activists. In reality, the large majority are embedded in family, friendship, and community networks, so that many more people are actually affected by the obstacles the undocumented face.

The report emphasizes the corrosive effect of permanent legal limbo for such a large portion of the state population, and recommends a variety of concrete steps designed to reduce insecurity and increase community integration, including the creation of a "Golden State Residency" program. We concur with the report's observation that such a large undocumented, and largely low-income, population creates immense difficulties for the individuals in question, their children and other family members, and ultimately for the state. Local, state, and federal policies that ignore the presence of this community are ultimately doomed to failure.

A host of long-run, medium-term, and immediate issues are affected by legal status. A long-range concern is that as undocumented workers reach retirement age they face bleak prospects because they are unlikely to have accumulated material assets and will not have the safety net of Social Security. In the medium and short term, undocumented status contributes to the already serious economic barriers to Latino homeownership. On an immediate, day-to-day basis, we see that undocumented status inhibits access to health care and higher education for immigrants and their U.S.-born children. Whatever one's personal attitude toward "illegal" immigration, this circumstance has played a role in the Mexican-American community since the 1920s; if it is perceived as being a greater "problem" today, it is because undocumented residents are denied many opportunities and protections that would otherwise facilitate their and their children's integration into California society.

An Agenda for Opportunity

California's severe budget crisis of the early 2000s will certainly affect the way state government can address the issues discussed in this volume. Because of an unprecedented deficit, the state is unable to provide resources for new initiatives and is likely to reduce expenditures in key areas such as education and health for the foreseeable future. Consequently, elected and civic leaders as well as community-based organizations will need to scrutinize expenditures of scarce public dollars, monitor program effectiveness, and develop innovative strategies to address the needs of the Latino population, particularly in health, education (preschool through adult), and social services. Reduced state expenditures, along with the effects of recession, could easily aggravate existing inequalities in access to education, health care, and other services.

Over the last decade, the emergence of Latinos as an electoral force has helped focus state policy attention to the concerns of moderate- and low-income Californians and the interests of immigrant communities. As discussed in the Fraga and Ramirez chapter, the 1990s saw a substantial expansion of the Latino electorate and the emergence of state legislative leadership that has achieved the capacity to frame public agendas and shape law-making on major statewide issues. Although the Latino electorate lags behind Latinos' share of the state's overall population, it nonetheless represents a significant and growing constituency for elected officials of all ethnic backgrounds. The enhanced presence of Latinos in California civic and political life provides an important foundation for advancing approaches to educational achievement, immigrant integration, affordable housing, employment opportunities, and health-care access—the focus of this book and the issues that constitute an "agenda for opportunity."

The authors of this volume have delineated a variety of strategies for addressing current inequalities and improving the quality of life for the state's Latino population. A number of these strategies involve actions by state government, others by school districts, local government, or the private sector. Clearly, proposals to improve adult education, enhance the educational achievement of low-income schoolchildren, or increase the availability of affordable housing would benefit not only Latinos or immigrants but other groups as well. In this sense, a number of the potential remedies to Latino inequality also have wider appeal, allowing for consensus and coalition-building among California's diverse groups. At the same time, persistent inequalities facing Latinos should also be a statewide concern, given both their significant and growing demographic presence and the negative implications for the state's well-being of its largest group lagging in educational achievement, earning power, and health-care access. Ultimately, the prosperity of California and its Latino population are closely linked, and will remain so for decades to come.

About the Authors

José A. Canela-Cacho, Ph.D., Carnegie Mellon University, is co-founder and CEO of The Ergo Group, Inc., a public-policy consulting firm, and research fellow at UC Berkeley's Earl Warren Legal Institute. His teaching and research experience spans the areas of criminal justice policy, Mexico-U.S. policy relations, and quantitative methods for public-policy analysis. Recent publications include co-authoring *Incapacitation Effect of Imprisonment in California, 1983–1998* (forthcoming), "Incapacitation" in Joshua Dressler, ed., *Encyclopedia of Crime and Justice* (2002), and *Gang Suppression in East Oakland, an Evaluation of the Oakland's Police Department 1996–97 Anti-Gang Initiative* (1998).

Lisa Chávez, Ph.D., UC Berkeley, is currently research associate at WestEd, a nonprofit education research agency. Her dissertation explored the underrepresentation of Latinos in high-school advanced math courses. Previously she worked for MPR Associates, where she wrote and also co-authored three statistical reports under contract with the National Center for Education Statistics. She also served as research assistant to the Latino Eligibility Study, a task force that examined Latino students' access to the University of California. Chávez has worked at the Gaston Institute at the University of Massachusetts, Boston, where she co-authored reports on the increasing population of Latinos in Massachusetts and the state of educational achievement, access, and outcomes among Massachusetts Latino youth, with an emphasis on exploring the impact of the state's new high-school exit exam on Latino graduation rates.

Luis Ricardo Fraga, Ph. D., Rice University, is associate professor in the Department of Political Science at Stanford University. Professor Fraga's research interests are American urban politics, educational policy, politics of race and ethnicity, and voting rights. He has published in the *Journal of Politics, Urban Affairs Quarterly, Western Political Quarterly, West European Politics,* and the *Journal of State Government* as well as in many edited volumes. Fraga was co-editor of *Ethnic and Racial Minorities in Advanced Industrial Democracies* (1992), and is currently completing two book manuscripts: *The Changing Urban Regime: Toward an Informed Public Interest,* and *Missed Opportunities: The Politics of Schools in San Francisco.* Professor Fraga also co-edits a book series entitled *Race, Ethnicity and Politics.*

Patricia Gándara, Ph.D., UCLA, is professor of education at UC Davis, and associate director of the University of California Linguistic Minority Research Institute. Her research and publications focus on access and equity in education for underrepresented students and English learners. Recent publications include

"What We Have Learned about Preparing Latino Youth for Higher Education," in *Educational Policy* (2002), and co-authoring "The Schooling of English Learners" in Burr, et al., *Crucial Issues in California Education*.

Eugene E. García, Ph.D., University of Kansas, is professor of education and dean of the College of Education at Arizona State University, following similar appointments at UC Berkeley from 1995–2001. He has published extensively on language teaching and bilingual development. His most recent books include *Hispanic Education in the United States: Raices y Alas* (2001) and *Student Cultural Diversity: Understanding and Meeting the Challenge* (2001).

David E. Hayes-Bautista, Ph.D., UCSF, is a professor in the School of Medicine and director of the Center for the Study of Latino Health and Culture at UCLA. His research focuses on the dynamics and processes of the health of the Latino population using both quantitative data and qualitative observations. The Center for the Study of Latino Health combines these research interests with teaching medical students, residents, and health-care providers to manage the care of a Latino patient base effectively, efficiently, and economically. His publications have appeared in *Family Medicine*, the *American Journal of Public Health*, *Family Practice*, *Medical Care*, and *Salud Pública de México*.

Andrés Jiménez is director of the California Policy Research Center (CPRC), and prior to that coordinated research programs at UC Berkeley's Institute of International Studies and Institute for the Study of Social Change. His areas of interest include political participation in the United States and Mexico, race and ethnic relations, immigration policy, and U.S.-Latin American relations. Jiménez serves on a number of advisory committees concerning public policy and has consulted with various governmental bodies in the United States and Mexico. He received a BA in politics and Latin American studies from UC Santa Cruz, and pursued doctoral studies in political science at UC Berkeley.

Edward Kissam, Ph.D., State University of New York, is a senior research associate at Aguirre International/The Aguirre Group, where he works on a range of applied research projects addressing issues related to farmworkers and other Latino immigrants. His social policy and program-planning interests include adult and K–12 education, employment training, immigrant civic engagement, Latino public radio, and community health. He is currently directing a national study sponsored by the Fund for Rural America on how immigration is transforming rural communities and strategies for responding. He is co-author of *Working Poor: Farmworkers in the United States* (1995), and has written several research studies on migrant and seasonal farmworkers for the U.S. Commission on Agricultural Workers and the Department of Labor.

David López, Ph.D., Harvard University, is professor of sociology at UCLA, where for three decades he has served as associate dean of the Graduate School, chair and director of Chicano Studies, and chair of the Latin American Studies Program. He has published extensively on issues relating to language and ethnicity in the United States, with a special focus on Latinos. Recent publications include "Social and Linguistic Aspects of Assimilation Today," in Charles Hirschman, ed., *The Handbook of International Migration: The American Experience* (1999), and co-authoring "Who Does What? California's Emerging Plural Labor Force," in Ruth Milkman, ed., *Organizing Immigrants* (2000) and "Mexican Americans: A Second Generation at Risk," in Rubén Rumbaut and Alejandro Portes, eds., *Ethnicities: Coming of Age in Immigrant America*.

Dowell Myers, Ph.D., MIT, is professor of urban planning and demography in the School of Policy, Planning, and Development at the University of Southern California, and also directs the Master of Planning program and the school's Population Dynamics Research Group. His research has focused on the upward mobility of immigrants to the United States and California, trajectories into homeownership, and projections for the future of the state's population. Myers is the author of the most widely referenced text on census analysis, *Analysis with Local Census Data: Portraits of Change* (1992), and has served on the Professional Advisory Committee of the United States Census Bureau. His most recent publication, "Demographic Futures as a Guide for Planning: California's Latinos and the Compact City," in *Journal of the American Planning Association* (2001), received an award for best article of the year from the journal's sponsors. Myers's web site is: http://www-rcf.usc.edu/~dowell/.

Kurt C. Organista, Ph.D., Arizona State University, is an associate professor of social welfare and director of the Center for Latino Policy Research at UC Berkeley. He teaches courses on psychopathology, stress and coping, and human diversity practice, including social work with Latino populations. He is interested in Latino health and mental health and conducts research on HIV/AIDS prevention with Mexican migrant laborers and the treatment of depression in Latinos. Organista currently serves on the editorial boards of the *Journal of Ethnic and Cultural Diversity in Social Work*, the *Hispanic Journal of the Behavioral Sciences*, and the *American Journal of Community Psychology*. Recent publications include "Cognitive-Behavioral Group Therapy with Latinos," in A. Freeman and J. White, eds., *Cognitive, Behavioral Group Therapy for Adults* (2000) and co-authoring "Predictors of Condom Use in Mexican Migrant Laborers," in the *American Journal of Community Psychology* (2000).

Manuel Pastor, Jr., Ph.D., University of Massachusetts, is professor of Latin American and Latino studies and director of the Center for Justice, Tolerance, and Community at UC Santa Cruz. His research on U.S. urban issues has been published in *Economic Development Quarterly*, *Review of Regional Studies*,

Social Science Quarterly, Journal of Economic Issues, Journal of Urban Affairs, Urban Affairs Review, Urban Geography, and elsewhere, and generally has focused on the labor market and social conditions facing low-income urban communities. Pastor co-authored *Searching for the Uncommon Common Ground: New Dimensions on Race in America* (2002). He is best known for co-authoring *Regions That Work: How Cities and Suburbs Can Grow Together* (2000), which has become a reference for those seeking to better link community and regional development.

Ricardo Ramírez, Ph.D., Stanford University, is an assistant professor in the Department of Political Science and the Program in American Studies and Ethnicity at the University of Southern California and an Adjunct Fellow at the Public Policy Institute of California. His research interests include state and local politics, political behavior, and the politics of race and ethnicity, especially as they relate to political participation and incorporation. His dissertation, The Changing Landscape of California Politics: 19902000, examined how contemporary racial and ethnic diversity and political context have affected three critical components of California s political landscape: white voter preferences, Latino political participation, and Latino mobilization. His writings include co-authoring Citizens by Choice, Voters by Necessity: Patterns in Political Mobilization by Naturalized Latinos. He is currently writing a book: *Continuity and Change: Latinos in American Politics Since 1990*.

Belinda I. Reyes, Ph.D., UC Berkeley, is a research fellow at the Public Policy Institute of California (PPIC). Her research focuses on immigration issues and the economic progress of the state's racial and ethnic groups. She was general editor of PPIC's *A Portrait of Race and Ethnicity in California: An Assessment of Social and Economic Well-Being* (2001), and has written and co-authored numerous reports and articles on immigration patterns, policy, and integration. Reyes has briefed various federal, state, and local governmental bodies and addressed numerous civic organizations. She has been a senior program associate at PolicyLink; a lecturer at UC Berkeley; a research fellow at the University of Michigan; and a visiting scholar at the Federal Reserve Bank of San Francisco.

Lonnie R. Snowden, Ph.D., Wayne State University, is professor in the School of Social Welfare at UC Berkeley, where he directs the Center of Mental Health Service Research, and also holds appointments in Health Services and Policy Analysis in the School of Public Health and in the Psychology Department. Recently, Snowden contributed to the surgeon general's report on mental health and served as a scientific editor of the recently issued supplement "Mental Health: Culture, Race, and Ethnicity." He has published many articles and book chapters, including these currently in press: "Bias in Mental Health Assessment and Intervention: Theory and Evidence," in the *American Journal of Public Health*; "Minority Youth in Foster Care: Managed Care and Access to Mental

Health Treatment," in *Medical Care*; "Mental Health Service Use by Racial and Ethnic Populations in Poverty Areas," in the *American Journal of Public Health*.

Robert Otto Burciaga Valdez, Ph.D., RAND Graduate School, conducts health policy analyses and research at RAND in Santa Monica and Washington, D.C. He previously served as dean and professor of Health Policy and Management of the MCP Hahnemann University School of Public Health, as professor at the Drexel University Lebow College of Business, and from 1985 to 2000 as professor of Health Services at the UCLA School of Public Health and director of doctoral studies for the Department of Health Services. Valdez has been active in health policy and health services research at the national, state, and local levels. From 1993 to 1996 he served in a dual capacity at the U.S. Department of Health and Human Services as Deputy Assistant Secretary for Health in the Public Health Service and Director of Interagency Health Policy in the Health Care Financing Administration. His responsibilities included managed-care developments and their effects on the public health-care system; care for the uninsured; and state health-care reforms. On the state and local levels, Dr. Valdez has provided policy analyses on issues of the uninsured and Medi-Cal. More recently he has worked with the states of California, Pennsylvania, New Jersey, and Delaware on public-health infrastructure rebuilding.